D0509754

Scala in Action

Scala in Action

NILANJAN RAYCHAUDHURI

MANNING

SHELTER ISLAND

For online information and ordering of this and other Manning books, please visit
www.manning.com. The publisher offers discounts on this book when ordered in quantity.
For more information, please contact

    Special Sales Department
    Manning Publications Co.
    20 Baldwin Road
    PO Box 261
    Shelter Island, NY 11964
    Email: orders@manning.com

©2013 by Manning Publications Co. All rights reserved.

No part of this publication may be reproduced, stored in a retrieval system, or transmitted, in
any form or by means electronic, mechanical, photocopying, or otherwise, without prior written
permission of the publisher.

Many of the designations used by manufacturers and sellers to distinguish their products are
claimed as trademarks. Where those designations appear in the book, and Manning
Publications was aware of a trademark claim, the designations have been printed in initial caps
or all caps.

♾ Recognizing the importance of preserving what has been written, it is Manning's policy to have
the books we publish printed on acid-free paper, and we exert our best efforts to that end.
Recognizing also our responsibility to conserve the resources of our planet, Manning books
are printed on paper that is at least 15 percent recycled and processed without the use of
elemental chlorine.

 Manning Publications Co.
20 Baldwin Road
PO Box 261
Shelter Island, NY 11964

Development editor: Cynthia Kane
Technical Proofreaders: Ivan Kirkpatrick, Clint Combs
Copyeditor: Corbin Collins
Proofreader: Elizabeth Martin
Typesetter: Dottie Marsico
Cover designer: Marija Tudor

ISBN 9781935182757
Printed in the United States of America
2 3 4 5 6 7 8 9 10 – MAL – 18 17 16 15 14 13

brief contents

contents

foreword

You're standing in front of a huge, steep wall of rock. Your neck is straining as you bend your head back as far as it will go to take it all in. If you squint, you can barely see something moving around at the top. There's probably some really good stuff up there. You've heard from people you trust that it's worth climbing this wall. But, you're damned sure going to hurt yourself on the way up. You can already see some of the jagged edges jutting out. And what if it turns out that you don't like what you see when you get there?

Learning difficult things is like this—and make no mistake: Scala *is* difficult to learn. And you may very well not like what you see when you get to the top. I'd guess that only a small fraction of developers learning a language like Scala ever put it to use. But it's almost always the climb that makes a challenge worth the effort. Scala is a lot to chew on. It's got what seems *way* too many features. It's going to appear, at least initially, overdesigned. You're going to hurt yourself on the way.

By the time you reach the top, you'll understand why those features exist, how they make your Scala programs better, and, more important, how they make you a more effective programmer. You'll still be sore from the bumps along the way but that pain will help you remember the lessons learned. You may even find yourself happily and productively working full-time in Scala for years to come!

As worthwhile as a journey like this may be, you don't want to climb a mountain this high alone, if you can help it. When covering unfamiliar—even alien—territory you want a guide who can make it look easy. That's Nilanjan Raychaudhuri. He has a way of putting people at ease when describing complex subjects. Scala itself isn't that complex—it's really just a bunch of simple pieces that join to form a deceptively capable whole. Nilanjan has a talent for making us believe that those pieces really *are* simple and are there for unearthing the underlying principles that bind them together. Indeed, even for the nuts and bolts of installation, configuration, and project compilation, reading this book is like having an experienced mentor accompany you every step of the way.

Some of the concepts in *Scala in Action* are going to be more foreign than others. When you hit these bumps, take your time. Musicians don't become great by playing the songs they know over and over. Elite athletes don't consistently stay in their comfort zones. It's the jagged edges that improve us.

If you approach this climb properly, you'll reach the top sharper, more open-minded, and, best of all, less afraid.

CHAD FOWLER
AUTHOR, SPEAKER, AND
PROGRAMMING LIFESTYLE ENGINEER

preface

Why write *Scala in Action* when there are plenty of other Scala books on the market? What sets this book apart?

Scala in Action targets developers who not only want to learn the language but also want to build real-world applications using Scala. This book, in other words, covers not only the language and its latest features but also its ecosystem. My goal was to pack a sufficient number of real-world examples along with the right mix of theory so readers can easily become comfortable with the language.

Scala is a feature-rich language and it is not possible to cover all of its features in one book, at least one of a reasonable size. For that reason, I deliberately avoided some of the more advanced features of Scala. I encourage you to think of this book as your first on Scala, a foundation on which to build, before you dive into the more advanced features Scala has to offer.

I had a great time writing this book and I hope you have a great time learning this new and exciting language. I know you had a choice when it comes to Scala books; thank you for choosing this one.

acknowledgments

First I thank Martin Ordesky, the creator of Scala, for his thoughtful creation, which takes language design to the next level. Without his work, this book would not exist.

I also thank all of the members of the Scala community. Without their help and comments, I never could have imagined writing this book.

At Manning, I give my thanks to Marjan Bace, Mike Stephens, my editors Cynthia Kane and Katharine Osborne for helping me improve my writing, and the production team of Corbin Collins, Elizabeth Martin, Dottie Marsico, Mary Piergies, Toma Mulligan, and Janet Vail. Special thanks go to Ivan Kirkpatrick and Clint Combs, my technical proofreaders, for their in-depth feedback on the text and the code.

Numerous reviewers read the book at various stages of its development and offered helpful comments and criticisms, and I acknowledge them here: Alexandre Alves, Andrew Rhine, Andy Dingley, Ben Hall, Cheryl Jerozal, Dan Dobrin, Daniel Bretoi, Dave Pawson, David Greco, Dennis Leung, Edmon Begoli, Eric Weinberg, Marco Ughetti, Mark Needham, Michael Smolyak, Peter Crosbie, Peter Thomas, Robert MacGregor, and Tom Belunis.

Thanks also to the readers of Manning's Early Access Program (MEAP). Their corrections and comments on the manuscript as it was being written were invaluable.

I extend a special thanks to Lutz Hankewitz for his help during the writing process. Without his thoughtful feedback, this book would have been incomplete. Special thanks also to Chad Fowler for contributing the foreword and for endorsing my work.

Last but definitely not least, I would like to thank my wife Manisha for her support and patience as I spent countless weekends working on this book while she took care of the family without any complaints.

about this book

If I were to pick a language to use today other than Java, it would be Scala.

—JAMES GOSLING

Congratulations for picking Scala as your next language. And if you are still undecided, please read the first chapter in this book, and I am sure that will change your mind.

The programming languages we use shape the way we think and how we solve programming issues. And when faced with new programming languages and paradigms we try to map them to the languages we know. I would discourage you from doing that when reading *Scala in Action*. Scala is a new programming language that brings myriad new ideas to the Java virtual machine platform.

Scala is unique. It is a multi-paradigm programming language that combines both functional and object-oriented languages. It has its own set of best practices and idioms and by the end of this book what you have learned will also be helpful in other programming languages.

Scala in Action has been updated to reflect the newest changes in Scala version 2.10.

Who should read this book?

This book is for all developers and hobbyists who like programming. Most of the concepts discussed can be easily absorbed without any knowledge of Java, but having a basic knowledge of Java is a definite plus. The book assumes that you are at least familiar with the JVM and its ecosystem. There are plenty of available resources for the JVM and its toolset that augment this book.

Roadmap

This book is divided into three parts. Part 1 introduces the language and its features. Part 2 makes use of the concepts and shows how to use them in real world. Part 3, updated to reflect the introduction of Scala 2.10, continues with real-world examples of building large-scale applications using Java and Akka.

It is recommended that you read the book from beginning to end. Having said that, if some chapters interest you more than others, feel free to jump ahead, but make certain you are familiar with the concepts introduced in the first five chapters (part 1). Chapter 6 is also important because it introduces the build tool used to compile and build the accompanying code samples.

When reading this book, and working with its examples, I recommend that you keep the Scala interpreter (REPL) open at all times. This is a programming book so keep programming as you read.

Part 1: Introducing Scala

Part 1 introduces Scala and the programming paradigms it supports.

Chapter 1 explores why Scala should be your next programming language. The chapter explores features of the language and compares them to other popular programming languages on the market. Picking up and learning a new language is a lot of work and you should read this chapter to understand what Scala has to offer and why Scala should be your next programming language.

Chapter 2 introduces basic Scala features you need to get started with the language. This chapter also introduces one of the most important Scala tools, the Scala REPL. If you have never used the REPL, this chapter will prepare you.

Chapter 3 explores the object-oriented programming side of things in Scala. It introduces traits, case classes, and companion objects, all new innovations in OOP.

Chapter 4 focuses on the Scala collection library, one of the most powerful features of Scala. The collection is one of the things that attracted me to this language. This chapter will introduce new concepts gently so that you can start using Scala collection classes as soon as possible. I promise once you get used to them there is no going back.

Chapter 5 introduces functional programming. This is the logical extension of the previous chapter. This chapter introduces what and why functional programming is important to learn. Even if you don't use Scala in your projects, some of the concepts introduced here can be used in any programming language.

Part 2: Working with Scala

Chapter 6 takes the first stab at building a large web application using Scala. This chapter will show you how to build and organize a Scala project and it introduces the popular Simple Build Tool (SBT).

Chapter 7, a continuation of the previous chapter, introduces Scala frameworks you can use to connect to the database.

Chapter 8 is about Scala's type system. No Scala book could be complete without exploration of Scala's type system. But it's no fun to talk about types unless you learn their value in design applications in the real world. This chapter introduces types available in Scala and how you can use them to build reusable components.

Chapter 9, extensively reworked after the release of Scala 2.10, introduces actors, one of the most popular aspects of Scala. An actor is a high-level abstraction over threads, allowing you to build and design concurrent applications.

Chapter 10 focuses on testing Scala applications and how you can use patterns to make your code more testable. If you are thinking of taking your Scala application to production you need to learn to write automated tests and to understand dependency injections.

Part 3: Advanced steps

Chapter 11 demonstrates integration with Java, one of the core features of Scala. Using Scala doesn't necessarily mean you have to use only Scala frameworks. In this chapter you will take Java frameworks like Spring, Hibernate, and Maven and use them with Scala

Chapter 12, also reworked after the release of Scala 2.10, introduces Akka, the most popular framework written in Scala. At the end of the chapter you will build a large distributed and scalable application using Akka. If you are interested in concurrent and parallel programming, this chapter is for you.

Code convention and downloads

This book contains numerous code examples. All the code is in a `fixed-width font like this` to separate it from ordinary text. Code members such as method names, class names, and so on are also in a fixed-width font.

Source code examples in this book are fairly close to the samples that you'll find online, but for the sake of brevity, we may have removed material such as comments from the code to fit it well within the text.

Code annotations accompany many of the source code listings, highlighting important concepts. In some cases, numbered bullets link to explanations that follow the listing.

The source code for the examples in the book is available for download from the publisher's website at www.manning.com/ScalainAction. To run the samples, you'll need to download some of the tools and languages used in this book. Links in the text point you to places where you can get the relevant files.

Software requirements

You can use any platform of your choice as long as you have a Java runtime version 1.5 or later running. I have used Java 6 on Mac OS X for running and building all the code examples.

Author Online forum

The purchase of *Scala in Action* includes free access to a private web forum run by Manning Publications, where you can make comments about the book, ask technical questions, and receive help from the author and from other users. To access the forum and subscribe to it, point your web browser at www.manning.com/ScalainAction. This page provides information on how to get on the forum once you are registered, what kind of help is available, and the rules of conduct on the forum.

Manning's commitment to our readers is to provide a venue where a meaningful dialogue between individual readers and between readers and authors can take place. It's not a commitment to any specific amount of participation on the part of the author, whose contribution to the forum remains voluntary (and unpaid). We suggest you try asking the author some challenging questions, lest his interest stray! The Author Online forum and archives of previous discussions will be accessible from the publisher's website as long as the book is in print.

about the cover illustration

The figure on the cover of *Scala in Action* is captioned "A woman from Senj, Family Vukasovic, Croatian Coast." The illustration is taken from a reproduction of an album of Croatian traditional costumes from the mid-nineteenth century by Nikola Arsenovic, published by the Ethnographic Museum in Split, Croatia, in 2003. The illustrations were obtained from a helpful librarian at the Ethnographic Museum in Split, itself situated in the Roman core of the medieval center of the town: the ruins of Emperor Diocletian's retirement palace from around AD 304. The book includes finely colored illustrations of figures from different regions of Croatia, accompanied by descriptions of the costumes and of everyday life.

Senj is the oldest town on the upper Adriatic coast, founded in the time before the Romans, some 3,000 years ago, on the hill Kuk, overlooking the sea. Through the centuries, Senj was a prosperous seaport which was ruled by many different tribes and nation states in its long history. In the eighteenth and nineteenth centuries, dress customs in the town indicated not only the social standing of a person, but also the family to which he or she belonged. The colors and embroidery patterns would tell the story of a person's class and family affiliation. The woman on the cover is wearing a richly embroidered blue dress and vest and a fancy lace apron and headscarf, which would have signaled both her status and her family ties.

Dress codes and lifestyles have changed over the last 200 years, and the diversity by region, town, or family, so rich at the time, has faded away. It is now hard to tell apart the inhabitants of different continents, let alone of different hamlets or towns separated by only a few miles. Perhaps we have traded cultural diversity for a more varied personal life—certainly for a more varied and fast-paced technological life.

Manning celebrates the inventiveness and initiative of the computer business with book covers based on the rich diversity of regional life of two centuries ago, brought back to life by illustrations from old books and collections like this one.

Part 1

Scala: the basics

First things first.

In *Scala in Action*, chapter 1 focuses on Scala and why you should pick it as your next language. You'll learn how Scala's high-level features compare with programming languages you may be very familiar with. If you're an object-oriented programmer, you'll quickly get comfortable with Scala; if you've used a functional programming language, Scala won't look much different because Scala supports both programming paradigms.

Scala is one of those rare languages that successfully integrates both object-oriented and functional language features. This makes it powerful because it gives you more in your toolbox to solve programming problems. If you have existing Java applications and are looking for a language that will improve your productivity and at the same time reuse your existing Java codebase, you'll like Scala's Java integration and the fact that Scala runs on the JVM platform.

It's important, when learning something new, to become comfortable in the heretofore unknown environment. Chapter 2 stays within the middle of the road, helping you become comfortable with the basics of Scala and its environment so you can start working with it and writing Scala programs. Early on, the focus is on only the Scala interpreter and its REPL environment to keep things simple, but you'll also learn about the basic Scala types, functions, for-comprehension, pattern matching, among other things.

Chapter 3 introduces the object-oriented features of Scala, including some not available in other statically typed languages.

You'll build a Scala driver for MongoDB, a scalable document-oriented database. You'll build this driver incrementally using the object-oriented constructs provided by Scala. You'll explore how to use traits when building Scala applications, and learn about the importance of Scala case classes.

In chapter 4 you'll learn Scala collections, which broadly support two categories of data structures—immutable and mutable.

To understand and benefit from Scala collections, you need to know two concepts: type parameterization and higher-order functions. Type parameterization allows you to create types that take another type as a parameter (similar to Java generics). Higher-order functions let you create functions that take other functions as parameters. These two concepts allow you to create generic and reusable components, like Scala collections.

The Scala collection is one of Scala's most powerful features. The library implements all the common data structures you need, making it essential for every Scala developer. A recent addition to the collection library is parallel collections. Scala parallel collections allow you to solve data parallelism problems in Scala with ease.

Chapter 5, the end of part 1, focuses on functional programming, although you've been doing functional programming if you've been following the examples in the book. In some cases functional programming is obvious; other times it is mixed with object-oriented constructs of Scala. The chapter also touches on monads and practical examples.

Why Scala?

This chapter covers
- What Scala is
- High-level features of the Scala language
- Why you should pick Scala as your next language

Scala is a general-purpose programming language that runs on Java Virtual Machine (JVM) and .NET platforms. But the recent explosion of programming languages on JVM, .NET, and other platforms raises a question that every developer faces today: which programming language to learn next? Which languages are ready for mainstream development? Among the heap of programming languages like Groovy, Ruby, Clojure, Erlang, and F#, why should you learn Scala?

Learning a new language is merely a beginning. To become a useful and productive developer, you also need to be familiar with all the toggles and gizmos that make up the language infrastructure.

Before I make the case for why Scala should be your next programming language, it's important to understand what Scala is. It's a feature-rich language that's used in various types of applications, starting with building a large messaging layer for social networking sites such as Twitter[1] to creating an application

---

[1] "Twitter on Scala: A Conversation with Steve Jenson, Alex Payne, and Robey Pointer," *Scalazine*, April 3, 2009, www.artima.com/scalazine/articles/twitter_on_scala.html.

build tool like SBT[2] (Simple Build Tool). Because of this *scala-bility*, the name of the language is *Scala*.

This chapter explores the high-level features of the language and shows how they compare to the programming languages you may be very familiar with. This will help you to choose Scala as your next programming language.

If you're an object-oriented programmer, you'll quickly get comfortable with the language; if you've used a functional programming language, Scala won't look much different because Scala supports both programming paradigms. Scala is one of those rare languages that successfully integrates both object-oriented and functional language features. This makes Scala powerful because it gives you more in your toolbox to solve programming problems. If you have existing Java applications and are looking for a language that will improve your productivity and at the same time reuse your existing Java codebase, you'll like Scala's Java integration and the fact that Scala runs on the JVM platform.

Now let's explore Scala a bit more.

1.1   *What's Scala?*

Scala is a general-purpose programming language designed to express common programming patterns in a concise, elegant, and type-safe way. It smoothly integrates features of object-oriented and functional programming languages, enabling programmers to be more productive. Martin Odersky (the creator of Scala) and his team started development on Scala in 2001 in the programming methods laboratory at EPFL (École Polytechnique Fédérale de Lausanne). Scala made its public debut in January 2004 on the JVM platform and a few months later on the .NET platform.

Even though Scala is fairly new in the language space, it has gained the support of the programming community, which is growing every day. Scala is a rich language in terms of features available to programmers, so without wasting time let's dive into some of them.

> **SCALA ON .NET** At present Scala's support for .NET isn't stable. According to the Scala language website (www.scala-lang.org), the current Scala distribution can compile programs for the .NET platform, but a few libraries aren't supported. The main difficulty to overcome is that Scala programs make heavy use of the Java JDK, which is not available out of the box in the .Net platform. To overcome this issue, the current strategy is to use IKVM (www.ikvm.net), which allows Java programs to convert to MSIL and the .NET library.[3] In this book I mainly focus on Scala for the JVM. The examples in this book are tested only on a JVM.

1.1.1   *Scala as an object-oriented language*

The popularity of programming languages such as Java, C#, and Ruby has made object-oriented programming (OOP) widely acceptable to the majority of programmers. OOP,

---

[2] Mark Harrah, "SBT, a Build Tool for Scala," 2012, https://github.com/harrah/xsbt/.

[3] "Scala comes to .Net," July 22, 2011, www.scala-lang.org/node/10299.

as its name implies, is a programming paradigm that uses objects. Think of objects as data structures that consist of fields and methods. Object orientation helps to provide structure to your application using classes and objects. It also facilitates composition so you can create large applications from smaller building blocks. There are many OOP languages in the wild, but only a few are fit to be defined as pure object-oriented languages.

What makes a language purely object-oriented? Although the exact definition of the term depends on whom you ask, most will agree a pure object-oriented language should have the following characteristics:

- Encapsulation/information hiding.
- Inheritance.
- Polymorphism/dynamic binding.
- All predefined types are objects.
- All operations are performed by sending messages to objects.
- All user-defined types are objects.

Scala supports all these qualities and uses a pure object-oriented model similar to that of Smalltalk[4] (a pure object-oriented language created by Alan Kay around 1980), where every value is an object, and every operation is a message send. Here's a simple expression:

```
1 + 2
```

In Scala this expression is interpreted as `1.+(2)` by the Scala compiler. That means you're invoking a + operation on an integer object (in this case, 1) by passing 2 as a parameter. Scala treats operator names like ordinary identifiers. An *identifier* in Scala is either a sequence of letters and digits starting with a letter or a sequence of operator characters. In addition to +, it's possible to define methods like <=, -, or *.

Along with the pure object-oriented features, Scala has made some innovations on OOP space:

- *Modular mixin composition*—This feature of Scala has traits in common with both Java interfaces and abstract classes. You can define contracts using one or more traits and provide implementations for some or all of the methods.
- *Self-type*—A mixin doesn't depend on any methods or fields of the class that it's mixed into, but sometimes it's useful to use fields or methods of the class it's mixed into, and this feature of Scala is called *self-type*.
- *Type abstraction*—There are two principle forms of abstraction in programming languages: parameterization and abstract members. Scala supports both forms of abstraction uniformly for types and values.

I cover these areas in detail in chapters 3 and 8.

---

[4] "Smalltalk," Wikipedia, http://en.wikipedia.org/wiki/Smalltalk.

> **DEFINITION**   A mixin is a class that provides certain functionality to be inherited by a subclass and isn't meant for instantiation by itself. A mixin could also be viewed as an interface with implemented methods.

1.1.2   *Scala as a functional language*

Before I describe Scala as a functional language, I'll define functional programming in case you're not familiar with it. *Functional programming* is a programming paradigm that treats computation as the evaluation of mathematical functions and avoids state and mutable data.

> **Mutable vs. immutable data**
>
> An object is called *mutable* when you can alter the contents of the object if you have a reference to it. In the case of an *immutable* object, the contents of the object can't be altered if you have a reference to it.
>
> It's easy to create a mutable object; all you have to do is provide access to the mutable state of the object. The disadvantage of mutable objects is keeping track of the changes. In a multithreaded environment you need lock/synchronization techniques to avoid concurrent access. For immutable objects, you don't have to worry about these situations.

Functional programming takes more of a mathematical view of the world, where programs are composed of functions that take certain input and produce values and possibly other functions. The building blocks of functional programming are neither objects nor procedures (C programming style) but functions. The simple definition of functional programming is programming with functions.

It's important to understand what is meant by *function* here. A function relates every value of the domain (the input) to exactly one value of the codomain (the output). Figure 1.1 depicts a function that maps values of type X to exactly one value of Y.

Another aspect of functional programming is that it doesn't have side effects or mutability. The benefits of not having mutability and side effects in functional programs are that the programs are much easier to understand (it has no side effects), reason about, and test because the activity of the function is completely local and it has no external effects. Another huge benefit of functional programming is ease of concurrent programming. Concurrency becomes a nonissue because there's no change (immutability) to coordinate

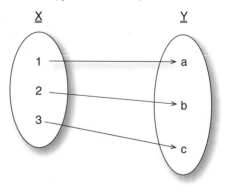

Figure 1.1   A pure function that maps values of X to exactly one value of Y

How do mathematical functions relate to functions in programming?

In mathematics, a function is a relation between a given set of elements called the *domain* (in programming we call this *input*) and a set of elements called the *codomain* (in programming we call this *output*). The function associates each element in the domain with exactly one element in the codomain. For example, `f(x) = y` could be interpreted as

```
x has a relationship f with y or x maps to y via f
```

If you write your functions keeping in mind the definition of the mathematical function, then for a given input your function should always return the same output.

Let's see this in a programming context. Say you have the following function that takes two input parameters and produces the sum of them:

```
def addFunction(a: Int, b: Int) = a + b
```

For a given input set `(2, 3)` this function always returns `5`, but the following function `currentTime` doesn't fit the definition:

```
def currentTime(timezone: TimeZone) =
      Calendar.getInstance(timezone).getTime
```

For the given `timezone` GMT, it returns different results based on the time of day.

One other interesting property of a mathematical function is *referential transparency*, which means that an expression can be replaced with its result. In the case of `add-Function`, we could replace all the calls made to it with the output value, and the behavior of the program wouldn't change.

between processes or threads. You'll learn about the functional programming side of Scala throughout the book, particularly in chapter 10.

Now let's talk about functional programming languages. Functional programming languages that support this style of programming provide at least some of the following features:

- Higher-order functions (chapter 4)
- Lexical closures (chapter 3)
- Pattern matching (chapters 2 and 3)
- Single assignment (chapter 2)
- Lazy evaluation (chapter 2)
- Type inference (chapter 2)
- Tail call optimization (chapter 5)
- List comprehensions (chapters 2 and 4)
- Mondadic effects (chapter 5)

Some of these features are probably unfamiliar if you haven't done functional programming before.

Side effects

A function or expression is said to have a side effect if, in addition to producing a value, it modifies some state or has an observable interaction with calling functions or the outside world. A function might modify a global or a static variable, modify one of its arguments, raise an exception, write data to a display or file, read data, or call other functions having side effects. In the presence of side effects, a program's behavior depends on its history of execution.

Is Scala a pure functional language?

Scala, put simply, is not a pure functional language. In a pure functional language modifications are excluded, and variables are used in a mathematical sense, with identifiers referring to immutable and persistent values. An example of a pure functional language is Haskell.

Scala supports both types of variables: single-assignment variables (also called values) that don't change their value throughout their lifetime and variables that point to a mutable state or could be reassigned to other objects. Even though you should use immutable objects whenever possible, Scala as a language doesn't provide any restrictions. The restriction is purely conventional. A good rule of thumb is to always default to `val` and use variables when it's absolutely necessary.

To me, the fundamental property of a functional language is treating functions as values, and Scala does that well.

Scala supports most of them, but to keep it simple Scala is a functional language in the sense that functions are *first-class values.* That means that in Scala, every function is a value (like some integer value 1 or some string value `"foo"`), and like any values, you can pass them as parameters and return them from other functions. In Scala you can assign a function `(x: Int) => x + 1` to a `val inc` and use that to invoke that function:

```
val inc = (x : Int) => x + 1
inc(1)
```

Here `val` represents a single assignment variable (like Java final variables) with a value that can't be changed after the assignment. The output of the function call is 2.

In the following example you'll see how to pass functions as parameters to another function and get the result:

```
List(1, 2, 3).map((x: Int) => x + 1)
```

In this case you're passing an increment function to another function called `map`, and the output produced by the invocation of the `map` function will be `List(2, 3, 4)`. Based on the output you can see that `map` is invoking the given function for each element in the list. Don't worry about the syntax right now; you'll learn about it in detail in later chapters.

1.1.3   *Scala as a multi-paradigm language*

Scala is a multi-paradigm language because it supports both functional and OOP programming. Scala is the first to unify functional programming and OOP in a statically typed language for the JVM. The obvious question is why we need more than one style of programming.

The goal of multi-paradigm computing is to provide a number of problem-solving styles so a programmer can select the solution that best matches the characteristics of the problem to be solved. This provides a framework where you can work in a variety of styles and mix the constructs from different ones. Functional programming makes it easy to build interesting things from simple parts (functions), and OOP makes it easy to adopt and extend complex systems using inheritance, classes, and so on.

According to researcher Timothy Budd,[5] "Research results from the psychology of programming indicate that expertise in programming is far more strongly related to the number of different programming styles understood by an individual than it is the number of years of experience in programming."

How can Scala combine these two different and almost opposite paradigms into one programming language? In the case of OOP, building blocks are objects, and in functional programming building blocks are functions. In Scala, functions are treated as objects.

FUNCTIONS AS OBJECTS

One of the benefits of combining functional programming with object-oriented programming in Scala is treating functions as objects.

Scala, being a functional language, treats functions as values, and you saw one example of assigning a function to a variable. Because all values in Scala are objects, it follows that functions are objects too. Look at the previous example again:

```
List(1, 2, 3).map((x: Int) => x + 1)
```

You're passing the function `(x:Int) => x + 1` to the method `map` as a parameter. When the compiler encounters such a call, it replaces the function parameter with an object, as in the following:

```
List(1, 2, 3).map(new Function1[Int, Int]{ def apply(x:Int): Int = x + 1})
```

What's going on here? Without diving in too deeply for now, when the Scala compiler encounters functions with one parameter, it replaces that call with an instance of class `scala.Function1`, which implements a method called `apply`. If you look carefully, you'll see that the body of the function is translated into the `apply` method. Likewise, Scala has `Function` objects for functions with more than one parameter.

As the popularity of multi-paradigm programming increases, the line between functional and object-oriented programming will fade away.[6] As we continue to explore Scala, you will see how we blend both functional programming and OOP to solve problems.

1.1.4 *Scala as a scalable and extensible language*

Scala stands for *scalable language*.[7] One of the design goals of Scala is to create a language that will grow and scale with your demand. Scala is suitable for use as a scripting language, as well as for large enterprise applications. Scala's component abstraction,

[5] Timothy A. Budd's personal web page, http://web.engr.oregonstate.edu/~budd/.
[6] "A Postfunctional Language," www.scala-lang.org/node/4960.
[7] "Scala: A Scalable Language" by Martin Odersky, Lex Spoon, and Bill Venners, Scalazine, May 6, 2008, www.artima.com/scalazine/articles/scalable-language.html.

succinct syntax, and support for both object-oriented and functional programming make the language scalable.

Scala also provides a unique combination of language mechanisms that makes it easy to add new language constructs in the form of libraries. You could use any method as an infix or postfix operator, and closures in Scala can be passed as "pass by name" arguments to other functions (see the next listing). These features make it easier for developers to define new constructs.

Let's create a new looping construct called `loopTill`, which is similar to the `while` loop in the following listing.

Listing 1.1   Creating the loop construct `loopTill` in Scala

```scala
def loopTill(cond: => Boolean)(body: => Unit): Unit = {
  if (cond) {
    body
    loopTill(cond)(body)
  }
}
var i = 10

loopTill (i > 0) {
    println(i)
    i -= 1
}
```

In this code you're creating a new `loopTill` construct by declaring a method called `loopTill` that takes two parameters. The first parameter is the condition (i > 0) and the second parameter is a closure. As long as the condition evaluates to `true`, the `loopTill` function will execute the given closure.

> **DEFINITION**   *Closure* is a first-class function with free variables that are bound in the lexical environment. In the `loopTill` example, the free variable is `i`. Even though it's defined outside the closure, you could still use it inside. The second parameter in the `loopTill` example is a closure, and in Scala that's represented as an object of type `scala.Function0`.

Extending a language with a library is much easier than extending the language itself because you don't have to worry about backward compatibility. For example, Scala actor implementation (defined in section 1.2.2) is provided as a library and isn't part of the Scala language. When the first actor implementation didn't scale that well, another actor implementation was added to Scala without breaking anything.

1.1.5   *Scala runs on the JVM*

The best thing about Java is not the language but the JVM. A JVM is a fine piece of machinery, and the Hotspot team has done a good job in improving its performance over the years. Being a JVM language, Scala integrates well with Java and its ecosystem, including tools, libraries, and IDEs. Now most of the IDEs ship with the Scala plug-in so that you can build, run, and test Scala applications inside the IDE. To use Scala you don't have to get rid of all the investments you've made in Java so far. Instead you can reuse them and keep your ROI coming.

Scala compiles to Java byte code, and at the byte-code level you can't distinguish between Java code and Scala code. They're the same. You could use the Java class file disassembler javap to disassemble Scala byte code (chapter 11 looks into this in more detail) as you could for Java classes.

Another advantage of running Scala on a JVM is that it can harness all the benefits of JVM-like performance and stability out of the box. And being a statically typed language, Scala programs run as fast as Java programs.

I go through all these features of Scala in more detail throughout the book, but I still haven't answered the question—why Scala?

1.2 The current crisis

An interesting phenomenon known as "Andy giveth, and Bill taketh away" comes from the fact that no matter how fast processors become, we software people find a way to use up that speed. There's a reason for that. With software you're solving more and more complex problems, and this trend will keep growing. The key question is whether processor manufacturers will be able to keep up with the demand for speed and processor power. When will this cycle end?

1.2.1 End of Moore's law

According to Moore's law, the number of transistors per square inch on a chip will double every 18 months. Unfortunately, Intel and other CPU manufacturers are finally hitting the wall[8] with Moore's law and instead are taking the route of multicore processors. The good news is that processors are going to continue to become more powerful, but the bad news is that our current applications and programming environments need to change to take advantage of multicore CPUs.

1.2.2 Programming for multicores

How can you take advantage of the new multicore processor revolution?

Concurrency. Concurrency will be, if it isn't already, the way we can write software to solve our large, distributed, complex enterprise problems if we want to exploit the CPU throughputs. Who doesn't want efficient and good performance from their applications? We all do.

A few people have been doing parallel and concurrent programming for a long time, but it still isn't mainstream or common among enterprise developers. One reason is that concurrent programming has its own set of challenges. In the traditional thread-based concurrency model, the execution of the program is split into multiple concurrently running tasks (threads), and each operates on shared memory. This leads to hard-to-find race conditions and deadlock issues that can take weeks and

---

[8] "The Free Lunch Is Over: A Fundamental Turn Toward Concurrency in Software," by Herb Sutter, originally published in Dr. Dobb's Journal, March 2005, www.gotw.ca/publications/concurrency-ddj.htm.

months to isolate, reproduce, and fix. It's not the threads but the shared memory that's the root of all the concurrency problems. The current concurrency model is too hard for developers to grok, and we need a better concurrent programming model that will help developers easily write and maintain concurrent programs.

Scala takes a totally different approach to concurrency: the Actor model. An actor[9] is a mathematical model of concurrent computation that encapsulates data, code, and its own thread of control and communicates asynchronously using immutable (no side effects) message-passing techniques. The basic Actor architecture relies on a shared-nothing policy and is lightweight in nature. It's not analogous to a Java thread; it's more like an event object that gets scheduled and executed by a thread. The Scala Actor model is a better way to handle concurrency issues. Its shared-nothing architecture and asynchronous message-passing techniques make it an easy alternative to existing thread-based solutions.

History of the Actor model

The Actor model was first proposed by Carl Hewitt in 1973 in his paper "A Universal Modular ACTOR Formalism for Artificial Intelligence" and was later on improved by Gul Agha ("ACTORS: A Model of Concurrent Computation in Distributed Systems").

Erlang was the first programming language to implement the Actor model. Erlang is a general-purpose concurrent programming language with dynamic typing. After the success of the Erlang Actor model at Ericsson, Facebook, and Yahoo!, it became a good alternative for handling concurrency problems, and Scala inherited it. In Scala, actors are implemented as a library that allows developers to have their own implementation. In chapters 7 and 12 you'll look into various Scala actor implementations.

Traditionally, programming multicore processors is more complex than programming uniprocessors and it requires platform-specific knowledge. It's also harder to maintain and manage these codebases. To make parallel programming easier, Scala provides higher abstractions in the form of a parallel collections library that hides parallel algorithms. For example, to square up each element of a List in parallel, you can use parallel collections like the following:

```
List(1, 2, 3).par.map(x => x * x)
```

In this case the .par transforms the List into a parallel collection that implements the map method using a parallel algorithm. Behind the scenes a parallel collections library will fork threads necessary to execute the map method using all the cores available in a given host machine. The parallel collections library is a new addition to Scala and provides parallel versions of most collection types. I explore more about parallel collections in chapter 4.

---

[9] "Actor model," Wikipedia, http://en.wikipedia.org/wiki/Actor_model.

1.3 Transitioning from Java to Scala

> "If I were to pick a language to use today other than Java, it would be Scala."
>
> —James Gosling

When Java, released in May 1995 by Sun Microsystems, arrived on the programming language scene, it brought some good ideas, such as a platform-independent programming environment (write once, run anywhere), automated garbage collection, and OOP. Java made object-oriented programming easier for developers, compared with C/C++, and was quickly adopted into the industry.

Over the years Java has become bloated. Every new feature added to the language brings with it more boilerplate code for the programmer; even small programs can become bloated with annotations, templates, and type information. Java developers are always looking for new ways to improve productivity using third-party libraries and tools. But is that the answer to the problem? Why not have a more productive programming language?

1.3.1 Scala improves productivity

Adding libraries and tools to solve the productivity problem sometimes backfires, adding complexity to applications and reducing productivity. I'm not saying that you shouldn't rely on libraries; you should whenever it makes sense. But what if you had a language built from the ground up from ideas like flexibility, extensibility, scalability—a language that grows with you?

Developers' needs today are much different than they used to be. In the world of Web 2.0 and agile development, flexibility and extensibility in the programming environment are important. Developers need a language that can scale and grow with them. If you're from Java, then Scala is that language. It will make you productive, and it will allow you to do more with less code and without the boilerplate code.

1.3.2 Scala does more with less code

To see the succinctness of Scala, you have to dive into the code. The next two listings provide a simple example of finding an uppercase character in a given string, comparing Scala and Java code.

> **Listing 1.2   Finding an uppercase character in a string using Java**

```
boolean hasUpperCase = false;
for(int i = 0; i < name.length(); i++) {
    if(Character.isUpperCase(name.charAt(i))) {
        hasUpperCase = true;
        break;
    }
}
```

In this code you're iterating through each character in the given string name and checking whether the character is uppercase. If it's uppercase, you set the `hasUpper-Case` flag to `true` and exit the loop. Now let's see how we could do it in Scala.

Listing 1.3   Finding an uppercase character in a string using Scala

```
val hasUpperCase = name.exists(_.isUpper)
```

In Scala you can solve this problem with one line of code. Even though it's doing the same amount of work, most of the boilerplate code is taken out of the programmer's hands. In this case you're calling a function called `exists` on `name`, which is a string, by passing a predicate that checks whether the character is true, and that character is represented by `_`. This demonstrates the brevity of the Scala language and its readability. Now let's look at the following listing, where you create a class called `Programmer` with the properties `name`, `language`, and `favDrink`.

Listing 1.4   Defining a `Programmer` class in Java

```java
public class Programmer {

    private String name;
    private String language;
    private String favDrink;

    public String getName() {
        return name;
    }
    public void setName(String name) {
        this.name = name;
    }
    public String getLanguage() {
        return language;
    }
    public void setLanguage(String language) {
        this.language = language;
    }
    public String getFavDrink() {
        return favDrink;
    }
    public void setFavDrink(String favDrink) {
        this.favDrink = favDrink;
    }
}
```

This is a simple POJO (plain old Java object) with three properties—nothing much to it. In Scala you could create a similar class in one line, as in the following listing.

Listing 1.5   Defining a `Programmer` class in Scala

```scala
class Programmer(var name:String,var language:String,var favDrink:String
```

In this example you're creating a similar class called `Programmer` in Scala but with something called a *primary constructor* (similar to a *default constructor* in Java) that takes three arguments. Yes, you can define a constructor along with the class declaration—another example of succinctness in Scala. The `var` prefix to each parameter makes the Scala compiler generate a getter and setter for each field in the class. That's impressive, right? You'll look into more interesting examples throughout the book when you go deeper into Scala. For now, it's clear that with Scala you can do more with fewer lines of code. You could argue that the IDE will automatically generate some of this boilerplate code, and that's not a problem. But I'd argue that you'd still have to maintain the generated code. Scala's succinctness will be more apparent when you look into much more involved examples. In Java and Scala code comparisons, the same feature requires 3 to 10 times more lines in Java than Scala.

1.4 *Coming from a dynamic language*

It's hard to find developers these days who haven't heard of or played with Ruby, Groovy, or Python. The biggest complaint from the dynamic language camp about statically typed languages is that they don't help the productivity of the programmer and they reduce productivity by forcing programmers to write boilerplate code. And when dynamically typed languages are compared with Java, obvious things like closures and extensibility of the language are cited everywhere. The obvious question here is how Scala is different.

Before going into the issue of static versus dynamically typed languages, let's look into Scala's support for closures and mixin. The following listing shows how to count the number of lines in a given file in Ruby.

Listing 1.6   Counting the number of lines in a file in Ruby

```
count = 0
File.open "someFile.txt" do |file|
   file.each { |line| count += 1 }
end
```

You're opening the file someFile.txt and for each line incrementing the count with 1. Simple! The following listing shows how you can do this in Scala.

Listing 1.7   Counting the number of lines in a file in Scala

```
val src = scala.io.Source.fromFile("someFile.txt")
val count = src.getLines().map(x => 1).sum
```

The Scala code looks similar to the Ruby code. You could solve this in many ways in Scala; here you're using the map method to return 1 for each line, then using the sum method to calculate the total count.

Scala supports mixin composition with something called *traits*, which are similar to an abstract class with partial implementation. For example, you can create a new type of collection which allows users to access file contents as iterable, by mixing the Scala Iterable trait. The only contract is to implement an iterator method:

```
class FileAsIterable {
  def iterator = scala.io.Source.fromFile("someFile.txt").getLines()
}
```

Now if you mix in the Scala Iterable, your new FileAsIterable will become a Scala Iterable and will start supporting all the Iterable methods:

```
val newIterator = new FileAsIterable with Iterable[String]
newIterator.foreach { line => println(line) }
```

In this case you're using the foreach method defined in the Iterable trait and printing each line in the file.

Scala version 2.10 adds support for a Dynamic[10] type. Using this feature you can dynamically add methods and fields to a type at runtime. This is very similar to the method_missing feature of Ruby and is quite useful if you're building a domain-specific language (DSL). For example, Scala map is a collection of key value pairs and if you want to access the value associated with a key you can do something like the following:

```
val someMap = Map("foo" -> 1, "bar" -> 2)
someMap.get("foo")
```

Here someMap is a collection of two key value pairs and someMap.get("foo") will return 1. Using Dynamic we can easily change that so that we can access the keys as if they were part of a type:

```
class MyMap extends Dynamic {
  ...
  def selectDynamic(fieldName: String) = map.get(fieldName)
  private val map = Map("foo" -> "1", "bar" -> 2)
}

val someMap = new MyMap
someMap.foo
someMap.bar
```

The magic ingredient in this case is the selectDynamic method. (Scala methods are defined using the def keyword.) When the Scala compiler checks that foo is not part of the type it doesn't give up immediately. If the type is a subtype of Dynamic it looks for the selectDynamic method and invokes it. If the method is not provided, you will get a compilation error.

Scala also supports something called *implicit conversion*, which is similar to Ruby open classes but scoped and compile time checked. Examples of implicit conversions are available throughout the book.

1.4.1 *Case for static typing, the right way*

With all that said and done, Scala is still a statically typed language. But if you've gone through the examples in the previous section, you've probably already figured out that Scala's static typing doesn't get in your face, and it almost feels like a dynamically typed language. But still, why should you care about static typing?

> **DEFINITION** *Static typing* is a typing system where the values and the variables have types. A number variable can't hold anything other than a number. Types are determined and enforced at compile time or declaration time.

---

[10] "SIP-17 Type Dynamic," http://docs.scala-lang.org/sips/pending/type-dynamic.html.

DEFINITION   *Dynamic typing* is a typing system where values have types but the variables don't. It's possible to successively put a number and a string inside the same variable.

The size and the complexity of the software you're building are growing every day, and having a compiler do the type checking for you is great. It reduces the time you need to spend fixing and debugging type errors. In a statically typed language like Scala, if you try to invoke a length method on a number field, the Scala compiler will give you a compilation error. In a dynamically typed language you'll get a runtime error.

Another benefit of a statically typed language is that it allows you to have powerful tools like refactoring and IDEs. Having an IDE might not interest you because of powerful editing tools like Emacs and TextMate, but having refactoring support is great when working on large codebases.

All these benefits do come with a price. Statically typed languages are more constraining than dynamically typed languages, and some force you to provide additional type information when you declare or call a function. But having constraints is useful when building a large application because they allow you to enforce a certain set of rules across the codebase. Scala, being a type-inferred language, takes care of most of the boilerplate code for the programmer (that's what compilers are good for, right?) and takes you close to a dynamically typed language, but with all the benefits of a statically typed language.

DEFINITION   *Type inference* is a technique by which the compiler determines the type of a variable or function without the help of a programmer. The compiler can deduce that the variable s in s="Hello" will have the type string because "hello" is a string. The type inference ensures the absence of any runtime type errors without putting a declaration burden on the programmer.

To demonstrate how type inference works, create an array of maps in Scala:

```
val computers = Array(
            Map("name" -> "Macbook", "color" -> "white"),
            Map("name" -> "HP Pavillion", "color" -> "black")
        )
```

If you run this Scala code in the Scala REPL, you'll see the following output:

```
computers:
    Array[scala.collection.immutable.Map[java.lang.String,java.lang.String]]
    = Array(Map(name -> Macbook, color -> white), Map(name -> HP Pavillion,
    color -> black))
```

Even though you only specified an array of maps with key and value, the Scala compiler was smart enough to deduce the type of the array and the map. And the best part is that now if you try to assign the value of name to some integer type variable somewhere in your codebase, the compiler will complain about the type mismatch, saying that you can't assign String to an integer-type variable.

1.5   *For the programming language enthusiast*

One of the main design goals for Scala was to integrate functional and OOP into one language (see section 1.1.4 for details). Scala is the first statically typed language to fuse functional and OOP into one language for the JVM. Scala has made some innovations in OOP (mentioned previously) so that you can create better component abstractions.

Scala inherits lots of ideas from various programming languages of the past and present. To start with, Scala adopts its syntax from Java/C# and supports both JVM and Common Language Runtime (CLR). Some would argue that Scala's syntax is more dissimilar than similar to that of Java/C#. You saw some Scala code in previous sections, so you can be the judge of that. In Scala every value is an object, and every operation is a method call. Smalltalk influences this pure object-oriented model. Scala also supports universal nesting and uniform access principles (see the following listing), and these are borrowed from Algol/Simula and Eiffel, respectively. In Scala variables and functions without parameters are accessed the same way.

> **Listing 1.8   Universal access principles in Scala**

```
class UAPExample {
  val someField = "hi"
  def someMethod = "there"
}

val o = new UAPExample
o.someField
o.someMethod
```

Here you're accessing a field and a method of the instance of the `UAPExample` class, and to the caller of the class it's transparent.

Scala's functional programming constructs are similar to those of the metalanguage (ML) family of languages, and Scala's Actor library is influenced by Erlang's Actor model.

> **COMPILE MACROS** The Scala 2.10 release adds experimental support for compile-time macros.[11] This allows programmers to write macro defs: functions that are transparently loaded by the compiler and executed during compilation. This realizes the notion of compile-time metaprogramming for Scala.

Based on this list you may realize that Scala is a rich language in terms of features and functionality. You won't be disappointed by Scala and will enjoy learning this language.

1.6   *Summary*

In this chapter I quickly covered many concepts, but don't worry because I'm going to reiterate these concepts throughout the book with plenty of examples so that you can relate them to real-world problems.

---

[11] Eugene Burmako, "Def Macros," http://docs.scala-lang.org/overviews/macros/overview.html.

You learned what Scala is and why you should consider learning Scala as your next programming language. Scala's extensible and scalable features make it a language that you can use for small to large programming problems. Its multi-paradigm model provides programmers with the power of abstractions from both functional and OOP models. Functional programming and actors will make your concurrent programming easy and maintainable. Scala's type inference takes care of the pain of boilerplate code so that you can focus on solving problems.

In the next chapter you'll set up your development environment and get your hands dirty with Scala code and syntax.

Getting started 2

This chapter covers

- Working with the Scala REPL
- Scala basics
- For-comprehensions and pattern matching
- Building a complete REST client in Scala

In chapter 1 you learned what Scala is and how it compares to other programming languages. I described the concepts at a high level, and in the next few chapters you're going to revisit those concepts and explore them in detail using examples. In this chapter you learn about the basic Scala types, functions, for-comprehensions, pattern matching, and the other usual suspects.

Some of the concepts in this chapter, like pattern matching and for-comprehensions, are functional programming concepts. But because Scala is a multi-paradigm language, I cover them with the rest of the nonfunctional programming concepts. The objective of this chapter is for you to become comfortable with the basics of the Scala language and its environment so you can start writing Scala programs. Early on, I focus on only the Scala interpreter and its REPL environment (you'll see it in the next section) to keep things simple.

Before going any farther, make sure your Scala installation is working. Throughout the chapter you're going to work with various Scala examples, and it would be better if you tried them in the Scala interpreter at the same time. Now let's have some fun with the Scala interpreter.

2.1 REPL with Scala interpreter

The easiest way to get started with Scala is by using the Scala interpreter, an interactive shell for writing Scala expressions and programs. To start the Scala interpreter in interactive mode, type `scala` at the command prompt. If everything goes fine with your installation, you'll see something like the following:

```
Welcome to Scala version 2.10.0.final (Java ...).
Type in expressions to have them evaluated.
Type :help for more information.

scala>
```

This means your Scala installation is successful. I'm running Scala version 2.10.0, and all the code examples should work for this version and above. At the Scala prompt type 42 and press Enter, and you should see something like this:

```
scala> 42
res0: Int = 42
```

The first line is what you typed. The Scala interpreter reads the input 42, evaluates it as an integer literal, creates an `Int` type object representing the number 42, and prints it back to the console. `res0` is the name of the variable created by the Scala interpreter (the name of the variable could be different for you because the variable name is generated by the Scala interpreter at runtime) and it holds the value 42. If you type the variable name, in this case `res0`, at the prompt, you'll get similar output:

```
scala> res0
res1: Int = 42
```

These steps together are called read-evaluate-print loop (REPL). You could loop read-evaluate-print steps repeatedly inside the Scala interpreter. Now you'll write your first "Hello world" program in Scala:

```
scala> println("Hello world")
Hello world
```

You're evaluating the `println` function by passing the `"Hello world"` string as a parameter, and Scala outputs the same string.

> **DEFINITION** `println` is a function defined in `scala.Console`, which in turn uses `System.out.println` to print messages to the console. Scala `Predef` (part of the standard library) maps `println` to `Console.println` for you so you don't have to prefix it with `Console` when using it.

In chapter 1, I mentioned that Scala integrates well with Java but didn't provide an example. I'll fix that now:

```
scala> val myList = new java.util.ArrayList[String]()
myList: java.util.ArrayList[String] = []
```

In this case you're creating an instance of `java.util.ArrayList` that will hold `String`-type objects. If you don't remember all the methods that you could possibly invoke on `myList`, don't worry because the Scala interpreter will help you with that. Type in `myList`, followed by a period, and press Tab; the Scala interpreter lists all the methods you can invoke. Not only does it list all the methods associated with a data type, it also autocompletes variable names and class names that are known to the interpreter. I encourage you to spend some time with the Scala interpreter, explore the available options, and keep it handy when working through the examples in this book. Consider REPL as an essential part of learning a new language because it gives quick feedback. Table 2.1 explains the REPL options available to you.

Table 2.1   Important Scala interpreter commands

Command	Description
`:help`	This command prints the help message with all the commands available in the Scala interpreter.
`:cp`	Use this command to add a JAR file to the classpath for the Scala interpreter. For example, `:cp tools/junit.jar` will try to find a JUnit JAR file relative to your current location and, if found, it will add the JAR file to your classpath so that you can refer to the classes inside the JAR file.
`:load` or `:l`	Allows you to load Scala files into the interpreter. If you want to investigate existing Scala code, you could load the file into the Scala interpreter, and all the definitions will be accessible to you.
`:replay` or `:r`	Resets the interpreter and replays all the previous commands.
`:quit` or `:q`	Exits the interpreter.
`:type`	Displays the type of an expression without evaluating it. For example, `:type 1 + 2` will determine the type of the expression to `Int` without performing the add operation.

2.2   Scala basics

In this section I round out basic Scala information with examples so you can gradually get comfortable with the language. You'll use the Scala REPL to try out the examples, but you can use any of the development environments mentioned in the previous section that suit you.

In the following sections you'll explore basic Scala types, including `String` and the value types `Byte`, `Short`, `Int`, `Long`, `Float`, `Double`, `Boolean`, and `Char`. You'll learn about two types of Scala variables, `var` and `val`, how they're used, and how they're different. You'll also learn about the Scala functions, how to define them, and ways you can invoke them. Let's start with the basic data types in Scala.

2.2.1 Basic types

If you're a Java programmer, you'll be glad to know that Scala supports all the basic value types (primitives): Byte, Short, Int, Float, Double, Boolean, and Char. Table 2.2 shows all eight basic value types supported by Scala. In Scala all the basic types are objects, and they're defined under the scala package.

Table 2.2 Scala basic types

Value type	Description and range
Byte	8-bit signed 2's complement integer. It has minimum value of –128 and a maximum value of 127 (inclusive).
Short	16-bit signed 2's complement integer. It has a minimum value of –32,768 and maximum of 32,767 (inclusive).
Int	32-bit signed 2's complement integer. It has a minimum value of –2,147,483,648 and a maximum value of 2,147,483,647 (inclusive).
Long	64-bit signed 2's complement integer. It has a minimum value of -9,223,372,036,854,775,808 and a maximum value of 9,223,372,036,854,775,807 (inclusive).
Float	A single-precision 32-bit IEEE 754 floating point.
Double	A double-precision 64-bit IEEE 754 floating point.
Boolean	Two possible values: true and false.
Char	A single 16-bit Unicode character. It has a minimum value of '\u0000' (or 0) and a maximum value of '\uffff' (or 65,535 inclusive).

In Scala all the basic types are declared using initial caps. Instead of declaring something as int, in Scala it's declared as Int. In earlier versions of Scala, programmers could use lowercase and uppercase interchangeably, but from version 2.8 on, if you declare any variable with int, you'll get a compiler error:

```
scala> val x:int = 1
<console>:4: error: not found: type
    int
val x:int = 1
```

The following is fine with the compiler:

```
scala> val x:Int = 1
x: Int = 1
```

Even though the full qualifying name of Int is scala.Int, you can use only Int

A small fact about Scala Predef

The Scala compiler implicitly imports java.lang, the scala package, and an object called scala.Predef to every compilation unit or Scala program. In the case of .NET instead of java.lang, it imports the system package. The Predef object defines standard functions and type aliases for Scala programs. Because this object is imported automatically, all members of this object are available to you. Predef is interesting, and you can learn a lot about Scala by looking at the scaladoc or source of the scala.Predef object.

because the scala package is automatically imported into every Scala source, so you don't have to fully qualify the basic types.[1]

To see all packages that are automatically imported, use the :imports command inside REPL:

```
scala> :imports
 1) import java.lang._          (153 types, 158 terms)
 2) import scala._              (798 types, 806 terms)
 3) import scala.Predef._       (16 types, 167 terms, 96 are implicit)
```

In this case, java.lang, scala, and scala.Predef packages are automatically imported when you start a REPL session.

INTEGER LITERALS

Of the basic types defined in table 2.2, Byte, Short, Int, Long, and Char are collectively called *integral types*. The integer literals can represent decimal, hexadecimal, and octal numbers. They're determined by the way the literal is defined. If the literal is 0 or any nonzero digits, it's a decimal number:

```
scala> val decimal = 11235
decimal: Int = 11235
```

> **DEFINITION** A *literal* is a shorthand way to describe an object. The shorthand expression matches the structure of the project. You could create a string object by using the string literal "one" and also using the new keyword, as in new String("one").

Because integer literals are usually integers, Scala infers the type as integer, but if you want a Long type, you could add the suffix L or l:

```
scala> val decimal = 11235L
decimal: Long = 11235
```

Hexadecimal numbers start with 0x, and octal numbers should be prefixed with 0:

```
scala> val hexa = 0x23
hexa: Int = 35

scala> val octa = 023
hexa: Int = 19
```

One thing to note while using hexadecimal and octal numbers is that the Scala interpreter always evaluates the result as a decimal number. You can specify the type of variable (sometimes called only *value*; more on this later) that you want when you think Scala type inference isn't producing the result you are seeking. If you declare a variable with an integer literal, for example, Scala creates a variable of type integer unless it can't fit the value within the range of integer values. In that case the Scala compiler throws an error. What do you do if you want a Byte type variable? You declare the type Byte when creating the variable:

---

[1] Documentation for the Scala standard library, www.scala-lang.org/docu/files/api/index.html.

```
scala> val i  = 1
i: Int = 1

scala> val i2: Byte = 1
i2: Byte = 1
```

FLOATING-POINT LITERALS

Floating-point literals are composed of digits with a decimal point and an exponent part. But both the decimal point and the exponent part are optional. Floating-point literals are of type `Float` when they're suffixed with `F` or `f` and are `Double` otherwise:

```
scala> val d  = 0.0
d: Double = 0.0

scala> val f = 0.0f
f: Float = 0.0
```

You can also create a `Double` variable with an exponent part. To declare a variable with the value of 1 times 10 to the power of 30 (1 times 10^30), it would look like this:

```
scala>val exponent = 1e30
exponent: Double = 1.0E30
```

A corner case with floating literals

In floating literals you could define a `Double` value as `1.0` or as `1`, without the trailing zero or digits. In Scala you can invoke a method with a decimal point (.) followed by a method name, because all basic types (primitives) are objects in Scala, and like all other Scala objects they have a `toString` method. This raises an interesting corner case when invoking methods on floating literals. To invoke a `toString` method on the `1.` floating literal, what should you do? You have to put a space between the dot and the `toString` method, like this: `1. toString`. If you try it as `1.toString` without the space, it invokes the `toString` method defined in the `Int` object. This is necessary only when the method name starts with a letter. For example, `1.+1` works fine and produces the desired output, `2.0`.

CHARACTER LITERALS

A character literal is a single character enclosed in quotes. The character can be a printable Unicode character or an escape sequence:

```
scala> val capB = '\102'
capB: Char = B

scala> val capB = 'B'
capB: Char = B
```

You can also assign special character literal escape sequences to `Char` type variables:

```
scala> val new_line = '\n'
new_line: Char =
```

Because the `new_line` character is nonprintable, unlike others, the value of the `new_line` variable doesn't show up in the Scala interpreter. All the character escapes in Java and .NET are supported. Scala takes programming with Unicode characters to the next level. You can use not only literals but also printable Unicode characters as variable and method names. To create a variable name `ans` with the value 42 using Unicode characters, you would do something like the following:

```
scala> val \u0061\u006e\u0073 = 42
ans: Int = 42
```

Using Unicode characters for naming variables or functions in a program is a way to get yelled at by your peers, but in some contexts it improves the readability of the code.[2] In the following example Unicode characters are used in the variable and method name:

```
val ? = scala.math.Pi
def ?(x:Double) = scala.math.sqrt(x)
```

Before trying out these examples, make sure your editor supports Unicode encoding.

STRING LITERALS

A string literal is a sequence of characters in double quotes. The characters are either printable Unicode characters or escape sequences. If the string literal contains a double-quote character, it must be escaped with a slash (\):

```
scala> val bookName = "Scala in \"Action\""
bookName: java.lang.String = Scala in "Action"
```

The value of the string literal is of type `String`. Unlike other basic types, `String` is an instance of `java.lang.String`. As mentioned earlier, it's automatically imported for you. Scala also supports a special multiline string literal that's enclosed in triple quotes (`"""`). The sequence of characters is arbitrary, except that it may not contain a triple quote, and it doesn't even necessarily have to be printable:

```
scala> val multiLine = """This is a
     |                          multi line
     |                          string"""
multiLine: java.lang.String =
This is a
          multi line
          string
```

The output of the `multiLine` variable has leading whitespaces, and maybe you don't want that. There's an easy fix—invoking a method called `stripMargin` strips out the margin for you:

```
scala> val multiLine = """This is a
     | |multi line
     | |string""".stripMargin
multiLine: String =
This is a
multi line
string
```

---

[2] "Boolean Algebra Internal DSL in Scala," Gabriel's software development blog, June 2, 2009, http://mng.bz/ w2V3.

This code may seem a little confusing. The first | (vertical bar) or margin is added by the interpreter when you press Enter without completing the expression, and the second one is the one that you added as a margin for the multiline string. When the `stripMargin` method finds those margin characters, it strips out the leading whitespaces. I find multiline strings helpful when creating data sets for unit tests.

String interpolation

Scala 2.10 has support for `String` interpolation. You can use the feature like this:

```
scala> val name = "Nilanjan"
name: String = Nilanjan
scala> s"My name $name"
res0: String = My name Nilanjan
```

Here is a method invoked on a class `StringContext` by passing the string literal contained within the double quotes. Any token prefixed with $ or wrapped with ${...} within the string will be replaced with its corresponding values. Similarly prepending `f` to any string literal allows the creation of simple formatted strings, similar to printf in other languages:

```
scala> val height = 1.9d
height: Double = 1.9
scala> val name = "James"
name: String = James
scala> println(f"$name%s is $height%2.2f meters tall")
James is 1.90 meters tall
```

As a careful reader, you're probably a little surprised by this `stripMargin` method because I said that a Scala `String` object is nothing but a representative of a `java.lang.String` object; where did we get this new `stripMargin` method? There's no method called `stripMargin` in `java.lang.String`. Again `Predef` is doing a little bit of magic by wrapping `java.lang.String` to another type called `scala.collection.immutable.StringLike`. If you look up the Scala documentation,[3] you'll see the `stripMargin` method with many other useful methods that Scala provides to string objects, along with the ones defined in the `java.lang.String` class.

RichString vs. StringLike

If you've used previous versions of Scala, you'll recall an earlier class called `scala.RichString` that provided additional methods to Scala string objects, but from Scala 2.8 it's called `scala.collection.immutable.StringLike`. Treating a string as an immutable collection makes sense because it's a collection of characters, and a string is an immutable object. Scala still has `Rich` type wrappers for other basic types like `RichInt`, `RichBoolean`, `RichDouble`, and so on.

---

[3] Documentation for the Scala standard library, www.scala-lang.org/api/current/index.html.

XML LITERALS

Typically, working with XML means using third-party parsers and libraries, but in Scala it's part of the language. Scala supports XML literals, where you can have XML fragments as part of the code:

```
val book = <book>
              <title>Scala in Action</title>
              <author>Nilanjan Raychaudhuri</author>
              </book>
```

When you type this expression into the Scala interpreter, you'll get the following:

```
book: scala.xml.Elem =
    <book>
        <title>Scala in Action</title>
        <author>Nilanjan Raychaudhuri</author>
    </book>
```

Scala converts the XML literal to a `scala.xml.Elem` type object. It doesn't stop here. You can put valid Scala code inside curly braces, `{}`, within the XML tags, and it works out great when you have to generate the XML dynamically:

```
scala> val message = "I didn't know xml could be so much fun"
scala> val code = "1"
scala> val alert = <alert>
              <message priority={code}>{message}</message>
              <date>{new java.util.Date()}</date>
              </alert>

alert: scala.xml.Elem =
<alert>
      <message priority="1">
          I didn't know xml could be so much fun
        </message>
      <date>Fri Feb 19 19:18:08 EST 2010</date>
 </alert>
```

As you can see, Scala executes the code inside the curly braces and replaces it with the output of the code. The code defined within curly braces is called *Scala code blocks.*

When using Scala code to generate attribute values, make sure you don't put double quotes around it (`priority={code}`) because if you do, Scala will ignore it and treat it as a string value. Throughout the book you'll look into various uses of XML literals and other XML goodies supported by Scala.

2.2.2 *Defining variables*

You've already seen many examples about defining variables. In Scala there are two ways you can define variables: `val` and `var`. A `val` is a single assignment variable, sometimes called *value*. Once initialized a `val` can't be changed or reassigned to some other value (similar to final variables in Java). On the other hand, `var` is reassignable; you can change the value of the variable over and over again after initial assignment:

```
scala> val constant = 87
constant: Int = 87

scala> constant = 88
<console>:5: error: reassignment to val
       constant = 88
                ^
scala> var variable = 87
variable: Int = 87

scala> variable = 88
variable: Int = 88
```

The Scala interpreter does a good job of inferring the type of variable based on the value, but there are times when you'd like to, or have to, specify the type. You can specify the type of variable after the variable name, separating it by a colon (:).

There'll be situations where you want to declare a variable without assigning a value because you don't yet know the value. In cases like these you can use the Scala placeholder character (_) to assign a default value:

```
scala> var willKnowLater:String = _
willKnowLater: String = null
```

Because the default value for String is null, in this example the value of willKnow-Later is null. As an exercise, try using Scala placeholder characters with other basic types and see what values you get back. One point to note here is that when declaring variables (both val and var), you have to specify the value or _ (Scala placeholder); otherwise, the Scala interpreter will complain. The only case where you can have variables (only vars because val always needs a value when declared) without values assigned to them is when the variables are declared inside a class.

Sometimes you may want to declare a type whose value gets calculated based on some time-consuming operation, and you don't want to do that when you declare the variable; you want to initialize it lazily because by default Scala evaluates the value assigned to var or val when it's declared. To change this default behavior, use lazy val:

```
scala> lazy val forLater = someTimeConsumingOperation()
forLater: Unit = <lazy>
```

The someTimeConsumingOperation() will be called when the variable forLater is used in any expression. Here's another example that demonstrates the laziness:

```
scala> var a = 1
a: Int = 1

scala> lazy val b = a + 1
b: Int = <lazy>

scala> a = 5
a: Int = 5

scala> b
res1: Int = 6
```

In the last line, typing b forces the evaluation of the b, and because it wasn't evaluated when b was declared, it uses the latest value of a. The lazy keyword is allowed only with val; you can't declare lazy var variables in Scala.

The variable declaration can sometimes have a pattern on the left side. Say you want to extract the first element of a List and assign it to a variable. You can do that using a pattern on the left side along with the variable declaration:

```
scala> val first :: rest = List(1, 2, 3)
first: Int = 1
rest: List[Int] = List(2, 3)
```

List is an immutable sequence type of collection (similar to List in Java and C#) in Scala, and in this case it holds a collection of integers from 1 to 3. The pattern on the left side matches the first element of the List, in this case 1, to the variable first and the rest to the tail of the list, 2 and 3. The :: (called cons) is a method defined in List. I cover more about pattern matching later in this chapter.

Earlier I made the argument for immutability and why you should always prefer immutability to mutability. Keeping that in mind, always start with val when declaring variables in Scala and change to var when it's absolutely necessary.

2.2.3 Defining functions

Functions are building blocks in Scala, and in this section you're going to explore that topic. To define a function in Scala, use the def keyword followed by the method name, parameters, optional return type, =, and the method body. Figure 2.1 shows the syntax of the Scala function declaration.

Use a colon (:) to separate the parameter list from the return type. Multiple parameters are separated by commas (,). The equals sign (=) is used as a separator between the method signature and the method body.

Let's drop the parameter for the time being; you'll come back to parameters later. You'll create your first Scala function without parameters:

```
scala> def myFirstMethod():String = { "exciting times ahead" }
myFirstMethod: ()String
```

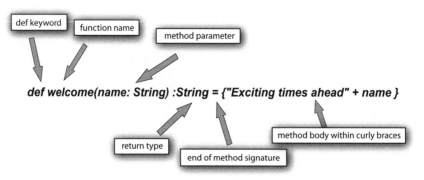

Figure 2.1   The syntax of the Scala function declaration

The return type of a Scala function is optional because Scala infers the return type of a function automatically. There are situations where it doesn't work, but don't worry about that until later. Improve the myFirstMethod method by removing the return type:

```
scala> def myFirstMethod() = { "exciting times ahead" }
myFirstMethod: ()java.lang.String

scala> myFirstMethod()
res6: java.lang.String = exciting times ahead
```

The significance of = after the method signature isn't only to separate the signature from the method body but also to tell the Scala compiler to infer the return type of your function. If you omit that, Scala won't infer your return type:

```
scala> def myFirstMethod(){ "exciting times ahead" }
myFirstMethod: ()Unit

scala> myFirstMethod()
```

In this case when you invoke the function using the function name and (), you'll get no result. In the REPL output, notice that the return type of your function is no longer java.lang.String; it's Unit. Unit in Scala is like void in Java, and it means that the method doesn't return anything.

> **TIP** Scala type inference is powerful, but use it carefully. If you're creating a library and plan to expose your functions as a public API, it's a good practice to specify the return type for the users of the library. In any case, if you think it's not clear from the function what its return type is, either try to improve the name so that it communicates its purpose better or specify the return type.

Your myFirstMethod is simple: it returns the string "exciting times ahead" and when you have a function like that, you also drop the curly braces from the method body:

```
scala> def myFirstMethod() = "exciting times ahead"
myFirstMethod: ()java.lang.String
```

If you invoke the function, you'll get the same result. In Scala it's always possible to take out unnecessary syntax noise from the code. Because you aren't passing any parameters, you can take out the unused () from the declaration, and it almost looks like a variable declaration, except that instead of using var or val you're using def:

```
scala> def myFirstMethod = "exciting times ahead"
myFirstMethod: java.lang.String
```

When calling the function you can also leave out the parentheses:

```
scala> myFirstMethod
res17: java.lang.String = exciting times ahead
```

If the function has side effects, the common convention is to use "()" even though it isn't required.

Returning to function parameters, the following function called max takes two parameters and returns the one that's the greater of the two:

```
scala> def max(a: Int, b: Int) = if(a > b) a else b
max: (a: Int,b: Int)Int

scala> max(5, 4)
res8: Int = 5

scala> max(5, 7)
res9: Int = 7
```

By now you probably have figured out that specifying return is optional in Scala. You don't have to specify the return keyword to return anything from the function. It will return the value of the last expression. In the previous case, if the if condition evaluates to true, then a is the last expression that is executed, so a is returned; otherwise b is returned. Even though the return type is optional, you do have to specify the type of the parameters when defining functions. Scala type inference will figure out the type of parameters when you invoke the function but not during the function declaration.[4,5]

> **Type inference**
>
> If you have a background in Haskell, OCaml, or any other type of inferred programming language, the way Scala parameters are defined could feel a bit weird. The reason is that Scala doesn't use the Hindley-Milner algorithm to infer type; instead Scala's type inference is based on declaration-local information, also known as local type inference. Type inference is out of the scope of this book, but if you're interested you can read about the Hindley-Milner type inference algorithm and why it's useful.

Sometimes it becomes necessary to create a function that will take an input and create a List from it. But the problem is you can't determine the type of input yet. Someone could use your function to create a List of Int, and another person could use it to create a List of String. In cases like this you create a function in Scala by parameterized type. The parameter type will be decided when you invoke the function:

```
scala> def toList[A](value:A) = List(value)
toList: [A](value: A)List[A]

scala> toList(1)
res16: List[Int] = List(1)

scala> toList("Scala rocks")
res15: List[java.lang.String] = List(Scala rocks)
```

When declaring the function, you denote the unknown parameterized type as A. Now when your toList is invoked, it replaces the A with the parameter type of the given parameter. In the method body you create an instance of immutable List by passing the parameter, and from the REPL output it's clear that List is also using a parameterized type.

4 "Type inference," Wikipedia, http://mng.bz/32jw.
5 Daniel Spiewak, posted at Code Commit, "What is Hindley-Milner? (and why is it cool?)," undated, http://mng.bz/H4ip.

NOTE If you're a Java programmer, you'll find lots of similarities between Java generics and Scala parameterized types. The only difference to remember for now is that Java uses angle brackets (<>) and Scala uses square brackets ([]). Another Scala convention for naming the parameterized types is that they normally start at A and go up to Z as necessary. This contrasts with the Java convention of using T, K, V, and E.

FUNCTION LITERALS

In Scala you can also pass a function as a parameter to another function, and most of the time in those cases I provide an inline definition of the function. This passing of functions as a parameter is sometimes loosely called *closure* (passing a function isn't always necessarily closure; you'll look into that in chapter 4). Scala provides a shorthand way to create a function in which you write only the function body, called *function literals*. Put that to a test. In this test you want to add all the elements of a List using function literals. This demonstrates a simple use of function literals in Scala. Here you're creating a List of even numbers:

```
scala> val evenNumbers = List(2, 4, 6, 8, 10)
evenNumbers: List[Int] = List(2, 4, 6, 8, 10)
```

To add all the elements of List (scala.collection.immutable.List), you can use the foldLeft method defined in List. The foldLeft method takes two parameters: an initial value and a binary operation. It applies the binary operation to the given initial value and all the elements of the list. It expects the binary operation as a function that takes two parameters of its own to perform the operation, which in our case will be addition. If you can create a function that will take two parameters and add them, you're finished with the test. The foldLeft function will call your function for every element in the List, starting with the initial value:

```
scala> evenNumbers.foldLeft(0) { (a: Int, b:Int) => a + b }
res19: Int = 30
```

In this case the function (a: Int, b:Int) => a + b is called an *anonymous* function, or a function without a predefined name. You can improve your function by taking advantage of Scala's type inference:

```
scala> evenNumbers.foldLeft(0) { (a, b) => a + b }
res20: Int = 30
```

Usually you have to specify the type of the parameter for top-level functions because Scala can't infer the parameter types when declared, but for anonymous functions Scala inference can figure out the type from the context. In this case you're using a list of integers and 0 as your initial value, and based on that Scala can easily infer the type of a and b as an integer. Scala allows you to go even further with your anonymous function: you can drop the parameters and only have the method body to make it a function literal. But in this case the parameters will be replaced with underscores (_). An underscore has a special meaning in Scala, and in this context it's a placeholder for a parameter; in your case, use two underscores:

```
scala> evenNumbers.foldLeft(0) { _ + _ }
res21: Int = 30
```

Each underscore represents a parameter in your function literal. You've already seen another use of the underscore when assigning a default value to variables. In Scala you can use underscores in various places, and their meaning is determined solely by the context and where they're used. Sometimes it gets a little confusing, so always remember that the value of the underscore is based on where it's being used. You'll see other uses of underscores throughout the book. Function literals are a common idiom in Scala, and you'll find occurrences of them in Scala libraries and codebases.

In chapter 1 you saw the following example but without enough explanation of what's going on with the code. Now, with your new knowledge of function literals, it should be pretty obvious that _.isUpper is a function literal:

```
val hasUpperCase = name.exists(_.isUpper)
```

In this case you're invoking the given function literals for each character in the name string; when it finds an uppercase character, it will exit. The underscore in this context represents a character of name string.

USING SCALA CLOSURE AND FIRST-CLASS FUNCTIONS: AN EXAMPLE

Before moving to the next section, leaving the "defining function" section without a small working example of closure would be unfair. A *closure* is any function that closes over the environment in which it's defined. For example, closure will keep track of any variable changes outside the function that are being referred to inside the function.

In the example you'll try to add support for the word break. I haven't talked about Scala keywords yet, but Scala doesn't have break or continue. Once you get comfortable with Scala, you won't miss them because Scala's support of functional programming style reduces the need for break or continue. But assume you have a situation where you think having break would be helpful. Scala is an extensible programming language, so you can extend it to support break.

Use the Scala exception-handling mechanism to implement break in Scala. Throwing an exception will help you break the sequence of execution, and the catch block will help you reach the end of the call. Because break isn't a keyword, you can use it to define your function so that it will throw an exception:

```
def break = new RuntimeException("break exception")
```

Another subject not yet covered is exception handling, but if you've used it in Java, C#, or Ruby, it should be easy to follow. In any case, you'll read about exception handling in a later part of the chapter. Now create the main function that will take the operation that needs a breakable feature. Make it obvious and call it breakable:

```
def breakable(op: => Unit) { ... }
```

What's this op: => Unit? The special right arrow (=>) lets Scala know that the breakable function expects a function as a parameter. The right side of the => defines the return type of the function—in this case it's Unit (similar to Java void)—and op is the name of the parameter. Because you haven't specified anything on the left side of the arrow, it means that the function you're expecting as a parameter doesn't take any parameter for itself. But if you expect a function parameter that takes two parameters, such as foldLeft, you have to define it as follows:

```
def foldLeft(initialValue: Int, operator: (Int, Int) => Int)= { ... }
```

The breakable function that you declared takes a no-parameter function and returns Unit. Now, using these two functions, you could simulate the break. Let's look at an example function that needs to break when the environment variable SCALA_HOME isn't set; otherwise, it must do the work:

```
def install = {
  val env = System.getenv("SCALA_HOME")
  if(env == null) break
  println("found scala home lets do the real work")
}
```

Now inside the breakable function we need to catch the exception that will get raised when break is called from the install function:

```
try {
    op
} catch { case _ => }
```

That's it. The following listing holds the complete code.

Listing 2.1 breakable, break, and install functions

```
val breakException = new RuntimeException("break exception")

def breakable(op: => Unit) {
  try {
    op
  } catch { case _ => }
}

def break = throw breakException

def install = {
  val env = System.getenv("SCALA_HOME")
  if(env == null) break
  println("found scala home lets do the real work")
}
```

To invoke the breakable function, pass the method name that needs a breakable feature, like breakable(install)—or you can inline the install function and pass it as a closure:

```
breakable {
  val env = System.getenv("SCALA_HOME")
  if(env == null) break
  println("found scala home lets do the real work")
}
```

In Scala if the last argument of a function is of function type, you can pass it as closure. This syntax sugar is useful in creating DSLs. In the next chapter you'll look into how closures are converted into objects; remember, everything in Scala is an object.

> **NOTE**   Scala already provides breakable as part of the library. Look for scala.util.control.Breaks. You should use Breaks if you have a need for break. Again, I'd argue that once you look into functional programming with Scala in detail, you'll probably never have a need for break.

2.3   *Working with Array and List*

Chapter 4 is dedicated to data structures, but until then I'll introduce List and Array so you can start writing useful Scala scripts.

In Scala, array is an instance of the scala.Array class and is similar to the Java array:

```
scala> val array = new Array[String](3)
array: Array[String] = Array(null, null, null)

scala> array(0) = "This"

scala> array(1) = "is"

scala> array(2) = "mutable"

scala> array
res37: Array[String] = Array(This, is, mutable)
```

Always remember that in Scala the type information or parameterization is provided using square brackets. The type parameterization is a way to configure an instance with type information when creating the instance.

Now iterating through each element in the array is easy; call the foreach method:

```
scala> array.foreach(println)
This
is
mutable
```

You're passing a function literal to the foreach method to print all the elements in the array. There are other useful methods defined for Array objects; for a complete list look in Scaladoc for scala.collection.mutable.ArrayLike. The most obvious question in your mind right now is probably why we have to check ArrayLike, which is a different class than the Array used to check methods that are available for an Array instance in Scala. The answer is Predef. Scala Predef provides additional array functionality dynamically using ArrayLike when you create an instance of an Array. Again, Predef is a great place to start to understand the Scala Library.

> **NOTE**   Predef implicitly converts Array to scala.collection.mutable .ArrayOps. ArrayOps is the subclass of ArrayLike, so ArrayLike is more like the interface for all the additional methods available to Array type collections.

When writing Scala scripts, you sometimes have to take command-like arguments. You can do that implicitly as a `val` type variable called `args`. In the following example you'll create a Scala script that takes input from a user and prints it to the console:

```
args.foreach(println)
```

Open your favorite editor and save this line in a file called myfirstScript.scala. Open a command prompt to the location where the file is saved and run the following command:

```
scala  myfirstScript.scala my first script
```

You'll see the following output:

```
my
first
script
```

You executed your first script. You're using the same command you used to start the Scala REPL environment. But in this case you're executing a Scala script by specifying the script filename and three parameters: `my`, `first`, and `script`. You'll see another script example at the end of this chapter.

The `Array` is a mutable data structure; by adding each element to the array, you're mutating the `array` instance and producing a side effect. In functional programming, methods should not have side effects. The only effect a method is allowed to have is to compute a value and return that value without mutating the instance. An immutable and more functional alternative to a sequence of objects like `Array` is `List`. In Scala, `List` is immutable and makes functional-style programming easy. Creating a list of elements is as easy as the following:

```
scala> val myList = List("This", "is", "immutable")
myList: List[java.lang.String] = List(This, is, immutable)
```

The `List` is shorthand for `scala.collection.immutable.List`, and again `Predef` automatically makes it available to you:

```
scala> val myList = scala.collection.immutable.List("This", "is",
    "immutable")
myList: List[java.lang.String] = List(This, is, immutable)
```

What is this scala.collection.immutable.$colon$colon?

If you call the `getClass` method on `myList` to see what type of object it is, you might be surprised. Instead of `scala.collection.immutable.List`, you'll see

```
scala> myList.getClass
res42: java.lang.Class[_] = class
        scala.collection.immutable.$colon$colon
```

That's because `scala.collection.immutable.List` is an abstract class, and it comes with two implementations: the `scala.Nil` class and `scala.::`. In Scala, `::` is a valid identifier, and you could use it to name a class. `Nil` represents an empty list, and `scala.::` represents any nonempty list.

Most of us are used to mutable collections where, when we add or remove elements, the collection instance expands or shrinks (mutates), but immutable collections never change. Instead, adding or removing an element from an immutable collection creates a new modified collection instance without modifying the existing one. The following example adds an element to an existing `List`:

```
scala> val oldList = List(1, 2)
oldList: List[Int] = List(1, 2)

scala> val newList = 3 :: oldList
newList: List[Int] = List(3, 1, 2)

scala> oldList
res45: List[Int] = List(1, 2)
```

In this example you're adding 3 to an existing `List` containing elements 1 and 2 using the `::` method. The job of the `::` method is to create a new `List` with all the existing elements plus the new element added at the front of the `List`. To add at the end of the `List`, invoke the `:+` method:

```
scala> val newList = oldList :+ 3
newList: List[Int] = List(1, 2, 3)
```

Scala provides a special object called `Nil` to represent an empty `List`, and you can use it to create new lists easily:

```
scala> val myList = "This" :: "is" :: "immutable" :: Nil
myList: List[java.lang.String] = List(This, is, immutable)
```

In this example you're using a new instance of `List` every time you add an element. To delete an element from a `List`, you could use the `-` method, but it's deprecated. A better way would be to use the `filterNot` method, which takes a predicate and selects all the elements that don't satisfy the predicate. To delete 3 from the `newList`, you can do something like the following:

```
scala> val afterDelete = newList.filterNot(_ == 3)
afterDelete: List[Int] = List(1, 2)
```

You'll delve deeper into Scala collections in chapter 4, section 4.3, but for now you know enough to play with Scala and script a few things. In the meantime I encourage you to look into methods defined for `List` and play with them.

2.4   *Controlling flow with loops and ifs*

It's a little hard to get into useful programming or scripting with Scala without the loops and ifs. Well, your wait is over. In Scala, `if` and `else` blocks work as they do in any other programming language. If the expression inside the `if` evaluates to `true`, then the `if` block gets executed; otherwise, the `else` block is executed. The interesting part about Scala is that every statement is an expression, and its value is determined by the last expression within the statement. Assigning a value depending on some condition in Scala could look like this:

```
val someValue = if(some condition) value1 else value2

scala> val useDefault = false
useDefault: Boolean = false

scala> val configFile = if(useDefault) "custom.txt" else "default.txt"
configFile: java.lang.String = default.txt
```

Scala doesn't support the ? operator as Java does, but I don't think you'll miss it in
Scala. You can nest if/else blocks, and you can combine multiple if/else blocks
using else if.

Loops in Scala have all the usual suspects like the while loop and do-while, but
the most interesting looping construct is for or for-comprehensions. The while and
do-while loops are pretty standard, and in Scala they aren't any different from Java or
C#. The next section looks at Scala for-comprehensions.

2.5   For-comprehensions

A for-comprehension in Scala is like a Swiss Army knife: you can do many things with
it using basic simple elements. The for expression in Scala consists of a for keyword
followed by one or more enumerators surrounded by parentheses and followed by an
expression block or yield expression (see figure 2.2).

Before I go into yield expression, let's look into the more traditional form of the
for loop. The common pattern used in a for loop is to iterate through a collection.
To print all the files in a directory that end with the .scala extension, for example, you
have to do something like the following:

```
val files = new java.io.File(".").listFiles
for(file <- files) {
    val filename = file.getName
    if(fileName.endsWith(".scala")) println(file)
}
```

The only thing that looks different from for loops in Java or C# is the expression file
<- files. In Scala this is called a *generator,* and the job of a generator is to iterate
through a collection. The right side of the <- represents the collection—in this case,
files. For each element in the collection (file in this case) it executes the for block.
This is similar to the way you define a for loop in Java:

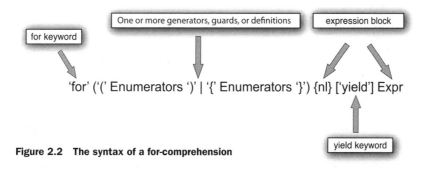

Figure 2.2   The syntax of a for-comprehension

```
for(File file: files) {
    String filename = file.getName();
    if(filename.endsWith(".scala")) System.out.println(file);
}
```

In the case of Scala, you don't have to specify the type of file object because Scala type inference will take care of it.

Apart from the generator, you can use other ingredients in a Scala `for` loop to simplify the previous example.

```
for(
    file <- files;
    fileName = file.getName;
    if(fileName.endsWith(".scala"))
) println(file)
```

Scala `for` loops allow you to specify definitions and guard clauses inside the loop. In this case you're defining a filename variable and checking whether the filename ends with .scala. The loop will execute when the given guard clause is `true`, so you'll get the same result as the previous example. Note that all the variables created inside a `for` expression are of the `val` type, so they can't be modified and hence reduce the possibility of side effects.

As mentioned earlier, it's possible to specify more than one generator in a Scala `for` loop control. The following example executes the loop for each generator and adds them:

```
scala> val aList = List(1, 2, 3)
aList: List[Int] = List(1, 2, 3)

scala> val bList = List(4, 5, 6)
bList: List[Int] = List(4, 5, 6)

scala> for { a <- aList; b <- bList } println(a + b)
5
6
7
6
7
8
7
8
9
```

The generators in this case are aList and bList, and when you have multiple generators, each generator is repeated for the other generator. When a = 1 for each value of b, that is, b = 4, b = 5, b = 6, the loop will be executed, and so on. I used curly braces to surround the `for` expression, but you don't have to; you could use `()`. I tend to use curly braces when I have more than one generator and guard clause.

The for-comprehension in Scala comes in two flavors. You've already seen one form in the previous examples: the *imperative form*. In this form you specify the statements that will get executed by the loop, and it doesn't return anything. The other form of for-comprehension is called the *functional form* (sometimes it's also called *sequence comprehension).* In the functional form, you tend to work with values rather than execute statements, and it does return a value. Look at the same example in functional form:

```
scala> for { a <- aList; b <- bList } yield a + b
res27: List[Int] = List(5, 6, 7, 6, 7, 8, 7, 8, 9)
```

Instead of printing the value of a + b, you're returning the value of the addition from the loop using the yield keyword. You're using the same aList and bList instances in the loop control, and it returns the result as a List. Now if you want to print the result, as in the previous example, you have to loop through the result List:

```
scala> val result = for { a <- aList; b <- bList } yield a + b
result: List[Int] = List(5, 6, 7, 6, 7, 8, 7, 8, 9)

scala> for(r <- result) println(r)
5
6
7
6
7
8
7
8
9
```

It does look like the functional form is more verbose than the imperative form, but think about it. You've separated the computation (the adding of two numbers) from how you're using it—in this case, printing the result. This improves the reusability and compatibility of functions or computations, which is one of the benefits of functional programming. In the following example you reuse the result produced by the for-yield loop to create an XML node:

```
scala> val xmlNode = <result>{result.mkString(",")}</result>
xmlNode: scala.xml.Elem = <result>5,6,7,6,7,8,7,8,9</result>
```

The mkString is a method defined in scala.collection.immutable.List. It takes each element in the List and concatenates each element with whatever separator you provide—in this case, a comma. Even though it doesn't make sense, what if you try to print inside the yield expression? What will happen? Remember, everything in Scala is an expression and has a return value. If you try the following, you'll still get a result, but the result won't be useful because it will be a collection of units. A *unit* is the equivalent of void in Java, and it's the result value of a println function used inside the yield expression:

```
scala> for { a <- aList; b <- bList } yield { println(a+b)}
5
6
7
6
7
8
```

```
7
8
9
res32: List[Unit] = List((), (), (), (), (), (), (), (), ())
```

You've only scratched the surface of for-comprehension, and I come back to this in chapter 4 to examine functional data structures, so hold on to your inquisitiveness until chapter 4 (or jump to that chapter). The next section moves into another functional concept: pattern matching.

2.6   *Pattern matching*

Pattern matching is another functional programming concept introduced in Scala. To start with, Scala pattern matching looks similar to `switch` case in Java. The example in the following listing, showing the similarity between Scala and Java, takes an integer and prints its ordinal number.

Listing 2.2   An ordinal class written in Java

```java
public class Ordinal {

  public static void main(String[] args) {
    ordinal(Integer.parseInt(args[0]));          ◁── Call ordinal method
  }

  public static void ordinal(int number) {
    switch(number) {                             ◁─┐ Go through cases for
      case 1: System.out.println("1st"); break;    │ given integer value
      case 2: System.out.println("2nd"); break;
      case 3: System.out.println("3rd"); break;
      case 4: System.out.println("4th"); break;
      case 5: System.out.println("5th"); break;
      case 6: System.out.println("6th"); break;
      case 7: System.out.println("7th"); break;
      case 8: System.out.println("8th"); break;
      case 9: System.out.println("9th"); break;
      case 10: System.out.println("10th"); break;
      default : System.out.println("Cannot do beyond 10");
    }
  }
}
```

Here the argument of the program is parsed to the integer value, and the ordinal method returns the ordinal text of a given number. Right now, it only knows how to handle numbers from 1 to 10. The following listing shows the same example in Scala.

Listing 2.3   An ordinal class in Scala

```scala
ordinal(args(0).toInt)

def ordinal(number:Int) = number match {        ◁─┐ Match cases
  case 1 => println("1st")                         │ from 1 to 10
  case 2 => println("2nd")
  case 3 => println("3rd")
```

```
    case 4 => println("4th")
    case 5 => println("5th")
    case 6 => println("6th")
    case 7 => println("7th")
    case 8 => println("8th")
    case 9 => println("9th")
    case 10 => println("10th")
    case _ => println("Cannot do beyond 10")
}
```

Default case
for > 10 and < 1

Here you're doing something similar to the previous Java example: taking an input integer value from a command like args and determining the ordinal value of the number. Because Scala can also be used as a scripting language, you don't have to define an entry point like the main method. And you no longer need to provide a break for each case because in Scala you can't overflow into other case clauses (causing multiple matches) as in Java, and there's no default statement. In Scala, default is replaced with case _ to match everything else. To run the Ordinal.scala script, execute the following command from a command prompt:

```
scala Ordinal.scala <your input>
```

The wildcard case is optional and works like a safe fallback option. If you remove it, and none of the existing cases match, you get a match error:

```
scala> 2 match { case 1 => "One" }
scala.MatchError: 2
    at .<init>(<console>:5)
    at .<clinit>(<console>)
   ...
```

This is great because it tells you that you're missing a case clause, unlike in Java, where if you remove the default and none of the existing cases match, it ignores it without providing any sort of feedback.

The similarity between Java and Scala pattern matching ends here because Scala takes pattern matching to the next level. In Java you can only use a switch statement with primitives and enums, but in Scala you can pattern match strings and complex values, types, variables, constants, and constructors. More pattern-matching concepts are in the next chapter, particularly constructor matching, but look at an example of a type match. The following example defines a method that takes an input and checks the type of the given object:

```
def printType(obj: AnyRef) = obj match {
  case s: String => println("This is string")
  case l: List[_] => println("This is List")
  case a: Array[_] => println("This is an array")
  case d: java.util.Date => println("This is a date")
}
```

In this example you're using a Scala type pattern consisting of a variable and a type. This pattern matches any value matched by the type pattern—in this case, String, List[AnyRef], Array[AnyRef], and java.util.Date. When the pattern matches with

the type, it binds the variable name to the value. You could do that in Java using the
instanceof operator and casting, but this is a more elegant solution. Save this
method into the file printType.scala and load the file into the Scala REPL:

```
scala> :load printType.scala
Loading printType.scala...
printType: (obj: AnyRef)Unit
```

Now try a printType function with various types of input:

```
scala> printType("Hello")
This is string

scala> printType(List(1, 2, 3))
This is List

scala> printType(new Array[String](2))
This is an array

scala> printType(new java.util.Date())
This is a date
```

Scala also allows the infix operation pattern, in which you can specify an infix operator in your pattern. In the infix style, operators are written between the operands—for
example, 2 + 2. In the following example, you're extracting the first and the second
elements from the List:

```
scala> List(1, 2, 3, 4) match {
        case f :: s :: rest => List(f, s)
        case _ => Nil
      }
res7: List[Int] = List(1, 2)
```

Here you're matching 1 to f, 2 to s, and 3 and 4 to the rest of the variables. Think of it
as what it will take to create a List of 1, 2 ,3, and 4 from the expression f :: s :: rest,
and then this will make more sense.

Sometimes you need to have a guard clause along with the case statement to have
more flexibility during pattern matching. In the following example you're determining the range in which the given number belongs:

```
def rangeMatcher(num:Int) = num match {
  case within10 if within10 <= 10 => println("with in 0 to 10")
  case within100 if within100 <= 100 => println("with in 11 to 100")
  case beyond100 if beyond100 < Integer.MAX_VALUE => println("beyond 100")
}
```

With this new information, revisit the ordinal problem. The previous Scala ordinal
example supported only 1 to 10, but the following listing implements that for all
integers.

> **Listing 2.4   Ordinal2.scala reimplemented**

```
val suffixes = List(
      "th", "st", "nd", "rd", "th", "th", "th", "th", "th",
th")
```

```
println(ordinal(args(0).toInt))

def ordinal(number:Int) = number match {
  case tenTo20 if 10 to 20 contains tenTo20 => number + "th"
  case rest => rest + suffixes(number % 10)
}
```

Here in the new implementation of ordinal you're using range, which is a collection of integer values between a given start and end. The expression 10 to 20 is 10.to(20) (remember that methods can be used as infix operators). You're calling the to method in RichInt, and it creates an inclusive range (scala.collection.immutable .Inclusive). You're calling the contains method on the range to check whether the number belongs to the range. In the last case you're mapping all the numbers below 10 and beyond 20 to a new variable called rest. This is called *variable pattern matching* in Scala. You can access elements of a List like array using index positions in the List. You'll revisit pattern matching in chapter 3 after looking at case classes. It's time to move on to the last topic of this chapter: exception handling.

2.7 *Exception handling*

You caught a glimpse of Scala exception handling in the breakable example. Scala's exception handling is little different from Java's. Scala allows you a single try/catch block, and in the single catch block you can use pattern matching to catch exceptions. The catch block is a match block under the surface, so all the pattern-matching techniques that you learned in the previous section are applicable to a catch block. Modify the rangeMatcher example to throw an exception when it's beyond 100:

```
def rangeMatcher(num:Int) = num match {
  case within10 if within10 <= 10 => println("with in 0 to 10")
  case within100 if within100 <= 100 => println("with in 11 to 100")
  case _ => throw new IllegalArgumentException(
          "Only values between 0 and 100 are allowed")
}
```

Now when calling this method you can surround it with a try/catch block and catch the exception:

```
scala> try {
         rangeMatcher1(1000)
       } catch { case e: IllegalArgumentException => e.getMessage }
res19: Any = Only values between 0 and 100 are allowed
```

The case statement isn't any different from the type pattern matching used in the printType example.

Scala doesn't have any concept like a checked exception; all exceptions are unchecked. This way is more powerful and flexible because as a programmer you're free to decide whether or not you want to catch an exception. Even though Scala exception handling is implemented differently, it behaves exactly like Java, with exceptions being unchecked, and it allows Scala to easily interoperate with existing Java libraries. You'll see the use of Scala exception handling in examples throughout the book.

2.8   *Command-line REST client: building a working example*

You've looked into a number of interesting concepts about Scala in this chapter, and it'll be nice to see some of these concepts in action together. In this section you'll build a command-line-based REST client in Scala script. You're going to use the Apache HttpClient[6] library to handle HTTP connections and various HTTP methods.

What is REST?

REST stands for REpresentational State Transfer. It's software architectural style for distributed hypermedia systems like the World Wide Web. The term first appeared in "Architectural Styles and the Design of Network based Software Architectures,"[7] the doctoral dissertation paper by Roy Fielding, one of the principal authors of the HTTP specification.

REST strictly refers to the collection of architectural principles[8] mentioned here. Systems that follow Fielding's REST principles are often referred to as RESTful.

- Application state and functionality are divided into resources.
- Every resource is uniquely addressable using a universal syntax.
- All resources share a uniform interface for transfer of state between client and resource, consisting of well-defined operations (GET, POST, PUT, DELETE, OPTIONS, and so on, for RESTful web services) and content types.
- A protocol that's client/server, stateless cacheable, and layered.

To make a REST call to a RESTful service, you have to be aware of the operations supported by the service. To test your client you need a RESTful web service. You could use free public web services to test the client, but to have better control of the operations on the service you'll create one. You could use any REST tool or a framework to build the REST service. I'll use a Java servlet (Java developers are familiar with it) to build the service to test the REST client. Understanding how the service is implemented isn't important for this example.

The simple way to create a RESTful service for now is to use a Java servlet, as shown in the following listing.

Listing 2.5   Java servlet as a RESTful service

```
package restservice;
import java.io.*;
import javax.servlet.*;
import javax.servlet.http.*;
```

---

[6] "HttpClient Overview," July 3, 2012, http://mng.bz/Q4Bf.

[7] Roy Thomas Fielding, "Architectural Styles and the Design of Network-based Software Architectures," doctoral dissertation, University of California, Irvine, 2000. http://mng.bz/2Xa4.

[8] Roy T. Fielding and Richard N. Taylor, "Principled Design of the Modern Web Architecture," University of California, Irvine, 2000, http://mng.bz/188g.

```
import java.util.*;

public class TestRestService extends HttpServlet {
  public void doGet(HttpServletRequest request,
                    HttpServletResponse response)
      throws ServletException, IOException {          ⟵── Handle HTTP GET
    PrintWriter out = response.getWriter();
    out.println("Get method called");
    out.println("parameters: " + parameters(request));
    out.println("headers: " + headers(request));
  }

  public void doPost(HttpServletRequest request,
                    HttpServletResponse response)
      throws ServletException, IOException {          ⟵── Handle HTTP POST
    PrintWriter out = response.getWriter();
    out.println("Post method called");
    out.println("parameters: " + paramaters(request));
    out.println("headers: " + headers(request));
  }

  public void doDelete(HttpServletRequest request,
                    HttpServletResponse response)
      throws ServletException, IOException {          ⟵── Handle HTTP DELETE
    PrintWriter out = response.getWriter();
    out.println("Delete method called");
  }                                                          Build
                                                             response
  private String parameters(HttpServletRequest request) {  ⟵┘ String
    StringBuilder builder = new StringBuilder();
    for (Enumeration e = request.getParameterNames() ; e.hasMoreElements();)
      {
      String name = (String)e.nextElement();
      builder.append("|" + name + "->" + request.getParameter(name));
    }
    return builder.toString();
  }                                                        Build response
                                                           String from
  private String headers(HttpServletRequest request) {   ⟵┘ headers
    StringBuilder builder = new StringBuilder();
    for (Enumeration e = request.getHeaderNames() ; e.hasMoreElements();) {
      String name = (String)e.nextElement();
      builder.append("|" + name + "->" + request.getHeader(name));
    }
    return builder.toString();
  }
}
```

In the servlet you're supporting three HTTP methods: GET, POST, and DELETE. These methods are simple and return the request parameters and headers in response, which is perfect when testing your REST client. The two helper methods I added are parameters and headers. The parameters method is responsible for parsing the HTTP request object for parameters that are passed from the client; in this case, it's the REST client. The headers method retrieves all the header values from the request object. Once the servlet is built, you must deploy the WAR file to a Java web container.

I've used Maven and Jetty[9] to build and run[10] the Java servlet, but you're free to use any Java web container.

2.8.1 *Introducing HttpClient library*

HttpClient is a client-side HTTP transport library. The purpose of HttpClient is to transmit and receive HTTP messages. It's not a browser, and it doesn't execute JavaScript or try to guess the content type or other functionality unrelated to the HTTP transport. The most essential function of HttpClient is to execute HTTP methods. Users are supposed to provide a request object like HttpPost or HttpGet, and the HttpClient is expected to transmit the request to the target server and return the corresponding response object, or throw an exception if the execution is unsuccessful.

HttpClient encapsulates each HTTP method type in an object, and they're available under the `org.apache.http.client.methods` package. In this script you're going to use four types of requests: GET, POST, DELETE, and OPTIONS.[11] The previous example implemented only GET, POST, and DELETE because the web container will automatically implement the OPTIONS method. HttpClient provides a default client and is good enough for our purpose. To execute an HTTP DELETE method you have to do the following:

```
val httpDelete = new HttpDelete(url)
val httpResponse = new DefaultHttpClient().execute(httpDelete)
```

The HTTP POST method is a little different because, according to the HTTP specification, it's one of the two entity-enclosing methods. The other one is PUT. To work with entities HttpClient provides multiple options, but in the example you're going to use the URL-encoded form entity. It's similar to what happens when you POST a form submission. Now you can dive into building the client.

To use the HttpClient in your script, you have to import all the necessary classes. I haven't talked about `import`, but for now think of it as similar to Java `import` except that Scala uses _ for importing all classes in a package, as in the following:

```
import org.apache.http._
import org.apache.http.client.entity._
import org.apache.http.client.methods._
import org.apache.http.impl.client._
import org.apache.http.client.utils._
import org.apache.http.message._
import org.apache.http.params._
```

You can do other interesting things with Scala imports, but that's in the next chapter.

---

[9] Getting started with Jetty: http://wiki.eclipse.org/Jetty/Howto.

[10] Jan Bartel, editor, "Maven Jetty Plugin Configuration Guide," Nov. 30, 2011, http://mng.bz/3ubj.

[11] HTTP method definitions, http://mng.bz/9qso.

2.8.2 Building the client, step by step

Now, because the service is up and running, you can focus on the client script. To make the script useful, you have to know the type of operation (GET or POST), request parameters, header parameters, and the URL to the service. The request parameters and header parameters are optional, but you need an operation and a URL to make any successful REST call:

```
require(args.size >= 2,
"at minimum you should specify action(post, get, delete, options) and url")

val command = args.head
val params = parseArgs(args)
val url = args.last
```

You're using a `require` function defined in `Predef` to check the size of the input. Remember that the command-line inputs are represented by an `args` array. The `require` function throws an exception when the predicate evaluates to `false`. In this case, because you expect at least two parameters, anything less than that will result in an exception. The first parameter to the script is the command, and the next ones are the request and header parameters. The last parameter is the URL. The input to the script will look something like the following:

```
post -d <comma separated name value pair>
     -h <comma separated name value pair> <url>
```

The request parameters and header parameters are determined by a prefix parameter, -d or -h. One way to define a `parseArgs` method to parse request and header parameters is shown in the following listing.

> **Listing 2.6   Parsing headers and parameters passed to the program**

```
def parseArgs(args: Array[String]): Map[String, List[String]] = {

  def nameValuePair(paramName: String) = {
    def values(commaSeparatedValues: String) =
      commaSeparatedValues.split(",").toList

    val index = args.findIndexOf(_ == paramName)
    (paramName, if(index == -1) Nil else values(args(index + 1)))
  }

  Map(nameValuePair("-d"), nameValuePair("-h"))
}
```

This listing has defined a function inside another function. Scala allows nested functions, and nested functions can access variables defined in the outer scope function—in this case, the `args` parameter of the `parseArgs` function. Nested functions allow you to encapsulate smaller methods and break computation in interesting ways. Here the nested function `nameValuePair` takes the parameter name, -d or -h, and creates a list of name-value pairs of request or header parameters. The next interesting thing about the `nameValuePair` function is the return type. The return type is a scala.Tuple2, a tuple of two elements. `Tuple` is immutable like `List`, but unlike `List` it can contain different types of elements; in this case, it contains a `String` and a `List`. Scala provides syntax sugar for creating a `Tuple` by wrapping elements with parentheses ():

```
scala> val tuple2 = ("list of one element", List(1))
tuple2: (java.lang.String, List[Int]) = (list of one element,List(1))
```

This is similar to:

```
scala> val tuple2 = new scala.Tuple2("list of one element", List(1))
tuple2: (java.lang.String, List[Int]) = (list of one element,List(1))
```

Here's how to create a tuple of three elements:

```
scala> val tuple3 = (1, "one", List(1))
tuple3: (Int, java.lang.String, List[Int]) = (1,one,List(1))
```

The last interesting thing I'd like to mention about the `parseArgs` method is the `Map`. A `Map` is an immutable collection of keys and values. Chapter 4 discusses `Map` in detail. In this example you're creating a `Map` of parameter name (`-d` or `-h`) and listing all the parameters as values. When you pass a tuple of two elements to `Map`, it takes the first element of the tuple as the key and the second element as the value:

```
scala> val m = Map(("key1", "value1"), ("key2", "value2"))
m: scala.collection.immutable.Map[java.lang.String,java.lang.String] =
    Map(key1 -> value1, key2 -> value2)

scala> m("key1")
res8: java.lang.String = value1
```

For now you'll support only four types of REST operations: POST, GET, DELETE, and OPTIONS, but I encourage you to implement other HTTP methods like PUT and HEAD. To check what type of operation is requested, you can use simple pattern matching:

```
command match {
  case "post"    => handlePostRequest
  case "get"     => handleGetRequest
  case "delete"  => handleDeleteRequest
  case "options" => handleOptionsRequest
}
```

Here `handlePostRequest`, `handleGetRequest`, `handleDeleteRequest`, and `handleOptionRequest` are functions defined in the script. Each needs to be implemented a little differently. For example, in the case of a GET call, you'll pass the request parameters as query parameters to the URL. POST will use a URL-encoded form entity to pass the request parameters. DELETE and OPTIONS won't use any request parameters. Look at the `handleGetRequest` method, shown in the following listing.

Listing 2.7   Preparing a GET request and invoking the REST service

```
def headers = for(nameValue <- params("-h")) yield {
  def tokens = splitByEqual(nameValue)
  new BasicHeader(tokens(0), tokens(1))
}
```

```
def handleGetRequest = {
  val query = params("-d").mkString("&")
  val httpget = new HttpGet(s"${url}?${query}")
  headers.foreach { httpget.addHeader(_) }
  val responseBody =
      new DefaultHttpClient().execute(httpget,
new BasicResponseHandler())
  println(responseBody)
}
```

In this method you're retrieving all the request parameters from the Map params and
creating the query string. Then you create the HttpGet method with the given URL
and query string. The DefaultHttpClient is executing the httpget request and giv-
ing the response. The handlePostRequest method is a little more involved because it
needs to create a form entity object, as shown in the following listing.

Listing 2.8 Preparing a POST request and invoking the REST service

```
def formEntity = {

  def toJavaList(scalaList: List[BasicNameValuePair]) = {
    java.util.Arrays.asList(scalaList.toArray:_*)
  }

  def formParams = for(nameValue <- params("-d")) yield {
    def tokens = splitByEqual(nameValue)
    new BasicNameValuePair(tokens(0), tokens(1))
  }                                                          Encode
                                                             POST
  def formEntity =                                           request
      new UrlEncodedFormEntity(toJavaList(formParams), "UTF-8")  ◁── parameters
  formEntity
}
def handlePostRequest = {
  val httppost = new HttpPost(url)
  headers.foreach { httppost.addHeader(_) }
  httppost.setEntity(formEntity)
  val responseBody = new DefaultHttpClient().execute(httppost, new
      BasicResponseHandler())
  println(responseBody)
}
```

Something interesting and unusual is going on here. First is the toJavaList method.
The Scala List and the Java List are two different types of objects and aren't directly
compatible with each other. Because HttpClient is a Java library, you have to convert it
to a Java type collection before calling the UrlEncodedFormEntity. The special :_*
tells the Scala compiler to send the result of toArray as a variable argument to the
Arrays.asList method; otherwise, asList will create a Java List with one element.
The following example demonstrates that fact:

```
scala> val scalaList = List(1, 2, 3)
scalaList: List[Int] = List(1, 2, 3)
```

```
scala> val javaList = java.util.Arrays.asList(scalaList.toArray)
javaList: java.util.List[Array[Int]] = [[I@67826710]

scala> val javaList = java.util.Arrays.asList(scalaList.toArray:_*)
javaList: java.util.List[Int] = [1, 2, 3]
```

The following listing contains the complete RestClient.scala script.

Listing 2.9   RestClient.scala

```
import org.apache.http._
import org.apache.http.client.entity._
import org.apache.http.client.methods._
import org.apache.http.impl.client._
import org.apache.http.client.utils._
import org.apache.http.message._
import org.apache.http.params._

def parseArgs(args: Array[String]): Map[String, List[String]] = {       ◁— Parse request parameters and headers

  def nameValuePair(paramName: String) = {
    def values(commaSeparatedValues: String) =
          commaSeparatedValues.split(",").toList

    val index = args.findIndexOf(_ == paramName)
    (paramName, if(index == -1) Nil else values(args(index + 1)))
  }

  Map(nameValuePair("-d"), nameValuePair("-h"))
}

def splitByEqual(nameValue:String): Array[String] = nameValue.split('=')

def headers = for(nameValue <- params("-h")) yield {              ◁— Create BasicHeader for each header name/value pair
  def tokens = splitByEqual(nameValue)
  new BasicHeader(tokens(0), tokens(1))
}

def formEntity = {                                               ◁— Create URL-encoded form entity
  def toJavaList(scalaList: List[BasicNameValuePair]) = {
    java.util.Arrays.asList(scalaList.toArray:_*)
  }

  def formParams = for(nameValue <- params("-d")) yield {
    def tokens = splitByEqual(nameValue)
    new BasicNameValuePair(tokens(0), tokens(1))
  }

  def formEntity =
new UrlEncodedFormEntity(toJavaList(formParams), "UTF-8")
  formEntity
}

def handlePostRequest = {
  val httppost = new HttpPost(url)
  headers.foreach { httppost.addHeader(_) }
  httppost.setEntity(formEntity)
  val responseBody =
new DefaultHttpClient().execute(httppost, new BasicResponseHandler())
```

```scala
    println(responseBody)
}

def handleGetRequest = {
  val query = params("-d").mkString("&")
  val httpget = new HttpGet(s"${url}?${query}")
  headers.foreach { httpget.addHeader(_) }
  val responseBody =
new DefaultHttpClient().execute(httpget, new BasicResponseHandler())
  println(responseBody)
}

def handleDeleteRequest = {
  val httpDelete = new HttpDelete(url)
  val httpResponse = new DefaultHttpClient().execute(httpDelete)
  println(httpResponse.getStatusLine())
}

def handleOptionsRequest = {
  val httpOptions = new HttpOptions(url)
  headers.foreach { httpOptions.addHeader(_) }
  val httpResponse = new DefaultHttpClient().execute(httpOptions)
  println(httpOptions.getAllowedMethods(httpResponse))
}

require(args.size >= 2, "at minmum you should specify
    action(post, get, delete, options) and url")
val command = args.head
val params = parseArgs(args)
val url = args.last

command match {
  case "post"    => handlePostRequest
  case "get"     => handleGetRequest
  case "delete"  => handleDeleteRequest
  case "options" => handleOptionsRequest
}
```

◁┐ **Validate the number of arguments** ❶

◁┐ **Pattern match command arguments** ❷

In this complete example you implemented the support for four types of HTTP requests: POST, GET, DELETE, and OPTIONS. The require function call ❶ ensures that your script is invoked with at least two parameters: the action type and the URL of the REST service. The pattern-matching block at the end of the script ❷ selects the appropriate action handler for a given action name. The parseArgs function handles the additional arguments provided to the script, such as request parameters or headers, and returns a Map containing all the name-value pairs. The formEntity function is interesting because the URL encodes the request parameters when the http request type is POST, because in POST request parameters are sent as part of the request body and they need to be encoded.

To run the REST client you can use any build tool that can build Scala code. This example uses a build tool called simple build tool (SBT). You'll learn about this tool in detail in chapter 6, but for now go ahead and install the tool following the instructions from the SBT wiki (http://www.scala-sbt.org). Take a look at the codebase for this chapter for an example.

2.9 *Summary*

This chapter covered most of the basic Scala concepts like data types, variables, and functions. You saw how to install and configure Scala. Most importantly, you learned how to define functions, an important building block in Scala, and functional concepts including pattern matching and for-comprehension. You also learned about exception handling and how Scala uses the same pattern-matching techniques for exception handling. This chapter also provided a basic introduction to List and Array collection types so you can start building useful Scala scripts. Chapter 4 covers Scala collections in detail. You worked with the Scala REPL throughout the chapter when trying out examples. The Scala REPL is an important and handy tool, and you'll use it throughout the book. The chapter finished by building a complete REST client using most of the concepts you learned in it. The example also demonstrated the flexibility Scala provides when building scripts. It's now time to move on to Scala classes and objects.

OOP in Scala

3

This chapter covers
- Building a MongoDB driver using Scala classes and traits
- Pattern matching with case classes
- Looking into named and default arguments

Up to this point the book has been focusing on Scala's fundamentals. This chapter introduces the object-oriented features of Scala. Object-oriented programming isn't new, but Scala has added a few new features that aren't available in other statically typed languages.

In this chapter you'll build a Scala driver for MongoDB (www.mongodb.org/display/DOCS/Home). MongoDB is a scalable, document-oriented database. You'll build this driver incrementally using the object-oriented constructs provided by Scala, and along the way I'll explain each concept in detail. Scala has made some object-oriented innovations, and one of them is the *trait*. Traits are similar to abstract classes with partial implementation. You'll explore how to use traits when building Scala applications. As you move through the chapter, you'll learn about Scala *case classes*. Case classes are useful when it comes to building immutable classes, particularly in the context of concurrency and data transfer objects. Case classes also allow Scala to bridge the gap between functional programming and OOP in terms of pattern matching. Without wasting any more time, let's learn OOP programming in Scala by building a MongoDB driver.

3.1   *Building a Scala MongoDB driver: user stories*

To explore Scala's object-oriented constructs and use, let's build a MongoDB driver. While building this example driver, you'll dive deep into concepts for a thorough understanding. You won't need to start from scratch because you'll use an existing Java driver for MongoDB. You'll build a Scala wrapper over the Java MongoDB driver. That way, you don't have to deal with the low-level MongoDB API and can focus on your objective of learning Scala.

The user stories you'll be implementing in your Scala wrapper driver are as follows:

As a developer, I want an easier way to connect to my MongoDB server and access document databases.

As a developer, I want to query and manage documents.

WHAT'S A USER STORY?   A good way to think about a user story is as a reminder to have a conversation with your customer (in Agile, project stakeholders are called *customers*), which is another way to say it's a reminder to do some just-in-time analysis. In short, user stories are slim and high-level requirements artifacts.

MongoDB is a scalable, high-performance, open source, schema-free, document-oriented database written in C++.[1] MongoDB is a document-based database that uses JSON (JavaScript Object Notation). The schema-free feature lets MongoDB store any kind of data of any structure. You don't have to define your database tables and attributes up front. You can add or remove attributes whenever you need them. This flexibility is achieved through the document-based model. Unlike relational databases, in a document-based model records are stored as documents in which any number of fields of any length can be stored. For example, you could have the following JSON documents in a single collection (a *collection* in MongoDB is like a table in a traditional RDBMS):

```
{ name : "Joe", x : 3.3, y : [1,2,3] }
{ name : "Kate", x : "abc" }
{ q : 456 }
```

In a schema-free environment, the concept of *schema* moves more toward the application than to the database. Like any other tool, there are pros and cons for using a schema-free database, and it depends on the solution you're trying to solve.

The format of the document in which the information is stored in MongoDB is BSON (binary JSON). Other document-based databases like Lotus Notes (IBM) and SimpleDB (Amazon.com) use XML for information storage. JSON has an added

---

[1]   "What is the Right Data Model?," July 16, 2009, http://mng.bz/1iT0.

advantage when working with web-based applications because JSON content can be easily consumed with little transformation. A great place to get a feel for MongoDB is http://try.mongodb.org. Go ahead and download MongoDB (www.mongodb.org/display/DOCS/Downloads). Then, unpack it and run the following command to start the MongoDB server:

```
$ bin/mongod
```

To connect to the MongoDB server, use the client shell that ships with the distribution of MongoDB:

```
$ bin/mongo
MongoDB shell version: 1.2.4
url: test
connecting to: test
type "help" for help
>
```

At this point you should be ready to start building the Scala wrapper driver. If you're interested in learning more about MongoDB, look at the MongoDB tutorial (www.mongodb.org/display/DOCS/Tutorial).

3.2 *Classes and constructors*

To connect to the already running MongoDB server, create a Mongo client class with a hostname and port number:

```
<scala> class MongoClient(val host:String, val port:Int)
```

The class declaration looks different from the way you declare in Java or C#—you're not only declaring the class, but also its primary constructor.

The *primary constructor* is a constructor that needs to be called directly or indirectly from overloaded constructors when creating the instance `MongoClient`. You'll look into overloaded constructors shortly. In Scala, the primary constructor for a class is coded inline with the class definition. In this case, the constructor takes two parameters: `host` and `port`. The `host` parameter specifies the address of the server, and `port` specifies the port in which the MongoDB server is waiting for the connection.

Because all the constructor parameters are preceded by `val`, Scala will create immutable instance values for each of them. The following example creates an instance of a Mongo client and accesses its properties:

```
scala> val client = new MongoClient("127.0.0.1", 123)
client: MongoClient = MongoClient@561279c8

scala> client.port
res0: Int = 123

scala> client.host
res1: String = 127.0.0.1
```

Like Java or C#, Scala also uses the `new` keyword for creating instances of a class. But wait a minute—where's the body of the `MongoClient` class? In Scala that's optional.

You can create classes without any class body. Creating a class like a JavaBean with only a getter and setter would be easy in Scala, as in the following:

```
scala> class AddressBean(
    var address1:String,
    var address2:String,
    var city:String,
    var zipCode:Int)
defined class AddressBean

scala> var localAddress = new AddressBean("230 43rd street", "", "Columbus",
    43233)
localAddress: (java.lang.String, java.lang.String, java.lang.String, Int) =
    (230 43rd street,,Columbus,43233)
```

When parameters are prefixed with var, Scala creates mutable instance variables. The val and var prefixes are optional, and when both of them are missing, they're treated as private instance values, not accessible to anyone outside the class:

```
scala> class MongoClient(host:String, port:Int)
defined class MongoClient

scala> val client = new MongoClient("localhost", 123)
client: MongoClient = MongoClient@4089f3e5

scala> client.host
<console>:7: error: value host is not a member of MongoClient
        client.host
```

Note that when Scala creates instance values or variables, it also creates accessors for them. At no point in time are you accessing the field directly. The following Mongo-Client definition is equivalent to the class MongoClient(val host:String, val port:Int) definition.

```
class MongoClient(private val _host:String, private val _port:Int) {
  def host = _host
  def port = _port
}
```

The reason I'm using private (you'll learn about access levels later in this chapter) is so the Scala compiler doesn't generate accessors by default. What val and var do is define a field and a getter for that field, and in the case of var an additional setter method is also created.

Most of the time you'll have MongoDB running on the localhost with default port 27017. Wouldn't it be nice to have an additional zero-argument constructor that defaults the host and port number so you don't have to specify them every time? How about this:

```
class MongoClient(val host:String, val port:Int) {
    def this() = this("127.0.0.1", 27017)
}
```

To overload a constructor, name it this followed by the parameters. Constructor definition is similar to method definition except that you use the name this. Also, you

How do you add a setter method to a class?

To add a setter, you have to suffix your setter method with _=. In the following `Person` class, age is `private` so I'll add both a getter and a setter:

```
class Person(var firstName:String, var lastName:String,
        private var _age:Int) {
    def age = _age
    def age_=(newAge: Int) = _age = newAge
}
```

Now you can use the `Person` class and change its `age` value:

```
val p = new Person("Nima", "Raychaudhuri", 2)
p.age = 3
```

The assignment `p.age = 3` could be replaced by `p.age_=(3)`. When Scala encounters an assignment like `x = e`, it checks whether there's any method defined like `x_=` and if so, it invokes the method. The assignment interpretation is interesting in Scala, and it can mean different things based on context. For example, assignment to a function application like `f(args) = e` is interpreted as `f.update(args)`. You'll read more about function assignments later.

can't specify a return type as you can with other methods. The first statement in the overloaded constructors has to invoke either other overloaded constructors or the primary constructor. The following definition will throw a compilation error:

```
class MongoClient(val host:String, val port:Int) {
  def this() = {
    val defaultHost = "127.0.0.1"
    val defaultPort = 27017
    this(defaultHost, defaultPort)
  }
}
```

When you compile this with scalac, you get the following compilation errors:

```
MongoClient.scala:3: error: 'this' expected but 'val' found.
    val defaultHost = "127.0.0.1"
      ^
MongoClient.scala:4: error: '(' expected but ';' found.
    val defaultPort = 27017
^
two errors found
```

This poses an interesting challenge when you have to do some operation before you can invoke the other constructor. Later in this chapter, you'll look into a companion object and see how it addresses this limitation.

To make a connection to the MongoDB you'll use the `com.mongodb.Mongo` class provided by the Mongo Java driver:

```
class MongoClient(val host:String, val port:Int) {
  private val underlying = new Mongo(host, port)
  def this() = this("127.0.0.1", 27017)
}
```

NOTE I have used the Mongo Java driver version 2.10.1 for all the code in this chapter. To run the Scala Mongo wrapper code you're going to develop in this chapter, you need to have the Java driver .jar file available in the classpath. For more information on the Java driver, visit www.mongodb.org/display/DOCS/Java+Language+Center. To compile the previous code, you have to import com.mongodb.Mongo above the class definition. You'll learn about importing in the next section.

The underlying instance value will hold the connection to MongoDB. When Scala generates the constructor, it instantiates the underlying instance value too. Because of Scala's scripting nature, you can write code inside the class like a script, which will get executed when the instance of the class is created (kind of like Ruby). The following example creates a class called MyScript that validates and prints the constructor input:

```
class MyScript(host:String) {
  require(host != null, "Have to provide host name")
  if(host == "127.0.0.1") println("host = localhost")
  else println("host = " + host)
}
```

And now load MyScript into Scala REPL:

```
scala> :load MyScript.scala
Loading MyScript.scala...
defined class MyScript

scala> val s = new MyScript("127.0.0.1")
host = localhost
s: MyScript = MyScript@401e9c3f

scala> val s = new MyScript(null)
java.lang.IllegalArgumentException: requirement failed:
    Have to provide host name
      at scala.Predef$.require(Predef.scala:117)
      at MyScript.<init>(<console>:5)
```

How is Scala doing this? Scala puts any inline code defined inside the class into the primary constructor of the class. If you want to validate constructor parameters, you could do that inside the class (usually at the top of the class). Let's validate the host in the MongoClient:

```
class MongoClient(val host:String, val port:Int) {
  require(host != null, "You have to provide a host name")
  private val underlying = new Mongo(host, port)
  def this() = this("127.0.0.1", 27017)
}
```

Right now the MongoClient is using an underlying instance to hold the connection to MongoDB. Another approach would be to inherit from the com.mongodb.Mongo class, and in this case you don't have to have any instance value to hold the connection to MongoDB. To extend or inherit from a superclass, you have to use the extends keyword. The following code demonstrates how it would look if you extended from the Mongo class provided by the Java driver:

```
class MongoClientV2(val host:String, val port:Int)
    extends Mongo(host, port){
  require(host != null, "You have to provide a host name")
  def this() = this("127.0.0.1", 27017)
}
```

As shown in the previous example, you can also inline the definition of the primary constructor of a superclass. One drawback of this approach is that you can no longer validate the parameters of the primary constructor before handing it over to the superclass.

> **NOTE** When you don't explicitly extend any class, by default that class extends the `scala.AnyRef` class. `scala.AnyRef` is the base class for all reference types (see section 3.1).

Even though extending `Mongo` as a superclass is a completely valid way to implement this driver, you'll continue to use the earlier implementation because that will give you more control over what you want to expose from the Scala driver wrapper, which will be a trimmed-down version of the complete Mongo Java API. Before going any further, I'll talk about Scala imports and packages. This will help you to work with the Mongo library and structure your code.

3.3 Packaging

A *package* is a special object that defines a set of member classes and objects. The Scala package lets you segregate code into logical groupings or namespaces so that they don't conflict with each other. In Java you're only allowed to have package at the top of the .java file, and the declaration defines the scope across the file. Scala takes a different approach for packaging. It combines Java's declaration approach with C#'s scoped approach. You can still use the traditional Java approach and define package at the top of the Scala file, or use a scoping approach, as demonstrated in the following listing.

Listing 3.1 Declaring packages using the scoping approach

```
package com {
  package scalainaction {
    package mongo {
      import com.mongodb.Mongo
      class MongoClient(val host:String, val port:Int) {
        require(host != null, "You have to provide a host name")
        private val underlying = new Mongo(host, port)
        def this() = this("127.0.0.1", 27017)

      }
    }
  }
}
```

Here you're creating the `com.scalainaction.mongo` package for the `MongoClient` class. The previous code is exactly equivalent to the following code, where you're declaring the package in traditional Java style:

```
package com.scalainaction.mongo
import com.mongodb.Mongo
class MongoClient(val host:String, val port:Int) {
  require(host != null, "You have to provide a host name")
  private val underlying = new Mongo(host, port)
  def this() = this("127.0.0.1", 27017)
}
```

You can also use curly braces with top-level package declarations like the following:

```
package com.scalainaction.mongo {
    import com.mongodb.Mongo
    class MongoClient(val host:String, val port:Int) {
      require(host != null, "You have to provide a host name")
      private val underlying = new Mongo(host, port)
      def this() = this("127.0.0.1", 27017)
    }
}
```

It's a matter of style; you can use either one of them. The scoping approach shown in listing 3.1 provides more flexibility and a concise way to lay out your code in different packages. But it might quickly become confusing if you start to define multiple packages in the same file. The most widely used way in Scala code bases is the traditional way of declaring a package at the top of the Scala file. The only large, open source project I know of that uses the package-scoping approach is the Lift web framework (http://liftweb.net).

One more interesting point to note here is that Scala package declaration doesn't have to match the folder structure of your filesystem. You're free to declare multiple packages in the same file:

```
package com.persistence {
  package mongo {
     class MongoClient
  }
  package riak {
    class RiakClient
  }
  package hadoop {
    class HadoopClient
  }
}
```

If you save this code in a file called Packages.scala and compile it using the Scala compiler (`scalac Packages.scala`), you'll notice that the Scala compiler generates class files in appropriate folders to match your package declaration. This ensures that your classes are compatible with the JVM, where package declaration has to match the folder structure in the filesystem.

> ### Building Scala code
> Scalac[2] is the compiler that comes bundled with the Scala distribution. If you've installed Scala as specified in chapter 2, you should have it available in your path. The Scala compiler provides lots of standard options, like deprecation, verbose, and classpath, and additional advanced options. For example, to compile the `MongoClient` you have to do the following:
>
> ```
> scalac -classpath mongo/mongo-2.10.1.jar MongoClient.scala
> ```
>
> Invoking the Scala compiler directly for smaller examples is okay, but for larger projects I tend to use build tools like Ant, Maven, or SBT. Ant and Maven are standard tools for building Java projects. You can easily use them to build Scala projects too, but the standard build tool for Scala projects is SBT[3]. Chapter 5 discusses how to use build tools to build Scala projects. For now, let's stick to scalac.

3.4   Scala imports

You've already seen some examples of `import` in previous chapters, but I haven't discussed it. At first glance, the Scala `import` looks similar to Java imports, and it's true they're similar, but Scala adds some coolness to it. To import all the classes under the package `com.mongodb`, you have to declare the import as follows:

```
import com.mongodb._
```

Here's another use for `_`, and in this context it means you're importing all the classes under the `com.mongodb` package. In Scala, `import` doesn't have to be declared at the top of the file; you could use `import` almost anywhere:

```
scala> val randomValue = { import scala.util.Random
        new Random().nextInt
      }
randomValue: Int = 1453407425
```

In this case you're importing the `Random` class defined in the `scala.util` package in the Scala code block, and it's lexically scoped inside the block and won't be available outside it. Because the Scala package is automatically imported to all Scala programs, you could rewrite the block by relatively importing the `util.Random` class:

```
scala> val randomValue = { import util.Random
      new Random().nextInt
      }
randomValue: Int = 619602925
```

In Scala, when you import a package, Scala makes its members, including subpackages, available to you. To import members of a class, you have to put `._` after the class name:

---

[2] "Scalac user commands," www.scala-lang.org/docu/files/tools/scalac.html.
[3] Mark Harrah, "SBT, a Build Tool for Scala," 2012, https://github.com/harrah/xsbt/.

```
scala> import java.lang.System._
import java.lang.System._

scala> nanoTime
res0: Long = 1268518636387441000
```

Here you're invoking the `nanoTime` method defined in the `System` class without a prefix because you've imported the members of the `System` class. This is similar to static imports in Java (Scala doesn't have the `static` keyword). Because imports are relatively loaded, you could import the `System` class in the following way as well:

```
scala> import java.lang._
import java.lang._

scala> import System._
import System._

scala> nanoTime
res0: Long = 1268519178151003000
```

You could also list multiple imports separated by commas. Scala also lets you map a class name to another class name while importing—you'll see an example of that soon.

The _root_ package in Scala

Consider the following example:

```
package monads { class IOMonad }
package io {
  package monads {
    class Console { val m = new monads.IOMonad }
  }
}
```

If you try to compile this code, you'll get an error saying that type `IOMonad` isn't available. That's because Scala is looking for the `IOMonad` type in the `io.monads` package, not in another top-level package called `monads`. To specify a top-level package you have to use `_root_`:

```
val m = new _root_.monads.IOMonad
```

Another point to note here is that if you create classes or objects without a package declaration, they belong to an empty package. You can't import an empty package, but the members of an empty package can see each other.

There's one handy feature of Scala import: it allows you to control the names that you import in your namespace, and in some cases it improves readability. In Java, for example, working with both `java.util.Date` and `java.sql.Date` in the same file becomes confusing; in Scala you could easily remap `java.sql.Date` to solve the problem:

```
import java.util.Date
import java.sql.{Date => SqlDate}
import RichConsole._
```

```
val now = new Date
p(now)
val sqlDate = new SqlDate(now.getTime)
p(sqlDate)
```

The `java.sql.Date` is imported as `SqlDate` to reduce confusion with `java.util` `.Date`. You can also hide a class using import with the help of the underscore:

```
import java.sql.{Date => _ }
```

The `Date` class from the `java.sql` package is no longer visible for use.

To finish the functionality required for the first user story, you still need to add methods for creating and dropping the database. To achieve that you'll add the methods shown in the following listing.

Listing 3.2 Completed `MongoClient`

```
package com.scalainaction.mongo

class MongoClient(val host:String, val port:Int) {
  require(host != null, "You have to provide a host name")
  private val underlying = new Mongo(host, port)
  def this() = this("127.0.0.1", 27017)

  def version = underlying.getVersion

  def dropDB(name:String) = underlying.dropDatabase(name)

  def createDB(name:String) = DB(underlying.getDB(name))

  def db(name:String) = DB(underlying.getDB(name))
}
```

Everything in this code should be familiar to you except the `createDB` and `db` methods. I haven't yet introduced DB objects (I do that in the next section). The `createDB` and `db` method implementations are identical because the `getDB` method defined in the Java driver creates a db if one isn't found, but I wanted to create two separate methods for readability.

3.5   *Objects and companion objects*

Before I show you the DB class used in the previous example, let's explore Scala objects. Scala doesn't provide any static modifier, and that has to do with the design goal of building a pure object-oriented language where every value is an object, every operation is a method call, and every variable is a member of some object. Having `static` doesn't fit well with that goal, and along with that there are plenty of down-sides[4] to using `static` in the code. Instead, Scala supports something called *singleton objects*. A singleton object allows you to restrict the instantiation of a class to one object.[5] Implementing a singleton pattern in Scala is as simple as the following:

---

[4] "Cutting out Static," Gilad Bracha blog, Room 101, Feb. 17, 2008, http://gbracha.blogspot.com/2008/02/cutting-out-static.html.

[5] "Singleton pattern," Wikipedia, http://en.wikipedia.org/wiki/Singleton_pattern.

```
object RichConsole {
  def p(x: Any) = println(x)
}
```

Here `RichConsole` is a singleton object. The object declaration is similar to a class declaration except instead of `class` you're using the `object` keyword. To invoke the new `p` method, you have to prefix it with the class name, as you'd invoke static methods in Java or C#:

```
scala> :l RichConsole.scala
Loading RichConsole.scala...
defined module RichConsole

scala> RichConsole.p("rich console")
rich console
```

You can import and use all the members of the `RichConsole` object as follows:

```
scala> import RichConsole._
import RichConsole._

scala> p("this is cool")
this is cool
```

The `DB` object introduced in listing 3.2 is nothing but a factory to create `DB` instances representing a database in MongoDB:

```
object DB {
  def apply(underlying: MongDB) = new DB(underlying)
}
```

What's interesting here is that when you use a `DB` object as a factory, you're calling it as if it's a function, `DB(underlying.getDB(name))`, whereas you'd expect something like `DB.apply(underlying.getDB(name))`. Scala provides syntactic sugar that allows you to use objects as function calls. Scala achieves this by translating these calls into the `apply` method, which matches the given parameters defined in the object or class. If there's no matching `apply` method, it will result in a compilation error. Even though calling an `apply` method explicitly is valid, a more common practice is the one I'm using in the example. Note also that an object is always evaluated lazily, which means that an object will be created when its first member is accessed. In this case, it's `apply`.

The Factory pattern in Scala

When discussing constructors I mentioned that sometimes working with constructors could create some limitations like processing or validating parameters because in overloaded constructors the first line has to be a call to another constructor or the primary constructor. Using Scala objects we could easily address that problem because the `apply` method has no such limitation. For example, let's implement a Factory pattern in Scala. Here you'll create multiple `Role` classes, and based on the role name you'll create an appropriate role instance:

(continued)

```
abstract class Role { def canAccess(page: String): Boolean }
class Root extends Role {
  override def canAccess(page:String) = true
}
class SuperAnalyst extends Role {
  override def canAccess(page:String) = page != "Admin"
}
class Analyst extends Role {
override def canAccess(page:String) = false }
object Role {
  def apply(roleName:String) = roleName match {
    case "root" => new Root
    case "superAnalyst" => new SuperAnalyst
    case "analyst" => new Analyst
  }
}
```

Now you can use the `role` object as a factory to create instances of various roles:

```
val root = Role("root")
val analyst = Role("analyst")
```

Inside the `apply` method you're creating an instance of the DB class. In Scala, both a class and an object can share the same name. When an object shares a name with a class, it's called a *companion object*, and the class is called a *companion class*. Now the DB.scala file looks like the following:

```
package com.scalainaction.mongo
import com.mongodb.{DB => MongoDB}

class DB private(val underlying: MongoDB) {
}

object DB {
  def apply(underlying: MongoDB) = new DB(underlying)
}
```

First, the DB class constructor is marked as `private` so that nothing other than a companion object can use it. In Scala, companion objects can access private members of the companion class, which otherwise aren't accessible to anything outside the class. In the example, this might look like overkill, but there are times when creating an instance of classes through a companion object is helpful (look at the sidebar for the factory pattern). The second interesting thing in the previous code is the mongodb import statement. Because of the name conflict, you're remapping the DB class defined by the Java driver to MongoDB.

Package object

The only things you can put in a package are classes, traits, and objects. But with the help of the package object, you can put any kind of definition in a package, such as a class. For example, you can add a helper method in a package object that will be available to all members of the package. Each package is allowed to have one package object. Normally you would put your package object in a separate file, called package.scala, in the package that it corresponds to. You can also use the nested package syntax, but that's unusual:

```scala
package object bar {
   val minimumAge = 18
   def verifyAge = {}
}
```

minimumAge and verifyAge will be available to all members of the package bar. The following example uses verifyAge defined inside the package object:

```scala
package bar
class BarTender {
    def serveDrinks = { verifyAge; ... }
}
```

The main use case for package objects is when you need definitions in various places inside your package, as well as outside the package when you use the API defined by the package.

In MongoDB, a database is divided into multiple collections of documents. Shortly you'll see how you can create a new collection inside a database, but for now add a method to retrieve all the collection names to the DB class:

```scala
package com.scalainaction.mongo
import com.mongodb.{DB => MongoDB}
import scala.collection.convert.Wrappers._

class DB private(val underlying: MongoDB) {
    def collectionNames =  for(name <- new
        JSetWrapper(underlying.getCollectionNames)) yield name
}
```

The only thing that looks somewhat new is the Wrappers object. You're using utility objects provided by Wrappers to convert a java.util.Set to a Scala set so you can use a Scala for-comprehension. Wrappers provides conversions between Scala and Java collections. To try out the mongodb driver, write this sample client code:

```scala
import com.scalainaction.mongo._

def client = new MongoClient
def db = client.createDB("mydb")

for(name <- db.collectionNames) println(name)
```

This sample client creates a database called mydb and prints the names of all the collections under the database. If you run the code, it will print test and system .indexes, because by default MongoDB creates these two collections for you.

Now you're going to expose CRUD (create, read, update, delete) operations in the Scala driver so that users of your driver can work with documents. The following listing shows the Scala driver code you've written so far.

Listing 3.3 Completed MongoClient.scala

```
package com.scalainaction.mongo

import com.mongodb._

class MongoClient(val host:String, val port:Int) {
  require(host != null, "You have to provide a host name")
  private val underlying = new Mongo(host, port)
  def this() = this("127.0.0.1", 27017)

  def version = underlying.getVersion
  def dropDB(name:String) = underlying.dropDatabase(name)
  def createDB(name:String) = DB(underlying.getDB(name))
  def db(name:String) = DB(underlying.getDB(name))
}
```

Using MongoClient, your driver will be able to connect to the running MongoDB server, to a given host and port, or to the local MongoDB server. You also added methods like dropDB, createDB, and db to manage MongoDB databases. The following listing shows the DB class you created to wrap the underlying MongoDB database.

Listing 3.4 DB.scala

```
package com.scalainaction.mongo

import com.mongodb.{DB => MongoDB}
import scala.collection.convert.Wrappers._

class DB private(val underlying: MongoDB) {
  def collectionNames =  for(name <- new
    JSetWrapper(underlying.getCollectionNames)) yield name
}

object DB {
  def apply(underlying: MongoDB) = new DB(underlying)
}
```

So far, you haven't added much functionality to the DB class. The only thing it provides is an easier way to access names of the collections of a given database. But that's about to change with Scala traits.

3.6   *Mixin with Scala traits*

A *trait* is like an abstract class meant to be added to other classes as a mixin. Traits can be used in all contexts where other abstract classes could appear, but only traits can be used as mixin. In OOP languages, a *mixin* is a class that provides certain functionality that could be used by other classes. You can also view a trait as an interface with imple-mented methods. You'll see shortly how Scala traits will help you in implementing the second user story.

> **NOTE** Another difference between traits and abstract classes in Scala is that an abstract class can have constructor parameters, but traits can't take any param-eters. Both can take `type` parameters, which I discuss in the next chapter.

The second user story you need to implement in your driver is an ability to create, delete, and find documents in a MongoDB database. MongoDB stores documents in a collection, and a database could contain multiple collections. You need to create a component that will represent a MongoDB collection. The common use case is to retrieve documents from a collection; another use case would be to perform adminis-trative functions like creating and deleting documents. The Java Mongo driver pro-vides a `DBCollection` class that exposes all the methods to operate on the collection, but you're going to take it and slice it into multiple views. In Scala, you could do that using a trait. You'll use different traits for different types of jobs.

In this implementation you'll wrap the existing `DBCollection` and provide three kinds of interfaces: a read-only collection, an administrable collection, and an updatable collection. The following listing shows how the read-only collection interface will look.

Listing 3.5 ReadOnly collection trait

```
import com.mongodb.{DBCollection => MongoDBCollection }
import com.mongodb.DBObject

trait ReadOnly {

  val underlying: MongoDBCollection

  def name = underlying getName
  def fullName = underlying getFullName
  def find(doc: DBObject) = underlying find doc
  def findOne(doc: DBObject) = underlying findOne doc
  def findOne = underlying findOne
  def getCount(doc: DBObject) = underlying getCount doc
}
```

The only abstract member defined in this trait is `underlying`, which is an abstract value. In Scala, it's possible to declare abstract fields like abstract methods that need to be inherited by subclasses.

> **NOTE** The difference between `def` and `val` is that `val` gets evaluated when an object is created, but `def` is evaluated every time a method is called.

It's not necessary to have an abstract member in a trait, but usually traits contain one or more abstract members. Note that you're invoking the `findOne` or `getCount` method on the underlying collection without using the . operator. Scala allows you to treat any method as you would the infix operator (+, -, and so on).

The DBObject parameter is nothing but a key-value map provided by the Mongo Java driver, and you're going to use the class directly. In the full-blown driver implementation, you'll probably want to wrap that class too, but for the toy driver you can live with this bit of leaky abstraction. I'll talk about the details of these methods shortly when you test the methods.

The next two traits you're going to look at are Administrable and Updatable. In the Administrable trait, you'll expose methods for drop collection and indexes; and in the Updatable trait you'll allow create and remove operations on documents—see the following listing.

Listing 3.6 Administrable and Updatable traits

```
trait Administrable extends ReadOnly {
  def drop: Unit = underlying drop
  def dropIndexes: Unit = underlying dropIndexes
}

trait Updatable extends ReadOnly {
  def -=(doc: DBObject): Unit = underlying remove doc
  def +=(doc: DBObject): Unit = underlying save doc
}
```

Both traits extend the ReadOnly trait because you also want to provide all the features of a read-only collection. If your trait extends another trait or class, then that trait can only be mixed into a class that also extends the same superclass or trait. This makes sense because you want to make sure that someone else implements the abstract members that your trait depends on. As with abstract classes, you can't create an instance of a trait; you need to mix it with other concrete classes. Here's a concrete implementation of the read-only collection:

```
class DBCollection(override val underlying: MongoDBCollection)
                 extends ReadOnly
```

You're overriding the underlying abstract value with whatever value will be passed to the primary constructor when creating the instance of DBCollection. Note that the override modifier is mandatory when overriding members of a superclass. The following adds three methods that return different flavors of the collection:

```
private def collection(name: String) = underlying.getCollection(name)

def readOnlyCollection(name: String) = new DBCollection(collection(name))
def administrableCollection(name: String) = new
                DBCollection(collection(name)) with Administrable
def updatableCollection(name: String) = new
                DBCollection(collection(name)) with Updatable
```

Here you're getting the underlying collection by name and wrapping it into a DBCollection instance. When building the administrable and updatable collection, you're mixing in the corresponding traits using a with clause. Using the with keyword, you can mix one or more traits into an existing concrete class. Another way of thinking about Scala mixins is as *decorators*. Like decorators, mixins add more functionality to existing classes. That allows you to widen a thin interface with additional traits when needed, as you did with the ReadOnly, Administrable, and Updatable traits. The next two listings show what the DB class (listing 3.7) and DBCollection class (listing 3.8) look like so far.

Listing 3.7   Completed DB.scala

```scala
package com.scalainaction.mongo

import com.mongodb.{DB => MongoDB}
import scala.collection.convert.Wrappers._

class DB private(val underlying: MongoDB) {
  private def collection(name: String) = underlying.getCollection(name)

  def readOnlyCollection(name: String) = new DBCollection(collection(name))
  def administrableCollection(name: String) = new
    DBCollection(collection(name)) with Administrable
  def updatableCollection(name: String) = new
    DBCollection(collection(name)) with Updatable
  def collectionNames = for(name <- new
    JSetWrapper(underlying.getCollectionNames)) yield name
}

object DB {
  def apply(underlying: MongoDB) = new DB(underlying)
}
```

Listing 3.8   DBCollection.scala

```scala
package com.scalainaction.mongo

import com.mongodb.{DBCollection => MongoDBCollection }
import com.mongodb.DBObject

class DBCollection(override val underlying: MongoDBCollection)
    extends ReadOnly

trait ReadOnly {                                        // <--- Create ReadOnly view
  val underlying: MongoDBCollection
  def name = underlying getName
  def fullName = underlying getFullName
  def find(doc: DBObject) = underlying find doc
  def findOne(doc: DBObject) = underlying findOne doc
  def findOne = underlying findOne
  def getCount(doc: DBObject) = underlying getCount doc
}

trait Administrable extends ReadOnly {                  // <--- Create Administrable view
  def drop: Unit = underlying drop
  def dropIndexes: Unit = underlying dropIndexes
}

trait Updatable extends ReadOnly {                      // <--- Create Updatable view
  def -=(doc: DBObject): Unit = underlying remove doc
  def +=(doc: DBObject): Unit = underlying save doc
}
```

If you've done any Ruby programming, you'll find lots of similarity with Ruby modules. One advantage of traits compared to module systems available in other languages is that the trait mixin is checked at compile time. If you make mistakes while stacking traits, the compiler will complain.

Now you'll build a client to demonstrate that the driver works. Ideally, you should always write unit tests to make sure your code works. Chapter 8 explores testing in Scala land. For now, the following listing shows the small client that validates your driver.

Listing 3.9   Test client for driver QuickTour.scala

```
import com.scalainaction.mongo._
import com.mongodb.BasicDBObject

def client = new MongoClient
def db = client.db("mydb")
for(name <- db.collectionNames) println(name)

val col = db.readOnlyCollection("test")
println(col.name)

val adminCol = db.administrableCollection("test")
adminCol.drop

val updatableCol = db.updatableCollection("test")        Create updatable
                                                         view of underlying
                                                         collection "test"
val doc = new BasicDBObject()
doc.put("name", "MongoDB")
doc.put("type", "database")
doc.put("count", 1)

val info = new BasicDBObject()
info.put("x", 203)
info.put("y", 102)
doc.put("info", info)                        ❶ Add document
updatableCol += doc                             to collection

println(updatableCol.findOne)

updatableCol -= doc
println(updatableCol.findOne)

for(i <- 1 to 100) updatableCol += new BasicDBObject("i", i)    Add 100
                                                               documents
val query = new BasicDBObject              Query for 71st   to "test"
query.put("i", 71);                        document in      collection
val cursor = col.find(query)          ❷    collection
while(cursor.hasNext()) {
  println(cursor.next());
}
```

In the test client you're creating collections using the methods exposed by the DB class. You're using BasicDBObject provided by the underlying MongoDB driver to test the find method. BasicDBObject is nothing but a wrapper around a Java map. MongoDB being a schema-free database, you can put any key-value pair on it and save it to the database ❶. At the end of the test, you're using the same `BasicDBObject` to query the database ❷.

To run the test client, make sure you have the Mongo Java driver .jar file in the classpath. To specify the classpath to the Scala interpreter, use the –cp option.

After the release of your driver, all the users are happy. But it turns out that the driver is slow in fetching documents, and users are asking whether there's any way we could improve the performance. One way to solve this problem immediately is by *memoization.*[6] To speed things up, you'll remember the calls made to the `find` method and avoid making the same call to the underlying collection again. The easiest way to implement the solution is to create another trait and mix it in with the other traits. By nature Scala traits are stackable, meaning one trait can modify or decorate the behavior of another trait down the stack. Here's how to implement the `Memoizer` trait:

```
trait Memoizer extends ReadOnly {
  val history = scala.collection.mutable.Map[Int, DBObject]()
  override def findOne = {
    history.getOrElseUpdate(-1, { super.findOne })
  }
  override def findOne(doc: DBObject) = {
    history.getOrElseUpdate(doc.hashCode, { super.findOne(doc) })
  }
}
```

You're keeping track of all the resulting `DBObject`s, and when the same request is made a second time, you're not going to make a call to MongoDB—instead, you'll return from the map. The `getOrElseUpdate` method is interesting; it allows you to get the value for the given key, and if it doesn't exist, it invokes the function provided in the second parameter. Then it stores the value with the key in the map and returns the result. You saved a complete `if` and `else` block with a single method. In the case of the parameterless `findOne` method, you're using `-1` as the key because the method doesn't take a parameter. To use this memoizer trait, you have to modify the existing `DB` class as follows:

```
def readOnlyCollection(name: String) =
    new DBCollection(collection(name)) with Memoizer
def administrableCollection(name: String) =
    new DBCollection(collection(name)) with Administrable with Memoizer
def updatableCollection(name: String) =
    new DBCollection(collection(name)) with Updatable with Memoizer
```

Now whenever the `findOne` method is invoked, the overridden version will be called, and the result will be cached.

There's a little problem with this `Memoizer` approach, though. If you remove documents from a collection, the `Memoizer` will still have them and return them. You could solve this by extending the `UpdatableCollection` trait and overriding the `remove` method. The next section discusses how stackable traits are implemented in Scala.

---

[6] "Memoization," Wikipedia, http://en.wikipedia.org/wiki/Memoization.

3.6.1 Class linearization

If you've worked with C++ or Common Lisp, then the mixin of traits will look like multiple inheritance. The next question is how Scala handles the infamous diamond problem (http://en.wikipedia.org/wiki/Diamond_problem). See figure 3.1. Before I answer that question, let's see how your hierarchy will look if you have a diamond problem for the following `UpdatableCollection`:

```
Class UpdatableCollection
    extends DBCollection(collection(name)) with Updatable
```

The problem with this hierarchy is that trying to invoke one of the `find` methods on `UpdatableCollection` will result in an ambiguous call because you could reach the `ReadOnly` trait from two different paths. Scala solves this problem using a something called *class linearization*. Linearization specifies a single linear path for all the ancestors of a class, including both the regular superclass chain and the traits. This is a two-step process in which it resolves method invocation by first using right-first, depth-first search and then removing all but the last occurrence of each class in the hierarchy. Let's look at this in more detail. First, all classes in Scala extend `scala.AnyRef`, which in turn inherits from the `scala.Any` class. (I explain Scala class hierarchy later in this chapter.) The linearization of the `ReadOnly` trait is simple because it doesn't involve multiple inheritance:

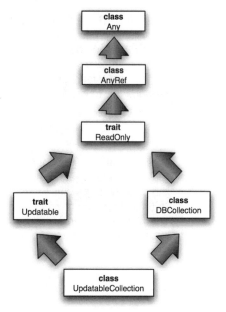

Figure 3.1 Class hierarchy of `UpdatableCollection` before class linearization

```
ReadOnly -> AnyRef -> Any
```

Similarly, `Updatable` and `DBCollection` also don't have that issue:

```
Updatable -> ReadOnly -> AnyRef -> Any
DBCollection -> ReadOnly -> AnyRef -> Any
```

When class linearization is applied to your `UpdatableCollection`, it puts the trait first after the class because it's the rightmost element and then removes duplication. After linearization, your `UpdatableCollection` looks like the following:

```
UpdatableCollection -> Updatable -> DBCollection -> ReadOnly -> AnyRef -> Any
```

Now if you add the `Memoizer` trait into the mix, it will show up before `Updatable` because it's the rightmost element:

```
UpdatableCollection -> Memoizer -> Updatable -> DBCollection -> ReadOnly ->
    AnyRef -> Any
```

Figure 3.2 illustrates how classes and traits are laid out for the UpdatableCollection class. The figure shows traits in a separate place because I want you to think differently about them. When traits have methods implemented, they work as a façade. Check the sidebar "Trait class files on JVM" for more details. The dotted lines show the hierarchy, and the solid lines with arrowheads show how methods will be resolved after linearization.

Trait class files on JVM

Depending on how you define a trait, the Scala compiler generates class files differently. When you define a trait with only a method declaration and without any method body, it produces a Java interface. You could use javap –c <class file name> to inspect class files generated by Scala. For example, trait Empty { def e: Int } will produce the following class file:

```
public interface Empty{
    public abstract int e();
}
```

When a trait declares concrete methods or code, Scala generates two class files: one for the interface (as shown in the previous code) and a new class file that contains the code. When a class extends a trait, the variables declared in the trait are copied to the class file, and the method defined in the trait becomes a façade method in the class. These façade methods in the class will call the methods defined in the trait code class.

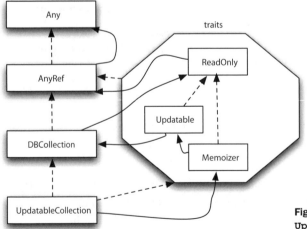

Figure 3.2   Class linearization of UpdatableCollection

3.6.2 *Stackable traits*

You've seen multiple uses for Scala traits. To recap, you've used a Scala trait as an interface using ReadOnly. You've used it as a decorator to expand the functionality of DBCollection using the Updatable and Administrable traits. And you've used traits as a stack where you've overridden the functionality of a ReadOnly trait with Memoizer. The stackable feature of a trait is useful when it comes to modifying the behavior of existing components or building reusable components. Chapter 7 explores abstractions provided by Scala in building reusable components. For now, let's look at another example and explore stackable traits in more detail.

You have another requirement for your driver; this time it's related to locale. The Scala Mongo driver is so successful that it's now used internationally. But the documents that you're returning aren't locale-aware. The requirement is to make your read-only interface locale-aware. Luckily, all the non-English documents have a field called locale. Now if only you could change your find to use that, you could address this problem.

You could change your find method in the ReadOnly trait to find by locale, but that would break all your users looking for English documents. If you build another trait and mix it with ReadOnly, you could create a new kind of Collection that will find documents using locale:

```
trait LocaleAware extends ReadOnly {
  override def findOne(doc: DBObject) = {
    doc.put("locale", java.util.Locale.getDefault.getLanguage)
    super.findOne(doc)
  }

  override def find(doc: DBObject) = {
    doc.put("locale", java.util.Locale.getDefault.getLanguage)
    super.find(doc)
  }
}
```

Now when creating a new Collection, you could mix in this trait:

```
new DBCollection(collection(name)) with Memoizer with LocaleAware
```

The traits could be reordered as follows, with the same result:

```
new DBCollection(collection(name)) with LocaleAware with Memoizer
```

As you can see, it's easy to use traits in a stack to add or modify the behavior of existing classes or traits. This kind of use is common in Scala code bases, and you'll see more on them throughout the second part of the book. Before we leave traits, there's one more thing I'd like to mention: the use of super. As you can see, when creating a trait you can't tell how your trait will get used and who will be above you. All you know is that it has to be of a type that your trait extends. In the previous code, you could mix in the LocaleAware trait before or after Memoizer, and in each case super would mean something different. The interpretation of super in traits is dynamically resolved in Scala.

> **ScalaObject trait**
>
> When discussing class linearization, I didn't give you the complete picture. Scala always inserts a trait called `scala.ScalaObject` as a last mixin in all the classes you create in Scala. The complete linearization of `UpdatableCollection` is as follows:
>
> > UpdatableCollection -> Memoizer -> Updatable -> DBCollection ->
> >   ReadOnly -> ScalaObject -> AnyRef -> Any
>
> Prior to Scala 2.8, `ScalaObject` used to provide methods like `$tag` to help with pattern matching, but from Scala 2.8 on, the `ScalaObject` trait is a marker (empty) trait.

3.7   *Case class*

Case classes are a special kind of class created using the keyword `case`. When the Scala compiler sees a case class, it automatically generates boilerplate code so you don't have to do it. Here's an example of a `Person` class:

```
scala> case class Person(firstName:String, lastName:String)
defined class Person
```

In this code example, you're creating a `Person` case class with `firstName` and `last-Name` parameters. But when you prefix a class with `case`, the following things will happen automatically:

- Scala prefixes all the parameters with `val`, and that will make them public value. But remember that you still never access the value directly; you always access through accessors.
- Both `equals` and `hashCode` are implemented for you based on the given parameters.
- The compiler implements the `toString` method that returns the class name and its parameters.
- Every case class has a method named `copy` that allows you to easily create a modified copy of the class's instance. You'll learn about this later in this chapter.
- A companion object is created with the appropriate `apply` method, which takes the same arguments as declared in the class.
- The compiler adds a method called `unapply`, which allows the class name to be used as an extractor for pattern matching (more on this later).
- A default implementation is provided for serialization:
  ```
  scala> val me = Person("Nilanjan", "Raychaudhuri")
  me: Person = Person(Nilanjan,Raychaudhuri)

  scala> val myself = Person("Nilanjan", "Raychaudhuri")
  myself: Person = Person(Nilanjan,Raychaudhuri)

  scala> me.equals(myself)
  res1: Boolean = true

  scala> me.hashCode
  res2: Int = 1688656232
  scala> myself.hashCode
  res4: Int = 1688656232
  ```

Now think about how many times you've created a data transfer object (DTO) with only accessors for the purpose of wrapping some data. Scala's case classes will make that easier for you the next time. Both `equals` and `hashCode` implementations also make it safer to use with collections.

> **NOTE** You're allowed to prefix the parameters to the case class with `var` if you want both accessors and mutators. Scala defaults it to `val` because it encourages immutability.

Like any other class, a case class can extend other classes, including trait and case classes. When you declare an abstract case class, Scala won't generate the `apply` method in the companion object. That makes sense because you can't create an instance of an abstract class. You can also create case objects that are singleton and serializable:

```
trait Boolean
case object Yes extends Boolean
case object No extends Boolean
```

Scala case classes and objects make it easy to send serializable messages over the network. You'll see a lot of them when you learn about Scala actors.

> **NOTE** From Scala 2.8 on, case classes without a parameter list are deprecated. If you have a need, you can declare your case class without a parameter. Use `()` as a parameter list or use the case object.

Let's put your recently gained knowledge of case classes to use in the MongoDB driver. So far, you've implemented basic `find` methods in your driver. It's great, but you could do one more thing to the driver to make it more useful. MongoDB supports multiple query options like `Sort`, `Skip`, and `Limit` that you don't support in your driver. Using case classes and a little pattern matching, you could do this easily. You'll add a new `finder` method to the collection to find by query and query options. But first, let's define the query options you're going to support:

```
sealed trait QueryOption

case object NoOption extends QueryOption

case class Sort(sorting: DBObject, anotherOption: QueryOption)
    extends QueryOption

case class Skip(number: Int, anotherOption: QueryOption)
    extends QueryOption

case class Limit(limit: Int, anotherOption: QueryOption)
    extends QueryOption
```

Here you're creating four options: `Sort`, `Skip`, `Limit`, and `NoOption`. The `NoOption` case is used when no option is provided for the query. Each query option could have another query option because you'll support multiple query options at the same time. The `Sort` option takes another `DBObject` in which users can specify sorting criteria.

Note that all the option case classes extend an empty trait, and it's marked as sealed. I'll talk about modifiers in detail later in the chapter, but for now a sealed modifier stops everyone from extending the trait, with a small exception. To extend a sealed trait, all the classes need to be in the same source file. In this case, I've defined all the previous classes in the DBCollection.scala file.

For the `Query` class, you'll wrap your good old friend `DBObject` and expose methods like `sort`, `skip`, and `limit` so that users can specify query options:

```
case class Query(q: DBObject, option: QueryOption = NoOption) {
  def sort(sorting: DBObject) = Query(q, Sort(sorting, option))
  def skip(skip: Int) = Query(q, Skip(skip, option))
  def limit(limit: Int) = Query(q, Limit(limit, option))
}
```

Here each method creates a new instance of a query object with an appropriate query option so that, like a fluent interface (http://martinfowler.com/bliki/Fluent Interface.html), you can chain the methods together as in the following:

```
var rangeQuery = new BasicDBObject("i", new BasicDBObject("$gt", 20))
var richQuery = Query(rangeQuery).skip(20).limit(10)
```

Here you're searching documents for which the `i > 20` condition is `true`. From the result set you skip 20 documents and limit your result set to 10 documents. The most extraordinary part of the code is the last parameter of the `Query` class: `option: Query-Option = NoOption`. Here you're assigning a default value to the parameter so that when the second parameter isn't specified, as in the previous snippet, the default value will be used. You'll look at default parameters in the next section. I'm sure that, as a focused reader, you've already spotted the use of the companion object that Scala generates for case classes. When creating an instance of a case class, you don't have to use new because of the companion object. To use the new query class, add the following new method to the `ReadOnly` trait:

```
def find (query: Query) = { "..." }
```

Before discussing implementation of the find-by-query method, let's see how case classes help in pattern matching. You'll be using pattern matching to implement the method.

You learned about pattern matching in chapter 2, but I haven't discussed case classes and how they could be used with pattern matching. One of the most common reasons for creating case classes is the pattern-matching feature that comes free with case classes. Let's take the `Person` case class once again, but this time you'll extract `firstName` and `lastName` from the object using pattern matching:

```
scala> case class Person(firstName:String, lastName: String)
defined class Person

scala> val p = Person("Matt", "vanvleet")
p: Person = Person(Matt,vanvleet)

scala> p match {
```

```
            case Person(first, last) => println(">>>> " + first + ", " + last)
        }
>>>> Matt, vanvleet
```

Look how you extracted the first and last names from the object using pattern matching. The `case` clause should be familiar to you; here you're using a variable pattern in which the matching values get assigned to the first and last variables. Under the hood, Scala handles this pattern matching using a method called `unapply`. If you have to hand-code the companion object that gets generated for `Person`, it will look like following:

```
object Person {

  def apply(firstName:String, lastName:String) = {
    new Person(firstName, lastName)
  }
  def unapply(p:Person): Option[(String, String)] =
    Some((p.firstName, p.lastName))
}
```

The `apply` method is simple; it returns an instance of the `Person` class and it is called when you create an instance of a case class. The `unapply` method gets called when the case instance is used for pattern matching. Typically, the `unapply` method is supposed to unwrap the case instance and return the elements (parameters used to create the instance) of the case class. I'll talk about the `Option` type in Scala in detail in the next chapter, but for now think of it as a container that holds a value. If a case class has one element, the `Option` container holds that value. But because you have more than one, you have to return a tuple of two elements.

> **NOTE** Sometimes instead of `unapply`, another method called `unapplySeq` could get generated if the case class parameters end with a repeated parameter (variable argument). I'll discuss that in a later chapter.

In the discussion of for-comprehensions in chapter 2, I didn't mention that the generator part of for-comprehensions uses pattern matching. I can best describe this with an example. Here you're creating a list of persons and looping through them using pattern matching:

```
scala> val people = List(
     | Person("Simon", "kish"),
     | Person("Phil", "Marzullo"),
     | Person("Eric", "Weimer")
     | )
people: List[Person] = List(Person(Simon,kish), Person(Phil,Marzullo),
     Person(Eric,Weimer))

scala> for(Person(first, last) <- people) yield first + "," + last
res12: List[java.lang.String] =
     List(Simon,kish, Phil,Marzullo, Eric,Weimer)
```

You'll see more examples of extractors and pattern matching throughout the book. Before we leave this section, I still owe you the implementation of the find-by-query method, so here you go (see the following listing).

Listing 3.10 ReadOnly trait

```
trait ReadOnly {
  val underlying: MongoDBCollection
  def name = underlying getName
  def fullName = underlying getFullName

  def find(query: Query): DBCursor = {
    def applyOptions(cursor:DBCursor, option: QueryOption): DBCursor = {
      option match {
        case Skip(skip, next) => applyOptions(cursor.skip(skip), next)
        case Sort(sorting, next)=> applyOptions(cursor.sort(sorting), next)
        case Limit(limit, next) => applyOptions(cursor.limit(limit), next)
        case NoOption => cursor
      }
    }
    applyOptions(find(query.q), query.option)
  }

  def find(doc: DBObject): DBCursor = underlying find doc
  def findOne(doc: DBObject) = underlying findOne doc
  def findOne = underlying findOne
  def getCount(doc: DBObject) = underlying getCount doc
}
```

Find method takes query object

Explicitly specify return type

Here you're using pattern matching to apply each query option to the result returned by the `find` method—in this case, `DBCursor`. The nested `applyOptions` function is applied recursively because each query option could wrap another query option identified by the `next` variable, and you bail out when it matches `NoOption`.

When it comes to overload methods (methods with the same name), you have to specify the return type; otherwise, the code won't compile. You have a similar limitation for recursive method calls. Scala type inference can't infer the type of recursive methods or functions. In case of type errors, it's always helpful to add type information. Using the test client in the following listing, you could test your new finder method.

Listing 3.11 TestFindByQuery.scala

```
import com.scalainaction.mongo._
import com.mongodb.BasicDBObject

def client = new MongoClient
def db = client.db("mydb")
val col = db.readOnlyCollection("test")
val updatableCol = db.updatableCollection("test")
for(i <- 1 to 100) updatableCol += new BasicDBObject("i", i)

val rangeQuery = new BasicDBObject("i", new BasicDBObject("$gt", 20))
val richQuery = Query(rangeQuery).skip(20).limit(10)
val cursor = col.find(richQuery)
while(cursor.hasNext()) {
  println(cursor.next());
}
```

Search for where i > 20

Skip first 20 docs, return 10 docs

When you run this client, you'll see output similar to the following:

```
{ "_id" : "4ba0df2c2771d753375f4aa7" , "i" : 41}
{ "_id" : "4ba0df2c2771d753385f4aa7" , "i" : 42}
{ "_id" : "4ba0df2c2771d753395f4aa7" , "i" : 43}
{ "_id" : "4ba0df2c2771d7533a5f4aa7" , "i" : 44}
{ "_id" : "4ba0df2c2771d7533b5f4aa7" , "i" : 45}
{ "_id" : "4ba0df2c2771d7533c5f4aa7" , "i" : 46}
{ "_id" : "4ba0df2c2771d7533d5f4aa7" , "i" : 47}
{ "_id" : "4ba0df2c2771d7533e5f4aa7" , "i" : 48}
{ "_id" : "4ba0df2c2771d7533f5f4aa7" , "i" : 49}
{ "_id" : "4ba0df2c2771d753405f4aa7" , "i" : 50}
```

The id values in the output might be different for you because they're autogenerated by MongoDB.

Common arguments against pattern matching

Pattern matching is common in functional programming languages, but not in the world of OOP languages. Common arguments against pattern matching by object-oriented developers are that pattern matching could be replaced by a Visitor pattern, pattern matching isn't extensible, and pattern matching breaks encapsulation.

First, pattern matching reduces lots of boilerplate code when compared to the Visitor pattern. The extensibility argument enters the picture when pattern matching is supported only for basic datatypes like Int, Long, or String. But Scala takes pattern matching much further and beyond basic datatypes with case classes. Pattern matching implemented for case classes matches only the constructor parameters provided for the case classes. This way, you don't have to expose hidden fields of the class, and you ensure encapsulation.

3.8   *Named and default arguments and copy constructors*

Scala lets you specify method arguments using a named style. When you have methods or class constructors taking similar types of arguments, it becomes difficult to detect errors if you swap them by mistake. Let's take the example of Person again. Instead of passing in an order of first name, last name, if we swap the order, Scala won't complain:

```
scala> case class Person(firstName:String, lastName:String)
defined class Person

scala> val p = Person("lastname", "firstname")
p: Person = Person(lastname,firstname)
```

Unfortunately, both parameters are of the same type, and the compiler can't detect the mistake at compile time. But now, using named style arguments, you can avoid the problem:

```
scala> val p = Person(lastName = "lastname", firstName = "firstname")
p: Person = Person(firstname,lastname)
```

The named arguments use the same syntax as a variable assignment, and when you use named arguments, the order doesn't matter. You can mix the named arguments with positional arguments, but that's usually a bad idea. When going for named arguments, always try to use a named style for all the arguments. The following example uses a named style for the first argument but not for the second. As mentioned earlier, it's good practice to avoid this:

```
scala> val p = Person(firstName = "firstname", "lastname")
p: Person = Person(firstname,lastname)
```

When using a named style, if the parameter name doesn't match, the Scala compiler will complain about the value not being found. But when you override a method from a superclass, the parameters' names don't have to match the names in the superclass method. In this case, the static type of the method determines which names have to be used. Consider this example, where you have the Person trait and SalesPerson overriding the grade method and changing the parameter name in the process from years to yrs:

```
scala> trait Person { def grade(years: Int): String }
defined trait Person
scala> class SalesPerson extends Person {  def grade(yrs: Int) = "Senior" }
defined class SalesPerson

scala> val s = new SalesPerson
s: SalesPerson = SalesPerson@42a6cdf5

scala> s.grade(yrs=1)
res17: java.lang.String = Senior

scala> s.grade(years=1)
<console>:12: error: not found: value years
        s.grade(years=1)
                ^
```

Here years won't work because the type of the s instance is SalesPerson. If you force the type variable to Person, then you can use years as a named argument. I know this is a little tricky to remember, so watch out for errors like this:

```
scala> val s: Person = new SalesPerson
s: Person = SalesPerson@5418f143

scala> s.grade(years=1)
res19: String = Senior
```

The value of the named argument could be an expression like a method or block of code, and every time the method is called, the expression is evaluated:

```
scala> s.grade(years={val x = 10; x + 1})
res20: String = Senior
```

The complementing feature to named arguments is default arguments. You've already seen one example of a default argument in the query example, where the last argument of the case class defaulted to NoOption:

```
case class Query(q: DBObject, option: QueryOption = NoOption) {
  def sort(sorting: DBObject) = Query(q, Sort(sorting, option))
  def skip(skip: Int) = Query(q, Skip(skip, option))
  def limit(limit: Int) = Query(q, Limit(limit, option))
}
```

The default argument has the form arg: Type = expression, and the expression part is evaluated every time the method uses the default parameter. If you create a Query instance using Skip, the default won't be used:

```
val skipOption = Skip (10, NoOption)
val newQuery = Query(new BasicDBObject(), skipOption)
```

One of the interesting uses of default arguments in Scala is in the copy method of case classes. Starting from Scala 2.8 on, along with the usual goodies, every case class has an additional method called copy to create a modified instance of the class. This method isn't generated if any member exists with the same name in the class or in one of its parent classes. The following example uses the copy method to create another instance of the skip query option, but with a Limit option instead of NoOption:

```
scala> val skipOption = Skip(10, NoOption)
skipOption: Skip = Skip(10,NoOption())

scala> val skipWithLimit = skipOption.copy(anotherOption = Limit(10,
                          NoOption))
skipWithLimit: Skip = Skip(10,Limit(10,NoOption))
```

The copy method is using a named argument to specify the parameter that you'd like to change. The copy method generated by the Scala compiler for the Skip case class looks like the following:

```
case class Skip(number: Int, anotherOption: QueryOption)
      extends QueryOption {
  def copy(number: Int = number,
        anotherOption: QueryOption = anotherOption) = {
    Skip(number, anotherOption)
  }
}
```

As you can see, in the generated method all the parameters are defaulted to the value provided to the constructor of the class, and you can pick and choose the parameter value you want to change during the copy. If no parameters are specified, copy will create another instance with the same values:

```
scala> Skip(10, NoOption) == Skip(10, NoOption).copy()
res22: Boolean = true
```

In Scala, invoking the == method is the same as calling the equals method. The == method is defined in the scala.Any class, which is the parent class for all classes in Scala.

3.9   *Modifiers*

You've already seen a few modifiers in action, but let's look deeper into them. Along with standard modifiers like private and protected, Scala has more modifiers and new abilities.

The private modifier can be used with any definition, which means it's only accessible in an enclosed class, its companion object, or a companion class. In Scala, you can qualify a modifier with a class or a package name. In the following example, the private modifier is qualified by class and package name:

```
package outerpkg.innerpkg

class Outer {
  class Inner {
    private[Outer] def f()   = "This is f"
    private[innerpkg] def g() = "This is g"
    private[outerpkg] def h() = "This is h"
  }
}
```

Here, access to the f method can appear anywhere within the Outer class, but not outside it. The method g is accessible anywhere within outerpkg.innerpkg. It's like the package private in Java. You could use it to make your methods available for unit tests in the same package. Because the h method is qualified with outerpkg, it can appear anywhere within outerpkg and its subpackages.

Scala also lets you qualify the private modifier with this: private[this]. In this case, it means object private. And object private is only accessible to the object in which it's defined. When members are marked with private without a qualifier, they're called *class-private*.

The protected modifier is applicable to class member definitions. It's accessible to the defining class and its subclasses. It's also accessible to a companion object of the defining class and companion objects of all the subclasses. Like the private modifier, you can also qualify the protected modifier with class, package, and this. By default, when you don't specify any modifier, everything is public. Scala doesn't provide any modifier to mark members as public.

Like Java, Scala also provides an override modifier, but the main difference is that in Scala the override modifier is mandatory when you override a concrete member definition from the parent class. The override modifier can be combined with an abstract modifier, and the combination is allowed only for members of traits. This modifier means that the member in question must be mixed with a class that provides the concrete implementation. An example will demonstrate this fact. The following creates a DogMood trait (dogs are moody, you know) with an abstract greet method and an AngryMood trait that overrides it:

```
trait DogMood {
  def greet
}
```

```
trait AngryMood extends DogMood {
  override def greet = {
    println("bark")
    super.greet
  }
}
```

The problem with this code is the `super.greet` line. You can't invoke the `super` `greet` method because it's abstract. But `super` calls are important if you want your trait to be stackable so that it can get mixed in with other traits. In cases like this, you can mark the method with `abstract override`, which means it should be mixed in with some class that has the concrete definition of the greet method. To make this code compile, you have to add `abstract` along with `override`, as in the following:

```
trait AngryMood extends DogMood {
  abstract override def greet = {
    println("bark")
    super.greet
  }
}
```

Scala has introduced a new modifier called `sealed`, which applies only to class definitions. It's a little different from the `final` modifier; classes marked `final` in Scala can't be overridden by subclasses. But classes marked `sealed` can be overridden as long as the subclasses belong to the same source file. You used `sealed` in a previous section when you created `QueryOption` case classes:

```
sealed trait QueryOption
```

This is a common pattern when you want to create a defined set of subclasses but don't want others to subclass it.

3.10 *Value classes: objects on a diet*

Starting with version 2.10, Scala allows user-defined value classes (which could be case classes as well) that extend `AnyVal`. Value classes are a new mechanism to avoid runtime allocation of the objects. To create a value class you need to abide by some important rules, including:

- The class must have exactly one `val` parameter (`vars` are not allowed).
- The parameter type may not be a value class.
- The class can not have any auxiliary constructors.
- The class can only have `def` members, no `vals` or `vars`.
- The class cannot extend any traits, only universal traits (we will see them shortly).

These are big constraints, so why bother? Value classes allow you to add extension methods to a type without the runtime overhead of creating instances. Look at the following example:

```
class Wrapper(val name: String) extends AnyVal {
def up() = name.toUpperCase
}
```

Here `Wrapper` is a custom value class that wraps the `name` parameter and exposes an `up()` method. To invoke the `up` method create the instance of the `Wrapper` class as in the following:

```
val w = new Wrapper("hey")
w.up()
```

This is only true at compile time. At runtime the expression will be optimized to the equivalent of a method class on a static object: `Wrapper.up$extension("hey")`. So what is going on? Behind the scenes the Scala compiler has generated a companion object for the value class and rerouted the `w.up()` calls to the `up$extension` method in the companion object. The `"$extension"` is the suffix added to all the methods extracted from the companion class. The contents of the `up$extension` method are the same as the `up()` method except all the references to `name` are changed to use the parameter. Here is an equivalent implementation of a `Wrapper` companion object:

```
object Wrapper {
 def up$extension(_name: String) = _name.toUpperCase
}
```

A value class can only extend a universal trait, one that extends `Any` (normally traits by default extend `AnyRef`). Universal traits can only have `def` members and no initialization code:

```
trait Printable extends Any {
 def p() = println(this)
}

case class Wrapper(val name: String) extends AnyVal with Printable {
 def up() = name.toUpperCase
}
...
val w = Wrapper("Hey")
w.p()
```

Even though now you can invoke the `p` method on a `Wrapper` instance at runtime an instance will also be created because the implementation of the `p` method prints the type. There are limitations when allocation is necessary; if you assign a value class to an array, the optimization will fail.

Nonetheless this is a very nice way to add extension methods to an existing type. We will see examples of value classes later in the book. For now let's explore the rest of the Scala type hierarchy.

3.11   *Implicit conversion with implicit classes*

Implicit conversion is a method that takes one type of parameter and returns another type. Here is an example of a conversion from `Double` to `Int`:

```
scala> val someInt: Int = 2.3
<console>:7: error: type mismatch;
 found    : Double(2.3)
 required: Int
        val someInt: Int = 2.3
                           ^

scala> def double2Int(d: Double): Int = d.toInt
double2Int: (d: Double)Int
scala> val someInt: Int = double2Int(2.3)
someInt: Int = 2
```

Usually you cannot assign a `Double` value to an `Int` type, but here we are explicitly converting `Double` to `Int` using the `double2Int` method before then assigning it to `someInt`. We can make the conversion implicit by using the `implicit` keyword:

```
implicit double2Int(d: Double): Int = d.toInt
```

The advantage of implicit conversion is that the compiler will find the appropriate implicit conversion and invoke it for you:

```
scala> val someInt: Int = 2.3
<console>:7: error: type mismatch;
 found    : Double(2.3)
 required: Int
        val someInt: Int = 2.3
                           ^

scala> implicit def double2Int(d: Double): Int = d.toInt
warning: there were 1 feature warnings; re-run with -feature for details
double2Int: (d: Double)Int

scala> val someInt: Int = 2.3
someInt: Int = 2
```

What is going on here? The first time we assigned a `Double` value to an `Int` type variable it failed, but it succeeds the second time. When the compiler encounters a type error, it doesn't immediately give up; instead, it looks for any implicit conversions that might fix the error. In this case, `double2Int` is used to convert `Double` to `Int`. The last line will be rewritten by the compiler:

```
val someInt: Int = double2Int(2.3)
```

This conversion happens at compile time, and, if no appropriate conversion method is found, the compiler throws a compilation error. The compiler will also throw an error if there is ambiguity in an implicit resolution; for example, more than one implicit conversion is found that matches the given criteria. It is quite safe compared to the runtime extension available in some dynamically typed languages. For now, ignore the warning. We will learn more about this later.

One of the common uses of implicit conversion is to add extension methods to existing types. For example, we know we can create a range by using the `to` method:

```
val oneTo10 = 1 to 10
```

But what if we want to create a range of numbers using the `-->` method?

```
val oneTo10 = 1 --> 10
```

This will fail because there is no `-->` method defined for `Int`. We can easily fix this by following two simple steps:

- Create a type that has a `-->` method defined for the `Int` type
- Provide an implicit conversion

Let's create a class that defines a `-->` method for `Int` and creates a `Range` of integers:

```
scala> class RangeMaker(left: Int) {
     |    def -->(right: Int) = left to right
     | }
defined class RangeMaker

scala> val range: Range = new RangeMaker(1).-->(10)
range: Range = Range(1, 2, 3, 4, 5, 6, 7, 8, 9, 10)
```

Here the left operand becomes the constructor parameter and the right operand the parameter to the `-->` method. The implicit conversion method takes `Int` and returns `RangeMaker`:

```
scala> implicit def int2RangeMaker(left: Int): Range = new RangeMaker(left)
```

To understand why we designed our type this way, we need to understand how the compiler will parse the `1 --> 10` expression. By default, the Scala compiler always evaluates expressions from left to right. So the expression is translated to `1.-->(10)`. Since there is no `-->` method defined for `Int`, the Scala compiler will look for an implicit conversion that can convert `Int` to some type that defines the `-->` method. In this case, the compiler will use the `int2RangeMaker` method by passing 1 as a parameter, then 10 as a parameter, to the `-->` method. After the implicit conversion, the `1 --> 10` expression will be converted to `int2RangeMaker(1).-->(10)`.

Since implicit conversion is so commonly used by libraries and applications, Scala provides implicit classes. Implicit classes reduce boilerplate code by combining the steps required for implicit conversion. We can combine the `RangeMaker` and conversion methods by making the class implicit:

```
implicit class RangeMaker(left: Int) {
  def -->(right: Int): Range = left to right
}
```

Behind the scenes, the compiler will "desugar" the implicit class into a simple class and an implicit conversion method, as we did earlier. Note that implicit classes must have a primary constructor with one argument.

Looking up an appropriate implicit conversion takes time, but it's not much of an issue because it happens at compile time. The only runtime cost comes from creating an additional instance of `RangeMaker` for each implicit conversion. The good news is that we can avoid the runtime cost by turning our implicit classes into value classes:

```
implicit class RangeMaker(val left: Int) extends AnyVal {
  def -->(right: Int): Range = left to right
}
```

Implicit conversion is a very powerful language feature, but overusing it can reduce the readability and maintenance of the code base.

3.12 Scala class hierarchy

Figure 3.3 illustrates the Scala class hierarchy. The root class in the hierarchy is the class scala.Any. Every class in Scala inherits directly or indirectly from this class. The Scala Any class defines two subclasses: AnyVal and AnyRef. All the values that are represented by an object in the underlying host system (JVM or CLR) are a subclass of AnyRef. Every user-defined Scala class also inherits from a trait called scala.Scala-Object (see section 3.6 for more details). AnyRef is mapped to java.lang.Object in the JVM and to system.Object in .NET.

The subclasses for AnyVal aren't represented as objects in the underlying host system. This is interesting because all this while I've been saying that everything in Scala is an object. It's still true that everything in Scala is an object, but not at the host system level. When Scala compiles to Java bytecode, it takes advantage of the Java primitive types for efficiency, but converts them to objects when required by the Scala application.

In figure 3.3, along with the subtypes, you have *views*. Views are implicit type converters that allow Scala to convert from Char to Int to Long and so on. You'll look into implicit functions later in the book.

Type Scala.Null is the subtype of all reference types, and its only instance is the null reference. The following code creates an instance of scala.Null, and the only way to create an instance of Null is by assigning null to an instance:

```
scala> val x: Null = null
x: Null = null
```

You'll still get an exception when you try to access any method on a Null object. Because it's subclassed from AnyRef, you can't assign null to any value type in Scala:

```
scala> val x: Int = null
<console>:8: error: type mismatch;
 found    : Null(null)
 required: Int
       val x: Int = null
```

On the other hand, scala.Nothing is at the bottom of the Scala hierarchy, and it's a subtype of everything in Scala. But you can't create an instance of Nothing, and there's no instance of this type in Scala. You'll learn about Nothing in more detail in chapter 4 because it does solve some interesting problems for Scala.

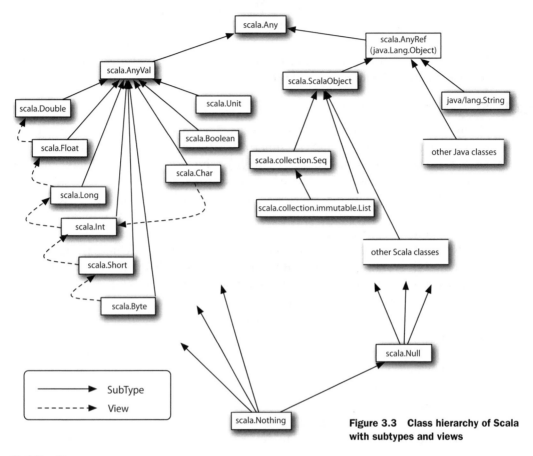

Figure 3.3   Class hierarchy of Scala with subtypes and views

3.13   Summary

This chapter covered a lot of ground, including how Scala empowers traditional OOP. You learned about new features introduced in Scala 2.8, like named and default arguments. On the one hand, you worked with traits and classes that provide interesting ways to structure your code in Scala; on the other hand, I introduced you to case classes that are handy and useful for building immutable data objects. You'll work with case classes again when you learn about Actors and concurrency. You also learned about singleton objects and companion objects and how they're used in Scala.

For the first time you also explored the Scala hierarchy and some of the important base classes. This knowledge will help you easily browse scaladoc when looking for library classes and how they fit into the Scala hierarchy.

This chapter provided a foundation for the things that will follow in consecutive chapters. You'll revisit object-oriented concepts in Scala in chapter 7, where you'll explore other abstraction techniques provided by Scala. Remember, a great way to familiarize yourself with Scala concepts is to load up the Scala REPL and try out all the features for yourself. The interactive approach is a good way to learn Scala and understand its concepts. The next chapter should be interesting, because you begin to tackle the various functional data structures in Scala.

Having fun with
functional data structures

In this chapter you'll switch gears to begin a fun and interesting part of the Scala language: Scala collections which broadly support two categories of data structures—immutable and mutable.

To understand and benefit from Scala collections, you need to know two concepts: type parameterization and higher-order functions. Type parameterization allows you to create types that take another type as a parameter (similar to Java generics). Higher-order functions let you create functions that take other functions as parameters. These two concepts allow you to create generic and reusable components, like Scala collections.

The Scala collection is one of Scala's most powerful features. The library implements all the common data structures you need, making it essential for every Scala developer. A recent addition to the collections library is parallel collections. Scala parallel collections allow you to solve data parallelism problems in Scala with ease. You'll see how the Scala parallel collections library helps when working with large datasets, so buckle up! This will be a fun and exciting ride.

4.1 *Introducing type parameterization*

In programming, type parameterization allows you to define methods or classes in terms of a type that will be specified later. It's like creating a placeholder for the type. Parameterized types should not be a new concept to you if you've worked with Java or C# generics. Scala provides additional extensions to generics because of its sound and powerful type system.

In chapter 3 you implemented the query interface to the MongoDB driver, and one of the methods you exposed was findOne, which retrieves a single document from the collection. The problem with that method is that it returns null when the collection is empty, but this little fact isn't clear from the method declaration. One way to solve the problem would be to add a comment, although adding a comment to a method is the weakest form of documentation. Wouldn't it be better if you could explicitly communicate that sometimes the method might not work as intended?

In a situation like this, Scala developers use something called an Option. Option is a collection type in Scala. Unlike other collection types, an Option contains a maximum of one element. It represents one of two possible values: None and Some. None means "no value" and Some represents "some value." By returning Option from a method, you can communicate that the method might not return a value at all times.

For this section, forget that Scala provides an Option type so that you can build something similar on your own. You'll create a function that will return the index position of an element in a list. It also needs to work for all kinds of lists. The list could contain integers, longs, or strings. How can you build a function that works for all types of lists? Using type parameterization, you can make the type information configurable. Here's how the position function looks with type parameterization:

```
def position[A](xs: List[A], value: A): Int = {
  xs.indexOf(value)                    ◁——|  Find index of first element occurrence
}
```

Here A denotes a type that could only be determined when the function is invoked. Both List and the value you're looking for need to be of the same type. Unlike Java and C#, Scala uses square brackets ([]) to declare the type parameter. When this function is invoked with a list of integers, A represents the type Int. Similarly if you invoke it with a list of strings, the type parameter A is replaced with String. Now test your position method with different types of parameters:

```
scala> val xs = List("one", "two", "three")
xs: List[java.lang.String] = List(one, two, three)
```

```
scala> position(xs, "two")
res2: Int = 1

scala> val ys = List(20, 30, 40)
ys: List[Int] = List(20, 30, 40)

scala> position(ys, 40)
res6: Int = 2

scala> position[Int](ys, 300)
res11: Int = -1
```

Even though you can explicitly specify the type value for the type parameter as in the last example, it's optional. Scala type inference determines the value of the type parameter based on the arguments passed to the function.

Currently your position function returns -1 when there's no matching element. Here, instead of returning the Int result, you'll return a new type that clearly expresses the behavior of the method. You'll create a container called Maybe that will wrap the result. Your position method will look like this:

```
def position[A](xs: List[A], value: A): Maybe[Int] = {
  val index = xs.indexOf(value)
  if(index != -1) Just(index) else Nil
}
```

In the case of a valid index (not -1), the position method returns Just (you'll see it shortly); otherwise Nil. Just and Nil are two implementations of the Maybe container, and the following listing shows how they're implemented.

Listing 4.1   Version 1 of Maybe.scala

```
sealed abstract class Maybe[+A] {
  def isEmpty: Boolean
  def get: A
}

final case class Just[A](value: A) extends Maybe[A] {
  def isEmpty = false
  def get = value
}
case object Nil extends Maybe[Nothing] {
  def isEmpty = true
  def get = throw new NoSuchElementException("Nil.get")
}
```

Most of this code should be familiar to you, except the type parameter part. The Maybe class is declared as a covariant on type A. The next section explores type variance in detail.

4.2   *Type variance with covariance and contravariance*

Type variance complements type parameterization with a mechanism to specify constraints like covariant and contravariant to the type system. The subtyping relationship gives rise to the question of variance—how do two types with a subtype relationship relate in type parameterization with each other? In Scala, you can use type parameters with classes and traits, as demonstrated previously. When using type parameters for classes or traits, you can use a + sign along with the type parameter to make it covariant (like the `Maybe` class in the previous example). Covariance allows subclasses to override and use narrower types than their superclass in covariant positions such as the return value. Here the `Nil` object is a subclass of `Maybe` with `scala.Nothing` as a type parameter. The reason you're using `scala.Nothing` here is that the `get` method in the `Nil` object throws an exception. Because the A type of `Maybe` is covariant, you can return a narrower type from its subclasses. There's no narrower type than `Nothing` in Scala because it's at the bottom of the hierarchy.

Usefulness of Nothing in Scala

In Scala all methods and functions need to have a return type. There's no `void` in Scala. In situations where you have methods that don't return anything, you use `scala.Unit` as a return type of the method. Scala uses `scala.Nothing` as a return type in situations where the return type isn't clear, such as when an exception is thrown:

```
scala> def throwException = throw new RuntimeException(
                   "Always throws exception")
throwException: Nothing
```

When you see a method returning `Nothing`, that means that method won't return successfully. Here's another example of invoking `exit` (`System.exit`) to terminate the runtime:

```
scala> def kill = sys.exit(1)
kill: Nothing
```

In Scala, an immutable `List` is covariant in its type parameter, so `List[String]` is a subtype of `List[Any]`. You can take an instance, `List[String]`, and assign it to a `List` of Any:

```
scala> val everything: List[Any] = List("one", "two", "three")
everything: List[Any] = List(one, two, three)
```

Covariance has lots of useful advantages. Look at the following method:

```
def ++(that: GenTraversableOnce [A]): List[A]
```

That method takes a type of iterator (`GenTraversableOnce` is a template trait for all objects that could be iterated once) and returns a concatenated collection. Similarly the `collection.Seq`, `collection.Iterable` and `collecton.Traversable` also provide the same method:

```
def ++(that: GenTraversableOnce[A]): Traversable[A]
def ++(that: GenTraversableOnce[A]): Iterable[A]
def ++(that: GenTraversableOnce [A]: Seq[A]
```

Traversable is the parent trait for all the collection types in Scala, and the ++ method is only defined in this trait. In the preceding example Seq, Iterable, and List inherit the definition from Traversable. Still, depending on the type of collection you're dealing with, it returns the same type of collection back, because Traversable is defined with a covariant parameter. You'll explore Scala collection hierarchy later in this chapter.

The opposite of covariance is contravariance. In the case of covariance, subtyping can go downward, as you saw in the example of List, but in contravariance it's the opposite: subtypes go upward. Contravariance comes in handy when you have a mutable data structure.

Mutable objects need to be invariant

A type parameter is *invariant* when it's neither covariant nor contravariant. All Scala mutable collection classes are invariant. An example can explain why mutable objects need to be invariant. By now, you should be comfortable using collection.immutable.List; the mutable counterpart of List is collection.mutable.ListBuffer. Because ListBuffer is mutable, it's declared as invariant as follows:

```
final class ListBuffer[A]  ...{ ... }
```

Notice that when you declare an invariant type, you drop the - or + sign. Because it's declared as invariant, you can't assign ListBuffer from one type to another. The following code will throw a compilation error:

```
scala> val mxs: ListBuffer[String] = ListBuffer("pants")
mxs: scala.collection.mutable.ListBuffer[String] =
        ListBuffer(pants)
scala> val everything: ListBuffer[Any] = mxs
<console>:6: error: type mismatch;
 found   : scala.collection.mutable.ListBuffer[String]
 required: scala.collection.mutable.ListBuffer[Any]
        val everything: ListBuffer[Any] = mxs
```

Even though String is a subtype of scala.Any, Scala still doesn't let you assign mxs to everything. To understand why, assume ListBuffer is covariant and the following code snippet works without any compilation problem:

```
scala> val mxs: ListBuffer[String] = ListBuffer("pants")
mxs: scala.collection.mutable.ListBuffer[String] =
        ListBuffer(pants)
scala> val everything: ListBuffer[Any] = mxs

scala> everything += 1
res4: everything.type = ListBuffer(1, pants)
```

Can you spot the problem? Because everything is of the type Any, you can store an integer value into a collection of strings. This is a disaster waiting to happen. It's exactly what happens to Java arrays. To avoid these kinds of problems, it's always a good idea to make mutable objects invariant. The next question is what happens in case of an immutable object for collections. It turns out that for immutable objects, covariance isn't a problem at all. If you replace ListBuffer with the immutable List, you can take an instance of List[String] and assign it to List[Any] without a problem.

(continued)

```
scala> val xs: List[String] = List("pants")
xs: List[String] = List(pants)
scala> val everything: List[Any] = xs
everything: List[Any] = List(pants)
```

The only reason this assignment is safe is because List is immutable. You can add 1 to xs List, and it will return a new List of type Any.

```
scala> 1 :: xs
res5: List[Any] = List(1, pants)
```

Again, this addition is safe because the cons(::) method always returns a new List, and its type is determined by the type of elements in the List. The only type that could store an integer value and reference value is scala.Any. This is an important property to remember about type variance when dealing with mutable/immutable objects.

The best way to understand contravariance is to see the problem that comes when it's absent. Try to spot the problem in the following Java code example:

```
Object[] arr = new int[1];
arr[0] = "Hello, there!";
```

You end up assigning the string to an integer array. Java fortunately catches this error at runtime by throwing an ArrayStoreException. Scala stops these kinds of errors at compile time by forcing parameter types to be either contravariant or invariant. A type parameter is invariant when it's neither covariant nor contravariant. A good example of contravariance in action is the Function1 trait defined in Scala:

```
trait Function1[-P, +R] { ... }
```

Scala uses the minus sign (-) to denote contravariance and the plus sign (+) for covariance. In this case, Function1 is contravariant in P and covariant in R. In Scala, functions are also values and have type. For example, Function1 type represents any function that takes one parameter. The important question is why the Function1 trait is contravariant for the parameter and covariant for the return type.

To answer, consider what will happen when the opposite is the case—for instance, covariant for parameter and contravariant for return value. Now imagine you have a covariant parameter, as in the following example:

```
val addOne: Function1[Any, Int] = { x: Int => x + 1 }
```

Because Int is a subtype of scala.Any, the covariant parameter should allow the preceding code to compile. But the loophole in this code is that you can now invoke addOne with any type of parameter as long as it's a subtype of scala.Any. Doing so could cause all sorts of problems for a function that expects only Int. Scala, being a type-safe language, doesn't allow you to do that. The only other option you have is to declare the parameter type as invariant, but that would make the Function1 trait inflexible. A contravariant parameter type is the only viable option to create a type-safe function.

You can't use a contravariant return type because you again get into a problem. Consider the following example:

```
val asString: Int => Int = { x: Int => (x.toString: Any) }
```

This code is not valid because `Any` is a super type of `Int`, and a contravariant allows you to go from a narrower type to a more generic type. The following piece of code should also be valid then, right?

```
asString(10) + 20
```

But you end up adding `20` to a string value, and that could be problematic. Scala's strong type system implementation stops you from making these kinds of mistakes when dealing with parameter types and return types. To have a flexible and type-safe `Function1` trait, the only possible implementation would be to have the parameter contravariant and the return type covariant. In the next section you'll learn to set bounds for type parameters—another important concept associated with type parameters.

4.3   *Lower and upper type bounds*

In Scala, type parameters may be constrained by type bound. Such type bounds limit the concrete values of the type variables. An example will illustrate this concept more clearly. The `position` function in the following listing throws an exception if you invoke `get` method on the `Nil` object:

```
scala> val xs = List("one", "two", "three")
xs: List[java.lang.String] = List(one, two, three)

scala> position(xs, "two").get
res3: Int = 1

scala> position(List(), "two").get
java.util.NoSuchElementException: Nil.get
  at Nil$.get(<console>:7)
  at Nil$.get(<console>:5)
  at .<init>(<console>:10)
```

Wouldn't it better to pass a default value in case the element isn't found? That way you can control the outcome in case of error. You can add a new method to the `Maybe` abstract class that will take a default callback:

```
sealed abstract class Maybe[+A] {
  def isEmpty: Boolean
  def get: A
  def getOrElse(default: A): A = {
    if(isEmpty) default else get
  }
}
```

Here `getOrElse` returns the default value if the `isEmpty` method returns true. In case of a `Nil` instance, `isEmpty` will always return true. But if you try to compile this code, you'll get the following compiler error:

```
covariant type A occurs in contravariant position in type => A of value default
```

Because A is a covariant type, Scala doesn't allow the covariant type as an input parameter. You'll also get the following compilation error if A is contravariant because it's
used as a return type for get:

```
contravariant type A occurs in covariant position in type => A of method get
```

You could solve this problem in two ways: make the Maybe class an invariant and lose
all the subtyping with Just and Nil, or use type bound. I'm not willing to give up nice
subtyping, so let's go with the local type bound.

Scala provides two types of type bound: lower and upper. An upper type bound T <:
A declares that type variable T is a subtype of a type A, and A is the upper bound. To
create a function that can only take subclasses of Maybe, you can write something like
the following:

```
def defaultToNull[A <: Maybe[_]](p: A) = {
  p.getOrElse(null)
}
```

The function defaultToNull takes parameter A, and it's constrained to one of the
subtypes of Maybe.

Because Maybe takes a type parameter, you have to declare the type parameter
when defining the upper type bound. If you don't care about the type parameter, you
can use the _ placeholder as in the last example.

A lower bound sets the lower limit of the type parameter. The lower bound T >: A
declares that the type parameter T is constrained to some super type of type A. You can
use the lower type bounds to implement the getOrElse method. The lower bound
helps you restrict the type of the parameter to A to some super type. The following listing shows the complete Maybe classes.

Listing 4.2   Complete Maybe.scala

```
sealed abstract class Maybe[+A] {                      ◁┐ Maybe class defined
  def isEmpty: Boolean                                    with a covariant
  def get: A                                              parameter type A
  def getOrElse[B >: A](default: B): B = {
    if(isEmpty) default else get
  }
}

final case class Just[A](value: A) extends Maybe[A] {   ◁┐ The Just subclass
  def isEmpty = false                                     holds the success
  def get = value                                         value of an operation
}

case object Nil extends Maybe[scala.Nothing] {          ◁┐ Nil is opposite of Just
  def isEmpty = true                                       and denotes an error
  def get = throw new NoSuchElementException("Nil.get")   condition
}
```

The Maybe class is defined with a covariant parameter type A so that its subclasses can
return more specialized types. The getOrElse method returns the value contained by

Just or the default value when it's empty. Because the default value is taken as a parameter, you have to set the lower bound to A to satisfy the contravariant rule.

Just and Nil are the two subclasses that represent success and error situations. The sealed modifier restricts anyone else from creating a subclass of Maybe (modifiers are covered in chapter 3).

When getting the index, you can always invoke the getOrElse method and avoid any unnecessary exceptions:

```
scala> position(List(), "something").getOrElse(-1)
res6: Int = -1

scala> position(List("one", "two", "three"), "three").getOrElse(-1)
res8: Int = 2
```

Scala's type system prevents you from making mistakes that could be easily caught during the compilation phase. You've learned the important role that covariance and contravariance play in building nice, type-safe applications. But remember that the approaches discussed here work only for immutable objects. When it comes to mutable objects, it's always safer to make them invariant.

You've only scratched the surface of Scala's type system. But I think you have enough to understand the data structures discussed in this chapter. You'll see more examples and explanations of Scala's type system throughout the book.

4.4 Higher-order functions, including map, flatMap, and friends

A function is called higher order if it takes a function as an argument or returns a function as a result. You've already seen some examples of Scala immutable.List. Now consider one of its methods called map. This method allows you to build a new list by applying a function to all elements of a given List:

```
class List[+A] ...  {
    def map[B](f: A => B) : List[B]
}
```

Here A represents the type of List in which the map is defined, and B is the type of the new List. To define a function argument, you have to use the => sign. In this case, f is a function that takes a single parameter of type A and returns a result of type B. In the following examples you're creating a new List by adding 1 to all the elements of a given list in various ways:

```
scala> List(1, 2, 3) map { (x: Int) => x + 1 }
res12: List[Int] = List(2, 3, 4)

scala> List(1, 2, 3) map { _ + 1 }
res13: List[Int] = List(2, 3, 4)

scala> def addOne(num:Int) = num + 1
addOne: (num: Int)Int

scala> List(1, 2, 3) map addOne
res11: List[Int] = List(2, 3, 4)
```

In the first case you're passing an anonymous function that takes x as a parameter and adds 1 to it. In the second case you're using a function literal, where a placeholder represents the parameter. In the last example, you're passing an existing function without referring to the parameters that are passed between the map function and the addOne function. This is a good example of pointfree-style[1] programming and functional composition. It's also an example of a call-by-name invocation, where the parameters of the function are wrapped inside another function. The function addOne is invoked every time map accesses the function.

You haven't looked at an example where a function returns another function. Let's fix that by refactoring the addOne function to add a nested function that abstracts our increment to 1 operation:

```
def addOne(num: Int) = {
  def ++ = (x:Int) => x + 1
  ++(num)
}
scala> List(1, 2, 3) map addOne
res15: List[Int] = List(2, 3, 4)
```

Call-by-value, call-by-reference, and call-by-name method invocation

Java supports two types of method invocation: call-by-reference and call-by-value. In call-by-reference invocation, a function is invoked with a reference to an object. In the case of Scala, it's any subtype of AnyRef. In the case of call-by-value invocation, the function is invoked with a value type. In Scala these are value types like Int or Float. Remember, Scala unboxes and boxes value types from and to an object depending on how it's used in the code. Along with these standard ones, Scala also provides additional method invocation mechanisms called call-by-name and call-by-need. In call-by-name method invocation, Scala passes a method parameter as a function. Let's look at an example that demonstrates this feature. In the following example, you have a log function, which logs a message when log is enabled:

```
def log(m: String) = if(logEnabled) println(m)
```

But to retrieve a log message, you have to look it up in the error queue—a time-consuming operation:

```
def popErrorMessage = { popMessageFromASlowQueue() }
log("The error message is " + popErrorMessage).
```

Here the parameter will always be evaluated even if log isn't enabled, and maybe you don't want that. You can use call-by-name to avoid the unnecessary computation:

```
def log(m: => String) = if(logEnabled) println(m)
```

Now by using =>, you've made the parameter a call-by-name, and it won't affect the way you're invoking the log function. But Scala will pass the parameter as a function that will be evaluated every time the parameter is accessed. If the log isn't enabled, the parameter will never be evaluated. Later in this chapter you'll see how lazy collections like Stream use the call-by-name method invocation pattern.

[1] "Pointfree," June 5, 2011 (last modified), www.haskell.org/haskellwiki/Pointfree.

Here the nested function ++ returns another function that takes Int as a parameter and returns Int. If you evaluate the ++ function in REPL, you'll see that the return type of the function is Int => Int:

```
scala> def ++ = (x:Int) => x + 1
$plus$plus: (Int) => Int
```

How can you implement a function like map that works for any type of list? You have a couple of ways to implement the map function—one uses recursion and the other uses a for-comprehension. The following is the implementation based on recursion, where using pattern matching you're extracting elements from the list and applying the supplied function:

```
def map[A, B](xs: List[A], f: A => B): List[B] = {
  xs match {
    case List() => Nil
    case head :: tail => f(head) :: map(tail, f)
  }
}
```

You're returning Nil (empty List) when the List is empty, and when the List isn't empty you're using pattern matching to separate List into head and tail. The head is assigned to the first element in the List, and the tail is the remaining list. You're using cons (::) to append the result of the f function recursively.

   If you try the map function with List(1, 2, 3) and the addOne function as parameters, the execution steps look like this:

```
case 1 :: List(2, 3) => addOne(1) :: map(List(2, 3), addOne)
case 2 :: List(3) => 2 :: addOne(2) :: map(List(3), addOne)
case 3 :: List() => 2 :: 3 :: addOne(3) :: map(List(), addOne)
```

At this point the empty list will match the first case, and the final expression will look like this:

```
2 :: 3 :: 4 :: Nil
```

Now the result of the each function f will be prepended to the empty list, resulting in a new list:

```
scala> map(List(1, 2, 3), addOne)
res0: List[Int] = List(2, 3, 4)
```

How does head :: tail work?

This pattern is called the *Infix Operation* pattern, where the expression head :: tail is shorthand for the constructor pattern ::(head, tail). The immutable List in Scala is defined as an abstract sealed class, and its only two subclasses are Nil and ::. Both are case classes. As you already know, one of the biggest benefits of Scala case classes is that they can participate in pattern matching. So ::(head, tail) matches the constructor of the :: case class that takes head as the first element and the list as the second element, which in this case is tail.

The associativity of the cons (::) is right instead of left. In the expression 2 :: 3 :: 4 :: Nil you're invoking :: (cons) on Nil first, and then on the result you return by the first cons operation, and so on. You could write the expression the following way too: Nil.::(2).::(3).::(4). In Scala, the associativity of an operator is determined by the operator's last character. If the operator ends with :, then it's right-associative. All other operators are left-associative. The associativity of the operator confuses many Scala newcomers. Always remember that associativity is determined by the last character of the operator.

Another simple way to implement the map function is to use a for-comprehension; here's the implementation:

```
def map1[A, B](f: A => B, xs: List[A]): List[B] = for(x <- xs) yield f(x)
```

Another interesting method defined for List is flatMap. This method builds a new collection by applying a function to all elements of this list and concatenating the result. The following shows how the flatMap method is declared in the List class:

```
class List[+A] { ...
    def flatMap[B](f: A => GenTraversableOnce[B]): List[B]
}
```

GenTraversableOnce represents all collection types that could be iterated either sequentially or in parallel. All the traits that start with Gen are introduced to the collection library to implement operations that are applicable to both sequential and parallel collections. Here you're focusing on sequential collections—later you'll learn about parallel collections.

The flatMap method works similarly to the map method with the added ability to flatten a collection of collections into a single collection. In the following example you're creating a list of characters from a list of strings:

```
scala> List("one","two", "three", "") flatMap { _.toList }
res5: List[Char] = List(o, n, e, t, w, o, t, h, r, e, e)
```

As mentioned earlier, String is treated as a Seq-like collection in Scala, and it exposes a method called toList to convert to a List. In the previous example you invoked toList on each element in the list. If you use map instead of flatMap, you get the following result:

```
scala> List("one","two", "three", "") map { _.toList }
res7: List[List[Char]] = List(List(o, n, e), List(t, w, o), List(t, h, r, e,
    e), List())
```

As you can see, flatMap takes the result of the map and flattens it to a single list. Here's how you could implement the flatMap function for List:

```
def flatten[B](xss: List[List[B]]): List[B] = {
  xss match {
    case List() => Nil
    case head :: tail => head ::: flatten(tail)
  }
}
```

```
def flatMap[A, B](xs: List[A])(f: A => List[B]) : List[B] = {
  flatten(map(xs, f))
}
```

Here `flatMap` is implemented by combining `map` with a new function called `flatten` that takes a `List` of `List` and flattens it to a single `List`. The `:::` is another method defined for `List` that appends the contents of one `List` to another. Let's try the `flatMap` function:

```
scala> flatMap(List("one", "two", "three")) { _.toList }
res9: List[Char] = List(o, n, e, t, w, o, t, h, r, e, e)
```

The `flatMap` function in that example is declared a little differently, as if it has two sets of parameters, one for the `List` and another for the `f` parameter:

```
def flatMap[A, B](xs: List[A])(f: A => List[B]) : List[B]
```

This is called *currying*.[2] Currying allows you to chain functions one after another with a single parameter. You'll explore currying in detail in chapter 5. An additional benefit of separating parameters of functions is that it allows you to pass functions as closures `{ _.toList }`.

What's the difference between a lambda and a closure?

A *lambda* is an anonymous function—a function without a name. You've already seen some examples of it. *Closure* is any function that closes over the environment in which it's defined. Let's use an example to explore this fact, applying a percentage to a list of amounts:

```
scala> List(100, 200, 300) map { _ * 10/100 }
res34: List[Int] = List(10, 20, 30)
```

In this case the function you're passing to the `map` function is a lambda. Now assume that the percentage value could change over time, so save the current percentage value in a variable.

```
scala> var percentage = 10
percentage: Int = 10
scala> val applyPercentage = (amount: Int) =>
amount * percentage/100
applyPercentage: (Int) => Int = <function1>
```

In this case `applyPercentage` is a closure because it keeps track of the environment in which it's created, like a percentage variable:

```
scala> percentage = 20
percentage: Int = 20
scala> List(100, 200, 300) map applyPercentage
res33: List[Int] = List(20, 40, 60)
```

Lambdas and closures are different concepts, but they're closely related.

---

[2]   Daniel Spiewak (blog), "Function Currying in Scala," March 2008, http://mng.bz/u0sJ.

The downside of using a recursive solution is that it can throw a stack overflow error on large datasets. An alternative is to implement the function using tail recursion so that the Scala compiler could do tail call optimization and transform the recursion into a loop. In tail recursion you perform your calculation first and then execute the recursive call by passing the result of the current step to the next step. Here's the implementation of the flatten function using tail recursion:

```
def flatten3[B](xss: List[List[B]]): List[B] = {
def _flatten3(oldList: List[List[B]], newList: List[B]): List[B] =
oldList match {
  case List() => newList
  case head :: tail => _flatten3(tail, newList ::: head)
}
_flatten3(xss, Nil)
}
```

In this case the flatten function is implemented using a nested function that uses the tail recursion pattern. The result of newList ::: head is passed as a parameter to the function so that the Scala compiler can optimize it. You'll learn more about tail call recursion in the next chapter. In the next section you'll explore another new concept called *fold* that allows you to process a data structure in some order and build a return value.

4.5   *Using foldLeft and foldRight*

Two other interesting methods defined in List are foldLeft and foldRight. These two operations allow you to perform binary operations on all the elements of the List. Both of these methods in List are declared as follows:

```
class List[+A] {
    ...
    def foldLeft[B](z: B)(f: (B, A) => B): B
    def foldRight[B](z: B)(f: (A, B) => B): B
}
```

The main difference between these methods is the way the parameters are passed to the function f. In foldLeft, z represents the start value, and it's passed as the first parameter to f. For foldRight the start value is passed as the second parameter. The function f is a combining function that takes two parameters and produces a single result value. To understand how fold works, look at the previous flatten implementation one more time. Notice that it's similar to the recursive implementation of map:

```
def map[A, B](xs: List[A], f: A => B): List[B] = {
  xs match {
    case List() => Nil
    case head :: tail => f(head) :: map(tail, f)
  }
}

def flatten[B](xss: List[List[B]]): List[B] = {
```

```
xss match {
  case List() => Nil
  case head :: tail => head ::: flatten(tail)
}
}
```

There's a common pattern in these functions: you do one thing when `List` is empty and something else when `List` isn't empty. The only thing that's different between these functions is the binary operation. You can avoid this duplication by using `fold-Right`:

```
def map2[A, B](xs: List[A])(f: A => B): List[B] = {
  val startValue = List.empty[B]
  xs.foldRight(startValue) { f(_) :: _ }
}

def flatten2[B](xss: List[List[B]]): List[B] = {
  val startValue = List.empty[B]
  xss.foldRight(startValue) { _ ::: _ }
}
```

The `startValue` is set to an empty `List`, and the combining function lets you apply the binary operator to all elements. The reason for using `foldRight` here is the right-associativeness of the `::` and `:::` operators. Both the cases start with an empty `List` and invoke either `::` or `:::` on the parameters. I'm sure by now you're familiar with the underscore (`_`) as a placeholder for parameters. This is a good example of how having higher-order functions helps libraries build common operations that can be used in many different ways without duplicating code.

Avoid `foldRight` as much as possible as it uses recursion and can potentially throw a stack overflow error. In some cases the Scala compiler transforms recursive functions to loops—you'll learn about them in the next chapter. One alternative approach is to use `foldLeft` and reverse the result. For example, you can implement `map2` using `foldLeft` and reverse the result:

```
def map3[A, B](xs: List[A])(f: A => B): List[B] = {
  val startValue = List.empty[B]
  xs.foldLeft(startValue)((a, x) => f(x) :: a).reverse
}
```

The `foldLeft` method applies a binary operator to a start value and all elements of a `List` going from left to right. Here's how to use `foldLeft` to calculate the sum and length of a `List`:

```
scala> List(1, 2, 3, 4).foldLeft(0) { _ + _ }
res25: Int = 10

scala> List(1, 2, 3, 4).foldLeft(0) { (a, b) => a + 1 }
res27: Int = 4
```

The first example calculates the sum of all the elements, and the second calculates the length of the `List`. The second example can't use underscore because you aren't using all the function parameters to compute the length of the List.

Both `foldLeft` and `foldRight` have an alias version, `/:` (foldLeft) and `:\` (fold-Right), that you can use instead. But Scala programmers tend to prefer `foldLeft` and `foldRight` to symbolic versions.

Folding is a great way to process collections of data to build a return value. Where map and `flatMap` allow you to transform contents of a collection, folding allows you to do structural transformations. You can use folding in many interesting ways to solve your day-to-day programming problems. The following example uses `foldLeft` to determine whether an element exists in a `List`:

```
def exists[A](xs: List[A], e: A) =
xs.foldLeft(false)((a, x) => a || (x == e))
```

It must be obvious by now that higher-order functions provide a nice way to encode common programming idioms as a part of the library. Using `foldLeft` and `fold-Right`, you can perform any type of binary operation without creating additional functions. Next time you feel the need to create a loop, step back and think about ways you could use higher abstractions like maps or folds.

Just because the Scala `List` collection is used for all the examples doesn't mean it should be your go-to collection type. For a given problem, always try to choose the right collection type. Later in this chapter I introduce you to other Scala collection types.

All the goodness of higher-order functions is possible in Scala because of its function objects. The next section explores how function objects work in Scala.

4.6   *Building your own function objects*

A *function object* is an object that you can use as a function. That doesn't help you much, so why don't I show you an example? Here you create a function object that wraps the `foldLeft` method you saw in the previous example:

```
object foldl {
  def apply[A, B](xs: Traversable[A], defaultValue: B)(op: (B, A) => B) =
          (defaultValue /: xs)(op)
}
```

Now you can use the `foldl` function object like any function you've used before:

```
scala> foldl(List("1", "2", "3"), "0") { _ + _ }
res0: java.lang.String = 0123

scala> foldl(IndexedSeq("1", "2", "3"), "0") { _ + _ }
res24: java.lang.String = 0123

scala> foldl(Set("1", "2", "3"), "0") { _ + _ }
res25: java.lang.String = 0123
```

You've already seen a few examples of `apply` and how to use them. It's no different when creating a function object. To treat an object as a function object, all you have to do is declare an `apply` method. In Scala, `<object>(<arguments>)` is syntactic sugar for `<object>.apply(<arguments>)`. You can also have multiple sets of arguments.

Because you've defined the parameter `Traversable`, the parent trait for all collection types in Scala, you can pass any collection type as a parameter.

The expression `(defaultValue /: xs) (op)` might look a little cryptic, but the idea is to demonstrate the alternative syntax for `foldLeft`, `/:`. Remember that when an operator ends with `:`, the right associativeness kicks in.

When declaring function objects, it's a good idea to extend one of the `Function` traits defined in the Scala library. In Scala, the `Functon1` trait is declared as follows:

```
trait Function1[-T1, +R] extends AnyRef {
  def apply(v: T1): R
}
```

Here 1 stands for "function with one parameter." Similarly, Scala defines a function trait for two or more parameters. In the following example, you're building an increment function that takes an integer parameter and increments its value by 1:

```
object ++ extends Function1[Int, Int]{
  def apply(p: Int): Int = p + 1
}
```

The shorthand and equivalent implementation of this function would be:

```
val ++ = (x: Int) => x + 1
```

There's one more way you could define your function object: using the alternative notation of function `=>`.

```
object ++ extends (Int => Int) {
  def apply(p: Int): Int = p + 1
}
```

In the last case you're using the shorthand notation of `Function1`; that is, `Int => Int`. You use a similar syntactic notation when declaring higher-order functions. You can use function objects anywhere you've used lambdas or closures before. Here you're invoking your `map` function with your new `++` function:

```
scala> map(List(10, 20, 30), ++)
res1: List[Int] = List(11, 21, 31)
```

This is the same as invoking it with an anonymous function:

```
scala> map(List(10, 20, 30), (x: Int) => x + 1)
res2: List[Int] = List(11, 21, 31)
```

It's also the same as passing the `Function` trait:

```
scala> map(List(10, 20, 30), new Function1[Int, Int] {
           def apply(p: Int) = p + 1
       })
res3: List[Int] = List(11, 21, 31)
```

When passing an existing function (not a function object) as a parameter, Scala creates a new anonymous function object with an `apply` method, which invokes the original function. This is called *eta-expansion*.

One interesting subtrait of the Function1[-P, +R] trait is PartialFunction, which allows you to define a function that's not defined for all P and allows you to compose with other partial functions to create a complete function that's defined for all values of input parameter(s). You'll explore PartialFunction in the next chapter, where you'll have a good use case for it.

Function1 is also defined as Function

Because the Function1 trait is used so often, Scala defines a type alias called Function. You won't find any reference to this trait in scaladoc because this type alias is defined inside the Predef class as follows:

```
type Function[-A, +B] = Function1[A, B]
```

type is a keyword in Scala, and it's used to create type aliases. It's similar to typedef in C. I discuss type variables at length in chapter 6, where we'll explore using them to create abstract members in Scala.

Another helpful use of type variables is as a representation of a complicated type:

```
type MILS = Map[Int, List[String]]
val mapping: MILS = Map(
    1 -> List("one", "uno"), 2 -> List("two", "dos"))
```

Function traits also let you compose two functions to create a new function. This is important because in functional programming you tend to solve problem by combining functions. The following example composes the same function twice to create a new one:

```
val addOne: Int => Int = x => x + 1
val addTwo: Int => Int = x => x + 2
val addThree = addOne compose addTwo
```

Composing the addOne and addTwo functions together creates the addThree function. This is similar to the following implementation:

```
val addThree: Int => Int = x => addOne(addTwo(x))
```

The compose method allows you to chain functions together to create new functions. You'll look into function composition in much more detail in the next chapter. Now it's time for you to explore the Scala collection hierarchy.

4.7   *Scala collection hierarchy*

One of the major features of the new Scala 2.8 release is its new, improved collection library.[3, 4] You're going to explore Scala collections in detail in this section.

The Scala collection classes are part of the scala.collection package and its sub-packages. The scala.collection.mutable package defines collection classes that

---

[3] Martin Odersky, SID#3 "New collection classes," revised, July 2010,www.scala-lang.org/sid/3.

[4] Martin Odersky, A. Moors, "Fighting Bit Rot with Types," 2009, http://mng.bz/104f.

provide side-effect operations that could change the state of the collection in place. On the other hand, `scala.collection.immutable` is guaranteed to be immutable for everyone. The immutable collections are sometimes called *persistent data structures* because you can be certain that accessing the same collection will yield the same result over time. Here *persistent* has nothing to do with a database or anything like that, but over time an immutable collection stays unchanged during the current program execution. Any change in an immutable collection produces a new collection without touching the existing collection.

The generic subpackage provides building blocks for implementing various collections. Typically, collection classes in mutable and immutable packages use the classes in the generic package for implementation of some of their operations. Normally you don't have to deal with the classes in the generic package unless you're planning to create custom collection classes on your own.

A collection class defined in the package `scala.collection` can be either mutable or immutable. For example, `scala.collection.Map[A, +B]` is a super class for both `collection.mutable.Map[A, B]` and `collection.immutable.Map[A, +B]`. Generally, the root collections in the package `scala.collection` define the same interface as the immutable collections, and the mutable collections add additional methods on top of the immutable collections that allow mutation of the collection. In the case of mutable `map`, it provides methods like `+=` and `-=` that add and remove elements from the collection and hence change the collection in the process. Even though you can use a root collection type as a reference to an immutable collection, it's always better to be explicit about the type of collection (mutable or immutable) when dealing with collections so that users can figure out the code easily. Here you're assigning both mutable and immutable collections to the `collection.Map` type value, and it's not clear from the type of the `mapping` whether or not the `map` it refers to can be changed by others:

```
scala> val mapping: collection.Map[String, String] = Map("Ron" -> "admin",
    "Sam" -> "Analyst")
mapping: scala.collection.Map[String,String] =
Map(Ron -> admin, Sam -> Analyst)

scala> val mapping: collection.Map[String, String] =
    collection.mutable.Map("Ron" -> "admin", "Sam" -> "Analyst")
mapping: scala.collection.Map[String,String] = Map(Sam -> Analyst, Ron ->
    admin)
```

Scala automatically imports immutable collections, but you have to explicitly import mutable collection types, as you did for `collection.mutable.Map`. Figure 4.1 shows a simplified version of the Scala collection library.

The root of the hierarchy is the trait `Traversable`. This base trait implements the behavior common to all collection types in Scala (see table 4.1). The only abstract method defined in the `Traversable` trait is `foreach`:

```
def foreach[U](f: Elem => U)
```

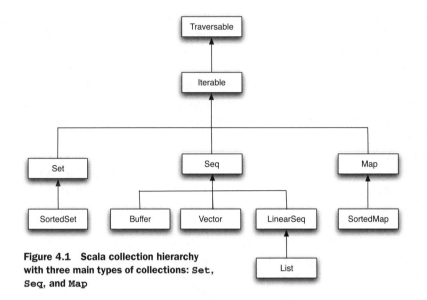

Figure 4.1   Scala collection hierarchy with three main types of collections: `Set`, `Seq`, and `Map`

Table 4.1   Useful methods defined in the `Traversable` trait

Methods	Description
`xs.size`	The number of elements in the collection.
`xs ++ ys`	A collection consisting of the elements of both `xs` and `ys`.
`xs map f`	The collection obtained from applying the function `f` to every element in `xs`.
`xs flatMap f`	The collection obtained from applying the collection valued function `f` to every element in `xs` and concatenating the results.
`xs filter p`	The collection consisting of those elements of `xs` that satisfy the predicate `p`.
`xs find p`	An option containing the first element in `xs` that satisfies `p`, or `None` if no element qualifies.
`(z /: xs)(op)`	Apply binary operation `op` between successive elements of `xs`, going left to right and starting with `z`. `/:` is alias for `foldLeft`.
`(xs :\ z)(op)`	Apply binary operation `op` between successive elements of `xs`, going right to left and starting with `z`. `:\` is alias for `foldRight`.
`xs.head`	The first element of the collection (or some element, if no order is defined).
`xs.tail`	The rest of the collection except `xs.head`.
`xs mkString sep`	Produces a string that shows all elements of `xs` between separators `sep`.

Let's see an example where you can use this knowledge. You've already seen examples of how to use Java collections with Scala, but here's another simple example where you could wrap any Java collection to `Traversable` so that you could use it in Scala freely:

```
import java.util.{Collection => JCollection, ArrayList }

class JavaToTraversable[E](javaCollection: JCollection[E]) extends
                                                       Traversable[E] {

  def foreach[U](f : E => U): Unit = {
    val iterator = javaCollection.iterator
    while(iterator.hasNext) {
      f(iterator.next)
    }
  }
}
```

You're providing a concrete implementation of only an abstract method in the Traversable trait, foreach. Now with just one concrete method, you can use all the methods defined in the Traversable trait, such as map, foldLeft, or filter:

```
scala> val jCol = new ArrayList[Int]
jCol: java.util.ArrayList[Int] = []

scala> (1 to 5) foreach { jCol.add(_) }

scala> jCol
res3: java.util.ArrayList[Int] = [1, 2, 3, 4, 5]

scala> val jtoT = new JavaToTraversable(jCol)
jtoT: JavaToTraversable[Int] = line3(1, 2, 3, 4, 5)

scala> jtoT map { _ * 10 } filter { _ > 20 }
res10: Traversable[Int] = List(30, 40, 50)
```

In Scala you can define a traversable object as finite or infinite; hasDefiniteSize determines whether a collection is finite or infinite. You'll see examples of an infinite collection later in this chapter.

4.8   *Mutable and immutable collections*

A collection in a scala.collection can be both mutable and immutable. You read about the difference between mutable and immutable collection classes in the previous section. Here you'll focus on both mutable and immutable collections. But before I start looking into specific collection classes, let's peek at the Iterable trait. This trait comes after Traversable. It provides the implementation of foreach that you learned in the last section and it exposes a new abstract method called iterator. It also adds methods like takeRight and dropRight along with the methods defined in the Traversable trait. takeRight returns a collection consisting of the last n elements for a given n, and dropRight does the opposite:

```
scala> Iterable(1, 2, 3, 4, 5) dropRight 2
res0: Iterable[Int] = List(1, 2, 3)

scala> Iterable(1, 2, 3, 4, 5) takeRight 2
res1: Iterable[Int] = List(4, 5)
```

The most interesting things about the Iterable trait are its three base classes: Seq, Set, and Map. One thing common among these subclasses is that they all implement the PartialFunction trait, and that means that all of them have the apply method. You'll now explore these base classes and their subclasses in detail.

4.9   *Working with List and ListBuffer*

The elements in a sequence are indexed, and they're indexed from 0 to length – 1, where length is the number of elements in the sequence collection. Because Seq also implements PartialFunction, it has an apply method (the Function trait defines an apply method), and it's a partial function from Int to an element. The reason it's partial is because for all values of Int you may not have elements in the collection. In the following example you're trying to access an element that exists in the sequence and one that doesn't:

```
scala> val languages = Seq("Scala", "Haskell", "OCaml", "ML")
languages: Seq[java.lang.String] = List(Scala, Haskell, OCaml, ML)

scala> languages(1)
res11: java.lang.String = Haskell

scala> languages(10)
java.lang.IndexOutOfBoundsException
    at scala.collection.LinearSeqLike$class.apply(LinearSeqLike.scala:78)
    at scala.collection.immutable.List.apply(List.scala:46)
```

Using a collection as PartialFunction

Along with the standard apply method, the PartialFunction trait in Scala defines a couple of interesting methods, including andThen and orElse. For example, to avoid situations where your Seq doesn't have elements, you could use orElse, which works as a fallback when the partial function isn't defined for a given value. Here's how to use orElse:

```
val default: PartialFunction[Int, String] = {
  case _ => "Is it a functional language?" }
val languagesWithDefault = languages orElse default
```

Now if you try to access an index that doesn't exist, your default is used instead.

```
languagesWithDefault(10) will produce "Is it a functional language?"
```

This is a good example of function composition and how to use it in Scala. You'll explore PartialFunction and other function composition parts and their usage throughout the book.

If the sequence is mutable like ListBuffer, then along with the apply method it offers an update method. An assignment is turned into an update method call. In the following code snippet you're creating a ListBuffer and updating it:

```
scala> import scala.collection.mutable.ListBuffer
import scala.collection.mutable.ListBuffer

scala> val buf = ListBuffer(1.2, 3.4, 5.6)
buf: scala.collection.mutable.ListBuffer[Double] =
ListBuffer(1.2, 3.4, 5.6)

scala> buf(2) = 10
```

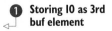 **1** Storing 10 as 3rd buf element

```
scala> buf
res30: scala.collection.mutable.ListBuffer[Double] =
ListBuffer(1.2, 3.4, 10.0)

scala> buf.update(2, 20)

scala> buf
res32: scala.collection.mutable.ListBuffer[Double] =
ListBuffer(1.2, 3.4, 20.0)
```

❷ Storing 20 as 3rd
buf element

The assignment at ❶ and the update method called at ❷ are identical. The two main subclasses for Seq are LinearSeq and Vector. These classes provide different performance characteristics. Vector provides efficient apply and length operations, whereas LinearSeq has efficient head and tail operations. The most common subclasses of LinearSeq are List and Stream. You've already seen examples of List. You'll explore Stream shortly.

What type of collection should I use?

Scala collections provide various types of collections, and every collection type has different performance characteristics. Making sure that you select the appropriate collection type to solve your problem is important. In case you're not sure what type of collection to use, always reach out for Vector. Overall, Vector has better performance characteristics compared to other collection types.

One interesting subcategory of Sequences in Scala is Buffers. Buffers are always mutable, and most of the collections I talk about here are internally built using Buffers. The two common subclasses of Buffers are mutable.ListBuffer and mutable.ArrayBuffer.

4.9.1   *Working with Set and SortedSet*

Set is an iterable collection type that contains no duplicate elements. Set provides the contains method to check whether the given element exists in the Set, and the apply method that does the same thing. Here's how to use them:

```
scala> val frameworks = Set("Lift", "Akka", "Playframework", "Scalaz")
frameworks: scala.collection.mutable.Set[java.lang.String] =
Set(Lift, Playframework, Akka, Scalaz)

scala> frameworks contains "Lift"
res36: Boolean = true

scala> frameworks contains "Scalacheck"
res37: Boolean = false

scala> frameworks("Lift")
res38: Boolean = true
```

To add or remove elements to or from an immutable Set, use + and -, respectively. Using these methods for a mutable Set isn't a good idea because it will create a new

Table 4.2 Useful methods defined in immutable and mutable Sets

Methods	Description
xs contains x	Test whether x is an element of xs.
xs ++ ys	Set containing all elements of xs and additional elements from ys. It won't add the duplicate entries from ys.
xs & ys, xs intersect ys	The set intersection of xs and ys.
xs | ys, xs union ys	The set union of xs and ys.
xs &~ ys, xs diff ys	The set difference of xs and ys.
xs ++= ys	Add elements from ys to set xs as a side effect and return xs itself. Only for mutable Set.
xs(x) = b, xs.update(x, b)	If Boolean argument b is true, add x to xs; otherwise remove x from xs.
xs.clear()	Remove all elements from xs.

Set. It will not update itself. A better way to change mutable Sets is using the += and -= methods (for other useful methods available for Set, see table 4.2). Here are some examples of adding and removing elements from both immutable and mutable Sets:

```
scala> val frameworks = Set() + "Akka" + "Lift" + "Scalaz"
frameworks: scala.collection.immutable.Set[java.lang.String] = Set(Akka,
    Lift, Scalaz)

scala> val frameworks = Set("Akka",  "Lift", "Scalaz") - "Lift"
frameworks: scala.collection.immutable.Set[java.lang.String] = Set(Akka,
    Scalaz)

scala> val mFrameworks = collection.mutable.Set[String]()
mFrameworks: scala.collection.mutable.Set[String] = Set()

scala> mFrameworks += "Akka" += "Lift"
res5: mFrameworks.type = Set(Lift, Akka)

scala> mFrameworks += "Scalacheck"
res12: mFrameworks.type = Set(Lift, Akka, Scalacheck)
```

Along with the add and remove methods, you can perform other Set operations, such as union, intersect, and diff. One interesting subtrait of Set is SortedSet. When iterator or foreach is called on SortedSet, it produces its elements in a certain order. In the following code snippet you're adding two sets, one using Set and the other using SortedSet. In the case of SortedSet, the order of the elements is maintained:

```
scala> Set(1, 2, 3) ++ Set(3, 4, 5)
res15: scala.collection.immutable.Set[Int] = Set(5, 1, 2, 3, 4)

scala> import collection.immutable.SortedSet
import collection.immutable.SortedSet

scala> SortedSet (1, 2, 3) ++ SortedSet(3, 5, 4)
res18: scala.collection.immutable.SortedSet [Int] = TreeSet(1, 2, 3, 4, 5)
```

4.9.2   *Working with Map and Tuple*

Maps are iterable pairs of keys and values. The key-value pair is represented by scala.Tuple2, a tuple of two elements. Unlike other collections, a Tuple is a heterogeneous collection where you can store various types of elements. Here's how you can create an instance of an immutable Map with two key-value pairs:

```
scala> val m = Map((1, "1st"), (2, "2nd"))
m: scala.collection.immutable.Map[Int,java.lang.String] =
    Map(1 -> 1st, 2 -> 2nd)
```

An alternative way to create a similar Map would be to use the key -> value syntax:

```
scala> val m = Map(1 -> "1st", 2 -> "2nd")
m: scala.collection.immutable.Map[Int,java.lang.String] =
                                    Map(1 -> 1st, 2 -> 2nd)
```

Most of the operations of Map are similar to those of Set. In the case of Map, the apply method returns the value of a given key, and if the value doesn't exist, it throws an exception. Here's an example of how to use the apply method:

```
scala> m(1)
res20: java.lang.String = 1st

scala> m(3)
java.util.NoSuchElementException: key not found: 3
    at scala.collection.MapLike$class.default(MapLike.scala:226)
    at scala.collection.immutable.Map$Map2.default(Map.scala:88)
```

The better way to retrieve a value associated with a key is to use the get method defined in Map. Instead of returning the value, it wraps the value in a container called Option:

```
def get(key: A): Option[B]
```

Option is similar to the Maybe construct you created at the beginning of the chapter. The Scala Option provides more features than you built for the Maybe. You can think of Option as a List of one element. When an element exists in the Map, it returns Some of the elements; otherwise, it returns None. In the following example you're using get to retrieve the value for a key:

```
scala> m.get(1)
res22: Option[java.lang.String] = Some(1st)

scala> m.get(3)
res23: Option[java.lang.String] = None
```

You can use get to extract the element from Option or use getOrElse to retrieve a value from Option. To get all the keys and values from the Map, you can use m.keys and m.values (table 4.3 lists some of the useful methods defined in mutable and immutable maps), and both of them return Iterator. Scala Map also defines methods like filter, which takes a predicate and returns a Map of all the key values for which the predicate was true. In the following code snippet, you're filtering out all the rock artists:

```
scala> val artists = Map(
"Pink Floyd" -> "Rock", "Led Zeppelin" -> "Rock",
"Michael Jackson" -> "Pop", "Above & Beyond" -> "Trance")
artists: scala.collection.immutable.Map[java.lang.String,java.lang.String] =
    Map(Pink Floyd -> Rock, Led Zeppelin -> Rock, Michael Jackson -> Pop,
    Above & Beyond -> Trance)

scala> artists filter { (t) => t._2 == "Rock" }
res26: scala.collection.immutable.Map[java.lang.String,java.lang.String] =
    Map(Pink Floyd -> Rock, Led Zeppelin -> Rock)
```

Table 4.3   Useful methods defined in immutable and mutable `Map`

Methods	Description
`ms getOrElse (k, d)`	The value associated with key `k` in map `ms`, or the default value `d` if not found.
`ms + (k -> v)`	The map containing all mappings of `ms` as well as the mapping `k -> v` from key `k` to value `v`.
`ms ++ kvs`	The map containing all mappings of `ms` as well as all key-value pairs of `kvs`.
`ms filterKeys p`	A map view containing only those mappings in `ms` where the key satisfies predicate `p`.
`ms mapValues f`	A map view resulting from applying function `f` to each value associated with a key in `ms`.
`ms(k) = v, ms.update(k, v)`	Adds mapping from key `k` to value `v` to map `ms` as a side effect, overwriting any previous mapping of `k`.
`ms getOrElseUpdate(k, d)`	If key `k` is defined in map `ms`, return its associated value. Otherwise, update `ms` with the mapping `k -> d` and return `d`.
`xs.clear()`	Removes all mappings from `ms`.

The `filter` method in `Map` calls the predicate by passing the key-value pair as an instance of `scala.Tuple2`. The Scala `Tuple2` defines the methods `_1` and `_2` to retrieve the first and second elements from the `Tuple`. Another way you could filter out all the rock artists would be to use for-comprehension, like so:

```
scala> for(t <- artists; if(t._2 == "Rock")) yield t
res31: scala.collection.immutable.Map[java.lang.String,java.lang.String] =
    Map(Pink Floyd -> Rock, Led Zeppelin -> Rock)
```

This brings up an interesting point of how a for-comprehension is similar to the `map`, `filter`, and `foreach` methods you've learned about so far. In the next section you'll see how a for-comprehension is translated in Scala.

4.9.3   *Under the hood of for-comprehension*

You've learned that for-comprehensions are made up of generators, value definitions, and guards. But I haven't talked about the under-the-hood translation that happens and how a for-comprehension combines pattern matching with `filter`, `map`, `flatMap`, and `foreach`. This knowledge will help you understand how to combine simple functions to create something powerful. As always, a better way is to look at what's going on underneath. This time you'll create a case class to represent the artists and use a for-comprehension to create a list of rock artists. Here's the code snippet:

```
case class Artist(name: String, genre: String)

val artists = List(Artist("Pink Floyd", "Rock"),
                   Artist("Led Zeppelin", "Rock"),
                   Artist("Michael Jackson", "Pop"),
                   Artist("Above & Beyond", "trance")
                  )
for(Artist(name, genre) <- artists; if(genre == "Rock"))
yield name
```

Under the hood, this for-comprehension will get translated to something like the following:

```
artists withFilter {
  case Artist(name, genre) => genre == "Rock"
} map {
  case Artist(name, genre) => name
}
```

How does this translation work? Every generator `p <- e` gets translated to a call to `withFilter` on e like `e.withFilter { case p => true; case _ => false }`. In the generator, the first part of `Artist(name, genre)` is nothing but pattern matching, and because you can use case classes in pattern matching, you used them for the `Artist` example. The `withFilter` method returns an instance of class `List.WithFilter` that supports all the filtering operations. The `yield` part of the for-comprehension is turned into a call to the `map` method on the output of the filter. For example, `for(Artist(name, genre) <- artists) yield name` gets translated into something like the following:

```
artists withFilter {
  case Artist(name, genre) => true; case _ => false
} map {
  case Artist(name, genre) => name
}
```

For-comprehensions without yield (imperative version) are translated into a `foreach` method call on the output of the filter. Here's an example:

```
for(Artist(name, genre) <- artists) println(name + "," + genre)

artists withFilter {
  case Artist(name, genre) => true; case _ => false
} foreach {
  case Artist(name, genre) => println(name + "," + genre)}
```

When you have multiple generators in the for-comprehension, things become a little more involved and interesting. Let's say that along with the artists you also like to store

Why use withFilter but not filter?

The answer lies in strict versus nonstrict processing of the filter. The `filter` method processes all the elements of the list and selects only those elements that satisfy the predicate/condition, whereas nonstrict processing means that computation is done on a need-to basis. Starting with Scala 2.8, for-comprehensions are nonstrict. In this example you have a list of numbers, and you want to control the processing based on a flag:

```
val list = List(1, 2, 3)
var go = true
val x = for(i <- list; if(go)) yield {
    go = false
    i
}
println(x)
```

You'd expect that x would be `List(1)`, but if you run the same code in Scala 2.7.*, you'll see that x is `List(1, 2, 3)`. The reason is that prior to Scala 2.8, for-comprehensions were translated into something like the following:

```
val y = list filter {
  case i => go
} map {
  case i => {
    go = false
    i
  }
}
println(y)
```

As you can see, when the filter processes the elements, `go` is true; hence it returns all the elements. The fact that you're making the `go` flag `false` has no effect on the filter because the filter is already done. In Scala 2.8 this problem is fixed using `withFilter`. When `withFilter` is used, the condition is evaluated every time an element is accessed inside a `map` method.

albums produced by those artists, and you're only interested in rock albums. Create another case class to store the artists with their albums, and using a for-comprehension you can easily filter out all the rock albums. Here's the code:

```
case class Artist(name: String, genre: String)
case class ArtistWithAlbums(artist: Artist, albums: List[String])

val artistsWithAlbums = List(
                ArtistWithAlbums(Artist("Pink Floyd", "Rock"),
                    List("Dark side of the moon", "Wall")),
                ArtistWithAlbums(Artist("Led Zeppelin", "Rock"),
                    List("Led Zeppelin IV", "Presence")),
                ArtistWithAlbums(Artist("Michael Jackson", "Pop"),
                    List("Bad", "Thriller")),
                ArtistWithAlbums(Artist("Above & Beyond", "trance"),
                    List("Tri-State", "Sirens of the Sea"))
                )
```

```
for { ArtistWithAlbums(artist, albums) <- artistsWithAlbums
      album <- albums
      if(artist.genre == "Rock")
    } yield album
```

For each artist you're iterating through all the albums and checking to see if the genre is Rock. When you have multiple generators, Scala uses flatMap instead of map. The preceding code gets translated to the following:

```
artistsWithAlbums flatMap {
  case ArtistWithAlbums(artist, albums) => albums withFilter {
                                     album => artist.genre == "Rock"
                           } map { case album => album }
}
```

The reason you use flatMap here is because you have to flatten the output of map for each generator. Using flatMap you get List(Dark side of the moon, Wall, Led Zeppelin IV, Presence) as the result, and with map you get List(List(Dark side of the moon, Wall), List(Led Zeppelin IV, Presence), List(), List()) as output.

Before leaving Scala collections, I'd like to discuss one more thing, and that's the usage of Scala Option. You've already seen some of the methods defined in Scala collections that return Option, and it's time to see what they are.

4.9.4 *Use Option not Null*

If you've worked with Java or a Ruby-like language, then you understand the pain of working with null or nil (in the case of Ruby) in code. In Ruby, things are a little better in the sense that Nil is a singleton object, and you can invoke methods on Nil. But in Java if a variable reference is null, you get a NullPointerException. To avoid the issue many programmers clutter their codebase with null checks and make the code difficult to read.

Scala takes a different approach to solving this problem, using something called Option.[5] Option implements the Null Object pattern. Option is also a Monad. I talk about Monads at length in the next chapter, but for now think of a Monad as a simple container. Option is an abstract class in Scala and defines two subclasses, Some and None. You implemented something similar in listing 4.2. Every now and then you encounter a situation where a method needs to return a value or nothing. In Java or Ruby you typically do this by returning null or nil. But in the case of Scala, Option is the recommended way to go when you have a function return an instance of Some or otherwise return None. The get method in Scala map does exactly that. When the given key exists, it returns the value wrapped in Some or returns None when the key doesn't exist. Here's an example:

```
val artists  = Map("Pink Floyd" -> "Rock", "Led Zeppelin" -> "Rock", "Michael
     Jackson" -> "Pop", "Above & Beyond" -> "Trance")
```

---

[5] Daniel Spiewak (blog), "The 'Option' Pattern," 2008, http://mng.bz/AsUQ.

```
artists: scala.collection.immutable.Map[java.lang.String,java.lang.String] =
    Map(Pink Floyd -> Rock, Led Zeppelin -> Rock, Michael Jackson -> Pop,
    Above & Beyond -> Trance)
scala> artists.get("Pink Floyd")
res33: Option[java.lang.String] = Some(Rock)

scala> artists.get("Abba")
res34: Option[java.lang.String] = None
```

You can use `Option` with pattern matching in Scala, and it also defines methods like
`map`, `filter`, and `flatMap` so that you can easily use it in a for-comprehension.

When should you use Either rather than Option?

scala.`Either` represents one of the two possible meaningful results, unlike
`Option`, which returns a single meaningful result or `Nothing`. `Either` provides two
subclasses: `Left` and `Right`. By convention, `Left` represents failure and `Right` is
akin to `Some`. In the following code you're trying to make a socket connection, and as
you know, it might fail or return a connection based on whether a server is available
to accept it. You could easily wrap these kinds of operations in a function called
`throwableToLeft`:

```
def throwableToLeft[T](block: => T):Either[Throwable, T] =
  try {
    Right(block)
  } catch {
    case ex Throwable => Left(ex)
  }
```

When creating a new `Socket` connection, you can wrap using `throwableToLeft` as
in the following:

```
scala> val r = throwableToLeft {
  new java.net.Socket("localhost", 4444)
}
scala> r match {
        case Left(e) => e.printStackTrace
        case Right(e) => println(e)
        }
```

When an exception occurs, you create an instance of `Left` otherwise `Right`. Most
programmers are used to throwing exceptions, and using `Either` could take some
getting used to. In particular, throwing an exception isn't a good idea in concurrent
programming, and using `Either` like a pattern is a good way to send and receive failures between processes and threads.

4.10 *Working with lazy collections: views and streams*

To understand *lazy collections*, step back and examine their opposite—*strict collections*.
So far you've looked at collections that are strict, meaning they evaluate their elements eagerly. The following example adds 1 to all the elements of the `List` but only
returns the `head` from the `List`:

```
scala> List(1, 2, 3, 4, 5).map( _ + 1).head
res43: Int = 2
```

The problem with this code is that even though you're looking for only the `head` element of the output (another instance of `List`) produced by `map`, you're still processing all the elements from 1 to 5 in the `List`. To make it clearer, break the previous line like this:

```
scala> val newList = List(1, 2, 3, 4, 5).map( _ + 1)
newList: List[Int] = List(2, 3, 4, 5, 6)

scala> newList.head
res44: Int = 2
```

Sometimes this isn't a big issue, but other times you may want to save space and time by not creating intermediate collections and operations unless required. Scala offers a couple of interesting and useful ways to create more on-demand collections using `View` and `Stream`. Let's start with views.

4.10.1 *Convert a strict collection to a nonstrict collection with views*

The more technical term for on-demand collections is *nonstrict collections*. You'll see an example shortly. Sometimes nonstrict collections are called *lazy collections*, but *lazy* usually refers to nonstrict functions that cache results.

> **TIP** Prior to Scala 2.8, `Views` were called `Projections`. This is one of the migration issues you may face when moving to `Views` from `Projections`.

Almost all collections expose a method called `view`, which returns a nonstrict view of the collection you're working on. To process the previous `List` **example** on demand, you could do the following:

```
scala> List(1, 2, 3, 4, 5).view.map( _ + 1).head
res46: Int = 2
```

In this case, a call to `map` produces another view without doing the calculation, and the calculation is deferred until you invoke `head` on it. Another interesting way to look at laziness is how sometimes you can avoid errors with lazy processing.[6] The following example processes elements of `List` by using each element as a divisor of 2. But one of the elements will result in a divide-by-zero error:

```
scala> def strictProcessing = List(-2, -1, 0, 1, 2) map { 2 / _ }
strictProcessing: List[Int]

scala> strictProcessing(0)
java.lang.ArithmeticException: / by zero
    at $anonfun$strictProcessing$1.apply(<console>:6)
```

Even though you're interested in only the first element of the list, the entire collection is processed, causing the exception for the third element. Using `View` would avoid the exception when accessing the first element:

```
scala> def nonStrictProcessing = List(-2, -1, 0, 1, 2).view  map { 2 / _ }
nonStrictProcessing: scala.collection.SeqView[Int,Seq[_]]
```

---

[6]   Daniel Sobral (blog), "Strict Ranges?," October 2009, http://mng.bz/nM4s.

```
scala> nonStrictProcessing(0)
res50: Int = -1
```

You can skip the error element and process the other elements, but the moment you access the error element you'll get an exception:

```
scala> nonStrictProcessing(3)
res52: Int = 2

scala> nonStrictProcessing(2)
java.lang.ArithmeticException: / by zero
    at $anonfun$nonStrictProcessing$1.apply(<console>:6)
```

To force strict processing on a view, invoke the `force` method on it, which, like the strict version, will throw `ArithmeticException`:

```
scala> nonStrictProcessing.force
java.lang.ArithmeticException: / by zero
...
```

The nonstrict method of processing collection elements is a useful and handy way to improve performance, especially when the operation is time-consuming. In lazy functional languages like Haskell and Clean, almost every construct is evaluated lazily. But because Scala isn't a lazy functional programming language, you have to take extra steps to simulate the equivalent type of laziness by using call-by-name functions or partial functions. An example will demonstrate this idea. The following code snippet has a time-consuming operation called `tweets`, which takes a handle and searches for Twitter messages that have the handle name:

```
import scala.io._
import scala.xml.XML

def tweets(handle: String) = {
  println("processing tweets for " + handle)

  val source = Source.fromURL(new
    java.net.URL("http://search.twitter.com/search.atom?q=" + handle))
  val iterator = source.getLines()
  val builder = new StringBuilder
  for(line <- iterator) builder.append(line)
  XML.loadString(builder.toString)
}
```

Using `Source` you get the Twitter search result in XML and create an XML node instance from it. Even though it doesn't take that much time, for argument's sake let's consider this operation to be expensive and time-consuming. Now you need to process these Twitter search results for multiple users. The most obvious solution would be to create a `Map` that stores the tweets with the handle name, as in the following:

```
scala> val allTweets = Map("nraychaudhuri" -> tweets("nraychaudhuri"),
                    "ManningBooks" -> tweets("ManningBooks"),
                    "bubbl_scala" -> tweets("bubbl_scala")
                    )
processing tweets for nraychaudhuri
```

```
processing tweets for ManningBooks
processing tweets for bubbl_scala
```

The problem with this approach is that while creating the Map, you're invoking the tweets function for all users. But because the tweets function is time-consuming, you'd like to invoke it only when you need it for a user. An alternative way to solve the problem would be to use a partial function, as discussed previously:

```
scala> val allTweets = Map(
"nraychaudhuri" -> tweets _ , "ManningBooks" -> tweets _,
"bubbl_scala" -> tweets _)

allTweets: scala.collection.immutable.Map[java.lang.String,(String) =>
    scala.xml.Elem] = Map(nraychaudhuri -> <function1>, ManningBooks ->
    <function1>, bubbl_scala -> <function1>)
```

In this case you've created the map using a partial function. A function becomes a partial function when you don't specify all the arguments it needs. For example, if you invoke tweets with an argument you get messages, but if you omit the argument you get a function back:

```
scala> tweets("ManningBooks")
processing tweets for ManningBooks

scala> tweets _
res73: (String) => scala.xml.Elem = <function1>
```

To omit an argument you have to specify _; otherwise, you'll get an error from Scala:

```
scala> tweets
<console>:19: error: missing arguments for method tweets in object $iw;
follow this method with '_' if you want to treat it as a partially applied
    function
        tweets
```

In the example if you use view, you can achieve the laziness you're looking for, and your tweets function will get called when you need the value:

```
scala> allTweets.view.map{ t => t._2(t._1)}.head
processing tweets for nraychaudhuri
```

Inside a Map, values are stored as Tuple2, a tuple of two elements. _1 is the handle and _2 is the value, and in this case it's a partial function. You're invoking the tweets function by passing the handle name. If you want to process the messages for Manning Books, you can use a for-comprehension, as in the following:

```
for(t <- allTweets; if(t._1 == "ManningBooks")) t._2(t._1)
```

Note that starting with Scala 2.8, for-comprehensions are now nonstrict for standard operations.

4.10.2 *Working with Streams*

The class Stream implements lazy lists in Scala where elements are evaluated only when they're needed. Stream is like List, in which elements are stored in two parts, head and tail. The `tail` for `Stream` isn't computed until it's needed. If you want, you can build an infinite list in Scala using `Stream`, and it will consume memory based on your use. Because `Stream` extends from `LinearSeq`, you have almost all the `List` methods available to you. The following example zips each element of the `List` with its index:

```
scala> List("zero", "one", "two", "three", "four",
        "five").zip(Stream.from(0))

res88: List[(java.lang.String, Int)] = List((zero,0), (one,1), (two,2),
      (three,3), (four,4), (five,5))
```

Here the `from` method defined in the `Stream` object creates an infinite stream starting at 0 and incrementing by 1. Scala `Stream`s also enjoy the same benefits as views when it comes to memory consumption and performance. Let's look at an example to demonstrate that, using the Fibonacci sequence.[7] In mathematics, the Fibonacci numbers are the numbers in the following sequence:

```
0, 1, 1, 2, 3, 5, 8, 13, 21, 34 ...
```

By definition, the first two numbers are 0 and 1, and each remaining number is the sum of the previous two. The most common way to implement the Fibonacci sequence is to use recursion; here's the code:

```
def fib(n: Int): Int = n match {
  case 0 => 0
  case 1 => 1
  case n => fib(n - 1) + fib(n - 2)
}
```

This function will return the Fibonacci number for a given n value. To see the efficiency problem of this implementation, you have to try the function for a value of n greater than 20. To clearly understand why it's not an efficient solution, look at what happens for `fib 8`:

```
fib(8)
fib(7) + fib(6)
(fib(6) + fib(5)) + (fib(5) + fib(4))
((fib(5) + fib(4)) + (fib(4) + fib(3))) + ((fib(4) + fib(3)) + (fib(3) +
    fib(2)))
...
```

As you can see, the calculation is growing exponentially, and unfortunately many of the steps are computed repeatedly. One way to implement the Fibonacci sequence is to build it using an infinite stream. If you take a Fibonacci sequence starting from 0 (0, 1, 1, 2, 3...) and zip with its `tail`, you get a sequence of pairs (tuples): ((0, 1), (1, 2), (2, 3)...). If you use map to sum the two parts of the pair, you get a number in the Fibonacci series. To implement this, use recursive streams. Here's the code snippet:

```
val fib: Stream[Int]  = Stream.cons(0, Stream.cons(1,
                          fib.zip(fib.tail).map(t => t._1 + t._2)))
```

---

[7]   The Fibonacci sequence example is taken from www.haskell.org/soe/.

You're using the `apply` method of the `cons` object with a head of `0` and another `Stream` as a `tail`. Now if you compare the timing of both implementations, you'll see that the stream-based solution performs better than the previous one.

The question that remains is how `Stream` can manage to evaluate the `tail` when it's required and not eagerly evaluated. The answer is a call-by-name parameter. A close look at the signature of the `apply` method in the `cons` object will show that the second parameter is declared as a function that takes no arguments and returns a stream:

```
def apply[A](hd: A, tl: => Stream[A]) = new Cons(hd, tl)
```

Here `tl` is a call-by-name parameter, which is encoded by turning it into a no-arg function. Note that when pattern matching a `Stream`, the usual `cons(::)` doesn't work; you have to use `#::`.

4.11 *Divide and conquer with parallel collections*

So far you've looked at collections that use either an eager or lazy evaluation strategy, and the elements of the collection are processed sequentially. Now you'll learn about Scala parallel collections, in which elements of a collection are evaluated in parallel.

The Scala parallel collections are implemented in terms of split and combine operations. The split operation divides parallel collections into small `Iterable` collections until it hits some threshold defined for a given collection. Then a set of tasks is created to perform the operation in parallel on small `Iterable` collections. These tasks are implemented in terms of a Fork/Join framework.[8] The Fork/Join framework figures out the number of CPU cores available to perform the operation and uses threads to execute the task. At the end, the output of the each task combines to produce the final result. Figure 4.2 shows how a `map` operation is performed on `ParVector`, a parallel version of `Vector` collection.

In figure 4.2 the `ParVector(10, 20, 30, 40, 50, 60, 70, 80, 90)` is split into smaller `Iterable` collections, and each small `Iterable` collection implements the `scala.collection.parallel.Splitter` trait. The threshold operation defined for each parallel collection provides an estimate on the minimum number of elements the collection has before the splitting stops. Once the split operation is over, each collection is handed over to a task to perform the operation. For example `TaskA` takes `10, 20` as an input and performs a `map` operation on them to produce `5, 10`. At the end, the output of each task is combined into the final result. Each parallel collection type provides a combiner that knows how to combine smaller collections to produce the output. To figure how many workers are used to perform the operation, you could try the following snippet inside the REPL:

```
scala> import scala.collection.parallel.immutable._
import scala.collection.parallel.immutable._

scala> ParVector(10, 20, 30, 40, 50, 60, 70, 80, 90).map {x =>
     println(Thread.currentThread.getName); x / 2 }
```

---

[8] Java Tutorials, "Fork/Join," http://mng.bz/0dnU.

```
ForkJoinPool-1-worker-2
ForkJoinPool-1-worker-2
ForkJoinPool-1-worker-3
ForkJoinPool-1-worker-3
ForkJoinPool-1-worker-3
ForkJoinPool-1-worker-3
ForkJoinPool-1-worker-1
ForkJoinPool-1-worker-0
ForkJoinPool-1-worker-0
res2: scala.collection.parallel.immutable.ParVector[Int] = ParVector(5, 10,
    15, 20, 25, 30, 35, 40, 45)
```

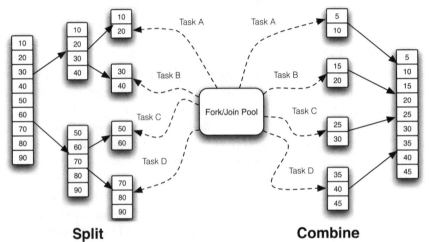

ParVector(10, 20, 30, 40, 50, 60, 70, 80, 90).map(x => x / 2)

Split   **Combine**

Figure 4.2   Parallel collections implemented in terms of split and combine operations using the Fork/Join framework

I've changed the map method a little bit to print out the name of the thread executing the operation. Because I'm running on a quad-core Macbook Pro, the Fork/Join framework used four different worker threads to execute the map operation in parallel. The details of Fork/Join are completely taken care of for you so you can focus on solving problems.

Configuring parallel collections

The engine responsible for scheduling the parallel collection operations is called TaskSupport. Each parallel collection is configured with a task support object that is responsible for keeping track of the thread pool, load-balancing, and scheduling of tasks.

Scala provides a few implementations of task support out of the box:

- "ForkJoinTaskSupport—This uses the fork-join thread pool used by JVM 1.6.

- "ThreadPoolTaskSupport—Less efficient than ForkJoinTaskSupport; it uses the normal thread pool to execute tasks.

- "ExecutionContextTaskSupport—This is the default task support for all the parallel collection types in Scala. This is implemented in the `scala.concurrent` package and uses the fork-join thread pool behind the scene.

To change the task support associated with a given collection, simply change the taskSupport property as in the following:

```
import scala.collection.parallel._
val pv = immutable.ParVector(1, 2, 3)
pv.tasksupport = new ForkJoinTaskSupport(new
scala.concurrent.forkjoin.ForkJoinPool(4))
```

In this case tasksupport is changed to ForkJoinTask with four working threads.

Parallel collections are well-suited for data parallel problems and improve the performance of the overall operation considerably without your worrying about concurrency. The `map` operation is a perfect example of an operation that you could parallelize because it doesn't depend on the order in which elements of a collection are processed. Scala parallel collections don't guarantee any order of execution. On the other hand, `foldLeft` isn't suited for parallel collections because the elements need to be processed in a certain order. The following example demonstrates that `foldLeft` is executed by a single thread even if performed on `ParVector`:

```
scala> ParVector(10, 20, 30, 40, 50, 60, 70, 80, 90).foldLeft(0) {(a,x) =>
    println(Thread.currentThread.getName); a + x }
Thread-14
Thread-14
Thread-14
Thread-14
Thread-14
Thread-14
Thread-14
Thread-14
Thread-14
res3: Int = 450
```

Note that in the absence of side effects, parallel collections have the same semantics as the sequential collections. The next section explores the types of available parallel collections.

4.11.1 *Parallel collection hierarchy*

Parallel collections were added to the collections library in Scala 2.9. All the parallel collection classes are implemented in a separate class hierarchy (see figure 4.3). At the top of the parallel collection library is `ParIterable`. This trait implements the common behavior of all the parallel collections.

Why there are Gen* classes in the scala.collection package

The `Gen*` classes implement operations that could be implemented both in a sequential and parallel collections library. These classes form a hierarchy similar to the class hierarchy in figure 4.1. If you want your code to *not care* whether it receives a parallel or sequential collection, you should prefix it with `Gen`: `GenTraversable`, `GenIterable`, `GenSeq`, and so on. These can be either parallel or sequential.

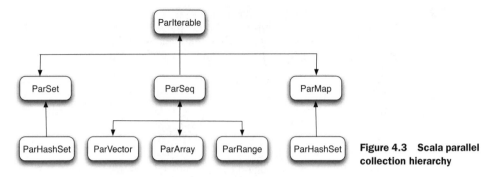

Figure 4.3   Scala parallel collection hierarchy

The Scala parallel collections library implements parallel versions of almost all the collection types available in the `scala.collection` package, both mutable and immutable types. I say *almost* because you won't find parallel implementation of `LinearSeq` type collections like `List` because they aren't well-suited for parallel execution.

To use any of these collection types you have to import the `scala.collection.parallel.immutable` or `scala.collection.parallel.mutable` package:

```
scala> import scala.collection.parallel.mutable._
import scala.collection.parallel.mutable._

scala> ParArray(1, 2, 3, 4).sum
res4: Int = 10
```

You don't always have to start with a parallel collection implementation; you can easily switch between sequential and parallel as you need them.

4.11.2 *Switching between sequential and parallel collections*

Scala collections provide the `par` method to all sequential collection types to create a parallel version of the collection. And on the other side, all the parallel collection types implement the `seq` method to create sequential versions of the collection. The following example filters out all the odd numbers by converting the sequential version of Vector to ParVector using the par method:

```
val vs = Vector.range(1, 100000)
vs.par.filter(_ % 2 == 0)
```

In this case the output will be an instance of `ParVector` of even numbers. To get back the sequential version of `Vector`, you have to invoke the seq method. The following example converts `Vector` to its parallel counterpart to perform a filter operation and then converts back to `Vector` again:

```
Vector.range(1, 100000).par.filter(_ % 2 == 0).seq
```

This kind of conversion has the additional benefit that you can optimize part of a codebase to use parallel collections without changing the type of the collection used across the code.

But parallel collections aren't a silver bullet. You shouldn't expect that everything will perform better by switching to parallel collections. In fact, in some cases it might perform worse than the sequential version. Consider two points before switching to parallel collections:

- Type of operation
- Overhead of conversion

First, not all operations are parallelizable, so switching to parallel collection won't improve the performance of these operations. An ideal candidate would be the one that doesn't assume any order of execution and doesn't have any side effects. Operations like `map`, `flatMap`, `filter`, and `forall` are good examples of methods that would be easily parallelized.

Second, there's an overhead of creating a parallel version of a sequential collection and using the Fork/Join framework. If it takes less time to perform the operation than to create a parallel collection, then using the parallel version will reduce your performance. It also depends on the type of collection you're using. Converting `Seq` to `ParSeq` is much faster than converting `List` to `Vector` because there's no parallel `List` implementation, so when you invoke `par` on `List` you get `Vector` back.

4.12 *Summary*

You've learned a few important concepts in this chapter. The knowledge of type parameterization helped in exploring type-variance concepts and the type-safety features of Scala. Understanding this concept is important for building generic, type-safe, reusable components in Scala. The chapter also explored the use and importance of higher-order functions such as `map` and `filter` and how they help users of the Scala library—in particular the collection library that provides rich and useful APIs. Using higher-order functions, you can easily encapsulate common programming idioms.

This chapter also introduced the Scala collections library and the new changes made to the API starting with Scala 2.8. The Scala collections library is a vast set of APIs, and you saw only the most important and commonly used ones. You need to explore the scaladoc for other `Collection` classes and APIs, because almost all common, useful functions are already encoded in the library.

When working with collections it's also important to understand the performance and memory requirements of individual collection types. Knowing the difference between strict and nonstrict processing will help you decide which type of collection would be useful and when.

The next chapter explores functional programming. You'll learn what functional programming is and how to do functional programming in Scala. Understanding functional programming will help you build functional, immutable, and simple solutions.

Functional programming

5

This chapter covers

- Why functional programming matters
- Mixing functional programming with OOP
- Functions in various forms
- Monads and their practical examples

You're already doing functional programming using Scala if you've been following the examples in the book. In some cases it's explicitly mentioned or visible and in other cases it's mixed with object-oriented constructs of the Scala language. This chapter focuses on functional programming concepts and how they can be implemented in Scala. The goal of the chapter is to make you comfortable with functional programming and help you to write code in functional programming style.

Functional programming is a programming paradigm that models computation as the evaluation of expressions. And expressions are built using functions that don't have mutable state and side effects. Exploring the roots of functional programming is valuable.[1] Believe it or not, functional programming started around 1930 when Alonzo Church introduced lambda calculus.[2] A lambda calculus (λ calculus) is a

---

[1] Slava Akhmechet, "Functional Programming for the Rest of Us," June 19, 2006, www.defmacro.org/ramblings/fp.html.

[2] Lloyd Anderson, "Lambda Calculus," http://mng.bz/tWaV.

formal mathematical system to investigate functions, function application, and function recursion. In lambda calculus functions are first-class values; functions can take other functions as a parameter and return functions as an output (higher-order functions). A function that adds two input parameters could be written like the following in lambda calculus:

```
λx. λy. x + y
```

Here λx. λy. x + y represents an anonymous function that takes x as a parameter and returns the new anonymous function λy. x + y that takes y as a parameter and returns the result of x + y. In lambda calculus all the functions are anonymous and represented by the symbol λ (hence the name lambda).

Lambda calculus is the main inspiration behind functional programming. Functional programming languages implement lambda calculus with some constraints and types. Not all programming languages have features like first-class functions, pattern matching, and so on, but it's possible to do functional programming in almost all programming languages. The next section explains functional programming in detail.

5.1 What is functional programming?

Functional programming is programming with functions. There's nothing much to it except understanding what's meant by function in this context. A function relates every value of type X to exactly one value of Y (see figure 5.1). A type is associated with a set of values. Here type X represents the set of values (1, 2, 3) and Y represents the set of values (a, b, c).

In Scala you could write the signature of such a function as follows:

```
def f: X => Y
```

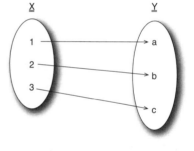

Figure 5.1 A pure function where each value of X is mapped to exactly one value of Y

A function provides the predictability that for a given input you will always get the same output. The following function is an example of that:

```
scala> def add(a: Int, b: Int): Int = a + b
add: (a: Int,b: Int)Int

scala> add(10, 10)
res0: Int = 20
```

Here the function add: (Int, Int) => Int fits the definition of the function because for a given input, it's always going to return the same result.

But what about the functions that depend on some external state and don't return the same result all the time? They're functions but they're not pure functions. A pure function doesn't have side effects. Any observable behavior change after the function finishes is considered a side effect. Updating global or static variables, writing data to the filesystem, displays on screen, calling other "side-effecting" functions, and throwing exceptions are all examples of side effects. The behavior of a pure function doesn't depend on any external behavior or state. You're also not allowed to mutate the arguments to the function or invoke a function that has side effects. The add function is a perfect example of a pure function, but the following weather function isn't a pure function because the weather will change based on when you invoke the function:

```
def weather(zipCode: String) = {
  val url =
    "http://api.wunderground.com/auto/wui/geo/GeoLookupXML/index.xml?query="
  Source.fromURL(url + zipCode)
}
```

Here I use the Weather Underground API[3] to get the weather information for a given ZIP code. Why care about pure functions? What's the value of programming with pure functions?

The value is referential transparency. *Referential transparency* is a property whereby an expression could be replaced by its value without affecting the program. Let's see an example of how referential transparency works. Assume the following is a part of a functional program:

```
...
val v = add(10, 10) + add(5, 5)
...
```

Because add is a pure function, I can replace the function call add(10, 10) with its result, which is 20, without changing the behavior of the program. And similarly I could replace add(5, 5) with 10 without affecting the behavior of the program. Why should you care about referential transparency? What advantage does it give you?

5.1.1 *The benefits of referential transparency*

Referential transparency provides the ability to reason about your code. You can provide proof that your program works correctly by replacing pure functions with their values and reducing a complex expression to a simpler expression. Sometimes you can even compute the result of a program in your head. This ability to reason about code helps programmers to debug and solve complex problems easily. And therein lies the essence of functional programming. With varying difficulty you can do functional programming in any programming language. The essence of functional programming is referential transparency, and its benefit is referential transparency—the safety net that allows you to easily find and fix problems. When you add that to the fact that Scala is a type-safe language, you can catch lots of problem ahead of time during compilation.

In Scala, functional programming is baked in with Scala's object-oriented features, so sometimes it's difficult to distinguish it when you have a language that allows you to define both methods and functions. You will explore this in detail, but for now

---

[3] Weather Underground, "A Weather API Designed for Developers," http://mng.bz/VtC8.

remember that methods in Scala don't have any type; type is only associated with the enclosing class, whereas functions are represented by a type and object.

Unfortunately, coming up with a definition of a functional programming language[4] is still hard. Everyone has his or her own definition, and I'm sure you'll also come up with your own one day. But even if functional programming is possible in all languages, it doesn't necessarily mean you should use it. It can be like trying to do OOP in a procedural language—it's possible, but probably hard and painful. There is good news: writing functional programs in Scala is easy. The next section builds one from scratch.

5.1.2 A pure functional program

A pure functional program is a single referentially transparent expression. An expression is constructed with a combination of subexpressions created using the language. An expression always evaluates to a result. The following is an example of a pure functional program:

```
object PureFunctionalProgram {
  def main(args: Array[String]):Unit = singleExpression(args.toList)

  def singleExpression: List[String] => (List[Int], List[Int]) = { a =>
    a map (_.toInt) partition (_ < 30)
  }
}
```

Here the main method is the entry point to our purely functional program, and the rest of the program is defined by a single expression that takes a collection of strings and returns a `Tuple` of two collections based on some partition criteria. The single expression is in turn built on two subexpressions: a `map (_.toInt)` and `<result of first sub expression> partition (_ < 30)`. If you can start thinking about your program as a collection of subexpressions combined into one single referentially transparent expression, you have achieved a purely functional program. Yes, you still may have to read inputs from the console or from the filesystem, but think of those as implementation details. It doesn't matter how the inputs are read—the behavior of your purely functional program should not change.

5.2 Moving from OOP to functional programming

Programmers in Java and C# as well as C++ are already familiar with the concepts of classes and objects and are probably comfortable with OOP. But how can one transition to a more functional programming style from a more OOP experience? Scala is a great language for this because it allows you to combine the styles in an elegant and well-engineered fashion. It's perfectly okay to start with Scala and focus on only its object-oriented features, but as you become more comfortable with the language and its library, you may slowly transition to a more functional programming style as discussed in the previous section. In this section I highlight a few techniques that you can

---

[4] David R. MacIver, "A Problem of Language," May 15, 2009, http://mng.bz/nsi2.

use to move to a more functional programming style and yet retain OO techniques and style as appropriate.

5.2.1 *Pure vs. impure programming*

At first glance it may seem odd to compare object-oriented and functional programming at a pure versus impure level. Although it's true that you can write object-oriented code without side effects, in practice OOP easily becomes riddled with undesirable side effects. Typically, OO-style applications are built around the idea of mutable state (produces side effects) managed by various objects inside the application.

Object-oriented solutions are modeled around classes and objects where data tends to carry collections of methods, and these methods share and at times mutate the data. A functional programming style only deals with values where problems are solved by the application of functions to data. Because data is only represented by value, each application of a function results in a new value without any side effects.

Another way to differentiate them is that functional programming raises the abstraction level over OOP. Object-oriented programming sometimes feels machine-dependent—concepts like pass by value, pass by reference, equality, and identity are defined based on how the program is interpreted or executed at runtime. If you only work with values, then how your functional program is interpreted and executed becomes irrelevant. Remember, you can compute the result of a purely functional program using paper and pen; running it using a machine is an implementation detail.

In languages where you have only functions, such as Haskell and Clojure, you don't have to worry about impurity. But Scala bakes both object-oriented and functional programming into one language, so you have to be extra careful about side effects. In Scala you still have to define classes (or traits) and objects to group your methods and function values. And it's your responsibility as a developer to make sure you don't rely on mutable data defined inside the class.

Take the following example, where you have a class that represents a square with one method that computes the area:

```
class Square(var side: Int) {
  def area = side * side
}
```

The problem with this class is that the `side` property is mutable, and the area method depends on the value of the `side` to compute the area of the square. It's clearly not a pure solution because the result of the area method depends on some external state—in this case, the value of the `side` property. It's also hard to reason about the area method because now you have to keep track of the value of the side property at a given point in time. To implement `Square` in a pure functional way, you'll use a Successor Value pattern[5] (sometimes called a functional object), where each change of state returns a copy of itself with the new state:

---

[5] Michael Feathers, "The Successor Value Pattern, March 22, 2009, http://mng.bz/b27e.

```
class PureSquare(val side: Int) {
  def newSide(s: Int): PureSquare = new PureSquare(s)
  def area = side * side
}
```

In this new solution, every time the side property is modified, a new copy of Pure-Square is returned, so you don't have to worry about a mutable state and the result of the area method because now it's associated with a new object, PureSquare. This common pattern is used when you have to model a state that could change over time. The Java String class we've been using throughout the book is an example of a Functional Object pattern. Now your challenge is to design all your objects in a similar fashion because it's easy to introduce side effects unintentionally. Watch out for all the vars and setters that your methods depend on and make them as pure as possible. Remember going forward: referential transparency is a criterion of a good design.

5.2.2 *Object-oriented patterns in functional programming*

Design patterns are just as useful in functional programming as they are in OOP as tools for communication. Some design patterns like Singleton, Factory, and Visitor are already implemented as part of the language. You can easily implement Singleton and Factory patterns using Scala objects. You could implement the Visitor pattern using the pattern-matching feature of Scala. Take a look at the Strategy pattern.[6] This pattern allows you to select algorithms at runtime and can easily be implemented using a higher-order function:

```
def calculatePrice(product: String, taxingStrategy: String => Double) = {
  ...
  ...
  val tax = taxingStrategy(product)
  ...
}
```

Because taxingStrategy is defined as a function, you can pass different implementations of the strategy. Similarly you can also implement the template method pattern using the higher-order functions.

Higher-order functions are also useful when dealing with dependency injection (DI). You can use function currying to inject dependencies. For example, you can define a type for tax strategy and have a function that calculates a tax based on strategy and the product code:

```
trait TaxStrategy {def taxIt(product: String): Double }
class ATaxStrategy extends TaxStrategy {
  def taxIt(product: String): Double = ...
}
class BTaxStrategy extends TaxStrategy {
  def taxIt(product: String): Double = ...
}

def taxIt: TaxStrategy => String => Double = s => p => s.taxIt(p)
```

---

[6] "Strategy pattern," February 2011, http://en.wikipedia.org/wiki/Strategy_pattern.

Here I have two implementations of the `TaxStrategy` trait, `ATaxStrategy` and `BTax-Strategy`. The interesting code here is the `taxIt` function. This function takes an instance of `TaxStrategy` and returns a function of type `String => Double`, which encapsulates the taxing strategy. With this setup you can easily create new functions by injecting different types of tax strategy:

```
def taxIt_a: String => Double = taxIt(new ATaxStrategy)
def taxIt_b: String => Double = taxIt(new BTaxStrategy)
```

Your knowledge of OO design patterns is still valuable in Scala, but its style of implementation has changed. Functional programming brings new sets of patterns that you haven't encountered before, and those are mainly related to recursive programming.

5.2.3 *Modeling purely functional programs*

So far, I've been focusing on implementing pure functional solutions, but what if you have to deal with side effects like writing to a socket or to a database? You can't avoid that, and in fact any useful program you write for an enterprise probably has a side effect. Are you doomed? No! The trick is to push the side effects as far down as possible. You can create an impure layer, as shown in figure 5.2, and keep the rest of your application as pure and functional as possible. In section 5.5 you'll learn how to build abstractions around code that by necessity include side effects.

To demonstrate how this works, you're going to build a simple HTTP server that only serves files from a directory in which the server is started. You're going to implement the HTTP GET command. Like any server, this HTTP server is full of side effects, like writing to a socket, reading files from the filesystem, and so on. Here are your design goals for the server you're building:

- Separate the code into different layers, pure code from the side-effecting code.
- Respond with the contents of a file for a given HTTP GET request.
- Respond with a 404 message when the file requested is missing.

The essence of the problem is to parse the request to figure out the name of the requested file, locate the resource, and return the response. Let's represent them with appropriate types and functions. The HTTP request is nothing but a stream of

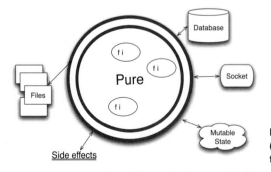

Figure 5.2   Separating pure and side-effecting (impure) code. The side-effecting code should form a thin layer around the application.

characters received from the client, and when building the pure model you don't have to worry about how we receive them—all you care about is that it's a collection of characters:

```
type Request = Iterator[Char]
```

Similarly the response could also be represented as a collection of characters. For simplicity, represent that using List[String]:

```
type Response = List[String]
```

The resource locator type should be able to check whether the file exists, retrieve the file contents, and check the content length. The first one would be used to determine whether to return the 200 response code or 404 error code. Here's how the ResourceLocator type looks:

```
type ResourceLocator = String => Resource
trait Resource {
  def exists: Boolean
  def contents: List[String]
  def contentLength: Int
}
```

The ResourceLocator is a function type that takes the name of a resource and returns the resource. The resource is represented by a trait Resource and provides all the methods you need to create the appropriate HTTP response. The important point here is that you're building an abstract layer that will allow you to design your application using values and pure functions. The following listing gives the complete implementation of the pure side of things, where the GET method returns success (HTTP 200) or failure (HTTP 404) response.

Listing 5.1 A pure implementation of an HTTP server

```
object Pure {
  trait Resource {
    def exists: Boolean
    def contents: List[String]
    def contentLength: Int
  }
  type ResourceLocator = String => Resource
  type Request = Iterator[Char]
  type Response = List[String]
```
Parse HTTP request for filename ⊳
```
  def get(req: Request)(implicit locator: ResourceLocator): Response = {
    val requestedResource = req.takeWhile(x => x != '\n')
                               .mkString.split(" ")(1).drop(1)
    (_200 orElse _404)(locator(requestedResource))
  }
```
◁ Return success/failure based on file existence
Create HTTP 200 response ⊳
```
  private def _200: PartialFunction[Resource, Response] = {
    case resource if(resource.exists) =>
           "HTTP/1.1 200 OK" ::
           ("Date " + new java.util.Date) ::
```

```
                "Content-Type: text/html" ::
                ("Content-Length: " + resource.contentLength) ::
                System.getProperty("line.separator") ::
                resource.contents                                    Create
    }                                                                HTTP 404
                                                                 ◁── response
    private def _404: PartialFunction[Resource, Response] = {
      case _ => List("HTTP/1.1 404 Not Found")
    }
}
```

The GET method first retrieves the requested filename, then locates the file based on the given locator. The _200 and _404 are partial functions and are defined for success and failure cases respectively. The _200 function is invoked if the file exists; otherwise, the _404 function is invoked.

Now that the core of the server is implemented, you need to hook it to the real world so it can be useful and practical. First you have to open a server socket at an appropriate port and listen for requests. You also have to handle each request in a separate thread so that you can listen for a new request while you're processing the old one. You can find the complete working copy in the code base for the chapter as NanoHttpServer.scala. Here let's focus on the implementation of Resource and ResourceLocator:

```
import Pure._
case class IOResource(name: String) extends Resource {
  def exists = new File(name).exists
  def contents = Source.fromFile(name).getLines.toList
  def contentLength = Source.fromFile(name).count(x => true)
}
implicit val ioResourceLocator: ResourceLocator =
                          name => IOResource(name)
```

The IOResource reads files from the local filesystem using the scala.io.Source, and the ResourceLocator is a function that takes the name of the file and creates an instance of IOResource. The only thing left now is reading and writing to the socket. You've successfully separated the side effects from pure functional code. This is an important technique to remember when designing your application: push the side effects to the edge of the world. You can refer to the nano-http-server project in the code base of this chapter for the complete implementation. To run the example, you need to install the simple build tool covered in the next chapter. In the next section you'll explore various types of functions and their applications.

5.3   *Functions in all shapes and forms*

Functional programming is all about functions, and Scala lets you create functions in various forms. Functions in Scala are first-class values. That means you can treat functions like Int or String as type values in Scala. You can create them as a value, pass them to functions as parameters, and compose them to create new functions.

5.3.1 Methods vs. functions

The common form of a function in Scala is defined as a member of a class. It's called a method:

```
class UseResource {
  def use(r: Resource): Boolean = {...}
}
```

Here use is a method defined in the class UseResource. One downside of using methods is that it's easy to depend on the state defined by the enclosing class without explicitly passing the dependencies as parameters—be careful about that because that will take you away from having pure methods. Unlike functions, methods don't have any type associated with them. Scala infuses functional programming with OOP by transforming functions into objects. For example, you can assign a function literal (anonymous function) to a value like the following:

```
val succ = (x: Int) => x + 1
```

Here succ is associated with a function Int => Int and it's nothing but a shorthand definition of the following:

```
val succFunction = new Function1[Int, Int] {
  def apply(x:Int) : Int = x + 1
}
```

Both of those definitions are equivalent. Functions in Scala are represented by a type and object, but methods aren't. Methods are only associated with the enclosing class. The good news is that Scala lets you convert methods to functions using a transform process called Eta expansion. You can take any existing method and append _ (underscore) to create the function. The following code creates a function version of the use method from the previous example:

```
val use_func: Resource => Boolean = (new UseResource).use _
```

It's common in Scala to convert methods into functions and pass them around to other functions. In the next section you'll look into examples of higher-order functions and how they help you in solving problems.

5.3.2 Higher-order functions

Higher-order functions are those that take functions as parameters or return functions as a return value. You've already seen plenty of examples of higher-order functions throughout the book. In the Scala collections you'll notice the use of higher-order functions everywhere. For example, to filter out all the even numbers from a List, you write something like the following:

```
scala> val l = List(1, 2, 3, 5, 7, 10, 15)
l: List[Int] = List(1, 2, 3, 5, 7, 10, 15)

scala> l.filter(_ % 2 == 0)
res0: List[Int] = List(2, 10)
```

Here `% 2 == 0` is a function literal (I'm sure you already knew that). Now let's see how you can use higher-order functions to solve a day-to-day problem. One of the most common programming problems is managing resources. For example, to send data over a TCP connection, you have to open a socket, send data, and, hopefully, remember to close the socket. Similarly, to read data from a file in a filesystem, you have to open the file, read data, and then close the file handle. The typical way to manage these resources is to wrap them in a `try-finally` block like the following:

```
val r: Resource = getResource()
try {
  useResourceToDoUsefulStuff(r)
} finally {
  r.dispose()
}
```

You get a handle to the resource (socket or file) and use the resource in the `try-finally` (sometimes `catch`) block to dispose of the resource once you're done using it. Now let's see how you can easily separate the resource-management part (try-finally) from the use:

```
def use[A, B <: Resource ](r: Resource)(f: Resource => A): A = {
  try {
    f(r)
  } finally {
    r.dispose()
  }
}
```

Here the `use` function is taking care of the resource management, and the function parameter `f` allows you to use the resource without worrying about releasing or disposing of it. Now the code for sending data through a socket will be like the following:

```
use(socketResource) { r=>
  sendData(r)
}
```

This abstraction for managing resources will remove duplication from your code and centralize the way you manage and dispose of resources after use, without cluttering the code base with `try-finally` blocks. To make this work you have to define a common type like `Resource` so you can create abstraction around the implementation. This is a common pattern in Scala known as the Loan pattern[7] (the object-oriented counterpart is called the Template Method pattern).

Another example will demonstrate the power of higher-order functions in terms of the design flexibility it provides to programmers. One of the common pieces of logic that you'll see across code bases goes something like the following:

---

[7] Kevin Wright (added), "Loan pattern," last edited May 25, 2011, https://wiki.scala-lang.org/display/SYGN/Loan.

1 Create or find some existing instance.
2 Perform some side-effect-inducing operation for the instance.
3 Use the instance in the other parts of the code.

You have to perform steps 1 and 2 before you can start using the instance. The problem is, there's structure to isolate the side-effect-inducing code, and it gets mixed with steps 1 and 3. Let's take a look at the following pseudo Scala code:

```
val x  = Person(firstName, lastName)
x.setInfo(someInfo)
println("log: new person is created")
mailer.mail("new person joined " + x)
x.firstName
```

Because steps 1 and 2 need to be done together before you can start using the instance, it would be nice if you could do it all as part of step 1 when you create an instance (like inside the constructor). But the problem with that approach is that you might not have everything that's accessible to the context of the caller namespace. For example, the reference to `mailer` in the previous code snippet is only available to the context of the caller and not available inside the `Person` instance. One way you can address this problem is to use higher-order functions. I will define a function called `tap` that will take an instance and a side-effect-inducing function. This function will apply the side-effecting function to the instance and return the instance. Here's how you could write it:

```
def tap[A](a: A)(sideEffect: A => Unit): A = {
   sideEffect(a)
   a
}
```

With this new `tap` function, your code will get some structure:

```
val x  = Person(firstName, lastName)
tap(x) { p =>
   import p._
   setInfo(someInfo)
   println("log: new person is created")
   mailer.mail("new person joined " + x)
}.firstName
```

This is better than what you had, but you can still improve on it using Scala's implicit conversion. Because this is so common, you'll make this function available to all the types. The following listing gives the complete working example.

Listing 5.2 Kestrel combinator

```
package chap10.fp.examples

object Combinators {
  implicit def kestrel[A](a: A) = new {          ◁─┐ Defines tap method
    def tap(sideEffect: A => Unit): A = {             for all types
      sideEffect(a)
```

```
        a
      }
    }
  }

  case class Person(firstName: String, lastName: String)
  case class Mailer(mailAddress: String) {
    def mail(body: String) = {println("send mail here...") }
  }
  object Main {
    import Combinators._
    def main(args: Array[String]): Unit = {
      Person("Nilanjan", "Raychaudhuri").tap(p => {
        println("First name " + p.firstName)
        Mailer("some address")
      }).lastName
    }
  }
```

Code keeps side effects from ❶ leaking through

Compare the code inside the main method ❶ with the pseudo code you started with, and you should see the difference. Now the code is more concise and well-structured, and the side effects are not leaking through. The best part of this pattern is that it lets you compose without relying on sequences of instructions. This is also a common combinator (higher-order function) in functional programming called Kestrel.[8] Kestrel is one of the many combinators defined in Raymond Smullyan's book *To Mock a Mockingbird* (Knopf, 1985). The combinatory logic is beyond the scope of this book, but I highly recommend *To Mock a Mockingbird*. I'd like to highlight that once you start thinking in higher-order functions, you'll see opportunities for extracting reusable code that you never thought possible. Think, for example, about foldRight and foldLeft defined in the Scala collection library, which let you apply any binary function. The application of higher-order functions lets you write don't-repeat-yourself (DRY) code and you should use it as much as possible. The next section discusses partial functions and how they help in the composition of functions.

5.3.3 *Function currying*

Function currying is a technique for transforming a function that takes multiple parameters into a function that takes a single parameter. Look at the following function definition that takes two parameters:

```
scala> trait TaxStrategy { def taxIt(product: String): Double }
defined trait TaxStrategy

scala> val taxIt: (TaxStrategy, String) => Double = (s, p) => s.taxIt(p)
taxIt: (TaxStrategy, String) => Double = <function2>
```

The taxIt function takes TaxStrategy and String parameters and returns Double value. To turn this function into a curried function, you can invoke the built-in curried method defined for function types:

---

[8] Reg Braithwaite, "Kestrels," http://mng.bz/WKns.

```
scala> taxIt.curried
res2: TaxStrategy => String => Double = <function1>
```

It turned the `taxIt` function into a function that takes one parameter and returns another function that takes the second parameter:

```
scala> class TaxFree extends TaxStrategy { override def taxIt(product:
    String) = 0.0 }
defined class TaxFree

scala> val taxFree = taxIt.curried(new TaxFree)
taxFree: String => Double = <function1>

scala> taxFree("someProduct")
res3: Double = 0.0
```

What's the benefit of using function currying? It allows you to turn generalized functions into specialized ones. For example, turning the `taxIt` function to function currying allows you to create a more specialized function like `taxFree`. This is similar to how DI works in OOP. Here I injected the `taxStrategy` as a dependency to the curried function to create a new function that uses the dependency. You can also turn existing methods to curried functions using an underscore (_). The following code example redefines the `taxIt` function as a method and then converts it to a curried function:

```
scala> def taxIt(s: TaxStrategy, product: String) = { s.taxIt(product) }
taxIt: (s: TaxStrategy, product: String)Double

scala> val taxItF = taxIt _
taxItF: (TaxStrategy, String) => Double = <function2>

scala> taxItF.curried
res4: TaxStrategy => String => Double = <function1>
```

You can also define methods in currying style using multiple parameters set:

```
scala> def taxIt(s: TaxStrategy)(product: String) = { s.taxIt(product) }
taxIt: (s: TaxStrategy)(product: String)Double

scala> val taxFree = taxIt(new TaxFree) _
taxFree: String => Double = <function1>
```

You've used multiple parameters set for higher-order functions to pass anonymous function like closures, but now you've learned another benefit of function currying: dependency injection.

5.3.4 *Function composition and partial functions*

A *partial function* is a function that's only defined for a subset of input values. This is different from the definition of a pure function (see section 5.1), which is defined for all input parameters. Figure 5.3 shows a partial function f: X -> Y which is only defined for X=1 and X=3, not X=2.

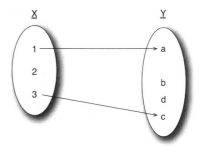

Figure 5.3   A partial function that's only defined for a subset of parameter values, in this case only for 1 and 3. Compare this figure with figure 5.1.

In Scala partial functions are defined by trait `PartialFunction[-A, +B]` and extend `scala.Function1` trait. Like all function types, `PartialFunction` declares the `apply` method and an additional method called `def isDefinedAt(a: A):Boolean`. This `isDefinedAt` method determines whether the given partial function is defined for a given parameter.

The easiest way to create a partial function is by defining an anonymous function with pattern matching. The following code example defines the partial function shown in figure 5.3:

```
def intToChar: PartialFunction[Int, Char] = {
  case 1 => 'a'
  case 3 => 'c'
}
```

In this case the Scala compiler will translate the preceding code snippet to something like the following:

```
new PartialFunction[Int, Char] {
    def apply(i: Int) = i match {
      case 1 => 'a'
      case 3 => 'c'
    }

     def isDefinedAt(i: Int): Boolean = i match {
      case 1 => true
      case 3 => true
      case _ => false
    }
  }
```

The `PartialFunction` trait provides two interesting combinatory methods called `orElse` and `andThen`. The `orElse` method lets you combine this partial function with another partial function. It's much like `if-else`, where if the current partial function isn't defined for a given case, then the other is invoked. You can chain multiples of them to create `if-else if` patterns. On the other hand, `andThen` lets you compose transformation functions with a partial function that works on the result produced by the partial function. An example will demonstrate the power of functional composition.

> **NOTE** It's important to understand the usefulness of partial functions. They let you write smaller functions, keeping in mind the single responsibility principle, and then compose them together to create a complete function that provides the solution. Be aware of the performance penalty. When composing partial functions, always remember that the `isDefinedAt` method of each composing partial function might get invoked multiple times.[9]

Assume you're building a pricing system for all the patient claims for which you need to invoice your providers. Typically these systems are complicated, so I'll simplify things a little. The pricing depends on the type of the claim and location. Further-

---

[9] Vassil Dichev, "Speaking My (Programming) Language?," July 31, 2011, http://mng.bz/9yOx.

more, the location is divided by state codes or ZIP codes. Each of these factors could influence the final price you'll charge your providers. Also, not all claims have specific pricing logic associated with them, so you have to have a catch-all default so that you can always calculate the price. I'm sure this sounds similar to some of the business rules you implement for your enterprise. Let's implement this small problem using partial functions. First define the claim types you're going to work with:

```
sealed trait Claim { val claimId: Int }
case class Full(val claimId: Int) extends Claim
case class Partial(val claimId: Int, percentage: Double) extends Claim
case class Generic(val claimId: Int) extends Claim
```

Each claim takes a `claimId` that uniquely identifies it in the system and optionally some additional properties associated with the claim. Understanding how each claim is different isn't important for this exercise, but remember that they're different.

To request a price, the requestor has to provide the claim information, the location, and the product identifier. In this application you can easily represent that using case classes:

```
case class Location(stateCode: Option[String], zipCode: Option[String])
case class Req(productId: String, location: Location, claim: Claim)
```

Except for `Generic` claim, the pricing for each claim is determined by specific business logic, and all the calculations start with some base prices associated with the product. To determine the final price of a product and the claim, you have to provide the request information and the base price. You can capture that with a type variable called `PC` (Pricing Criteria):

```
type PC = Tuple2[Req, Option[Double]]
```

Here the `Option[Double]` represents the base price of the product. The following code example implements the business logic associated with each `Full` and `Partial` claim:

```
def handleFullClaim: PartialFunction[PC, PC] = {
    case (c@Req(id, 1, Full(claimId)), basePrice)  =>
        ...
}

 def handlePartialClaim: PartialFunction[PC, PC] = {
    case (c@Req(id, 1, Partial(claimId, percentage)), basePrice)  =>
        ...
}
```

Similarly, the final price to the provider is also influenced by the location of the claim. Both state code and ZIP code could change the price. The separate location-based logic could also be implemented as separate partial functions, as in the following:

```
def handleZipCode: PartialFunction[PC, PC] = {
  case (c@Req(id, Location(_, Some(zipCode)), _), price) =>
      ...
}
```

```
def handleStateCode: PartialFunction[PC, PC] = {
  case (c@Req(id, Location(Some(stateCode), _), _), price) =>
    ...
}
```

To create the final solution to calculate the price for a provider, you can combine these smaller partial functions and be done with it. According to the business rules, you should first determine the price based on the claim and further refine the calculated price based on location. You can easily combine these functions with the `orElse` and `andThen` combinators you learned at the beginning of this section:

```
def claimHandlers = handleFullClaim orElse handlePartialClaim
def locationHandlers = handleZipCode orElse handleStateCode
def priceCalculator: PartialFunction[PC, PC] =
    claimHandlers andThen locationHandlers
```

The preceding code implements the business rules the way they've been described. Calculate the price using the claim, then refine it based on location. As the business rules or new claim types get added to the system, you can easily modify the combinations and add new partial functions. For example, you aren't handling the `Generic` claim type yet. You can easily add it to the final solution by adding another `orElse` block to the `claimHandlers`.

The partial functions are applicable to more situations than you might think. For example, throwing exceptions from a function or a method could be considered a partial function. The function that's throwing an exception isn't defined for the case that raises the exception. Instead of throwing an exception, you could consider making the function partial and combining it with some other function that knows how to handle the exception case. In Scala, partial functions are powerful when it comes to function composition. Keep that in mind when you write your code.

5.3.5 *Recursion*

Recursion is where a function calls itself. Recursion is a useful tool in your functional programming toolbox. It lets you break problems into subproblems and subproblems further down into sub-subproblems.[10] This allows for solving these smaller subproblems and then combining them together to produce the final solution. Think of recursion as the assembly language of functional programming.

One of the main benefits of recursion is that it lets you create solutions without mutation. In the next small exercise, you have to calculate the sum of all the elements of a `List` without using any mutation. You can solve the problem in many ways using library functions, but let's try to build it from scratch. The imperative solution to this problem looks something like the following:

```
scala> var sum = 0
scala> for(e <- List(1,2,3)) { sum += e }
```

---

[10] James O. Coplien, "To Iterate is Human, to Recurse, Divine," C++ Report 10(7), July/August 1988, pp 43-51, http://mng.bz/wXr4.

You declare a mutating variable and accumulate the result by iterating through all the elements of the collection. And the recursion-based solution would look something like the following:

```
def sum(xs: List[Int]): Int = xs match {
  case Nil => 0
  case x :: ys => x + sum(ys)
}
```

The difference is that a recursion-based solution doesn't use any mutable temporary variables and it lets you break the problem into smaller pieces. A typical way to implement recursive functions in Scala is to use pattern matching. Pattern matching helps you break the problem into subproblems where each case potentially represents a subproblem. Recursion always looks easy when someone else is doing it, but it can be hard when you have to do it. The next section explains how you can start thinking recursively by following simple steps.

5.4   *Thinking recursively*

Suppose you're given a list of elements, and your job is to remove the duplicates. For example, if you're given `List(0,1,2,3,2,1,0)`, the output should be `List(0, 1, 2, 3)`. I'm going to show you a step-by-step process to come up with a recursion-based solution.[11]

The first step is to identify the type. Thinking in terms of type will help you think about the input parameter and the return value of the function. Don't generalize yet, but think about what you have and what you want to achieve. Sometimes using a concrete example helps. The type of the `removeDups` function will look like the following:

```
removeDups: List[Int] => List[Int]
```

The next step is to declare all the cases that you need to handle. In the case of `removeDups`, you have to handle the following cases:

```
  case Nil =>
  case x :: ys if(ys.contains(x)) =>
  case x :: ys =>
```

The first case checks for an empty list, the second case is for a duplicate element in the list, and the third case is for a nonduplicate element. Depending on the type of the problem you're trying to solve, you might end up with many cases. Don't worry—you'll refactor the solution later into a more elegant solution after it's working.

The next step is to implement the simple cases. Here you have only one simple case, and that's case `Nil`. Because empty lists can't have any duplicates, you can safely return an empty list back:

```
case Nil => Nil
case x :: ys if(ys.contains(x)) =>
case x :: ys =>
```

---

[11] Graham Hutton, *Programming in Haskell* (Cambridge University Press, 2007), www.cs.nott.ac.uk/~gmh/book.html.

The next step is to implement the other case(s) when you have a nonempty list. For this step, it's useful to consider which constructs and functions you have that you could use to implement these cases. For the second case, you want to throw out the x because it's a duplicate and continue with the processing for the rest of the elements in the list. The easiest way to do that is to invoke removeDups again by passing the ys as a parameter.

```
case Nil => Nil
case x :: ys if(ys.contains(x)) => removeDups(ys)
case x :: ys =>
```

For the last case you want to continue with the rest of the list and append the non-duplicate element to the list:

```
case Nil => Nil
case x :: ys if(ys.contains(x)) => removeDups(ys)
case x :: ys => removeDups(ys) :+ x
```

The final step is to generalize and simplify the solution. Start with your type signature and see whether you can generalize the solution. In this case, you started with List[Int] => List[Int], but do you need to specify Int here? Are you using anything that's specific to the Int?

In the removeDups solution, you don't care about the type of List as long as there is a way to compare two elements. You can generalize the type signature of removeDups as in the following:

```
def removeDups[A](xs: List[A]): List[A] = xs match {
   case Nil => Nil
   case x :: ys if(ys.contains(x)) => removeDups(ys)
   case x :: ys => removeDups(ys) :+ x
}
```

Next comes the refactoring. Let's see whether you can simplify the implementation. In this case, it looks simple so you don't need to go any farther. But sometimes foldl or foldr could simplify the solution.

The best way to get better at recursion is practice. Once you become comfortable, these steps will come naturally to you, but until then let them guide you in how to implement recursive solutions.

5.4.1   *Tail recursion*

Before I talk about tail recursion, let me explain how head recursion works. *Head recursion* is the more traditional way of doing recursion, where you perform the recursive call first and then take the return value from the recursive function and calculate the result.

In *tail recursion* you perform your calculation first and then execute the recursive call by passing the result of the current step to the next step. I'll provide an example shortly to demonstrate how you can write recursive functions, keeping tail recursion in mind. But first it's useful to consider why recursion is avoided in Java and other similar languages.

Generally when you call a function an entry is added to the call stack of the currently running thread. The downside is that the call stack has a defined size, and once you violate that boundary you get a StackOverflowError exception. This is why Java developers prefer to iterate rather than recurse. Because Scala runs on the JVM, Scala programs also suffer from this problem. But the good news is that starting with Scala 2.8.1, Scala overcomes this limitation by doing tail call optimization. Here's a tail call optimization example. In the following code snippet you're calculating the length of a given List:

```
def length[A](xs: List[A]): Int = xs match {
    case Nil => 0
    case x :: ys => 1 + length(ys)
}
```

This is a classic example of head recursion where you call length recursively and then add all the ones at the end. If you try to execute this function with a large List (100,000 elements, for example), you will get a StackOverflowError. Now rewrite the preceding function in tail recursion:

```
def length2[A](xs: List[A]): Int = {
    def _length(xs: List[A], currentLength: Int): Int = xs match {
      case Nil => currentLength
      case x :: ys => _length(ys, currentLength + 1)
    }
    _length(xs, 0)
}
```

In this version you aren't doing any calculation after the recursive call. You do the calculation at each step and pass the result to the next step of the recursion. The question is, which one should you prefer? For Scala, you should always prefer the version that uses tail recursion because Scala tries to optimize tail recursive functions. Scala does tail call optimization at compile time, and the compiler transforms a tail recursive function into a loop. This way tail recursive functions don't add additional entries to the call stack and don't blow up. Scala can't optimize every tail recursion—it can optimize functions but not nonfinal methods. The best way to know whether the Scala compiler can optimize your tail recursion is to use the @tailrec annotation because that way you'll get a compiler warning if the Scala compiler fails to optimize your tail recursive functions or methods. The following listing has the complete length function with the @tailrec annotation.

Listing 5.3 Tail recursive function with @tailrec annotation

```
import scala.annotation.tailrec

def length2[A](xs: List[A]): Int = {                    Marker to
    @tailrec                                        ◁── optimize tail
    def _length(xs: List[A], currentLength: Int): Int = xs match {   recursion
      case Nil => currentLength
      case x :: ys => _length(ys, currentLength + 1)
    }
    _length(xs, 0)
  }
```

The common pattern for implementing a tail recursive function is to use a local function like _length. This local function approach allows you to have an additional parameter by which you can pass the result of the current step to the next step. Always remember when going for tailrec optimization that your recursion should be the last step in your function or final method.

5.5 *Algebraic data types*

Algebraic data type (ADT) is a classification. A *data type* in general is a set of values (think of Int as a type that identifies all the integer values). You can define an algebraic type by enumerating all the values of the set, except each value could have its own constructor. It also allows you to decompose the type using pattern matching. If that sounds like an abstract concept, let's look at an example. So far you've learned that ADT is a kind of type that represents a set of values. ADTs could represent a finite or an infinite set of values. First, look at an example of a closed ADT (finite set of values) that explores why they're valuable.

The easiest way to define an algebraic type in Scala is to use case classes. The following example code defines an Account type and its possible values:

```
object ADT {
  sealed trait Account

  case class CheckingAccount(accountId: String) extends Account
  case class SavingAccount(accountId: String, limit: Double)
          extends Account
  case class PremiumAccount(corporateId: String, accountHolder: String)
          extends Account
}
```

Here you've defined three account types, each with its own constructor taking various numbers of parameters. It also declares Account trait as sealed, and that means no one else can extend the trait and create a new type of Account unless it's defined in the same source file. You've managed to create a finite ADT, but why case classes are a good implementation choice for ADTs is still not clear. The reason is pattern matching. Once you've created ADTs, you use them in functions. ADTs become much easier to deal with if they're implemented as case classes because pattern matching works out of the box. In the following snippet printAccountDetails prints the details of each account:

```
object ADT {
    ...
  def printAccountDetails(account: Account): Unit = account match {
    case CheckingAccount(accountId) =>
        println("Account id " + accountId)
    case SavingAccount(accountId, limit) =>
        println("Account id " + accountId + " , " + limit)
  }
}
```

Along with the values and constructors, ADTs also come with a way to decompose the type through pattern matching so that you can easily use them in your functions. A powerful concept: once you create an algebraic data type, you get pattern matching support to readily use them in functions.

In the `printAccountDetails` function I intentionally left out the case for `Premium-Account` in order to show you what happens when you compile the previous code. You'll see the following warning for the missing case:

```
[warn] missing combination PremiumAccount
[warn]   def printAccountDetails(account: Account): Unit = account match {
```

Another advantage of using the finite algebraic data type is that it provides hints to the Scala compiler to check whether the functions are handling all possible values of algebraic data types. There are two ways you can get rid of the warning: provide the case for the `PremiumAccount` or make the `Account` type nonsealed. The downside of removing the `sealed` keyword is that anybody can extend `Account` trait and create a new account type. In that case, how can you write functions that handle all possible account types like `printAccountDetails`? I'm fond of finite (closed) algebraic types and always prefer to use them because I can get a lot of mileage from Scala at compilation time.

One of the biggest benefits is writing total functions. A *total function* is one that knows how to handle all the values of an algebraic data type and always produces a result. That means you know at compile time that the function will work for all inputs. You've been using ADT types in this book for a while now without knowing it. A couple of well-known examples of ADT in Scala are `scala.Either` and `scala.Option`.

5.6 *Why does functional programming matter?*

You've explored quite a bit of theory and seen many examples of functional programming in this chapter. Functional programming, as I've mentioned, is different from imperative programming. It's another way of thinking about programming. Why bother to learn this new technique? What will this buy you?

First, it's good to learn a new programming paradigm because it makes you a better programmer (see section 1.1.4). But this reason alone isn't good enough—what other benefits does functional programming provide? The popular answer is concurrency and multicore programming. Functional programming helps you write concurrent applications more effectively and easily. Enterprise software developers have to deal with complex business problems and large-scale software development, and although concurrency is an important part of it, it's not enough to convince all developers. In the rest of the section I make a case for why functional programming matters and how it can help you better handle complexity.

John Hughes, a renowned computer scientist, in his excellent paper on why functional programming matters[12] describes how functional programming helps in

---

[12] John Hughes, "Why Functional Programming Matters," 1990, http://mng.bz/8KxU.

handling complexity. In fact, the content and the title of this section were influenced by this paper.

Take the example of Unix pipes. Unix pipes are analogous to a pipeline where processes are chained together (by their input/output streams) to form a pipeline. For example, the following command retrieves the size of the file identified by the URL www.manning.com/raychaudhuri/:

```
curl -s "http://www.manning.com/raychaudhuri/" | wc -c
```

Here I combine the `curl` process to get data from the server and the `wc` process to count the bytes I get back from the server. The | is the Unix pipe command, which indicates the output from one process is to be "piped" as input to the next one. I'm pretty sure the authors of `curl` and `wc` would have never thought that someone would combine these processes to perform an action. In fact, you can almost take any number of Unix processes and combine them to create new commands. This is one of the most useful and powerful ideas of the Unix-like OSs. What's the design philosophy behind all these Unix processes?[13] All Unix processes follow two simple rules:

- Write programs that do one thing and do it well.
- Write programs to work together.

So what do you gain by following these simple rules? The answer is *composability*. Unix processes show us the power of composability. Unix processes are like LEGO blocks. You can pick them in any order, combine them to create new processes, name these processes, build new processes on top of them, and so on. How does all of this map to functional programming? A Unix pipe is like a functional programming language. If you think of each process as a function, a Unix pipe lets you compose these functions using | notation; in Scala it's functional composition. Similarly, let's say the following set of functions is available to you in Scala:

```
def even: Int => Boolean = _ % 2 == 0
def not: Boolean => Boolean = !_
def filter[A](criteria: A => Boolean)(col: Traversable[A])=
    col.filter(criteria)
def map[A, B](f: A => B)(col: Traversable[A]) = col.map(f)
```

These functions are like Unix processes in that each one does exactly one thing. The `even` function returns `true` if the given element is an even integer value. The `not` function toggles the input `Boolean` parameter. The `filter` function, on the other hand, takes a `Traversable` type collection (super trait for all traversable collection types in Scala) and additional criteria function to return a collection with all the elements that match the criteria. The `map` function traverses the collection and applies the given function `f`. Now, suppose you have a problem where you have to find all the even numbers in a given collection and double them. With the functions at your disposal, you can easily build the solution by composing them into a multistep

---

[13] Eric S. Raymond, *The Art of Unix Programming*, Addison-Wesley, 2008, www.catb.org/esr/writings/taoup/.

process. First build a filter that knows how to find even elements and a function that can double a value:

```
def evenFilter = filter(even) _
def double: Int => Int = _ * 2
```

In the case of `evenFilter` I'm using function currying to create a specific version of the filter that knows how to filter even numbers. To compose the two functions together, Scala provides a method called `andThen`, available to all function types except those with zero arguments. This `andThen` method behaves similarly to Unix pipes—it combines two functions in sequence and creates one function. Because all Scala functions get compiled to a `scala.Function` trait, you'll use this compose method to join two functions. To filter out odd elements and double them, create the following function:

```
def doubleAllEven = evenFilter andThen map(double)
```

Here `evenFilter` creates a collection of even elements, and the map function invokes the `double` function for each element in the collection. Job done. But what if you have to double all the odd numbers? You have all the ingredients you need, just compose them slightly differently:

```
def odd: Int => Boolean = not compose even
def oddFilter = filter(odd) _
def doubleAllOdd = oddFilter andThen map(double)
```

Here for the `odd` function I use another combinatory method defined for function types, called `compose`. The only difference between `andThen` and `compose` is that the order of evaluation for `compose` is right to left. `odd` will find all the even elements and negate them.

The example in hand is naïve and simple, but one point is clear: composability allows you to build solutions from smaller building blocks, which is important because that's how you solve complex problems. When you design a solution for a large, complex problem, you break the problem into smaller problems and further break them down into even smaller problems until you get to a point where comprehension is easy. Solving these individual pieces and then gluing them together to build the final piece is a centuries-old technique.

This breaking down of problems into smaller digestible pieces happens across all the layers of software development. Functional composability lets you build these mathematical microworlds in your application. In these microworlds you can be certain about things because they're all made of pure functions, and you can easily build them using function composition. The good news is that you can implement most of the application complexity in these microworlds, and functional composability gives you a clear, well-defined path to break the problem into smaller functions and compose them later.

In today's enterprises, delivering software is not enough. You have to deliver as fast as possible. And therein lies the benefits of abstraction and composability. You as a developer can save time by composing smaller functions without reinventing and duplicating implementations.

Another benefit of this pure functional world is debugging. You no longer have to worry about the sequence of events that happened before the problem occurred because there's no side effect. You also don't have to worry about the sequence in which the functions are executed because the behavior of the function is only driven by the set of input parameters. It's much easier to find defects in the functional programming world than in the imperative programming world. To make all this possible, follow the Unix design philosophy:

- Write pure functions that do one thing and do it well.
- Write functions that can compose with other functions.

The first rule is the Single Responsibility Principle. The second rule is a by-product of following the first rule. Keeping functions small and pure automatically helps you compose them together with other functions, as you saw in the previous example. One way to keep functions small is to have them only take one parameter (although the reality is you're going to have functions that take multiple parameters and do a combination of things).

The second rule is to write functions while keeping function currying in mind, or use partial functions. When declaring functions, make sure you order your parameters from most specific to most generic. It will help others to use functions in more places and to replace the generic parameters—or even better, have functions that take only a single parameter.

As an object functional language, Scala offers the benefits of both object-oriented and functional programming. Functional programming gives you the additional benefit of composition that makes the core and more complex parts of your application easier to write and maintain.

So what about those functions with side effects? Are they hopeless in terms of composition? No. In the next section I show how you can build abstractions around them so that they can participate in composition.

5.7   *Building higher abstractions with monads*

If you come from an OOP background you've probably encountered design patterns. In this section I describe a functional programming design pattern called monads. The problem with monads is the mysticism that comes along with them. The general misconceptions about monads are that they're hard to understand and that you need a good mathematical background to fully appreciate them. It's true that monads originated from tenets of category theory,[14] a branch of mathematics that formalizes abstract mathematical concepts into collections and arrows. But they provide a nice abstraction layer (like design patterns) to help structure your code.

---

[14] "Category Theory," http://en.wikipedia.org/wiki/Category_theory.

Many implementations of monads exist, and each solves a specific kind of problem. You've already used monads, in fact—the two common ones so far are List and Option. The List monad abstracts out the computation that might return 0, 1, or more possible results. The Option monad abstracts out the computation that may not return anything (Some or None). Monads are usually considered an advanced functional programming concept, but I feel strongly enough about them to put them in this book because they have enough practical benefits that you as an application developer should know them. The two most important benefits are

1 Monads let you compose functions that don't compose well, such as functions that have side effects.
2 Monads let you order computation within functional programming so that you can model sequences of actions.

Both of these are critical and powerful properties to be aware of when designing applications using functional programming techniques. First I'll explore the second benefit because it's commonly used even if you're building smaller mathematical microworlds without side effects. In the later part of this section I show you how to compose side-effecting functions in functional programming style.

5.7.1 Managing state using monads

When I introduced functional programming I mentioned that it doesn't care about the sequencing of functions or operations, because functions are pure. Let's challenge that with another retail pricing example. This application needs to calculate a price for a product by following a sequence of steps:

1 Find the base price of the product.
2 Apply a state code-specific discount to the base price.
3 Apply a product-specific discount to the result of the previous step.
4 Apply tax to the result of the previous step to get the final price.

This pattern should be common in enterprise software. It's clear that you have to maintain the price generated by each action and pass it to the next action in the sequence. How will you do that? The imperative answer is to use a mutable variable shared by each action—bad idea, for all the reasons I've mentioned throughout the book. What about implementing all these actions in one function? Yikes! That could result in a large function, because each step could potentially be 10–20 lines of code. A better answer would be to implement each step as a function and pipe the result of the current action to the next action. The following listing shows how the implementation would look.

Listing 5.4 Sequencing methods by passing back the state

```
object PriceCalculatorWithoutMonad {                    ⎤  Import stub
                                                        ⎦  implementations
  import Stubs._                                      ⎦
  case class PriceState(productId: String, stateCode: String,price: Double)
```

Find base price of product ▷

```
def findBasePrice(productId: String, stateCode: String): PriceState = {
  val basePrice = findTheBasePrice(productId: String)
  PriceState(productId, stateCode, basePrice)
}
```

State-specific logic ▷

```
def applyStateSpecificDiscount(ps: PriceState): PriceState = {
  val discount = findStateSpecificDiscount(ps.productId, ps.stateCode)
  ps.copy(price = ps.price - discount)
}
```

Product-specific discount ▷

```
def applyProductSpecificDiscount(ps: PriceState): PriceState = {
  val discount = findProductSpecificDiscount(ps.productId)
  ps.copy(price = ps.price - discount)
}
def applyTax(ps: PriceState): PriceState = {
  val tax = calculateTax(ps.productId, ps.price)
  ps.copy(price = ps.price + tax)
}
```

Apply tax to calculated price ◁

Sequence functions ❶ ▷

```
def calculatePrice(productId: String, stateCode: String): Double = {
  val a = findBasePrice(productId, stateCode)
  val b = applyStateSpecificDiscount(a)
  val c = applyProductSpecificDiscount(b)
  val d = applyTax(c)
  d.price
}
}
```

I stubbed out the uninteresting parts of the code into a file called Stubs so that it doesn't clutter the code example. Here's the implementation with some hardcoded values:

```
object Stubs {
  def findTheBasePrice(productId: String) = 10.0
  def findStateSpecificDiscount(productId: String, stateCode: String) = 0.5
  def findProductSpecificDiscount(productId: String) = 0.5
  def calculateTax(productId: String, price: Double) = 5.0
}
```

The most interesting feature in listing 5.4 is the calculate price method ❶. It invokes each individual function and wires them together in a sequence by passing the result of one function to the next. Naming variables with a, b, and c is not a good idea, but it nicely shows how the instance of PriceState is passed around. This solution works and is implemented using a functional programming style, but the API of each individual function looks ugly. Instead of returning only the price, the applyStateSpecific-Discount, applyProductSpecificDiscount, and applyTax methods now have to return an instance of PriceState. The last line of each apply method in listing 5.4 shows the problem.

The next problem is in the calculatePrice method. It's easy to get something wrong while managing PriceState on your own, while wiring each individual method. In more complicated problems, this kind of approach becomes messy. Surely a higher abstraction that takes care of this state management would be helpful. Here comes the State monad. It is called a *State monad* because it threads the changing state across multiple operations transparently. In this case, you'll implement a State monad so that you don't have to manage the PriceState across multiple method calls. But you'll have enough of a generic implementation so that you can use it in other places where you have similar problems.

The Scalaz[15] library provides implementations of lots of monads—consider using them without reinventing the wheel. Here you'll implement the State monad.

Before I show you how to implement your State monad, let us change the signature of the findBasePrice, applyStateSpecificDiscount, applyProductSpecific-Discount, and applyTax methods so that the API looks cleaner:

```
def findBasePrice(ps: PriceState): Double
def applyStateSpecificDiscount(ps: PriceState): Double
def applyProductSpecificDiscount(ps: PriceState): Double
def applyTax(ps: PriceState): Double
```

All these methods now take an instance of PriceState and return the calculated price. Your job is to implement a State monad so you can sequence these methods or actions to calculate the final price.

The State monad encapsulates a transition function from an initial state to a (newState, value) pair. It could be easily represented as a trait in Scala, as in the following:

```
trait State[S, +A] {
    def apply(s: S): (S, A)
}
```

The apply method represents that transition function. To implement this trait all you have to do is provide a function that takes S and returns (S,A). You could easily implement that as the following:

```
object State {
    def state[S, A](f: S => (S, A)) = new State[S, A] {
      def apply(s: S) = f(s)
    }
}
```

You'll use this object as a place to keep all the handy methods you need to work with your State monad. While you're there, add a couple of methods to the State object to make life easier:

```
object State {
    def state[S, A](f: S => (S, A)) = new State[S, A] {
      def apply(s: S) = f(s)
    }
    def init[S]: State[S, S] = state[S, S](s => (s, s))
    def modify[S](f: S => S) =
       init[S] flatMap (s => state(_ => (f(s), ())))
}
```

---

[15] "Type Classes and Pure Functional Data Structures for Scala," http://github.com/scalaz/scalaz.

The init method lets you create State monads with a skeleton implementation of a transition function (s => (s, s)). Think of it as a default constructor of the State monad. The modify method is a bit more interesting. It lets you modify the current state inside the monad with a new state and return the given function and value part of the (S, A) pair with Unit. You'll use this method to implement your solution.

To treat the State trait as a first-class monad you also have to implement map and flatMap methods. Why will be clear once you're done with it, but for now remember that map and flatMap are critical parts of the monad interface—without them, no function can become a monad in Scala.

Implementing map and flatMap is easy because you know how to create an instance of the State monad. The following listing shows the trait that represents the State monad.

Listing 5.5 `StateMonad` in Scala

```
object StateMonad {
  import State._
  trait State[S, +A] {
    def apply(s: S): (S, A)                                      ◁─┐ Abstract method
    def map[B](f: A => B): State[S, B] = state(apply(_) match {  ◁─┐ represents state
      case (s, a) => (s, f(a))                                        transition
    })
    def flatMap[B](f: A => State[S, B]): State[S, B] =           ◁─┐ Modifies
      state(apply(_) match {                                          value part
        case (s, a) => f(a)(s)                                        of the pair
      })
  }                                                             ◁─┐ Creates new
                                                                     state and
  object State {                                                     value pair
    def state[S, A](f: S => (S, A)) = new State[S, A] {
      def apply(s: S) = f(s)
    }
    def init[S]: State[S, S] = state[S, S](s => (s, s))
    def modify[S](f: S => S) =
        init[S] flatMap (s => state(_ => (f(s), ())))
  }
}
```

The map method of the State monad helps transform the value inside the State monad. On the other hand, flatMap helps transition from one state to another. If all this feels a little abstract, don't worry—it will make sense when you use these constructs to implement the solution. Let's do that right now.

So far you've learned that State monads take care of threading the changing state across method calls without your being worried about it. But you still have to invoke individual pricing methods in sequence as specified by the business rules. The best place to sequence a series of method calls is in a for-comprehension. This guarantees that the steps you specify inside them will execute in sequence; it's also a great way to isolate things that need to be run in a sequence. In this case it will be something like the following:

```
      import StateMonad.State._
def modifyPriceState(f: PriceState => Double) =
      modify[PriceState](s => s.copy(price = f(s)))
      val stateMonad = for {
              _ <- modifyPriceState(findBasePrice)
              _ <- modifyPriceState(applyStateSpecificDiscount)
              _ <- modifyPriceState(applyProductSpecificDiscount)
              _ <- modifyPriceState(applyTax)
      } yield ()
```

Lots of things are going on in this small code example, so let me take it from the top. The `modifyPriceState` method is a handy method that takes one of the pricing methods and lifts it to a function so that you can invoke the `modify` method inside the `State` object.

Each `modifyPriceState` method creates an instance of a State monad. When you invoke them inside the for-comprehension, you get a State monad back that encapsulates this sequence of method calls and knows how to create a price state with a final price. Note that now `stateMonad` holds a transition function that's a composition of all the pricing methods defined inside the for-comprehension. And the benefit of this approach is that the threading of state is almost invisible from the application code and is hidden inside the monad. You can pass around this instance of a State monad, and when the time comes you can calculate the final price by passing the initial state:

```
val initialPriceState = PriceState(productId, stateCode, 0.0)
val finalPriceState = stateMonad.apply(initialPriceState)._1
val finalPrice = finalPriceState.price
```

How does this work? The magic is in `map` and `flatMap`. The for-comprehension is nothing but syntactic sugar for `map`/`flatMap`. You've used for-comprehensions for `List` and `Option`—because they both implement `map` and `flatMap`. Chapter 4 looked into this in great detail, and in this section I'll dissect the previous for-comprehension and show you how it gets translated to the `map`/`flatMap` combination.

Note in the previous code example those underscores on the left side of the for-comprehension. They represent the value part of the pair, and you don't need to worry about them for this example. I'll show you another example where this value would be used effectively—the following listing shows the complete reimplementation of the retail pricing using `StateMonad`.

Listing 5.6   Sequencing methods using `StateMonad`

```
package chap10.monads.example

object StateMonad {
  import State._                             Interface for
                                             State monad
  trait State[S, +A] {
    def apply(s: S): (S, A)
    def map[B](f: A => B): State[S, B] = state(apply(_) match {
      case (s, a) => (s, f(a))
    })
```

```scala
      def flatMap[B](f: A => State[S, B]): State[S, B] =
        state(apply(_) match {
          case (s, a) => f(a)(s)
        })
    }

  object State {
    def state[S, A](f: S => (S, A)) = new State[S, A] {
      def apply(s: S) = f(s)
    }
    def init[S]: State[S, S] = state[S, S](s => (s, s))
    def modify[S](f: S => S) =
        init[S] flatMap (s => state(_ => (f(s), ())))
  }
}

object PriceCalculator {
  import Stubs._
  import StateMonad.State._
  case class PriceState(productId: String, stateCode: String,price: Double)

  def findBasePrice(ps: PriceState): Double = {
    val basePrice = findTheBasePrice(ps.productId)
    basePrice
  }

  def applyStateSpecificDiscount(ps: PriceState): Double = {
    val discount = findStateSpecificDiscount(ps.productId, ps.stateCode)
    ps.price - discount
  }

  def applyProductSpecificDiscount(ps: PriceState): Double = {
    val discount = findProductSpecificDiscount(ps.productId)
    ps.price - discount
  }
  def applyTax(ps: PriceState): Double = {
    val tax = calculateTax(ps.productId, ps.price)
    ps.price + tax
  }

  def calculatePrice(productId: String, stateCode: String): Double = {
    def modifyPriceState(
      f: PriceState => Double) = modify[PriceState](s =>    // ◁ Chaining
        s.copy(price = f(s)))                               //   state using
      val stateMonad = for {                                //   stateMonad
        _ <- modifyPriceState(findBasePrice)
        _ <- modifyPriceState(applyStateSpecificDiscount)
        _ <- modifyPriceState(applyProductSpecificDiscount)
        _ <- modifyPriceState(applyTax)
      } yield ()
    val initialPriceState = PriceState(productId, stateCode, 0.0)
    val finalPriceState = stateMonad.apply(initialPriceState)._1
    val finalPrice = finalPriceState.price
    finalPrice
  }
}
```

State monad is a general abstraction layer that allows you to build computations for sequences of actions that require a shared state.

You've yet to see the relevance of having the pair of state and value in your State monad implementation. Although it's true that you don't always need them, if you have a computation that relies on the current state of the monad, you can use the state and value pair to do your computation. Suppose you need to implement logging for the retail-pricing example and log the result of each step.

To implement logging, you need to expose one more method to the State object, called gets. This method lets you access the current state so you can create the log message and save it as a value inside the monad. Here's how it's implemented:

```
def gets[S,A](f: S => A): State[S, A] =
    init[S] flatMap (s => state(_ => (s, f(s))))
```

It's similar to the modify method but allows you to provide a function that takes S and returns A. The gets method also creates a new instance of State monad with the value returned from the given function f. Now you can sequence the log steps after each pricing action inside the for-comprehension, as shown in the following listing, to log all the steps.

Listing 5.7   Calculating price and logging each step

```
def calculatePriceWithLog(productId: String, stateCode: String): Double = {
    def modifyPriceState f: PriceState => Double) =
        modify[PriceState](s => s.copy(price = f(s)))
    def logStep(f: PriceState => String) = gets(f)          ◁─┐ Helper
                                                               │ improves
    val stateMonad = for {                                     │ readability
        _ <- modifyPriceState(findBasePrice)                   │ over gets
        a <- logStep(s => "Base Price " + s)
        _ <- modifyPriceState(applyStateSpecificDiscount)
        b <- logStep(s => "After state discount " + s)
        _ <- modifyPriceState(applyProductSpecificDiscount)
        c <- logStep(s => "After product discount " + s)
        _ <- modifyPriceState(applyTax)
        d <- logStep(s => "After tax " + s)
    } yield a :: b :: c :: d :: Nil
    val (finalPriceState, log) = stateMonad.apply(PriceState(productId,
        stateCode, 0.0))                    ◁─┐
    finalPriceState.price                      │ Produce final price
}
```

Access current state, log it as List points to the block with `a <- logStep`.

First you create a logStep method to wrap the gets method to provide a little more readability. Secondly you've sequenced the logStep after each state modification so you can track the state changes. Finally you're combining the log of each step as part of the yield to create a list of log messages. See how easy it is to add behavior that relies on changing state using State monad?

5.7.2   *Building blocks for monads*

The building blocks for monads in Scala are the flatMap and map combination. If you think of a monad as a container, then flatMap and map are the only two possible ways to get into the value currently stored inside the container. Both flatMap and map take a function as a parameter and create a new instance of a monad by applying the function to allow composability. But in both cases you end up with another instance of a monad. To retrieve the value from the monad, you have to use a different technique. For our example I used the `apply` method defined inside the `StateMonad`. For some types of monads, you use pattern matching. For example, `scala.Option` is a monad, and you use pattern matching to retrieve the value from the `Some` instance.

The important part is to understand why you need both `flatMap` and `map` methods. They seem to have a similar kind of behavior. To clearly understand why both are important, reimplement the `calculatePrice` method from listing 5.6 without the for-comprehension:

```
def calculatePrice2(productId: String, stateCode: String): Double = {
  def modifyPriceState(f: PriceState => Double) =
      modify[PriceState](s => s.copy(price = f(s)))

  val stateMonad = modifyPriceState(findBasePrice) flatMap {a =>
      modifyPriceState(applyStateSpecificDiscount) flatMap {b =>
        modifyPriceState (applyProductSpecificDiscount) flatMap {c =>
          modifyPriceState (applyTax) map {d =>() }
          }
        }
      }
  val initialPriceState = PriceState(productId, stateCode, 0.0)
  val finalPriceState = stateMonad.apply(initialPriceState)._1
  val finalPrice = finalPriceState.price
  finalPrice
}
```

Here price state is chained together using `flatMap` without the syntactic sugar of for-comprehension. As you can see, I used both `flatMap` and `map` together. This is exactly how Scala will also translate the for-comprehension from listing 5.6. Now compare the previous code using the following signature of `map` and `flatMap`:

```
def map[B](f: A => B): State[S, B]
def flatMap[B](f: A => State[S, B]): State[S, B]
```

The `map` method lets you create an instance of State monad, and `flatMap` lets you flatten the nested state. Without `flatMap` you end up with a nested instance of State monad because each invocation of `modifyPriceState` returns back an instance of State monad. Try to change the previous code to use `map` instead of `flatMap` to see the difference.

Here's the recipe for building a monad on your own:

1 Define both `flatMap` and `map` for the interface.
2 Decide on a way to get the value of the monad (pattern matching or `apply`).
3 Conform to the monadic laws.[16]

Monads are almost everywhere—you've been using them without knowing it. One common monad you haven't seen here is the I/O monad. This one lets you compose

[16] Tony Morris, "Monad Laws using Reductio (Scala)", June 26, 2008, http://mng.bz/59P5.

functions with side effects. Explore the Scalaz library for its implementation. Now you know how to create monads on your own and identify them if you see them in the wild. Monads are a great way to raise the abstraction level that is composable. You could have invented monads[17] (and maybe you already have).

5.8   *Summary*

This chapter explored the functional programming side of Scala. Even though you've been using functional programming constructs provided by Scala, for the first time I explained functional programming in detail in this chapter. You looked into the roots of functional programming and into the example of a purely functional program.

Enterprise developers find it hard to not worry about side effects because any interesting program out there somehow has to talk to the outside world. You learned how you could still build pure functional modules and push the side effects as far as possible from the core code, which will help build the confidence in and correctness of your applications. Now no more hours of debugging will be required to isolate the mutable state that's causing your application to misbehave.

The critical benefit of functional programming is composition, the fundamental property that you apply when you construct large programs. And with the power of type abstractions available in Scala, you can finally build reusable functions and components.

You also learned about a functional programming design pattern called Monad. Monads let you compose in the face of side effects. At first they appear to be complex, but once you start using them you'll see this pattern in many places, including the standard Scala library. Using Monads you've merely scratched the surface of functional programming design patterns and concepts. I highly recommend exploring advanced functional programming concepts. A great place to start is *Scala in Depth* (www.manning.com/suereth/) by Joshua D. Suereth (Manning, 2012).

Functional programming isn't restricted to Scala. You can use the concepts you've learned here in any programming language. Always remember the key is to create a referentially transparent expression, and if that's possible in your language then go for it. Functional programming languages should also enable functional composition. In short, one language is more functional than another if it makes composing functions easier.

Chapter 6 explores how you can start taking advantage of the benefits of your Java code bases by integrating them with Scala.

---

[17] Dan Piponi (sigfpe), "You Could Have Invented Monads! (And Maybe You Already Have.)," August 7, 2006, http://mng.bz/96E6.

Part 2

Working with Scala

These five chapters in part 2 focus on working with Scala. You'll build applications using the Simple Build Tool (SBT), connect to a database using Squeryl, build scalable and reusable components in Scala, and use actors to make concurrent programming easy.

Chapters 6 and 7 are companions, or rather, chapter 7 is an extension of chapter 6. In chapter 6 you'll learn how to create a simple web application using the SBT and the Scalaz HTTP module. But the application you set out to build in chapter 6 won't be complete by chapter's end because to build a functional Kanban application, your application needs to store information such as stories and its status information into persistent storage. In chapter 7 you will complete the weKanban application and learn how to retrieve and store information in a relational database.

In chapter 8, in which you will learn how to build simple and reusable components, your focus will be on the type system—types of types. You'll also learn about a new kind of polymorphism using type classes that allows you to express and create abstractions that are easy to extend and scale—a powerful construct to help you solve your day-to-day programming problems.

In chapter 9 Scala's actor library takes center stage. Think of an actor as an object that processes a message (your request) and encapsulates state (state is not shared with other actors). The ability to perform action in response to an incoming message is what makes an object an actor. At a high level, actors are the way you should do OOP. The important thing to remember is that the actor model encourages no shared state architecture. I explain why that's an important property to have for any concurrent program.

The goal in chapter 10 is to make you comfortable writing automated tests in Scala so that you can build production-quality software. The path to writing well-crafted code is the path where you write tests for your code. Another goal is to dispel the common perception that writing tests is hard. Your first steps will be getting started with practices like test-driven development (TDD) and continuous integration for your Scala project.

Building web applications
in functional style

This chapter covers

- Building Scala projects with SBT (Simple Build Tool)
- Introduction to the Scalaz HTTP module
- Creating a web application in Scala called weKanban

This second part of the book switches focus to more real-world applications of the Scala programming language, and what could be more practical than building a web application in Scala? There are already web frameworks like Lift (http://liftweb.net) and Playframework (www.playframework.org) that Scala developers can use to build web applications. But this chapter introduces you to an interesting library called Scalaz (http://code.google.com/p/scalaz/). (The source code for Scalaz is hosted at http://github.com/scalaz/scalaz.) This simple library will allow you to focus on building a web application in functional style without worrying about the complexity of a full-stack web framework.

There are quite a few similarities between web applications and functional programming. Think of a web application as a collection of functions that takes an

HTTP request and produces an HTTP response. Each URL endpoint is mapped to a function that knows how to handle the request. Because you're building in functional programming style, the web application state (like user sessions) is explicitly specified in each request. The benefit of thinking in this style is that you can build web applications by composing functions or using higher-order combinators. Frameworks built using this strategy usually are stateless and scalable. In this chapter you'll learn to use functional programming to build a web application.

You're also quickly reaching a point where you have to start thinking about a build tool to compile and run Scala applications. Even though you could use almost any existing build tool for Scala applications, the de facto standard is SBT (introduced in chapter 1). This chapter will explore this tool and will show you how to configure and build Scala web projects using SBT. Get yourself a nice coffee and a sandwich before diving in to build your first web application in Scala.

6.1 Building weKanban: a simple web-based Kanban board

You're going to build a simple web-based Kanban[1] board. The word Kanban is derived from the Japanese language and it means "card-signal." In Kanban, the card-signaling is used to trigger action for new work. This mechanism is also known as a *pull system* because new work is pulled in only when there's available capacity to handle the work.

The essential idea behind the Kanban system is limiting the work in progress.[2] *Stop starting and start finishing* is an important mantra aimed at reducing the amount of work in progress and, ultimately, waste. Thanks to Agile software development methodology, the card wall (or notice board or whiteboard with index cards) has become popular, and you'll use it to visualize the work in progress for user stories and backlog, and to determine who is working on what. But card walls aren't necessarily a Kanban system unless there's an explicit limit on work in progress and a signaling system to pull new work.

The Kanban board you'll build (figure 6.1) has this limit in place for the ready, dev, and test phases. In figure 6.1 the number 3 at the top of the ready phase means that you can't have more than three stories in the ready state; similarly, you can have 2 stories at the most in the dev phase.

According to figure 6.1, you can move one more story from the ready phase to the dev phase. A pair of developers looking for new work can select a card from the ready phase and move that card to the dev phase. Once the development work is done, the card moves to the test phase where, in this stage, a tester, business analyst, or other members of the team will verify the work against the user story. When the story is approved or verified, it's moved to the deploy phase, which means it's ready for production deployment. This is how a card (work) flows through the system.

---

[1] "Kanban," http://en.wikipedia.org/wiki/Kanban.

[2] David J. Anderson, *Kanban: Successful Evolutionary Change for Your Technology Business*, Blue Hole Press, April 7, 2010.

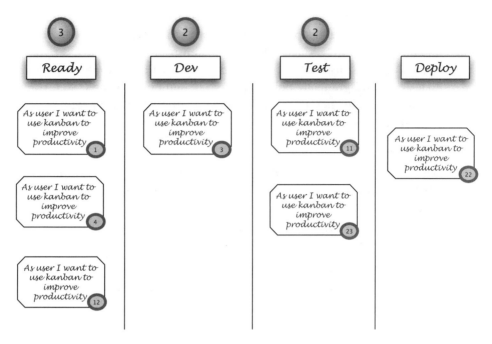

Figure 6.1 Kanban board with four phases.

You'll name your Kanban application weKanban, and here are the user stories you'll implement:

> *As a customer, I want to create a new user story so I can add stories to the ready phase.*

> *As a developer, I want to move cards (stories) from one phase to another so I can signal progress.*

In this chapter and the next, you'll implement these stories and build a full, working web application in Scala. But first you'll learn about SBT so you can compile and test your application.

6.2 *Building Scala applications using Simple Build Tool*

SBT[3] is a build tool for Scala and Java projects. It is entirely written in Scala, and you can write Scala code or use SBT's built-in DSL to configure your project and its dependencies. The benefit of using Scala for configuring your build definition is that you have the full power and type-safety of the language. This situation is quite different from Maven (http://maven.apache.org) or Ant (http://ant.apache.org), where the project build configuration is written in XML.

SBT provides support for continuous compilation and testing, meaning SBT will compile and run your tests automatically whenever there's a change in project source files. You're going to use this feature to your advantage to autodeploy changes to the web server.

---

[3] Install, features, and getting started, SBT 0.12.1, http://scala-sbt.org.

The following few sections introduce you to SBT, starting with installing to your environment. Then you'll explore the basics of SBT and learn how SBT projects are structured. I focus on creating and building web projects with SBT for your weKanban application. Because SBT is configured using Scala code, you'll see examples of how that works and gradually build a project definition for your weKanban application, including creating new tasks. Let's start with setting up SBT for your environment. Follow along!

6.2.1 Setting up SBT

The easiest way to get up and running with SBT is to download[4] the latest version of the SBT .jar file from the website and create the script file, depending upon your OS.

UNIX
Create a file called sbt with the following line:

```
java -Xms512M -Xmx1536M -Xss1M -XX:+CMSClassUnloadingEnabled
-XX:MaxPermSize=384M -jar `dirname $0`/sbt-launch.jar "$@"
```

To run SBT from any directory, put the sbt file in the ~/bin folder along with the downloaded .jar file and configure it in the PATH variable. You might have to set the permission to make the file executable using the following command:

```
Chmod u+x ~/bin/sbt
```

The `CMSClassUnloadingEnabled` flag allows the garbage collector (GC) to remove classes that are no longer used from PermGen memory.

WINDOWS
Create a batch file, sbt.bat, with the following lines:

```
Set SCRIPT_DIR=%~dp0
Java -Xmx512M -jar "%SCRIPT_DIR%sbt-launch.jar" %*
```

Put the downloaded .jar file and the batch file in the same directory and alter your path so that it's accessible from any directory.

MAC
For Mac users it's simple—use either Homebrew or MacPorts to install SBT:

```
brew install sbt
```

```
sudo port install sbt
```

You don't have to download a .jar file. If you're behind an HTTP proxy, you can set that by passing the `http.proxyUser` and `http.proxyPassword` properties:

```
java -Dhttp.proxyUser=username -Dhttp.proxyPassword=mypassword -Xmx512M
    -jar `dirname $0`/sbt-launch.jar "$@"
```

---

[4] SBT download, http://mng.bz/1E7x.

SBT will pick up the HTTP proxy settings from the `http.proxy` environment variable. SBT needs access to the internet to download the dependencies from external repositories (more on this in the next section). It's also at times useful to have the encoding of the terminal set to UTF-8 so that you can work with Unicode method names inside the SBT console (REPL).

To verify that your setup is working properly, type *sbt* in the command prompt and click Enter. If the setup is working, you'll see the sbt prompt and something similar to the following line as an output:

```
[info] Set current project to default-afcdbe (in build file:/Users/n/mybook/
    code/chap06/test/)
>
```

You can start SBT on any empty folder and you don't need a project structure to get up and running. In this case SBT created a new project called default-afcdbe under the /Users/n/mybook/code/chap06/test/ folder. In your case the project name and the location could be different. To make sure you're in an SBT prompt, type in the following command to print the version of SBT you're using:

```
> sbt-version
[info] 0.12.0
```

If you see an output, you know your installation is working correctly. SBT 0.7+ versions used to prompt you to create a New Project if one is not already defined. The definition of the project has changed in SBT 0.11+ so that any folder can be a root folder of the project. The benefit of the new approach is that now you can use SBT to build your Scala scripts without worrying about creating full-blown projects. Any folder with one Scala file can be treated as an SBT project. For now type `exit` to exit the SBT prompt. The next section explores the project structure and fundamentals of SBT.

6.2.2 *Understanding the basics of SBT*

It's important to understand the basics of SBT before you start using it. SBT is a feature-rich build tool, and I can't cover all its possible features. The goal of this section is make you aware of the basics so you can set up your Scala projects to use SBT. For more details on SBT, go to http://scala-sbt.org.

There are three ways to configure projects with SBT:

- Use the .sbt file to configure the build definition of the project.
- Use the .scala file for the build definition. This allows you to write Scala code to configure the build.
- Use both .sbt and .scala files to configure the project.

The first option is the easiest way to get started with SBT. It's a DSL to declare the build definition for the project. For a more complex build, you need to use .scala build files. That's why it's common to see both .sbt and .scala build files in typical Scala projects. Later I'll explain when to use the .scala version of the build file. For now let's start your journey with SBT with a simple build file.

BUILDING THE FIRST SBT BUILD FILE

SBT works purely by convention. It looks for Scala source files in the base directory, inside the `src/main/scala` and `src/main/java` folders. The minimum requirement for a valid SBT project is a source file under the base directory. Let's create a simple Hello world! program to play with SBT. The following snippet creates an empty folder called test and creates a hello world application:

```
$ mkdir test
$ cd test
$ echo 'object HW { def main(args: Array[String]): Unit = println("Hello
    world!") }' > hw.scala
```

Now fire up SBT to compile and run the application. Once in the SBT prompt, you can invoke the `compile` task to compile the source code. And once the source code is compiled, invoke the `run` task to run the hello world example. You should get output like the following:

```
> run
[info] Running HW
Hello world!
[success] Total time: 0 s, completed ...
```

SBT is smart enough to pick the source file from the base directory of the project, and the `run` task looks for classes in the `classpath` that define the main method. All the compiled classes are generated under the target directory. To see all the available SBT tasks, invoke the `tasks` task from the SBT prompt.

By default, SBT will use the Scala version that shipped with SBT to compile the source code of the project. In this case it is 2.10.2.

```
> scala-version
[info] 2.10.0
[info] Reapplying settings ...
[info] Set current project to default-afcdbe...
```

You can easily change the default Scala version to some other version by using the `set` command. The following commands will change the name and version of the project from within the SBT prompt:

```
> set name := "Testing SBT"
[info] Reapplying settings...
[info] Set current project to Testing SBT
> set version := "1.0"
[info] Reapplying settings...
[info] Set current project to Testing SBT
```

Each time you call `set`, it changes the settings of the project. To learn more about SBT settings, check the "Settings in SBT" sidebar; but in short: `scalaVersion`, `name`, and `version` are predefined keys in SBT that contain String type values associated with the build. The type of each of these keys is `SettingKey[T]`, where `T` is the type of the value it can accept.

Settings in SBT

Settings are the way SBT stores the build definition. A build definition defines a list of `Setting[T]` where `Setting[T]` is a transformation affecting SBT's key value pair. A `Setting` is created assigning value to `SettingKey`. There are three kinds of keys in the SBT:

- `SettingKey[T]` is a key with a value computed only once. Examples are `name` or `scalaVersion`.
- `TaskKey[T]` is a key with a value that has to be recomputed each time. `TaskKey` is used to create tasks. Examples are compile and package.
- `InputTask[T]` is a task key which takes command-line arguments as input.

All predefined keys are defined in the `sbt.Keys` object.

To persist these changes in the settings, invoke the `session save` task from the SBT prompt. This will take the settings changes and save them into the build.sbt file under the base directory:

```
$ cat build.sbt

scalaVersion := "2.10.0"

name := "Testing SBT"

version := "1.0"
$
```

Congratulations! You've created your first SBT build configuration file. Each line in the build file is an expression, and each needs to be separated by a blank line—otherwise, SBT can't distinguish them. The expressions in the build file create a list of settings for SBT. A build definition in SBT is nothing but a list of settings represented by `Setting[T]` (refer to the sidebar "Settings in SBT"). When all the settings are evaluated, SBT creates an immutable `Map` of key value pairs. And that's your build definition. The following expression will create a `Setting[String]` setting:

```
name := "Testing SBT"
```

Here `:=` is a method call on a key called `name`. You could have written that preceding line like this as well:

```
name.:=("Testing SBT")
```

All the available keys are defined in the sbt.Keys object, and it's automatically imported for you in the build.sbt file. You can also specify import statements inside build.sbt, but they should go at the top of the file. The build.sbt file is a great place to configure build settings. For example, you can enable unchecked and deprecation warnings for the Scala compiler by adding -unchecked and -deprecation values to the `scalacOptions` key:

```
scalacOptions ++= Seq("-unchecked", "-deprecation")
```

The ++= method lets you append multiple values to scalacOptions. One more important thing to note here is that SBT build files are type-safe. The type of key determines the type of the value. For example, organizationHomePage lets you set the homepage of the organization, and it expects Option[URL] as a value:

```
> set organizationHomepage := "22"
<set>:1: error: type mismatch;
 found    : java.lang.String("22")
 required: Option[java.net.URL]
organizationHomepage := "22"
```

Some argue about the benefits of type-safe build tools, but I say if type-safety is good for your code then surely it's also good for build files. In any medium or large project, you will write a considerable amount of code for your build system, and SBT can provide type-safety for faster feedback. In the next section you'll learn to build a more formal project structure for SBT.

BUILDING A PROJECT STRUCTURE FOR SBT

If you've used SBT 0.7+ before, you might be a little surprised to know that SBT doesn't create a Maven-style project structure for you. But don't worry, because now you have multiple ways to create your project structure. You can use the following snippet to create all the folders typically found in an SBT project:

```
$ mkdir -p src/{main,test}/{scala,java,resources} lib project
```

This will create all the folders you need for a typical Scala application. As a second option, you can use an SBT plug-in to create a new project. An SBT plug-in extends the build definition by adding new tasks and settings. Since the plug-in creates new SBT projects it makes sense to add it as a global plug-in. Global plug-ins are automatically added to all SBT projects; adding a plug-in to a project confines it to that project. To add a global plug-in create the following files:

```
$ touch <home-directory>/.sbt/plugins.sbt
$ touch <home-directory>/.sbt/build.sbt
```

You're going to use the np plug-in (https://github.com/softprops/np) to generate the new project. To use it, add the following lines to the plugins.sbt:

```
addSbtPlugin("me.lessis" % "np" % "0.2.0")

resolvers += Resolver.url("sbt-plugin-releases",
  url("http://scalasbt.artifactoryonline.com/scalasbt/sbt-plugin-releases/"))(
    Resolver.ivyStylePatterns)
```

The resolvers key tells SBT of the locations to find the dependencies. The += lets you append new resolvers to existing ones. The addSbtPlugin function adds a new plug-in to the SBT build system. Now add the following line to the build.sbt file:

```
seq(npSettings: _*)
```

The plug-in provides npSettings and by adding the above line to build.sbt this setting will be available to all the SBT projects. We'll explore SBT settings in detail shortly. Now to create a new project just execute the following commands:

```
$ mkdir <your project name>
$ cd <your project name>
$ sbt np
```

The np plug-in also generates a default build.sbt file that you can modify to add your settings.

The third option is to use giter8 (https://github.com/n8han/giter8). It's a command-line tool to generate files and directories from templates published in Github. This is slowly becoming a standard way of creating projects in Scala. Once giter8 is installed, you can choose a template to generate the project structure.

> **NOTE** You don't have to go to the SBT prompt to execute SBT tasks—you can execute them from the command line. For example, the `sbt compile run` command will execute both `compile` and `run`.

It doesn't matter how you've created the project structure; the structure should look familiar if you've used the Maven build tool previously because SBT uses the Maven project directory structure (figure 6.2). In fact, if you use Maven with a Scala plug-in (http://scala-tools.org/mvnsites/maven-scala-plugin/) to create a project, you'll end up with almost the same project directory structure as SBT. If your project has Java source files along with Scala source files, you need to have a folder called java under src/main and src/test.

Figure 6.2 shows a complete SBT project with all the possible build configurations. You've already seen build.sbt in action. It's a simple build configuration that allows you to set various build-related settings and dependencies. You haven't configured dependencies yet but you'll learn how to shortly.

> **NOTE** The convention is to name the build files *build*, like build.sbt or build.scala, but you can use any name. This also means you can have multiple .sbt and .scala build files in one project.

The build.scala file gives you the full power of SBT. Instead of using the DSL, you can write Scala code to configure your build using build.scala. In the old SBT world, this was the only way to configure build. But in the "new" SBT it's recommended that you start with the simple build definition (build.sbt file) and only when needed create the build.scala file. For your weKanban project, you'll use both of them together.

The build.properties file allows you to set the version of SBT used to build the project. For example, the contents of my build.properties are as follows:

```
sbt.version=0.12.0
```

This sets the version of SBT used by the project. The project/plugins.sbt is typically used to configure SBT plug-ins for the project. Please note that you don't need the build.scala and plugin.sbt files to build projects with SBT. Only add them to the project when the need arises. The target folder is used to store generated classes, .jars, and other artifacts produced by the build.

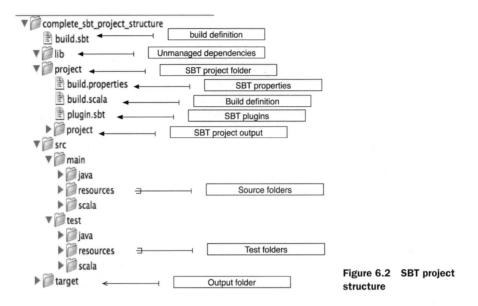

Figure 6.2   SBT project structure

NOTE   Always start with the .sbt file and only add the .scala file when needed. The rule of thumb is to define all the settings in the .sbt file and use .scala files when you need to factor out a val or object or method definition. For multiproject setup, the build.scala file is used to define common settings and tasks for multiple projects.

SBT project structure is recursive. The project directory is another project inside your project that knows how to build your project. And the project/project knows how to build the parent project. The .scala build configuration is an SBT project.

ADDING DEPENDENCIES AND CUSTOM TASKS

There are two ways you can manage dependencies with SBT: manual and automatic. To manually manage dependencies, copy the .jar files you want to the lib folder. SBT will put these .jar files on the `classpath` when compiling, running, and testing. The downside is now you're responsible for managing those .jars, updating them, or adding them. The most common and recommended way to manage dependencies in SBT projects is to allow SBT to do it for you. In automatic dependencies management, you specify the dependency in your build definition file, and SBT handles the rest. For example, the following build.sbt file adds a jetty server as a dependency:

```
libraryDependencies += "org.eclipse.jetty" % "jetty-server" %
    "7.3.0v20110203"
```

The `libraryDependencies` is setting a key to add dependencies to the project so that SBT can handle them automatically. This key holds the sequence of all the dependencies for a given project. The following is how you define dependency in SBT:

```
groupID % artifactID % version
```

This way of referring to dependencies is exactly how dependencies are resolved in Maven using Project Object Model (POM) files. Any dependency can be uniquely found using the three properties in the preceding code.

NOTE If you use `%%` after `groupID`, SBT will add the Scala version of the project to the artifact ID.

SBT uses a set of resolvers to locate project dependencies and download them. In SBT, a resolver is mapped to a URL that hosts dependencies (like Maven repositories). By default, SBT uses Maven2 and Typesafe ivy releases[5] to resolve dependencies. You can also easily add new resolvers to the list of existing resolvers using the `resolvers` key.

Using SBT on existing Maven Scala projects

Because SBT follows Maven project structure and uses Maven dependencies, setting up SBT for a Maven project is easy. SBT can read the dependencies defined in the POM file if you use the `externalPom()` method in your build file. Note you still have to specify the repositories.

Alternatively, you can create a project definition file configured to use a local Maven repository:

```
resolvers += "Local Maven Repository" at
"file://"+Path.userHome+"/.m2/repository"
```

SBT automatically picks up the build configuration changes, but you can also explicitly run the `reload` and `update` tasks to recompile and resolve dependencies.

NOTE SBT uses Apache Ivy to implement and manage dependencies. Apache Ivy is a dependency manager with flexibility and configurability.

You can also declare dependencies for a specific configuration (scope) by specifying an additional value after the version in the dependency declaration. The following line declares the dependency to specs (unit testing framework for Scala) but only for a test configuration:

```
libraryDependencies += "org.scala-tools.testing" % "specs" % "1.6.2" % "test"
```

Now this dependency is only available for classes under `src/main/test`. Here's how the build.sbt looks after all the changes:

```
scalaVersion := "2.10.0"
name := "Testing SBT"
version := "1.0"
scalacOptions ++= Seq("-unchecked", "-deprecation")
libraryDependencies ++= Seq(
```

---

[5] Index of ivy-releases, http://repo.typesafe.com/typesafe/ivy-releases.

```
"org.eclipse.jetty" % "jetty-server" % "7.0.0.RC2",
"org.scala-tools.testing" % "specs" % "1.6.2" % "test")
```

Another common thing you can do with SBT is create custom tasks for the project. For custom tasks, the .scala build definition file is used because the .sbt build file doesn't support it. To create custom tasks follow these steps:

1 Create a `TaskKey`.
2 Provide a value for the `TaskKey`.
3 Put the task in the .scala build file under project.

`TaskKey` is similar to `SettingKey`, but it's used to define tasks. The main difference is the value of `SettingKey` is evaluated only once, but the value of `TaskKey` is evaluated every time the key is accessed. It makes sense because you want to execute the task over and over again. But both `SettingKey` and `TaskKey` produce settings (key-value pairs) for the build. The following shows a simple Build.scala file that defines a hello world task:

```
import sbt._
import Keys._

object ExampleBuild extends Build {                              ❶ Create the
  val hello = TaskKey [Unit]("hello", "Prints 'Hello World'")        TaskKey

  val helloTask: Setting[Task[Unit]] = hello := {              ❷ Define
    println("Hello World")                                        the task
  }

  val project = Project (
    "example",
    file (".")).settings(helloTask)
}
```

If the name of the project is example, the Build.scala file should go under the example/project folder. ❶ creates a new `TaskKey` by passing the name and the description of the task. The name part will be used to invoke the task from the SBT prompt. ❷ defines the task by assigning a closure that implements the task, and this creates a setting that you can use in your project.

The build definition of the project should extend sbt.Build, and it gives access to default build settings. Each build definition should also define one or more projects. In this case you have only one project, but multiproject builds will declare all the subprojects here. Multiproject build definitions are beyond the scope of this book, but you can always check out http://scala-sbt.org for details. Because you want to add the hello task to the project, you set it by calling the settings method on the project. Now you have a new task available for the project:

```
> reload
[info] Loading project definition from ...
[info] Set current project to Testing SBT ...
> hello
Hello World
[success] Total time: 0 s, ...
```

> **Debugging project definition in interactive mode**
>
> Depending on the size of the Scala project you're working on, the build definition could become quite big. To troubleshoot any problems with a project definition, SBT provides a task called `console-project`. If you execute this build command inside the SBT console, SBT will load the Scala interpreter with your build definition. If you run `console-project` it will load all your build and plug-in definitions from your project and make them accessible. If you run the `console-project` task on your example project, you can access its settings and run tasks:
>
> ```
> scala> get(name)
> res2: String = Testing SBT
> scala> get(scalaVersion)
> res3: String = 2.10.0
> scala> runTask(hello, currentState)
> Hello World
> res11: (sbt.State, Unit) = (sbt.State@4fae46d5,())
> ```
>
> `runTask` runs any task defined in the build. In this case, you have the hello task. The `currentState` tracks SBT commands.
>
> Similarly, you can launch the Scala interpreter with your project classes using the `console` build command.

You should have all the basics you need to know about SBT to use it to build a web application. In the next section, you'll build the weKanban project structure and learn how to build web applications using SBT.

6.2.3 Setting up the weKanban project with SBT

To set up the weKanban project, first create the project structure as shown in figure 6.3. This structure will look similar to the structure in figure 6.2 with additional folders for web projects. As you build the project, you'll fill up these folders and build files.

Start by setting the SBT version you're going to use for the weKanban project in the project/build.properties file:

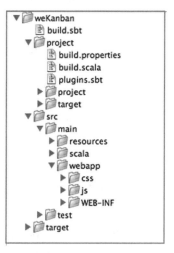

Figure 6.3   WeKanban project structure

```
sbt.version=0.12.0
```

The only purpose of the build.properties file is to set the value of the sbt.version key. In this case, it's set to version 0.12.0. SBT will automatically download the version specified in the properties file if it's not available locally. Next, add project-related build information inside the build.sbt file:

```
name := "weKanban"

organization := "scalainaction"

version := "0.1"
```

```
scalaVersion := "2.10.0"

scalacOptions ++= Seq("-unchecked", "-deprecation")
```

Remember to separate each setting expression with an empty new line so that SBT can parse each expression .sbt file. When SBT loads a .sbt file, it creates a `Seq[Setting[T]]` of all the expressions defined in the .sbt file.

To add web support for your project, you'll use the SBT web plug-in (https:// github.com/siasia/xsbt-web-plugin) that uses the Jetty web server (http://jetty .codehaus.org/jetty/). This plug-in adds tasks to the SBT build to start and stop the web server. Add the following line to the project/plugins.sbt file:

```
libraryDependencies <+= sbtVersion {v =>
  "com.github.siasia" %% "xsbt-web-plugin" % (v+"-0.2.11.1")
}
```

This adds the web plug-in as a dependency to the project. Adding the plug-in is nothing more than adding a library dependency to the build definition. The `<+=` method allows you to compute a new list element from other keys. Here the `sbtVersion` key is used to determine the exact version number for the plug-in. In fact, the `apply` method of the `sbtVersion` is used to compute the version of the plug-in:

```
libraryDependencies <+= sbtVersion.apply {v =>
  "com.github.siasia" %% "xsbt-web-plugin" % (v+"-0.2.11.1")
}
```

Before using the plug-in to start and stop the project, you have to add Jetty dependencies to the build definition inside build.sbt:

```
libraryDependencies ++= Seq(
  "org.eclipse.jetty" % "jetty-servlet" % "7.3.0.v20110203" % "container",
  "org.eclipse.jetty" % "jetty-webapp" % "7.3.0.v20110203" % "test,
    container",
  "org.eclipse.jetty" % "jetty-server" % "7.3.0.v20110203" % "container"
)
```

Note that the Jetty dependencies are added into the container scope. Additionally, `jetty-web` is added into test scope. The scope (http//scala-sbt.org) allows SBT keys to have values in more than one context. Think of scope as a name-spacing mechanism that allows a key to have different values in different scopes. For example, in a multi-project build, you could have the `sbtVersion` key value set to a different version of Scala for each project. This is useful for plug-ins because scoping allows plug-ins to create tasks that don't conflict with other task names. To include all the tasks from the plug-in to your project, you have to import the settings from the plug-in project into your build.sbt file as follows:

```
seq(com.github.siasia.WebPlugin.webSettings :_*)
```

If everything goes well in your SBT prompt, you should see additional tasks under the container scope (you might have to invoke the `reload` task):

```
> container:
apps                 classpath-types        configuration
configuration-files  configuration-xml      custom-configuration
discovered-contexts  full-classpath         managed-classpath      port
reload               start
state                stop                   streams                this-
project-ref          update
```

To start the web server, run the `container:start` task, and it will start the Jetty server at port number 8080. Because SBT forks a new process to run the Jetty server, you can execute other build actions in the SBT console while the server is running. In http:// localhost:8080/ you should see the directory listing of the webapp folder. At this point you're done with your build setup. You'll add more dependencies when you need them. Now let's switch gears and talk about Scalaz, a framework for building web applications in Scala.

6.3   *Introducing the Scalaz HTTP module*

Scalaz (pronounced "Scala-zed") is a library written in the Scala programming language. The idea behind Scalaz is to provide general functions that aren't provided by the standard Scala API. This section introduces you to the HTTP module that comes with the core Scalaz distribution. And while you're using the HTTP module, I'll touch on some of the Scalaz core APIs that are used by the Scalaz HTTP module. Let me first introduce you to the Scalaz HTTP module and how you'll use it for your weKanban application.

6.3.1   *How the Scalaz HTTP library works*

In a nutshell, the Scalaz HTTP library is a wrapper over Java Servlet APIs. What the Scalaz HTTP library exposes is a way to write functions that transforms an HTTP request into a response. This exactly matches what was discussed in section 6.1, where I talked about mapping HTTP URLs to functions that take requests and return responses. The following is an example of what a web `Application` trait looks like in Scalaz:

```
trait Application[IN[_], OUT[_]] {
  def apply(implicit req: Request[IN]): Response[OUT]
}
```

The `Application` trait defines a single `apply` method that takes an instance of `request` and returns an instance of `response`. The easiest way to implement this method would be to create a factory method that takes a function to transform `request` to `response`. Here's how that would look:

```
object Application {
  def application[IN[_], OUT[_]](f: Request[IN] => Response[OUT])
      = new Application[IN,OUT] {
      def apply(implicit req: Request[IN]) = f(req)
  }
}
```

The `application` method creates a new instance of the `Application` trait by passing the function that takes a request and returns an instance of response. The type parameters used by the `Application` trait look quite different than what you saw in section 4.1—they're called *higher-kinded types* in Scala. Think of higher-kinded types as a way to specify a type of a parameter type (type of types). I know this is little confusing, so let's break it down a bit.

Another example of higher-kinded types

You've already seen an application for higher-kinded types in the Scalaz library, so now let's study an example to understand why higher-kinded types are so powerful. You've learned that higher-kinded types are nothing but a group of types, and when you have to write a function that could operate on a group of types, higher-kinded types are a common way to implement it. How would you implement a sum function that could operate on various types of Scala collections? One way would be to implement `sum` for all the collection types:

```
def sumList(xs: List[Int]): Int = xs.foldLeft(0)(_ + _)
def sumArray(xs: Array[Int]): Int = xs.foldLeft(0)(_ + _)
```

This isn't an effective way to implement a `sum` function, but if you create an abstraction for all the collections as a type, then you could write a generic `sum` function that works with that type. Let me show you what I mean here. First make your `sum` function work with all types that implement the + function. To achieve that, create a trait called `Summable` that's parameterized for type A:

```
trait Summable[A] {
  def plus(a1: A, a2: A): A
  def init: A
}
```

Now for each type that supports the + function, I'll implement this trait. The following is the implementation for `Int` and `String` types:

```
object IntSummable extends Summable[Int] {
  def plus(a1: Int, a2: Int): Int = a1 + a2
  def init: Int = 0
}
object StringSummable extends Summable[String] {
  def plus(a1: String, a2: String): String = a1 + a2
  def init: String = ""
}
```

Similarly you can implement this for other types. Now, to implement the logic to sum all the elements of a collection, use the `foldLeft` function, but this time you'll create a trait to abstract the `foldLeft` function for any higher-kinded type:

```
trait Foldable[F[_]] {
  def foldLeft[A](xs: F[A], m: Summable[A]) : A
}
```

Note that you're using the `Summable` trait created a minute ago. Now, for each type of Scala collection, implement this trait:

```
      object ListFoldLeft extends Foldable[List] {
        def foldLeft[A](xs:List[A],m:Summable[A]) =
          xs.foldLeft(m.init)(m.plus)
      }
      object ArrayFoldLeft extends Foldable[Array] {
        def foldLeft[A](xs:Array[A],m:Summable[A]) =
          xs.foldLeft(m.init)(m.plus)
      }
```

Using these traits you'll implement your generic sum function. Your generic sum function will take three parameters: the collection, the appropriate implementation of the Foldable trait, and the Summable trait for a given type:

```
      def sum[F[_], A](xs: F[A], f: Foldable[F], m: Summable[A]): A =
        f.foldLeft(xs, m)
```

Here you're parameterizing the sum function for the type of collection and the type of the objects the collection holds. Now to sum the list of integers and array of strings, you can use the previous sum function as follows:

```
      sum(List(1, 2, 3), ListFoldLeft, IntSummable)
      sum(Array("one", "two", "three"), ArrayFoldLeft, StringSummable)
```

Admittedly, a sum function like that is a little verbose and not as clean as invoking sum(List(1, 2, 3)) and sum(Array("one", "two", "three")), but let's defer this for the next chapter, where you'll see how you can improve your sum function. In a smaller context, this approach might look like a lot of work, but in a large context this is a powerful way to create abstractions, and you'll see some real-world examples of it in the next chapter.

Both request and response objects need to talk to the input stream and output stream to read and write HTTP parameters. But wouldn't it be nice if we could think of this input or output stream as a collection? The request and response would have a collection of bytes, and we could use all the collection API methods. Scalaz allows exactly that, using type parameters. Out of the box, you can parameterize Request or Response using scala.collection.Stream or scala.collection.Iterator. Here's one way to use the application method:

```
Application.application { req: Request[Stream] =>
  new Response[Stream] {
    ...
  }
}
```

The advantage of this is that now you can use all the collection methods to read and write without worrying too much about the input and output stream. And because Scala Stream is a nonstrict collection (see section 4.5), you only read from the input stream when you need it. Why do you need a higher-kinded type again? Because Stream is a collection and has its own parameter type, you have to say Stream of something. In this case it's Stream of bytes. The IN[_] and OUT[_] type parameters will get evaluated to Stream[Byte] and Stream[Byte] during runtime. You'll shortly see this Application trait in action.

NOTE   The conversion from `inputStream` to `Request[Stream]` happens through a class called `scalaz.http.InputStreamer` defined in the Scalaz HTTP module. This class in turn uses the Scalaz core library to convert `inputStream` to Scala Stream.

To deploy your web application in Jetty or any Java web container, you have to conform to the Java Servlet API. I mentioned earlier that Scalaz provides a wrapper around Java servlets, so you don't have to worry about that too much. Figure 6.4 shows how HTTP requests are handled in Scalaz when deployed in a web container.

Like a standard Java web application, Scalaz is configured using `web.xml`. Typically you map all the URLs to any of the subclasses of `scalaz.http.servlet.Scalaz-Servlet`. In this application you'll use `scalaz.http.servlet.StreamStreamServlet`. Usually this servlet is configured with the name of the `application` class (similar to the `Application` trait we saw earlier) that will handle all the `request` and `response`. You have to write this `application` class for your weKanban application. The main responsibility of the `servlet` class is to instantiate the `application` class and transform between the HTTP servlet request and servlet response to Scalaz's `scalaz.http.request.Request` and `scalaz.http.response.Response` objects.

When the web server (we're using Jetty) receives an HTTP request (see figure 6.4) it calls the `service` method of `ScalazServlet`. Inside the `service` method it transforms the HTTP servlet request to the Scalaz `Request` object and then invokes the `application` method of the `Application` trait configured in web.xml. Once the `application` method returns the Scalaz `response`, it transforms that `response` object back to the HTTP servlet response so that the web server can send the response back to the caller. With this new knowledge, let's move on and configure Scalaz to your SBT build. After this, you'll be ready to implement stories for your weKanban application.

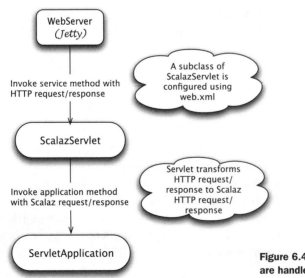

Figure 6.4   The way HTTP requests are handled by Scalaz

> ## Servlet lifecycle
>
> The lifecycle of the servlet is controlled by the web container (in this case, Jetty) in which the servlet is deployed. When the container receives a request that maps to a servlet, the container performs the following steps:
>
> - If the instance of the servlet doesn't exist, it creates one.
>
> - Initializes the servlet instance by calling the `init` method. You can override this `init` method to initialize anything you need before serving any request. You can also pass parameters to this `init` method. `ScalazServlet` overrides this `init` method to initialize the `application` class from the `init` parameter.
>
> - Servlet's `service` method is invoked by passing a `request` and `response` object. Typically servlet-based frameworks override this `service` method to invoke framework-specific classes. In the case of `ScalazServlet`, the `service` method transforms the HTTP request and response to Scalaz-specific request and response instances and invokes the `application` class to handle the request. Each Scalaz-based web application will provide the implementation of this application. (You'll see this class shortly.)

6.3.2 Configuring Scalaz with SBT

In order to configure Scalaz with SBT, Scalaz must be added as a dependency to your WeKanbanProjectDefinition.scala file. The following listing shows how it will look like after adding the Scalaz dependency.

Listing 6.1 build.sbt with Scalaz dependencies

```
name := "weKanban"

organization := "scalainaction"

version := "0.1"

scalaVersion := "2.10.0"

scalacOptions ++= Seq("-unchecked", "-deprecation")

libraryDependencies ++= Seq(
  "org.scalaz" %% "scalaz-core" % "6.0.3",
  "org.scalaz" %% "scalaz-http" % "6.0.3",
  "org.eclipse.jetty" % "jetty-servlet" % "7.3.0.v20110203" % "container",
  "org.eclipse.jetty" % "jetty-webapp" % "7.3.0.v20110203" % "test,
    container",
  "org.eclipse.jetty" % "jetty-server" % "7.3.0.v20110203" % "container"
)

seq(com.github.siasia.WebPlugin.webSettings :_*)
```

After adding Scalaz dependencies, if you reload and update your project from the SBT console, SBT will download the necessary Scalaz .jar files from the Scala snapshot repository. SBT will automatically look for dependencies that are compatible with the version of Scala your project is configured for. In the preceding project definition, notice that for `scalaz-core` and `scalaz-http` I'm using double `%%` rather than single `%`. This tells SBT to look for dependencies matching the Scala version of the project. If multiple Scala versions are configured, it will download dependencies for each configured version. Ideally you should use this pattern for declaring dependencies, but not all libraries in the Maven repository support the naming convention required by SBT to make the pattern work.

In the previous section you learned about Scalaz and how it works in the Java web server environment, but you haven't configured one. Let's do that right now. Start by creating web.xml. I'm not going to explain the entire web.xml file here, only the parts that are interesting for our purposes. The two most important things you need to configure in the web.xml file are the Scalaz servlet and the `application` class. The following listing shows what web.xml would look like.

Listing 6.2   Configuring web.xml for weKanban

```xml
<?xml version="1.0" encoding="utf-8"?>
<!DOCTYPE web-app PUBLIC
        "-//Sun Microsystems, Inc.//DTD Web Application 2.3//EN"
        "http://java.sun.com/dtd/web-app_2_3.dtd">
<web-app>
    <servlet>
        <servlet-name>Scalaz</servlet-name>
        <servlet-class>
            scalaz.http.servlet.StreamStreamServlet
        </servlet-class>
        <init-param>
            <param-name>application</param-name>
            <param-value>
                com.kanban.application.WeKanbanApplication
            </param-value>
        </init-param>
    </servlet>
    <servlet-mapping>
        <servlet-name>Scalaz</servlet-name>
        <url-pattern>/*</url-pattern>
    </servlet-mapping>
</web-app>
```

<- **Stream-based servlet to handle all HTTP servlet request**

<- **The application class**

Here you're using `StreamStreamServlet` as your `servlet` class. This servlet will create both a request and response of type `scala.collection.Stream` (discussed in the previous section). The `application` class you're going to use is `com.kanban.application.WeKanbanApplication`. When the Scalaz servlet is initialized, the `application` class that's passed as an `init-param` will be instantiated. Let's save this web.xml in the src/webapp/WEB-INF folder per the Java servlet convention.

Before you start the application, you have to create the missing `application` class `WeKanbanApplication`.

6.3.3 *Building your first web page using Scalaz*

Your `application` class needs to extend the `scalaz.http.servlet.StreamStream-`
`ServletApplication` trait. This trait declares an abstract value of type `scalaz.http`
`.servlet.ServletApplication`, which needs to be implemented, and then you're
done with the setup.

> **What if I want to roll out my own servlet?**
>
> It's somewhat easy to create a servlet that extends `ScalazServlet`. The only thing
> you have to do is provide parameter type values for the request, response, and type
> of `application` class you're going to use. For example, the `StreamStreamServlet`
> you're using looks like the following in the Scalaz codebase:
>
> ```
> final class StreamStreamServlet extends
>     ScalazServlet[Stream,Stream,StreamStreamServletApplication]
>     (classOf[StreamStreamServletApplication])
> ```
>
> Because `StreamStreamServletApplication` is used for the `application` class,
> you have to extend that for your `application` class. The only requirement for the
> `application` class or trait is to provide a method or value called `application` that
> is of type `ServletApplication`.

The only abstract method defined in the `ServletApplication` trait is this:

```
def application(implicit servlet: HttpServlet,
    servletRequest: HttpServletRequest,
    request: Request[IN]) : Response[OUT]
```

This `application` method isn't that much different from the one I started this discussion with (section 6.4.1). Because you're using a servlet to handle the HTTP request and response, Scalaz is providing access to the underlying `HttpServlet` and `HttpServletRequest`. But for this application we'll stick to Scalaz Request.

The only thing that will look new to you is the `implicit` keyword before the servlet parameter. The beauty of declaring the `implicit` parameter[6] is that, if such a method misses its arguments for implicit parameters, the compiler will automatically provide such an argument by looking up the implicit value matching the type of the argument in the enclosing scope. Implicits are a powerful concept in Scala. Chapter 7 looks into `implicit` in detail.

I think you're ready to implement your Scalaz `application` class. Here's how it looks right now:

```
final class WeKanbanApplication extends StreamStreamServletApplication {

  val application = new ServletApplication[Stream, Stream] {

    def application(implicit servlet: HttpServlet,
        servletRequest: HttpServletRequest,
```

---

[6] David R. MacIver, "An Introduction to Implicit Arguments," March 3, 2008, http://mng.bz/TqwD.

```
        request: Request[Stream]) = {
    }
  }
}
```

You're extending the `StreamStreamServletApplication` to create your `application` class because it's enforced by the Scalaz servlet you're using to handle all the HTTP request and response. The only abstract value you have to implement is `application`, and the preceding code does that by providing an implementation of the `application` method. Right now the method isn't doing anything. The quickest way to verify your configuration and setup is to add a static HTML file that you'll load using your `application` class. This way you'll know that your environment is working properly.

To load any static resource from the web context (in this case, src/main/webapp), Scalaz provides a useful method called `resource`. Using this method, you can load any existing resource requested:

```
HttpServlet.resource(x => OK << x.toStream, NotFound.xhtml)
```

Here the `resource` method will try to load the resource from the filesystem relative to your web context path and, if found, invoke the first parameter passed to it. The first parameter is a function that takes `Iterator[Byte]` and returns a `Response[Stream]`. You can invoke the `resource` method in the following way as well:

```
def found(x: Iterator[Byte]) : Response[Stream] = OK << x.toStream

resource(found, NotFound.xhtml)
```

`OK` (`scalaz.http.response.OK`) is one of the case classes created for HTTP status code, and it corresponds to status code 200. Now when you invoke the `<<` method on a Scalaz status code object, it converts that to an empty Scalaz `Response` object. Once it's converted to a `Response` object, `<<` appends the stream to the body of the response. With `OK << x.toStream`, you create a Scalaz `Response` object with the contents of the requested resource. Similarly, `NotFound` is a case class representing HTTP status code 404; when calling the `xhtml` method, it implicitly gets converted to a Scalaz `Response` object with an HTTP header value for a content-type of "application/ xhtml+xml." This is a good example of how you can use higher-order functions and combine functions to create nice APIs like the preceding example. Chapter 4 talks about higher-order functions and functional compositions at length. After putting all these pieces together, your application looks like the following listing.

Listing 6.3   WeKanban application so far

```
package com.kanban.application

import scalaz._
import Scalaz._
import scalaz.http._
import response._
import request._
import servlet._
```

```
import HttpServlet._
import Slinky._

final class WeKanbanApplication extends StreamStreamServletApplication {
  val application = new ServletApplication[Stream, Stream] {
    def application(implicit servlet: HttpServlet, servletRequest:
     HttpServletRequest, request: Request[Stream]) = {
      def found(x: Iterator[Byte]) : Response[Stream] = OK << x.toStream
      HttpServlet.resource(found, NotFound.xhtml)
    }
  }
}
```

WeKanbanApplication is the application class that you created by extending the
StreamStreamServletApplication trait. To create a valid Scalaz application class,
you have extended this trait.

The StreamStreamServletApplication trait defines a single abstract value called
application of type ServletApplication that you've overridden with the new ServletApplication.

The ServletApplication trait also defines an abstract method called application
that takes servlet, HTTP request, and Scalaz request as parameters. This method is the
core of the Scalaz-based web application and is invoked for each HTTP request that's
mapped to ScalazServlet.

So far, your application can only handle static content (you'll change this little fact
in the next chapter), and to load static content you're using the Scalaz library method
called resource that takes two parameters. The first parameter to the method is the
function Iterator[Byte] => A (here A is Stream) that looks for the static content for
the path specified in the request and loads the content as bytes. In the nested found
function, you're transforming the Iterator of bytes to a Scalaz response. The second
parameter is another function that gets called when no static content is found. Not-
Found is a status case class defined in Scalaz that represents the 404 HTTP status code,
and xhtml will create a 404 Scalaz response.

Let's create a simple index.html file under src/main/webapp as a placeholder for
your weKanban application, as follows:

```
<html>
    <body>
      <h1>weKanban board will come shortly</h1>
    </body>
</html>
```

Now go into your SBT console (you can always start the SBT console by typing sbt
under the project folder) and run the jetty-run build action. This will start the Jetty
server in the background, and your application should be deployed automatically provided all the steps have been followed properly. Point your browser at http://local-
host:8080/index.html, and you'll see the placeholder page.

Go ahead and pat yourself on the back, because you're done with the Scalaz and
SBT setup and are ready to implement your weKanban application.

6.4   *Summary*

This chapter was your first step in building a medium-sized Scala application. For the first time you moved outside the RPEL to build a Scala application. You used SBT. You learned how to work with it, configure it, and manage dependencies, which is important when it comes to building large Scala applications. You used Scalaz's HTTP module to build your web application. You also learned how functional programming concepts could be used in web applications. And you saw how Scalaz is using Scala's higher-order functions and pattern matching to expose nice APIs.

This chapter has provided enough background for you to work with various Scala tools to build your next application. In this chapter, you spent most of your time laying the groundwork for your weKanban application, and you haven't finished any of the stories you started with. To complete any of the stories mentioned in section 6.2, you have to figure out a way to talk to persistence storage. The next chapter explores some of the tools available for talking to databases from Scala and completing your application.

Connecting to a database

This chapter covers

- Setting up a database from SBT
- Connecting to a database from weKanban using Squeryl
- Finishing the weKanban application

In chapter 6 you learned how to create a simple web application using the Simple Build Tool (SBT) and the Scalaz HTTP module. But the application you set out to build in the previous chapter wasn't complete. The reason: to build a functional Kanban application, your application needs to store information such as stories and its status into persistent storage.

> **NOTE** This chapter is an extension of chapter 6, so if you haven't read that chapter, some parts in this chapter related to Scalaz and SBT could be hard to follow.

In this chapter you'll complete the weKanban application started in chapter 6. You'll learn how to retrieve and store information in a relational database. I introduce a Scala Object Relational Mapping (ORM) tool called Squeryl to communicate with the database. You'll also explore how to model database tables in a type-safe manner. You'll build a new screen for adding new stories to the application and a screen that displays all the stories added to the Kanban board. In the process of building these screens, you'll explore how to work with databases from Scala applications. Even though the focus of the chapter is working with a database, I will show you bits of Scalaz and SBT that are required to connect all the pieces. Before building our application, let's recap all the stories you need to implement the complete weKanban application:

> *As a customer I want to create a new user story so that I can add stories to the ready phase.*

> *As a developer I want to move cards (stories) from one phase to another to signal progress.*

Let's start by building a screen that will allow users to add a new story to the weKanban board.

7.1   Adding a new story to a weKanban board

The first thing to work on is adding a new story to the board, because without that it would be difficult to do anything with the board. Adding a story means you have to worry about the persistence store. Enterprise developers use relational databases to persist information in tables, and I suggest using the open source Java SQL database called H2 (www.h2database.com/html/main.html). Actually, you're free to pick any of the following databases: Postgres, Oracle, MySQL, and DB2. The reason I restrict you to this predefined list is because the Scala Object Relational Mapping (ORM) library you'll use for your application, called Squeryl (http://squeryl.org/ index.html), can only support those databases at the time of writing.

> **NOTE**   Using a schema-free database like MongoDB could be argued for this application, but I want to focus on a more traditional relational database solution to help you see how to work with the relational database management system (RDBMS) in Scala. You're free to experiment with other types of databases.

7.1.1   Connecting to a database using Squeryl

So why use Squeryl to access a database? First it's popular in the Scala community. It also provides a nice, simple DSL to talk to a database. Even though it's fine to use JDBC directly from Scala, you'll use Squeryl to learn an ORM tool that's completely written in Scala. Scala's strong type system is perfect for creating a type-safe ORM tool. I encourage you to play with other Scala ORM tools like ScalaQuery[1] and Querulous[2] to know your options.

For now, add Squeryl as an SBT dependency to `WeKanbanProjectDefinition` `.scala`—and while you're there, add H2 as well, as shown in the following listing.

---

[1]   A fork of SLICK to keep old links to the ScalaQuery repository alive, http://github.com/szeiger/scala-query.

[2]   Querulous, an agreeable way to talk to your database, http://github.com/nkallen/querulous.

Listing 7.1 Complete weKanban `build.sbt` project definition

```
name := "weKanban"

organization := "scalainaction"

version := "0.2"

scalaVersion := "2.10.0"

scalacOptions ++= Seq("-unchecked", "-deprecation")

libraryDependencies ++= Seq(
  "org.scalaz" %% "scalaz-core" % "6.0.3",
  "org.scalaz" %% "scalaz-http" % "6.0.3",
  "org.eclipse.jetty" % "jetty-servlet" % "7.3.0.v20110203" % "container",
  "org.eclipse.jetty" % "jetty-webapp" % "7.3.0.v20110203" % "test,
    container",
  "org.eclipse.jetty" % "jetty-server" % "7.3.0.v20110203" % "container",
  "com.h2database" % "h2" % "1.2.137",
  "org.squeryl" % "squeryl_2.10" % "0.9.5-6"
)
seq(com.github.siasia.WebPlugin.webSettings :_*)
```
◁ **Add Squeryl dependency**

◁ **Add H2 dependency**

By now you know what you have to do to update your SBT dependencies. For your Kanban board the story should have three attributes: a story number that identifies the story uniquely, a title describing the story, and the phase the story is in. The following is how you represent a story class in Scala:

```
class Story(val number: String, val title: String, val phase: String)
```

To make this class work with Squeryl, you have to do a couple of simple setups. First you have to tell Squeryl you need a table that will store all the stories for you in the database. The way to do that in Squeryl is to create a subclass of `org.squeryl.Schema`. Think of this class as equivalent to a database schema where you'll keep all the data definitions of an application. The following code defines the schema with a table called "STORIES" for your `Story` class:

```
package com.kanban.models

import org.squeryl._

object KanbanSchema extends Schema {
  val stories = table[Story]("STORIES")
}
```

Save this as the file KanbanSchema.scala under src/main/scala/com/kanban/models. One thing to note here is I'm defining the table in a type-safe manner. The `stories` value now represents the database table "STORIES," and you can invoke various types of queries on the `stories` object without worrying about type and always get back story type objects.

> **NOTE**   Most ORM tools use some kind of external configuration file to specify
> schema and domain model mapping information. But because Scala is a DSL-
> friendly and expressive language, it's common for Scala tools to use the Scala
> language itself for configuration. You've already seen examples of this in SBT
> and now in Squeryl. The next time you think you need to have an external con-
> figuration/properties file, think how you can express that in the Scala language.

Next, configure Squeryl to use the H2 database. Before connecting to the database,
make sure that the H2 database server is running. It's simple to start the H2 server—all
you have to do is provide the h2 .jar files in the path:

```
java -cp ~/.ivy2/cache/com.h2database/h2/jars/h2*.jar org.h2.tools.Server
```

This is a little ugly because you have to dig into the location where SBT stores all your
runtime dependencies (ivy cache). It would be better if you could start and stop the
H2 server as you can for the Jetty server. Unfortunately SBT doesn't come with built-in
support for H2, so you have to create new tasks for H2. The good news is that it's easy
to add new build tasks to SBT, but for that we have to make changes to the build.scala
file. SBT provides lots of helper methods to create custom tasks, but here the tasks are
implemented by methods in build.scala. Copy the code from the following listing into
your build.scala file.

Listing 7.2   build.scala file to define a custom task

```
import sbt._                                                 Explanation is in
import Keys._                                                the following
                                                         ◁   sidebar
object H2TaskManager {
  var process: Option[Process] = None
  lazy val H2 = config("h2") extend(Compile)

  val startH2 = TaskKey[Unit]("start", "Starts H2 database")
  val startH2Task = startH2 in H2 <<= (fullClasspath in Compile) map {
   cp =>
    startDatabase {
      cp.map(_.data)
        .map(_.getAbsolutePath())
        .filter(_.contains("h2database"))
    }
  }

  def startDatabase(paths: Seq[String]) = {
    process match {
      case None =>
        val cp = paths.mkString(System.getProperty("path.separator"))
        val command = "java -cp " + cp + " org.h2.tools.Server"
        println("Starting Database with command: " + command)
        process = Some(Process(command).run())
        println("Database started ! ")
      case Some(_) =>
        println("H2 Database already started")
    }
  }
```

```
    val stopH2 = TaskKey[Unit]("stop", "Stops H2 database")
    val stopH2Task = stopH2 in H2 :={
      process match {
        case None => println("Database already stopped")
        case Some(_) =>
          println("Stopping database...")
          process.foreach{_.destroy()}
          process = None
          println("Database stopped...")
      }
    }
}

object MainBuild extends Build {
 import H2TaskManager._
 lazy val scalazVersion = "6.0.3"
 lazy val jettyVersion = "7.3.0.v20110203"

 lazy val wekanban = Project(
   "wekanban",
   file(".")).settings(startH2Task, stopH2Task)
}
```

> **Build definition of weKanban** ⤶

> **1 Project definition with tasks** ⤶

The build.scala file is doing a couple of things here. First it defines the project **1** by providing name, locations, and settings. The project inherits settings from the build definition by default and along with that I've added two new tasks: `startH2Task` and `stopH2Task`. These tasks are now part of the project settings and can be used to start and stop the H2 database.

The second thing is the versions of the `scalazVersion` and `jettyVersion` are declared as a lazy val. The benefit of this is you don't have to repeat the version number multiple times when declaring dependencies in the build.sbt file:

```
libraryDependencies ++= Seq(
  "org.scalaz" %% "scalaz-core" % scalazVersion,
  "org.scalaz" %% "scalaz-http" % scalazVersion,
  "org.eclipse.jetty" % "jetty-servlet" % jettyVersion % "container",
  "org.eclipse.jetty" % "jetty-webapp" % jettyVersion % "test, container",
  "org.eclipse.jetty" % "jetty-server" % jettyVersion % "container",
  "com.h2database" % "h2" % "1.2.137",
  "org.squeryl" % "squeryl_2.10" % "0.9.5-6"
)
```

Yes, you can share the settings and vals from the build.scala file to build.sbt files. In fact it's a common practice to declare common things in build.scala files and use them in build.sbt files. In the end, all the settings from various files are combined into one sequence of settings.

After the build definitions are reloaded, you'll see two new tasks, `h2:start` and `h2:stop`:

```
> h2:st
start   stop
```

How h2:start and h2:stop tasks are implemented

Creating new tasks in SBT is simple: create a TaskKey and assign a closure that implements the task. Because you want to play nice with other custom tasks and plug-ins, a new scope is created for H2 tasks:

```
lazy val H2 = config("h2") extend(Compile)
```

This line creates a new config name "h2" and extends the `Compile` config. The `Compile` config will provide the necessary `classpath` setting you need to run the tasks. The new config will create a new scope for you, and the tasks will be available under it.

The `startH2` task is implemented by the `startDatabase` method. This method expects a sequence of paths that point to the H2 database .jar files you need to start the database. Because the `H2` config extends `Compile` config, you can easily use the `fullClasspath` setting at Compile scope to tap into the `classpath`. And the `<<=` method in SBT helps to create a new setting that depends on other settings. The following code snippet maps the path information from `fullClasspath` in Compile scope and creates a new function that will get executed for the start task:

```
val startH2Task = startH2 in H2 <<= (fullClasspath in Compile) map {
       cp =>
    startDatabase {
      cp.map(_.data)
        .map(_.getAbsolutePath())
        .filter(_.contains("h2database"))
    }
  }
```

The `startDatabase` method stores the reference of the process object so that it can be used in the `stopDatabase` method. The `stopDatabase` method is associated with the `h2:stop` task.

This will help you in working with H2 without leaving the comfort of the SBT console. When you run h2:start, it will automatically start the H2 database server at port 8082 and open your default browser with a login screen, as shown in figure 7.1.

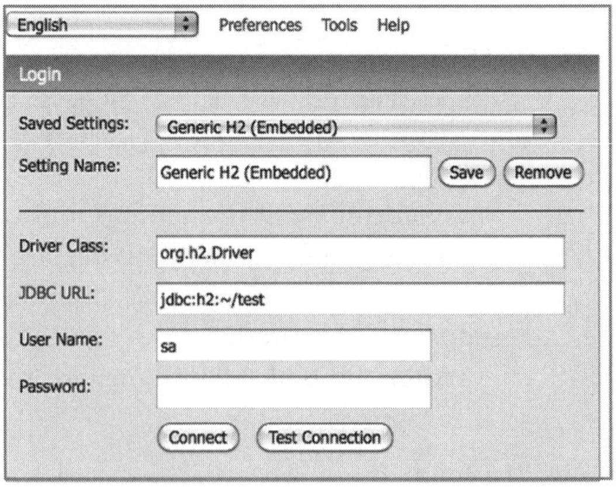

(If the browser doesn't open, try going to http://localhost:8082 directly from the browser.) Because the H2 server is running, let's switch focus to make Squeryl connect to this running server. To connect to the H2 server, use the following driver and database URL:

Figure 7.1 The H2 console

- JDBC Driver class: `org.h2.Driver`
- Database URL: `jdbc:h2:tcp://localhost/~/test`
- User name: `sa`

All this information and more is available in the H2 documentation (www.h2database.com/html/quickstart.html). The following listing adds an `init` method to the `KanbanSchema` class to connect to the H2 database.

Listing 7.3   KanbanSchema with init method for database connection

```scala
package com.kanban.models

import org.squeryl._
import org.squeryl.adapters._
import org.squeryl.PrimitiveTypeMode._
import java.sql.DriverManager

object KanbanSchema extends Schema {
  val stories = table[Story]("STORIES")

  def init = {
    import org.squeryl.SessionFactory
    Class.forName("org.h2.Driver")
    if(SessionFactory.concreteFactory.isEmpty) {
      SessionFactory.concreteFactory = Some(()=>
        Session.create(
          DriverManager.getConnection("jdbc:h2:tcp://localhost/~/test",
            "sa", ""), new H2Adapter))        ◁─┐ H2Adapter
    }                                              provided by
  }                                                SQueryl
}
```

The `KanbanSchema` represents the schema definition of the weKanban application. The first thing to do is map the Story DOM with the STORIES table in the database using the `table` method defined in the Squeryl `Schema` class.

The `init` method is responsible for establishing a connection with the running H2 database. In the `init` method, import `org.squeryl.SessionFactory`. `Session-Factory` is similar to the database connection factory and is used in Squeryl to create new connections. Next, load the Java Database Connectivity (JDBC) driver for the H2 database using `Class.forName("org.h2.Driver")`. This driver will be used when you create a new database connection.

Creating a new connection in Squeryl means creating a new `Session`. This approach is similar to the popular ORM mapping tool in Java called Hibernate (www.hibernate.org), where the connection is encapsulated as `Session`. Think of a Squeryl session as a wrapper to a database-based connection with which you can control database transactions. The Squeryl `Session` instance provides additional methods like `log` and methods for binding/unbinding the session to the current thread. Note that `Session` saves the database connection to a thread local[3] variable so that each

---

[3]   "Class `ThreadLocal<T>`," Java Platform Standard Ed. 6, http://mng.bz/cqt0.

thread in the application gets its own connection. This is useful in web applications where you can have multiple users accessing your application at any point.

In Squeryl, the mechanism for creating new sessions needs to be defined in a variable called `concreteFactory`, defined in the `SessionFactory` object. By default the value of this variable is `None`. If the value of the `concreteFactory` is something other than `None`, you know it's initialized. And Squeryl expects `concreteFactory` to be a function that will create new sessions. In this case the function looks like the following:

```
() =>
    Session.create(
      DriverManager.getConnection("jdbc:h2:tcp://localhost/~/test",
                              "sa", ""), new H2Adapter))
```

Here you're calling the utility method defined in the `Session` object called `create` by passing a database connection and the adapter. The Java `DriverManager` takes the connection URL to the H2 database, username, and password to create a new connection. Squeryl defines adapter classes for each supported database type, and in this case you're using `H2Adapter` for the H2 database. Because the type of the `concreteFactory` is `Option[()=>Session]`, you need to wrap your function with the `Option` value `Some`.

Because you've defined the `stories` object to represent the `"STORIES"` table, this won't create tables in the database. You have to explicitly do that. In some cases you'd rather create database tables using SQL scripts, but here you'll use Squeryl to create the schema for you. Do that by adding a main method to your `KanbanSchema` class so that you can use SBT to run it whenever you need it:

```
def main(args: Array[String]) {
    println("initializing the weKanban schema")
    init
    inTransaction { drop ; create }
}
```

Drop, create tables in weKanban schema

The `inTransaction` method defined by Squeryl runs the given closure in a database transaction. It creates a new transaction if none is in progress. Here in the transaction block, you're dropping all the tables and creating them back again. Right now the only table defined is `"STORIES."` Now when you execute the SBT run build action, it will invoke the main method and will create a fresh schema for you. Before running this action, make sure your H2 database is running (you can use `h2:start` to launch the H2 server). Now let's move on to saving a new story to the database.

7.1.2 *Saving a new story to the database*

To insert a row into the database using Squeryl, you have to call the `insert` method defined in the `org.squeryl.Table` class, which takes an instance of a model and saves it to the database. You already have a table object called `stories` in your `WeKanban-Schema` object that points to the "STORIES" table in the database. If you create an instance of `Story` and pass it to the `insert` method, you can save a `Story` to the database. So far the `Story` class looks like the following:

```
class Story(val number: String, val title: String, val phase: String)
```

Before saving an instance of Story to the database, you have to add validation. For example, both the number and title properties of Story should be nonempty, and because the story number should uniquely identify a story, you have to make sure that the number value is unique too. Checking whether a field is empty is simple; here's how it's implemented:

```
class ValidationException(message: String) extends RuntimeException(message)

private[this] def validate = {
   if(number.isEmpty || title.isEmpty) {
     throw new ValidateException("Both number and title are required")
   }
}
```

Add this `validate` method to the Story class and invoke it before saving it to the database. Here you've created a custom exception called ValidatationException that you'll use for all the validation failures.

> **NOTE** You didn't define any primary key for your Story class but instead used number as a unique key. This is okay for the small application you're building here, but in the real world you should have a surrogate key as primary key for your model classes. To add an autoincrement id field to your domain class, you can extend the KeyedEntity[A] trait. You can also use KeyedEntity to create composite keys. For more information, see the Squeryl documentation.

To check the uniqueness of the number field, you have to query the "STORIES" table to make sure there's no other story with the same number. Squeryl provides a nice method called where in table objects that you can easily use to achieve that. The where method takes a predicate function to filter out rows from the result. Here's how to check the uniqueness of a story number using the where method:

```
if(!stories.where(a => a.number === number).isEmpty) {
   throw new ValidationException ("The story number is not unique")
}
```

Here using the function a => a.number === number (=== is the equality operator defined by Squeryl), you're only selecting the stories that match the given story number. If that results in anything other than an empty collection, then the given number isn't unique. Note that the where method returns a lazy iterable called Query defined by the class org.squeryl.Query. The query is only sent to the database when you start the iteration. After adding this validation, the validate method now looks like the following:

```
private[this] def validate = {
   if(number.isEmpty || title.isEmpty) {
     throw new ValidationException ("Both number and title are required")
   }
   if(!stories.where(a => a.number === number).isEmpty) {
     throw new ValidationException ("The story number is not unique")
   }
}
```

Now, before inserting the new story into the database, you'll invoke this `validate` method to make sure the story is valid. You also have to run under a database transaction so you can commit or roll back your changes when saving the story instance (more on this later). For now, let's add a method called `save` to our `Story` class. But what should you return from the method? Well, you could return a success message that the story is created successfully, but what if something goes wrong while saving to the database? In those cases I prefer `scala.Either` (discussed in chapter 4), which allows you to return both success and error responses. This will also help the caller of the `save` method to handle both scenarios gracefully (you'll see that shortly). Here's the complete `Story` class after adding both the `validate` and `save` methods.

Listing 7.4   Story class with validate and save methods

```
package com.kanban.models

import org.squeryl._
import org.squeryl.PrimitiveTypeMode._
import org.squeryl.annotations._
import KanbanSchema._

class Story(val number: String, val title: String, val phase: String){

  private[this] def validate = {                                    ← Validate story
    if(number.isEmpty || title.isEmpty) {                              number, title ❶
      throw new ValidationException ("Both number and title are required")
    }
    if(!stories.where(a => a.number === number).isEmpty) {
      throw new ValidationException ("The story number is not unique")
    }
  }

  def save(): Either[Throwable, String] = {                          ← Validate,
    tx {                                                               insert new
      try {                                                            story
        validate
        stories.insert(this)
        Right("Story is created successfully")
      } catch {
        case exception: Throwable => Left(exception)
      }
    }
  }
}
object Story {                                                      ← Companion
  def apply(number: String, title: String) =                          object for
    new Story(number, title, "ready")                                 Story
}

class ValidationException(message: String) extends                  ← Extend
    RuntimeException(message)                                          RuntimeException
```

Here in the `Story` class you added two new methods, `validate` and `save`. Inside the `validate` method you do a couple of validation checks. First you're checking whether the story number or title is empty because neither can be empty. If either is empty, you throw the `ValidationException` created in ❶. The second validation involves going to the database and making sure that the given story number is unique. Here you're using the built-in method called `where`, available to all table objects. The `where` method takes a function that filters out stories based on a Boolean expression (similar to the `filter` method defined in the Scala collection library). In your function you're matching on story number `a => a.number === number`, where a represents a story saved in the database. If the `where` method results in a nonempty collection, you throw `ValidationException` for a nonunique story number.

The `save` method first calls the `validate` method to make sure the story is valid and then invokes the `insert` method defined in the `stories` table object to save it to the database. Both method calls are wrapped in a closure of the `tx` method. The `tx` method is responsible for initiating `SessionFactory.concrete` and the database transaction. This method is defined in `KanbanSchema`, and you'll see it shortly. Because `save` could result in both success and failure, I'm using `scala.Either` as a return type of the `save` method. This helps to communicate to the caller of the method that expects both success and failure. In Scala, using `scala.Either` is a more common idiom than throwing exceptions from public methods. Additionally, you created a companion object for `Story` to create new story instances. The default phase for a new story is "Ready," because that's the first phase in the Kanban board.

The `tx` method in the previous code snippet makes sure that the Squeryl `Session-Factory` is initialized properly and starts a new transaction if no transaction exists. The `tx` method takes a function as a parameter and returns the response of the function. This function could be any closure or block of code that you want to run within a transaction boundary. The following listing shows the complete `KanbanSchema` object.

Listing 7.5 Complete `KanbanSchema` object

```
package com.kanban.models

import org.squeryl._
import org.squeryl.adapters._
import org.squeryl.PrimitiveTypeMode._
import java.sql.DriverManager

object KanbanSchema extends Schema {
  val stories = table[Story]("STORIES")

  def init = {
    import org.squeryl.SessionFactory
    Class.forName("org.h2.Driver")
    if(SessionFactory.concreteFactory.isEmpty) {
      SessionFactory.concreteFactory = Some(()=>
        Session.create(
          DriverManager.getConnection("jdbc:h2:tcp://localhost/~/test",
            "sa", ""),
          new H2Adapter))
    }
  }
```

```
def tx[A](a: =>A): A = {
  init
  inTransaction(a)
}

def main(args: Array[String]) {
  println("initializing the weKanban schema")
  init
  inTransaction { drop ; create }
}

}
```

◁ Initializes
   SessionFactory, starts
   transaction if required

The tx method takes a function and runs that function in the transaction. The inTransaction method defined by Squeryl checks whether there's any transaction in progress and, if so, it participates in the in-progress transaction—otherwise it creates a new one. The tx method first invokes the init method to make sure that Session-Factory.concreteFactory is initialized properly before initiating the transaction. The inTransaction will roll back if the given function throws an exception—otherwise the transaction is committed if there's no in-progress transaction. In case of an in-progress transaction, the given function will be executed and the result returned. The init method is explained in listing 7.2.

7.1.3   *Building the Create Story web page*

In this section you'll build the screen with which the user will create a new story and add it to the Kanban board. You'll also hook your Story model object with the input from the screen and complete the following feature of the weKanban application:

> *As a customer, I want to create a new user story so I can add stories to the ready phase.*

You can create dynamic web pages in Scala in many ways. You can use JSP, the Scala template engine (Scalate[4]), or Scala's built-in support for XML to generate XHTML. Here you'll use Scala's XML support to your advantage to generate XHTML web pages. It's simple and testable and will demonstrate some of Scala's XML capabilities (covered in chapter 2). For complex and large applications, this approach doesn't scale. In chapter 12 you'll explore Scala web frameworks that make building large web applications easy.

To represent each screen as XML, you'll create a view object that will be used by your WeKanbanApplication (see listing 5.3) class when sending the response. Figure 7.2 shows what the Create a new Story screen looks like.

Create a new Story

Story Number (uniquely identifies a story)

Title (describe the story)

Go to Kanban board

Figure 7.2   The Create a new Story screen

---

4   "Scalate: Scala Template Engine," Scalate 1.5.3, http://scalate.fusesource.org.

To create the screen in figure 7.2, see the following listing to create a `CreateStory` object under src/main/com/kanban/views.

Listing 7.6 `CreateStory` view object

```scala
package com.kanban.views

object CreateStory {
  def apply(message: String = "") =
    <html>
      <head>
        <title>Create new Story</title>
        <link rel="stylesheet" href="/css/main.css" type="text/css"
          media="screen" charset="utf-8"/>
      </head>
      <body>
        <span class="message">{message}</span>
        <div class="createStory">
          <form action="/card/save" method="post" accept-charset="utf-8">
            <fieldset>
              <legend>Create a new Story</legend>
              <div class="section">
                <label for="storyNumber">Story Number
                    <span class="subtle">
                           (uniquely identifies a story)
                    </span>
                </label>
                <input type="text" size="10" maxlength="10" minlength="3"
                  name="storyNumber" id="storyNumber"/>
              </div>
              <div class="section">
                <label for="title">Title
                    <span class="subtle">
                           (describe the story)
                    </span>
                </label>
                <textarea rows="5" cols="30" name="title"
                    id="title"></textarea>
              </div>
              <div class="section">
                <button type="submit">Save</button>
              </div>
            </fieldset>
          </form>
          <span class="linkLabel">
            <a href="/kanban/board">Go to Kanban board</a>
          </span>
        </div>
      </body>
    </html>
}
```

> ⟵ Success/error message

Here, in the `apply` method of the view object, you have the necessary HTML that when rendered will create a view like figure 7.2. Even though it's HTML, it's also valid XML or XHTML and can be used easily as an XML fragment inside Scala code. The return type of the `apply` method is `scala.xml.NodeSeq`, which is a sequence of XML nodes, and when rendering the string representation of the `NodeSeq` will return exact HTML code. Now let's tie this view to a URL so you can render this view. Copy all the static resources like CSS and JavaScript files from the accompanying code base of this book. The main.css file should go in the `webapp/css` folder, and JavaScript files should go in the `webapp/js` folder.

> **NOTE**   To save typing, you can copy view objects from the code available for download at https://github.com/nraychaudhuri/scalainaction.

So far in your Scalaz `application` class you've handled static resources using the `resource` method:

```
def application(implicit servlet: HttpServlet, servletRequest:
    HttpServletRequest, request: Request[Stream]) = {
  def found(x: Iterator[Byte]) : Response[Stream] = OK << x.toStream
  resource(found, NotFound.xhtml)
}
```

To handle dynamic resources like view objects, create a method called `handle` in the `application` class. This method will take the same parameters as the `application` method but will match on the URL on the request object. Typically web frameworks use a separate configuration file to map a URL to a resource or function. In convention-based frameworks like Rails, the `playframework` URL contains enough information to map to the appropriate function or action. Scalaz takes a different approach—it uses Scala's powerful pattern matching, where the URL is broken into an HTTP method and URL parts as List. For example, a request object with the URL http://localhost:8080/card/create can be matched like this:

```
request match {
    case MethodParts(GET, "card" :: "create" :: Nil) => ...
    ...
}
```

The `MethodParts` is an extractor object (see section 3.7.1) that takes a Scalaz `Request` and returns `Option` with the HTTP method and URL parts as List. In the previous code snippet, `GET` is the HTTP method used to request the resource, and the second parameter is the URL broken into the List.

How an Extractor object works

In chapter 3 you learned how to use case classes for pattern matching, but pattern matching isn't restricted to case classes. You can use almost any object for pattern matching as long as it defines a method called `unapply`. Any object with the `unapply` method is called an Extractor object. For example, `MethodParts` in Scalaz is defined as the following:

```
object MethodParts {
   def unapply[IN[_]](r : Request[IN]) : Option[(Method,
    List[String])] = {
     Some(r.method, r.parts)
   }
  }
```

Here the unapply method takes an instance of the Scalaz request and returns a Some value of method and URL parts. The parts method returns all URL path elements separated by /.

When Scala encounters the pattern case MethodParts(...), it translates that to an invocation of MethodParts.unapply by passing the reference to the object that's used to match the pattern (in this case it's an instance of Scalaz request). Note that the apply method isn't necessary for pattern matching. It's typically used to mimic constructor calls. For example, you're using the apply method in the Story object to create a new instance of the Story class.

One rule to notice here is if you want to return some value from unapply, it then needs to be wrapped around the scala.Option type.

Sometimes you'll request this resource by passing a request parameter. For example, when a story is created successfully, you'll come back to the same "Create story" page but with a success message. To read a request parameter from a URL, use the ! method defined in the Scalaz Request object. Let's create a private method called param in your application class that will return a string value of the parameter or an empty string if the parameter isn't specified:

```
def param(name: String)(implicit request: Request[Stream]) =
    (request ! name).getOrElse(List[Char]()).mkString("")
```

The ! method of Scalaz Request returns Option[List[Char]] and you're converting that to a string. Now let's create the handle method by combining these pieces:

```
def handle(implicit request: Request[Stream],
    servletRequest: HttpServletRequest): Option[Response[Stream]] = {

  request match {
    case MethodParts(GET, "card" :: "create" :: Nil) =>
      Some(OK(ContentType, "text/html") << strict <<
    CreateStory(param("message"))))

   case _ => None
  }
}
```

Here, when the request matches both the HTTP method type and the URL, you're creating a response by invoking the CreateStory view object by passing the value of the request parameter message. OK(ContentType, "text/html") creates an empty Scalaz Response with the HTTP response header content-type represented by the Content-Type object. The << method allows you to add additional information to the response object. And because Scala encourages creating immutable objects, every time you call the << method, a new response object is created.

> **NOTE**   The strict used in the handle method is called the *doctype*. The doctype declaration isn't an HTML tag. It's an instruction to the web browser about what version of the markup language the page is written in. To adhere to strict HTML standards, the example is using the strict doctype.

In the application method (your entry point for all URLs) you'll invoke your new handle method. You can still keep the existing resource method so you can load static resources. The Scalaz core provides a method called | for the Option class and using it you can combine both handle and resource methods so that when the handle method returns None you can invoke the resource method as a fallback to load resources. Here's how the application method looks after changes:

```
def application(implicit servlet: HttpServlet,
    servletRequest: HttpServletRequest, request: Request[Stream]) = {

  def found(x: Iterator[Byte]) : Response[Stream] = OK << x.toStream
  handle | resource(found, NotFound.xhtml)
}
```

Because all the parameters to the handle method are implicit, you don't have to explicitly pass them, but you can. If the handle method returns None as a response, the resource method will be called, and you do that with the | method. If no resource is found matching the URL, then NotFound.xhtml is returned.

> **NOTE**   Scalaz uses Scala's implicit method conversion to add the | method to the Option class. If you're used to metaprogramming in Ruby, Groovy, or other programming languages, implicit conversions are Scala's way of doing metaprogramming but in a more controlled way. You'll explore implicit conversion in detail in the next chapter.

Now before going ahead with running the application, take a look at the following listing, showing the WeKanbanApplication class you have so far.

Listing 7.7   WeKanbanApplication with the handle method for creating a story

```
import scalaz._
import Scalaz._
import scalaz.http._
import response._
import request._
import servlet._
import HttpServlet._
import Slinky._
import com.kanban.views._
import com.kanban.models._

final class WeKanbanApplication extends StreamStreamServletApplication {
  import Request._
```

```
import Response._                                          │ Implicit charset value
implicit val charset = UTF8                              ◁┘ used by << method

def param(name: String)(implicit request: Request[Stream]) =      ◁┐ Return
    (request ! name).getOrElse(List[Char]()).mkString("")            │ parameter
                                                                     │ value as string
def handle(implicit request: Request[Stream],
    servletRequest: HttpServletRequest): Option[Response[Stream]] = {

    request match {
      case MethodParts(GET, "card" :: "create" :: Nil) =>
        Some(OK(ContentType, "text/html") << strict <<
      CreateStory(param("message"))))
      case _ => None
    }
}

val application = new ServletApplication[Stream, Stream] {

    def application(implicit servlet: HttpServlet,
      servletRequest: HttpServletRequest, request: Request[Stream]) = {
      def found(x: Iterator[Byte]) : Response[Stream] = OK << x.toStream
      handle | resource(found, NotFound.xhtml)          ◁┐ Invoke
    }                                                      │ handle
}                                                        ❶ method
}
```

Handle creates new story request ▷ (annotation pointing to `def handle` line)

Here you added two new methods to the existing `WeKanbanApplication` class to handle a new story request from the browser. The `handle` method matches the HTTP request to a function. So far, it only knows how to handle the create story request. Here you're using the Scalaz Extractor object called `MethodParts`, which breaks the Scalaz request into request type and URL parts. The HTTP `GET` request to the http://localhost:8080/card/create URL will be matched to `MethodParts(GET, "card" :: "create" :: Nil)`, where `GET` is the method type and `"card" :: "create" :: Nil` are the parts of the URL. And when it matches, it creates a new Scalaz response to render the create story screen using `Some(OK(ContentType, "text/html") << strict << CreateStory(param("message")))`. `CreateStory` is the name of the view object, and `OK(ContentType, "text/html") << strict` creates an empty Scalaz response with a strict HTML doctype.

The `param` method retrieves the parameter value for a given parameter name. You're using the `!` method defined in the Scalaz request to retrieve the parameter value and transform into a `String`. Scalaz by default uses `List[Char]` to represent a parameter value.

When the requested URL doesn't match the cases defined in the `handle` method, it returns `None` (default case). In case of `None`, the `application` method calls the `resource` method ❶ to load any static resource that matches the requested URL.

Now go to your SBT console and start the Jetty server using the `jetty-run` build action if it's not already running. This will start the server at port 8080. If you go to the http://localhost:8080/card/create URL, you'll see a screen similar to figure 7.2. That's great, but you still have to tie the Save button with the `save` method of the model object.

Clicking Save will result in an ugly error because you haven't linked the URL to any function in your `application` class. Fix that by adding a `MethodParts` to your `handle` method, which will match the URL ending with `/card/save` to the `saveStory` method defined in the `application` class:

```
def handle(implicit request: Request[Stream],
      servletRequest: HttpServletRequest): Option[Response[Stream]] = {
    request match {

      case MethodParts(GET, "card" :: "create" :: Nil) =>
        Some(OK(ContentType, "text/html") << strict <<
      CreateStory(param("message"))))

      case MethodParts(POST, "card" :: "save" :: Nil) =>
        Some(saveStory)

      case _ => None
   }
 }
```

> Match URL
> to saveStory
> method

The `saveStory` method will read the HTTP POST parameters from the request, instantiate an instance of the `Story` model class, and invoke the `save` method (see listing 7.3) on it. To read POST parameters from the request, add another utility method like the `param` method to your application class, but this time with a `!` because POST generally means a side-effect (section 5.1):

```
def param_!(name: String)(implicit request: Request[Stream]) =
    (request | name).getOrElse(List[Char]()).mkString("")
```

You know that the `save` method (see listing 7.3) in the `Story` class returns `scala.Either[Throwable, String]`, and in case of error it returns `Left` with the exception; otherwise `Right` with the success message. `Left` and `Right` are the only two subtypes of `Either`. You can easily use pattern matching and take appropriate actions. When `save` is successful, you'll redirect to the "Create story" screen with a success message so the user can create another story; in case of error you return to the "Create story" page, but this time with an error message. The following is how to implement the `saveStory` method:

```
private def saveStory(implicit request: Request[Stream],
      servletRequest: HttpServletRequest) = {
    val title  = param_!("title")
    val number = param_!("storyNumber")
    Story(number, title).save match {
      case Right(message) =>
        redirects[Stream, Stream]("/card/create", ("message", message))
      case Left(error) => OK(ContentType, "text/html") << transitional <<
          CreateStory(error.toString)
     }
   }
```

> To create
> screen with
> success

> To create
> screen with
> error

The `redirects` method is defined in the Scalaz `Response` object, which is already imported for the `application` class. The `redirects` method takes the relative URL and the parameters to the URL as a tuple.

NOTE It's always a good idea to redirect after a POST form submission to avoid double submission.

Before testing the save method, make sure the H2 database server is running (you can start H2 server using h2:start task). The next listing shows the complete application class you have so far.

Listing 7.8   Complete save story in `WeKanbanApplication`

```
final class WeKanbanApplication extends StreamStreamServletApplication {
  import Request._
  import Response._
  implicit val charset = UTF8

  def param_!(name: String)(implicit request: Request[Stream]) =
    (request | name).getOrElse(List[Char]()).mkString("")
  def param(name: String)(implicit request: Request[Stream]) =
    (request ! name).getOrElse(List[Char]()).mkString("")

  def handle(implicit request: Request[Stream],
      servletRequest: HttpServletRequest): Option[Response[Stream]] = {
    request match {
      case MethodParts(GET, "card" :: "create" :: Nil) =>
        Some(OK(ContentType, "text/html") << strict <<
      CreateStory(param("message")))
      case MethodParts(POST, "card" :: "save" :: Nil) =>          ◁─ POST request to /card/save
        Some(saveStory)
      case _ => None
    }
  }

  private def saveStory(implicit request: Request[Stream],     ◁─ Handle save new story request
      servletRequest: HttpServletRequest) = {
    val title  = param_!("title")
    val number = param_!("storyNumber")
    Story(number, title).save match {
      case Right(message) =>
            redirects[Stream, Stream]("/card/create", ("message", message))
      case Left(error) => OK(ContentType, "text/html") << strict <<
      CreateStory(error.toString)
    }
  }

  val application = new ServletApplication[Stream, Stream] {
    def application(implicit servlet: HttpServlet,
      servletRequest: HttpServletRequest, request: Request[Stream]) = {
      def found(x: Iterator[Byte]) : Response[Stream] = OK << x.toStream
      handle | resource(found, NotFound.xhtml)
    }
  }
}
```

Here you're extending the application class to handle the save story POST request. To handle the save story request, you added a new pattern matching expression to the handle method. Now the POST request made to /card/save will be matched by

`MethodParts(POST, "card" :: "save" :: Nil)`, and when it matches it invokes the `saveStory` method defined in the `application` class.

The `saveStory` method extracts the story number and title parameters from the Scalaz request and creates a new instance of the `Story` model object. The `save` method defined in the `Story` model object will validate and save the story in the database. In case of error, the `saveStory` method renders the `CreateStory` view object with the error message. When the save is successful it redirects to a new "Create story" screen. Here using the `scala.Either` type allows you to easily handle the error condition.

You're done adding new stories to the Kanban board. Next you'll build the Kanban board where all the stories will be displayed.

7.2   Building the Kanban board page

Now the focus will move to building the Kanban board. Your next user story:

> *As a developer I want to move cards (stories) from one phase to another so that I can signal progress.*

Figure 6.1 shows the prototype of the Kanban board you're supposed to build. To implement this story, you have to provide an ability to move cards from one phase to another. For example, a user of your Kanban board should be able to move a card from ready phase to development phase and vice versa. To implement drag-and-drop, use the jQuery-ui plug-in (http://jqueryui.com) for jQuery (http://jquery.com), a JavaScript framework that simplifies HTML, document traversing, event handling, and Ajax interactions for web development.

I don't focus on the jQuery library in detail here, but if you haven't used jQuery I encourage you to check the links. After you download the jquery-ui library, copy the JavaScript files to the js folder under the webapp folder of the weKanban project, as shown in figure 7.3. The main.js file is something you'll create shortly.

> **NOTE**   You can also copy the JavaScript files from the code that accompanies this book.

The draggable plug-in of jQuery adds draggable functionality to any DOM element, and all you have to do is invoke a `draggable` method to it. For example, if you want to make your stories draggable, invoke the `draggable` method on each DOM element that represents a story in the board. For now, you'll add a css class called `story` to each story to easily find them and make them draggable.

To make DOM elements droppable, call the `droppable` method by passing a function that can handle the drop event. In your board all the elements that represent phases (ready, dev, and so on) will be droppable.

But only implementing drag-and-drop in the web page isn't enough—you also have to update the database when a story moves from one phase to another so that when you come back to the board you can see the updated version. Because you've already decided to use jQuery, you'll use its Ajax features to make an HTTP POST call when a story moves from one phase to another. The next listing shows the completed main.js file that implements drag-and-drop for the Kanban board.

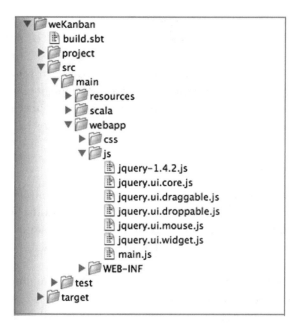

Figure 7.3 The weKanban project with JavaScript files for drag-and-drop

Listing 7.9 Implementing drag-and-drop for the weKanban board in the main.js file

```
function moveCard(storyNumber, phase) {

  $.post("/card/move",{storyNumber: storyNumber, phase: phase},
    function(message) {
           $('#message').html(message)                        ◁── Make POST
    });                                                            request
}

  function init() {
    $(function() {
            $(".story").each(function() {                     ◁── Add
              $(this).draggable();                                draggable
              });                                                 feature
            $("#readyPhase").droppable({                       ◁── Add
            drop: function(event, ui) {                           droppable
  moveCard(ui.draggable.attr("id"), "ready") }                    feature
            });
            $("#devPhase").droppable({
              drop: function(event, ui) {
  moveCard(ui.draggable.attr("id"), "dev") }
        });
            $("#testPhase").droppable({
              drop: function(event, ui) {
                      moveCard(ui.draggable.attr("id"), "test") }
            });
            $("#deployPhase").droppable({
              drop: function(event, ui) {
                      moveCard(ui.draggable.attr("id"), "deploy") }
        });
      });
}
```

In the init function you're making the element with the story class draggable and adding droppable functionality to all the phases identified by their ids. To implement droppable you've implemented the drop function, which gets invoked when an element is dropped. Inside the drop function you're calling the moveCard function by passing the id of the story that's dropped and the target phase. The job of moveCard is to make an Ajax POST call to the /card/move URL by passing both the story number and target phase. Now you'll create the view object for the Kanban board and the JavaScript code.

7.2.1 Creating the view for the Kanban board

To create the Kanban board view you have to retrieve all the stories from the database by phase. You have to show all the stories that are in the ready state, all the stories at dev state, and so on. At first all the stories that you create using the "Create story" view will be in the ready state. But once you implement the drag-and-drop features, you'll have stories in various phases.

At first, to select stories by phase, add a findAllStoriesByPhase method to the Story model object which will return a list of stories which you'd use to render the view. To implement the findAllStoriesByPhase method, use Squeryl's query DSL, which looks similar to SQL. First use Squeryl to find all the stories from the database and then apply a filter to the result to find stories matching a particular phase. To find all the stories from the database using Squeryl, you have to do the following:

```
from(stories)(s => select(s))
```

Here the from method returns an instance of Query, which takes a function that takes an instance of the story object and returns the same story object as select. But this isn't helpful because you want to filter the stories by phase; to do that, add a where method that will check for the phase, as in the following:

```
from(stories)(s => where(s.phase === phase) select(s))
```

The === method is added by an implicit method conversion to a String class so that the DSL looks like SQL's where clause. The Squeryl query returns an immutable instance of Query that's a lazy Iterable collection. At this point Squeryl has only created the query—it hasn't executed it in the database. It will execute the query the moment you try to access the first element in the collection. But because you're going to use this collection to render stories in your Kanban board view, let's change this to strict collection from lazy collection (covered in chapter 4) by invoking the map method, so that you access these instances of Story objects outside the transaction:

```
def findAllByPhase(phase: String) = tx {
  from(stories)(s => where(s.phase === phase) select(s)) map(s => s)
}
```

Here you're calling map on the Query object to create a collection of stories. But because you don't need to transform your story objects, the map is returning the parameter.

NOTE   You could use a different `method toXXX` methods defined in the Scala `Iterable` trait to transform to various types of collections. Here I'm using `map` to demonstrate that you can take the response from Squeryl and transform it if necessary.

Now in your `view` object you can invoke the `findAllByPhase` method by passing various phases to render the stories in the Kanban board. To create the view for the Kanban board, add a new `view` object under src/main/scala/com/kanban/views/ KanbanBoard.scala.

```
package com.kanban.views

import com.kanban.models._

object KanbanBoard {
}
```

The first thing you'll do is add a `header` method that will include all the JavaScript files you need to enable the drag-and-drop feature to your board:

```
private def header =
    <head>
        <meta charset="UTF-8" />
        <title>weKanban: A simple Kanban board</title>
        <script type="text/javascript" src="/js/jquery-1.4.2.js"/>
        <script type="text/javascript" src="/js/jquery.ui.core.js"/>
        <script type="text/javascript" src="/js/jquery.ui.widget.js"/>
        <script type="text/javascript" src="/js/jquery.ui.mouse.js"/>
        <script type="text/javascript" src="/js/jquery.ui.draggable.js"/>
        <script type="text/javascript" src="/js/jquery.ui.droppable.js"/>
        <script type="text/javascript" src="/js/main.js"/>
        <link type="text/css" href="/css/main.css" rel="stylesheet" />
        <script type="text/javascript">
        init()                                  ◁⌐ Invoke init method
        </script>                                  for drag-and-drop
    </head>
```

This `header` method, apart from adding all the JavaScript, also invokes the `init` method that's defined in the main.js to initialize the drag-and-drop functionality using jQuery. To render the stories you get back from the `findAllByPhase` method, add another method that will loop through the stories and create an `html div` element:

```
private def stories(phase: String) =
    for(story <- Story.findAllByPhase(phase)) yield
      <div id={story.number} class="story">
        <fieldset>
          <legend>{story.number}</legend>
          <div class="section">
            <label>{story.title}</label>
          </div>
        </fieldset>
      </div>
```

Here you're using a for-comprehension to loop through all the stories and creating a story `html` `div` element. This method returns a list of `scala.xml.NodeSeq` objects that you can easily insert into the body of HTML you're going to generate for the Kanban board. To tie all these pieces together, add the `apply` method to the `KanbanBoard` view object, which will create the Kanban board view, shown in the following listing.

Listing 7.10   Kanban board view

```scala
package com.kanban.views

import com.kanban.models._

object KanbanBoard {
  def apply()=
  <html>
  <head>{header}</head>                          ⟵ Add contents of header method
  <body>
    <h2 class="header">weKanban: Simple Kanban board</h2>
    <span id="message" class="message clearFloat"></span>
    <br/>
    <span class="linkLabel clearFloat"><a href="/card/create">[Add new story
     to Ready Phase]</a></span>
    <div class="phase" id="readyPhase">
      <h3 class="message" title="Stories ready for development. Limit is set
     to 3">Ready [3]</h3>
      {stories("ready")}                          ⟵ Render stories in ready phase
    </div>
    <div class="phase" id="devPhase">
      <h3 class="message" title="Stories in progress. Limit is set to 2">Dev
     [2]</h3>
      {stories("dev")}
    </div>
    <div class="phase" id="testPhase">
      <h3 class="message" title="Stories that are tested. Limit is set to
     2">Test [2]</h3>
      {stories("test")}
    </div>
    <div class="phase" id="deployPhase" title="Ready for production
     deployment">
      <h3 class="message">Deploy</h3>
      {stories("deploy")}
    </div>
  </body>
  </html>
                                                  ⟵ Create HTML to render stories
  private def stories(phase: String) =
    for(story <- Story.findAllByPhase(phase)) yield
      <div id={story.number} class="story">
        <fieldset>
          <legend>{story.number}</legend>
          <div class="section">
            <label>{story.title}</label>
          </div>
        </fieldset>
      </div>
```

```
private def header =                                    ⊲⌐ Include JavaScript
  <head>                                                   └ for drag-and-drop
      <meta charset="UTF-8" />
      <title>weKanban: A simple Kanban board</title>
      <script type="text/javascript" src="/js/jquery-1.4.2.js"/>
      <script type="text/javascript" src="/js/jquery.ui.core.js"/>
      <script type="text/javascript" src="/js/jquery.ui.widget.js"/>
      <script type="text/javascript" src="/js/jquery.ui.mouse.js"/>
      <script type="text/javascript" src="/js/jquery.ui.draggable.js"/>
      <script type="text/javascript" src="/js/jquery.ui.droppable.js"/>
      <script type="text/javascript" src="/js/main.js"/>
      <link type="text/css" href="/css/main.css" rel="stylesheet" />
      <script type="text/javascript">
      init()
      </script>
  </head>
}
```

The `KanbanBoard` view object is used to render the Kanban board in figure 7.4. Like the `CreateStory` view object, the `apply` method is responsible for rendering the Kanban board. The `apply` method calls the `header` method to add all the JavaScript files you need to add drag-and-drop functionality to your Kanban board. The contents of the `header` method get inserted in between the HTML head tags.

To render stories in each phase, the `apply` method invokes the `stories` method by passing the phase. The `stories` method is invoked for each phase in the Kanban board. The `stories` method uses a for-comprehension to generate the HTML required to render the result. The `findAllByPhase` method in the `Story` model class returns all the stories in a given phase from the database.

The last missing piece is to modify the `handle` method in the `WeKanbanApplication` class to handle the /kanban/board URL. Add the following case to the `handle` method:

```
case MethodParts(GET, "kanban" :: "board" :: Nil) =>
       Some(OK(ContentType, "text/html") << transitional << KanbanBoard())
```

If you rebuild and run the application again (if you're running ~prepare-webapp, the changes will be available to you automatically), the link "Go to Kanban board" will take you to the Kanban board screen displaying all the stories you created (figure 7.4).

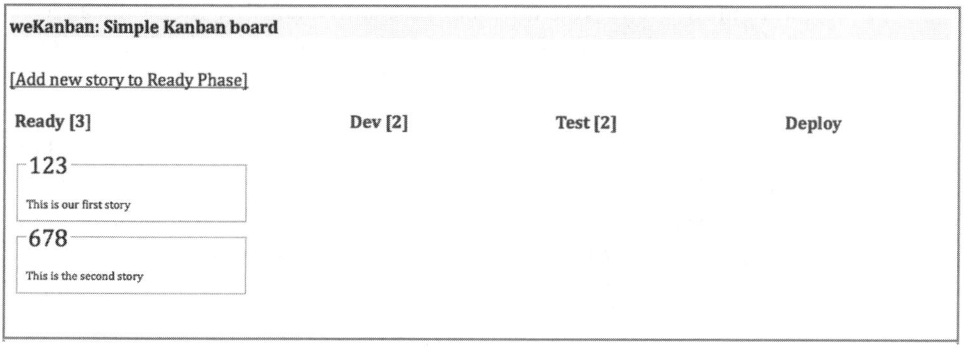

Figure 7.4   Kanban board with stories in ready phase

Even though you haven't implemented the move card functionality on the server side, in the UI you should be able to drag and drop cards from one phase to another. Because the server side logic isn't implemented, when you refresh the page all the stories will show up in ready phase again. To complete the move card story, you have to implement the move card logic in the server side.

7.2.2 *Moving cards in the Kanban board*

To implement moving cards from one phase to another, you have to update the phase of the story. For example, to move a story from the ready to the dev phase, you have to get the story number (the story number uniquely identifies a story) to find the story and update the phase. But the problem is, you aren't allowed to cross the limit set for the phase, so before updating the phase you have to check whether you're crossing the threshold of the phase you're moving to. The limit for ready is 3, for dev it's 2, and for test phase it's 2 stories. To validate that you aren't crossing the limit, add a validate method to the `Story` class; doing so will compute the total number of stories in a phase and throw an exception if you exceed the limit. For now, hardcode the limits for each phase inside the `Story` class:

```
private def phaseLimits = Map("ready" -> Some(3),
                    "dev" -> Some(2), "test" -> Some(2), "deploy" -> None)

private[this] def validateLimit(phase: String) = {
    val currentSize:Long =
            from(stories)(s => where(s.phase === phase) compute(count))
    if(currentSize == phaseLimits(phase).getOrElse(-1)) {
       throw new ValidationException("You cannot exceed the limit set for
            the phase.")
    }}
```

Set up limits for each phase ⊳ (annotation pointing to first two lines)

Compute number of rows ⊳ (annotation pointing to the from line)

Here you're selecting the number of stories in a given phase and checking with the hardcoded values in the `phaseLimits`. If the values match, you throw the validation exception. The `compute(count)` is a way to invoke a `count` function on the result of the `where` function. The `compute` Squeryl function is similar to the Squeryl `select` function except `compute` can invoke other aggregate functions like `count`. Check the Squeryl documentation[5] for all the available functions and operators.

Now, to move a story to a different phase, add another method, called `moveTo`, to the `Story` class. This method will take the target phase and validate whether you're crossing the limit. If everything is okay it will update the phase value of the story. This method will also return `Either[Throwable, String]` so that your Scalaz application class responds accordingly. To update a given row in the database, Squeryl provides an update method, which takes an instance of `table` (in this case it's the `stories` object defined in the `Schema` class) and a function that will update the row. To update a story identified by `this`, you can use the Squeryl update function like this:

---

[5] "Group and Aggregate Queries," http://squeryl.org/group-and-aggregate.html.

```
update(stories)(s =>
          where(s.number === this.number)
          set(s.phase := phase)
     )
```

Here, inside the function passed to update, you're first identifying the story you need to update using the where method and then invoking the set method by passing the target phase value. Here's the completed moveTo method defined in the Story class:

```
def moveTo(phase: String): Either[Throwable, String] = {
    tx {
      try {
        validateLimit(phase)                              Validate limit
        update(stories)(s =>                              for target phase
              where(s.number === this.number)             Update phase of
              set(s.phase := phase)                       story using set
        )
        Right("Card " + this.number + " is moved to " + phase + " phase
            successfully.")
      } catch {
        case exception: Throwable => Left(exception)
      }
    }
  }
```

To invoke this moveTo method from the application class you have to first find the story object using the story number. To find a story by its number, add a method called findByNumber to your singleton Story object. This method will query the "STORIES" table and find the one that matches the given story number. Here's how the method is implemented:

```
def findByNumber(number: String) =
tx { stories.where(s => s.number === number).single }
```

Here you're using the single method defined in the Squeryl Query object that returns the first row from the query. At this point you're all done with your model changes. Before you hook this new method to your application class, look at the following listing, which shows the complete implementation of the Story class.

Listing 7.11 Complete Story model implementation

```
package com.kanban.models

import org.squeryl._
import org.squeryl.PrimitiveTypeMode._
import org.squeryl.annotations._
import KanbanSchema._

class Story(val number: String, val title: String, val phase: String){

  private def phaseLimits = Map("ready" -> Some(3), "dev" -> Some(2),
      "test" -> Some(2), "deploy" -> None)                          Add limit
                                                                    per phase
  private[this] def validate = {
    if(number.isEmpty || title.isEmpty) {
      throw new ValidationException ("Both number and title are required")
```

Validate story number and title

```
    }
    if(!stories.where(a => a.number === number).isEmpty) {
      throw new ValidationException ("The story number is not unique")
    }
  }
```
Validate limit set for a phase
```
  private[this] def validateLimit(phase: String) = {
    val currentSize:Long =
            from(stories)(s => where(s.phase === phase) compute(count))
    if(currentSize == phaseLimits(phase).getOrElse(-1)) {
      throw new ValidationException ("You cannot exceed the limit set for
      the phase.")
    }
  }
```
Move card between phases
```
  def moveTo(phase: String): Either[Throwable, String] = {
    tx {
      try {
        validateLimit(phase)
        update(stories)(s =>
            where(s.number === this.number)
            set(s.phase := phase)
        )
        Right("Card " + this.number + " is moved to " + phase + " phase
            successfully.")
      } catch {
        case exception: Throwable =>
                        exception.printStackTrace ;
                        Left(exception)
      }
    }
  }
```
Save new story to table
```
  def save(): Either[Throwable, String] = {
    tx {
      try {
        validate
        stories.insert(this)
        Right("Story is created successfully")
      } catch {
        case exception: Throwable => Left(exception)
      }
    }
  }
}
```
Companion object for Story
```
object Story {
  def apply(number: String, title: String) =
    new Story(number, title, "ready")
```
Find all stories from table
```
  def findAllByPhase(phase: String): Iterable[Story] =
    tx { from(stories)(s => where(s.phase === phase) select(s)) map { s:
            Story => s } }
```
Find story from database
```
  def findByNumber(number: String) =
    tx { stories.where(s => s.number === number).single }}
```
Signal validation failure
```
class ValidationException(message: String) extends
    RuntimeException(message)
```

Now the only thing remaining is to handle the Ajax call in your `application` class so you can update the database when the card is moved in the UI. You do this with an Ajax call using the `moveCard` function defined in the main.js file (see listing 7.10):

```
function moveCard(storyNumber, phase) {
  $.post("/card/move", {storyNumber: storyNumber, phase: phase},
    function(message) {
      $('#message').html(message)
    });
}
```

This method gets called when you drop a card in a phase from the `drop` method (see listing 7.8). This function makes an HTTP POST call to the /card/move URL by passing the `storyNumber` and the target phase of the story that moved—and handles the response by appending the message to the DOM element identified by the id message.

In the `application` class add a `moveCard` function to handle the /card/move POST request. This function first finds an instance of the `Story` class by its number and then calls the `moveCard` method you added to the `Story` class. Based on whether the move failed or succeeded, you'll return a response message. Add the following `moveCard` method to the `WeKanbanApplication` class:

```
private def moveCard(implicit request: Request[Stream],
    servletRequest: HttpServletRequest) = {
    val number = param_!("storyNumber")
    val toPhase = param_!("phase")
    val story = Story.findByNumber(number)
    story.moveTo(toPhase) match {
      case Right(message) => OK(ContentType, "text/html") <<
            strict << message
      case Left(error) => OK(ContentType, "text/html") <<
            strict << error.getMessage
    }
}
```

The first thing you do in the `moveCard` method is retrieve both story number and phase from the Scalaz request. Here you're using the `param_!` method already defined in the `application` class. Next, using the story number, you retrieve the `Story` model object associated with it and invoke the `moveTo` method to update the phase. Listing 7.11 shows how these methods are implemented inside the `Story` model class. Based on the response from the `moveTo` method, you show either a success message or an error message.

To invoke this `moveCard` method, let's add another pattern matching case to the `handle` method to match the POST request to move a card:

```
case MethodParts(POST, "card" :: "move" :: Nil) =>
        Some(moveCard)
```

That's it. Now if you run the weKanban application with all the changes, you'll be able to move a card between phases, and your changes will persist. The following listing shows the complete `WeKanbanApplication` class.

Listing 7.12   Completed `WeKanbanApplication` class

```scala
package com.kanban.application

import scalaz._
import Scalaz._
import scalaz.http._
import response._
import request._
import servlet._
import HttpServlet._
import Slinky._
import com.kanban.views._
import com.kanban.models._

final class WeKanbanApplication extends StreamStreamServletApplication {
  import Request._
  import Response._
  implicit val charset = UTF8

  def param_!(name: String)(implicit request: Request[Stream]) = (request |
    name).getOrElse(List[Char]()).mkString("")
  def param(name: String)(implicit request: Request[Stream]) = (request !
    name).getOrElse(List[Char]()).mkString("")
  def handle(implicit request: Request[Stream], servletRequest:
          HttpServletRequest): Option[Response[Stream]] = {
    request match {
      case MethodParts(GET, "card" :: "create" :: Nil) =>
        Some(OK(ContentType, "text/html") << strict <<
      CreateStory(param("message")))
      case MethodParts(POST, "card" :: "save" :: Nil) =>
        Some(saveStory)
      case MethodParts(GET, "kanban" :: "board" :: Nil) =>
        Some(OK(ContentType, "text/html") << strict << KanbanBoard())
      case MethodParts(POST, "card" :: "move" :: Nil) =>
        Some(moveCard)
      case _ => None
    }
  }

  private def moveCard(implicit request: Request[Stream], servletRequest:
          HttpServletRequest) = {
    val number = param_!("storyNumber")
    val toPhase = param_!("phase")
    val story = Story.findByNumber(number)
    story.moveTo(toPhase) match {
      case Right(message) => OK(ContentType, "text/html") << strict <<
                  message
      case Left(error) => OK(ContentType, "text/html") << strict <<
                  error.getMessage
    }
  }

  private def saveStory(implicit request: Request[Stream], servletRequest:
          HttpServletRequest) = {
```

Retrieve value from POST request

Retrieve value from GET request

Transform Scalaz request to response

Move card from phase to phase

Create new story, save to database

```
        val title  = param_!("title")
        val number = param_!("storyNumber")
        Story(number, title).save match {
          case Right(message) => redirects[Stream, Stream]("/card/create",
              ("message", message))
          case Left(error) => OK(ContentType, "text/html") << strict <<
              CreateStory(error.toString)
      }
    }
```

Handle requests for resources ⟶
```
    val application = new ServletApplication[Stream, Stream] {
      def application(implicit servlet: HttpServlet, servletRequest:
                  HttpServletRequest, request: Request[Stream]) = {
        def found(x: Iterator[Byte]) : Response[Stream] = OK << x.toStream
        handle | resource(found, NotFound.xhtml)
      }
    }
  }
```

At this point I think we're done with the second story, and your application is ready to ship. You can use the package build action to create a WAR file deployable to any web container. You've implemented the most basic features of a web-based Kanban board. You can easily extend the application to make it more sophisticated.

7.3   *Summary*

In chapters 6 and 7 you took your first step in building medium-sized Scala applications. For the first time you moved outside the RPEL to build your Scala application. You used the SBT. You learned how to work with SBT, configure it, and manage dependencies—which is important when it comes to building enterprise-level Scala applications. You used Scalaz's HTTP module to build your web application and also learned how functional programming concepts can be used in web applications. You saw how Scalaz uses Scala's higher-order functions and pattern matching to expose nice APIs. Building enterprise-level applications most of the time means you have to work with relational databases. You looked into Squeryl, the Scala ORM tool, to understand how a relational database can be used and modeled in your Scala application.

This chapter has provided enough of a foundation to work with various Scala tools to build your next application. I encourage you to try different Scala ORM tools, view template engines, and web frameworks to build or extend this application. I hope the concepts and the tools you've learned in these two chapters will make you comfortable working with the various Scala tools available in the market.

In this chapter you got a glimpse of implicit conversion and implicit parameters. In the next chapter we'll take a deep dive into the Scala type system and see how we can build abstraction layers using types.

Building scalable and extensible components

8

This chapter covers

- Building components in Scala
- A tour of various types of types in Scala
- Ad hoc polymorphism with type classes
- Solving expression problems in Scala

So far we've been working with Scala without paying any serious attention to its *type system*. The type system is a tractable syntactic method for proving the absence of certain program behaviors by classifying phrases according to the kinds of values they compute.[1]

The challenge of learning about a type system is understanding the theory behind it. It's always helpful to learn the fundamentals behind a good type system, but in this chapter my focus is on the practical benefits of a good type system without going too much into theory. In the process I explore various types of the types

---

[1] Benjamin C. Pierce, *Types and Programming Languages,* 2002, The MIT Press, www.cis.upenn.edu/~bcpierce/tapl/.

Scala provides you, with examples so you can understand their applications. Why is the type system so important? It provides the following features:

- *Error detection*—Think of the compiler as a suite of test cases that can detect common type and other program errors.
- *Abstractions*—This is the focus of this chapter. You'll learn how the type system provides abstractions to build components.
- *Documentation*—The signature of a function or method tells you a lot about what it's doing.
- *Efficiency*—The type system helps the compiler generate optimized binary code.

My goal for this chapter is to show you how you can use Scala's type system to build reusable components. I'm using *component* as an umbrella term to refer to reusable libraries, classes, modules, frameworks, or web services.

Building reusable components is not easy. The goal of building software by assembling components is still a dream and isn't possible to the extent we'd like. The challenge of building something reusable is to make the components refer to the context in which they are built. Typically, you modify your component to suit the current need and end up with multiple versions of the same component. This results in a maintenance problem. In the first section of this chapter, you'll learn about building simple, reusable components using Scala's type system.

Next you'll learn about different kinds of types provided by Scala so that you're aware of all the building blocks you have to make your code more expressive and reusable.

You'll also learn about a new kind of polymorphism using type classes that allows you to express and create abstractions that are easy to extend and scale—a powerful construct to help you solve your day-to-day programming problems.

It's important to understand that a good type system doesn't work against you. Rather, it provides you with enough flexibility to be as creative as possible. Settle in with your coffee and don't worry if the ride feels a little bumpy. I promise, by the end of this chapter the results will be valuable.

8.1 Building your first component in Scala

As I mentioned, building scalable and reusable components is hard. By *scalable* I mean small or large components—particularly when you're trying to build one using a type-safe, object-oriented language. Table 8.1 explores three abstraction techniques provided by Scala.

I covered mixin composition in detail in chapter 3. Remember that Scala traits allow you to build small components and combine them to build larger components. Let's explore abstract type members and self type before you start building your component, because they're important building blocks.

Table 8.1   Scala abstraction techniques

Technique	Description
Modular mixin composition	This feature of Scala provides a mechanism for composing traits for designing reusable components without the problems of multiple inheritance. You could define contracts using it and have multiples of them (such as interfaces), or you could have concrete method implementations.
Abstract type members	Scala lets you declare abstract type members to class, trait, and subclasses that can provide concrete types. Similar to abstract methods and fields.
Self type	A mixin doesn't depend on any methods or fields of the class that it's mixed into. But sometimes it's useful to use fields or methods of the class it's mixed into. This feature of Scala is called *self type*.

8.1.1   *Abstract type members*

Scala takes the idea of abstract beyond methods and fields. You can also declare abstract type members inside a class or trait. *Abstract* types are those whose identity is unknown at the time of declaration. Unlike concrete types, the type of an abstract type member is specified during the concrete implementation of the enclosing class. The following example declares an abstract type member S inside a trait called `Calculator`:

```
trait Calculator { type S }
```

Any concrete class that mixes in this trait has to now provide a type for an S type member:

```
class SomeCalculator extends Calculator { type S = String }
```

The benefit of abstract type members is they can hide the internal information of a component. I'll use an example to demonstrate that fact. You're going to build a price calculator that can take a product ID and return the price of the product. There can be many ways to calculate the price, and each way could use a different type of data source to retrieve the price. You're building this for a retail company that sells various types of products from a number of manufacturers. The common steps across all the calculators are the following:

1   Connect to a data source (could be of many types)
2   Calculate the price using the data source
3   Close the connection to the data source

A fairly successful way to encode common steps and program skeletons is a Template Method pattern, which lets you follow a common algorithm across multiple subclasses. Here's how you could implement your parent `Calculator` trait using the Template Method pattern:

```
trait Calculator {
    def initialize: DbConnection
    def close(s: DbConnection): Unit
    def calculate(productId: String): Double = {
```

```
      val s = initialize
      val price = calculate(s, productId)
      close(s)
      price
    }
    def calculate(s: DbConnection, productId: String): Double
}
```

In this example, DbConnection is a component that knows how to retrieve data from a
database. Because all the necessary steps are implemented, each calculator can implement the overloaded calculate(s: DAO, productId: String) method. The problem with the current implementation is that it's hard-wired to a DAO, and a calculator
that uses a different kind of data source won't be able to use the calculator.

   You can easily fix the problem of the hard link to DbConnection by creating an
abstract type member that hides the type of component you use to retrieve the price
from the data source. The following listing shows the Calculator trait with the
abstract type member.

Listing 8.1   Calculator trait with abstract type member

```
package abstractMember {
  trait Calculator {
    type S
    def initialize: S
    def close(s: S): Unit
    def calculate(productId: String): Double = {
      val s = initialize
      val price = calculate(s, productId)
      close(s)
      price
    }
    def calculate(s: S, productId: String): Double
  }
}
```

The Calculator trait abstracts out the type that knows how to connect to the data
source. The initialize method makes the connection to a data source, and the
close method closes the connection. Now any concrete calculator implementation,
along with implementing all the abstract methods, needs to provide type information
for S. Here's one implementation of a calculator that uses MongoDB as a data source:

```
class CostPlusCalculator extends Calculator {
    type S = MongoClient
    def initialize = new MongoClient
    def close(dao: MongoClient) = dao.close

    def calculate(source: MongoClient, productId: String) = {
      ...
    }
  }
  class MongoClient {
    def close = ...
  }
```

The abstract type member concept is particularly useful to model a family of types that varies covariantly. The next section talks about self type, which helps in building components from smaller components.

8.1.2   *Self type members*

The self type annotation allows you to access members of a mixin trait or class, and the Scala compiler ensures that all the dependencies are correctly wired before you're allowed to instantiate the class. Self type makes mixin composition more powerful because it allows you to statically define dependencies defined by other classes and traits. In the following example, trait A is defining a dependency to trait B:

```
trait B {
    def b:Unit = ...               self: B declares
}                                  the self type
trait A { self: B =>               annotation
    def a:Unit = b
}
```

Trait A can't be mixed in with a concrete class unless that class also extends B. And because of that type-safety, you can access members of B as if it's defined in A, as shown in the preceding example. Also note that self is a name—it could be any valid parameter name. The most common names used for self type annotation are this and self.

I'll use an example to demonstrate how self type can work in a real-world application. In this example, you'll try to build a product finder that depends on a couple of required services: a way to access the database and a logger to log the result. Because traits let you easily compose features, separate the required services and the logic to find products into separate traits. Here are the required service traits:

```
trait Connection {
  def query(q: String): String
}

trait Logger {
  def log(l: String): Unit
}

trait RequiredServices {
  def makeDatabaseConnection: Connection
  def logger: Logger
}
```

The RequiredServices trait declares all the services that could be used by the product finder:

```
trait ProductFinder { this: RequiredServices =>
    def findProduct(productId: String) = {
      val c = makeDatabaseConnection
      c.query("find the lowest price")
      logger.log("querying database...")
    }
  }
```

Because the required services are annotated with self type `this`, you can still access those services, and the Scala compiler will ensure that the final class gets mixed with a trait or a class that implements `RequiredServices`. The following listing shows the complete example with test services.

Listing 8.2 Product finder with self type annotation

```
package selfTypeAnnotation {
  trait Connection {
    def query(q: String): String
  }
  trait Logger {
    def log(l: String): Unit
  }

  trait RequiredServices {
    def makeDatabaseConnection: Connection
    def logger: Logger                                    Implement
  }                                                        required services
                                                           for test
  trait TestServices extends RequiredServices {
    def makeDatabaseConnection =
        new Connection { def query(q: String) = "test" }
    def logger = new Logger { def log(l: String) = println(l) }
  }

  trait ProductFinder { this: RequiredServices =>
    def findProduct(productId: String) = {
      val c = makeDatabaseConnection
      c.query(productId)
      logger.log("querying database...")
    }                                                     Final object
  }                                                       that composes
  object FinderSystem extends ProductFinder with TestServices   all the traits
}
```

This example shows how to build large components by combining smaller components in Scala using self type annotation and mixin composition. We will explore self type once again in chapter 10 to help in unit testing. Now let's move on to build your first reusable component—a generic ordering system.

8.1.3 *Building a scalable component*

To see how to build a reusable component, let's build a generic product ordering system. It will be reusable in that a user can order any kind of product. A general ordering system is built using the following components (see figure 8.1):

■ An order component that represents the order placed by the customer.

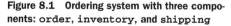

Figure 8.1 Ordering system with three components: order, inventory, and shipping

- An inventory component that stores the products. You need to check the inventory to make sure you have the product before you place the order.
- A shipping component that knows how to ship an order to customer.

A real-world ordering system is more complex than this, but let's stick to this simple system because you can easily scale it to fit into a larger context.

You can use abstract type members to abstract out the components your ordering system requires:

```
trait OrderingSystem {
  type O <: Order
  type I <: Inventory
  type S <: Shipping
}
```

The OrderingSystem declares three abstract members—O, I, and S—and at the same time sets the upper bounds for each type. The type O denotes a type that is a subtype of the Order type. Similarly I and S should be a subtype of Inventory and Shipping. And Order, Inventory, and Shipping define the contracts for each component:

```
trait OrderingSystem {
  type O <: Order
  type I <: Inventory
  type S <: Shipping

  trait Order {def placeOrder (i: I):Unit }
  trait Inventory { def itemExists(order: O): Boolean }
  trait Shipping {def scheduleShipping(order: O): Long }
}
```

The benefit of nesting all these components under a trait is that they're all aggregated and encapsulated in one place. So far you have the interfaces for each component, but you still need to implement the steps for placing the order. Here they are:

1 Check whether that item exists in inventory.
2 Place the order against the inventory. (Inventory will reduce the count by the amount of product in the inventory.)
3 Schedule the order for shipping.
4 If the item doesn't exist in inventory, return without placing the order and possibly notify Inventory to replenish the product.

Let's implement these steps as part of an Ordering trait that is defined inside the OrderingSystem:

```
trait Ordering {this: I with S =>
  def placeOrder(o: O): Option[Long] = {
    if(itemExists(o)) {
        o.placeOrder (this)
        Some(scheduleShipping(o))
    }
    else None
  }
}
```

> Self type annotation for two mixin traits

The `placeOrder` method implements all the steps mentioned with the help of the self type annotation. Ordering now relies on Inventory for `itemExists` and Shipping for the `scheduleShipping` method. Note that you can specify multiple self type annotations using the `with` keyword, similar to the way you mix in traits. All these pieces together make up the ordering system component. The following listing shows the complete code.

Listing 8.3   Generic ordering system with abstract type members and self type

```
trait OrderingSystem {
  type O <: Order
  type I <: Inventory                          Declares all the
  type S <: Shipping                           required services

  trait Ordering {this: I with S =>
    def placeOrder(o: O): Option[Long] = {     Logic to
      if(itemExists(o)) {                       place order
        o.placeOrder(this)
        Some(scheduleShipping(o))
      }
      else None
    }
  }

  trait Order {def placeOrder(i: I):Unit }
  trait Inventory { def itemExists(order: O): Boolean }
  trait Shipping { def scheduleShipping(order: O): Long }
}
```

The abstract type members of the `OrderingSystem` represent the required services that this component relies on without providing concrete implementation. This allows it to be reusable in various contexts. The mixin feature allows it to build the `Ordering` trait by composing `Inventory` and `Shipping` traits. And finally self type allows the `Ordering` trait to use services provided by the mixed in traits. As you can see, all these abstracts provide a building block to build scalable and reusable components in Scala. If you want to implement an ordering system for books, you could easily use the `OrderingSystem` as follows:

```
object BookOrderingSystem extends OrderingSystem {
  type O = BookOrder
  type I = AmazonBookStore
  type S = UPS

  class BookOrder extends Order {
    def placeOrder(i: AmazonBookStore): Unit = ...
  }
  trait AmazonBookStore extends Inventory {
    def itemExists(o: BookOrder) = ...
  }

  trait UPS extends Shipping {
    def scheduleShipping(order: BookOrder): Long = ...
  }
```

```
    object BookOrdering extends Ordering with AmazonBookStore with UPS
}
```

The `BookOrderingSystem` provides all the concrete implementations and creates the `BookOrdering` object to place orders for books. Now all you have to do to use the `BookOrderingSystem` is import it:

```
import BookOrderingSystem._
BookOrdering.placeOrder(new BookOrder)
```

The next section shows you how to use the concepts you learned here to solve the expression problem.

8.1.4   Building an extensible component

The ability to extend a software component and integrate it into an existing software system without changing existing source code is a fundamental challenge in software engineering. Many people have used the *expression problem* to demonstrate that object-oriented inheritance fails in terms of extensibility of a software component. The expression problem is one in which the challenge is to define a data type with cases, and in which one can add new cases of the type, and operations for the types, without recompiling and maintaining static type-safety. Usually this challenge is used to demonstrate strength and weakness of programming languages. Next I'll show you how to solve the expression problem in Scala with the constructs you've learned so far. But first lets look at the expression problem in detail.

THE EXPRESSION PROBLEM AND THE EXTENSIBILITY CHALLENGE

The goal is to define a data type and operations on that data type in which one can add new data types and operations without recompiling existing code, but while retaining static type safety.

Any implementation of the expression problem should satisfy the following requirements:

- Extensibility in both dimensions. You should be able to add new types and operations that work on all the types. (I look into this in detail in this section.)
- Strong static type-safety. Type casting and reflection are out of the question.
- No modification of the existing code and no duplication.
- Separate compilation.

Let's explore this problem with a practical example. You have a payroll system that processes salaries for full-time employees in the United States and Canada:

```
case class Employee(name: String, id: Long)

trait Payroll {
  def processEmployees(
    employees: Vector[Employee]): Either[String, Throwable]
}

class USPayroll extends Payroll {
  def processEmployees(employees: Vector[Employee]) = ...
```

```
}
class CanadaPayroll extends Payroll {
  def processEmployees(employees: Vector[Employee]) = ...
}
```

The `Payroll` trait declares the `processEmployees` method that takes a collection of employees and processes their salaries. It returns `Either` because it could succeed or fail. Both `USPayroll` and `CanadaPayroll` implement the `processEmployees` method based on the way the salary is processed in the individual country.

With current changes in the business, you also have to process salaries of full-time employees in Japan. That's easy—all you have to do is add another class that extends the `Payroll` trait:

```
class JapanPayroll extends Payroll {
  def processEmployees(employees: Vector[Employee]) = ...
}
```

This is one type of extension the expression problem talks about. The solution is typesafe, and you can add `JapanPayroll` as an extension and plug it in to an existing payroll system with a separate compilation.

What happens when you try to add a new operation? In this case the business has decided to hire contractors, and you also have to process their monthly pay. The new `Payroll` interface should look like the following:

```
case class Employee(name: String, id: Long)
case class Contractor(name: String)

trait Payroll extends super.Payroll {
  def processEmployees(
    employees: Vector[Employee]): Either[String, Throwable]
  def processContractors(
    contractors: Vector[Contractor]): Either[String, Throwable]
}
```

The problem is you can't go back and modify the trait because that will force you to rebuild everything—which you can't do because of the constraint put on you by the expression problem. This is a practical problem: how to add features to an existing system incrementally without doing modifications. To understand the difficulty of solving the expression problem, let's try another route: using the Visitor pattern to solve this problem. You'll have one Visitor to process salaries for employees:

```
case class USPayroll {
  def accept(v: PayrollVisitor) = v.visit(this)
}

case class CanadaPayroll {
  def accept(v: PayrollVisitor) = v.visit(this)
}

trait PayrollVisitor {
  def visit(payroll: USPayroll): Either[String, Throwable]
  def visit(payroll: CanadaPayroll): Either[String, Throwable]
}
```

```
class EmployeePayrollVisitor extends PayrollVisitor {
    def visit(payroll: USPayroll): Either[String, Throwable] = ...
    def visit(payroll: CanadaPayroll): Either[String, Throwable] = ...
}
```

Both the USPayroll and CanadaPayroll types accept a payroll visitor. To process salaries for employees, you'll use an instance of EmployeePayrollVisitor. To process monthly pay for contractors, you can easily create a new class called Contractor-PayrollVisitor, as in the following:

```
class ContractorPayrollVisitor extends PayrollVisitor {
    def visit(payroll: USPayroll): Either[String, Throwable] = ...
    def visit(payroll: CanadaPayroll): Either[String, Throwable] = ...
}
```

Using the Visitor pattern, it's easy to add new operations, but what about type? If you try to add a new type called JapanPayroll, you have a problem. You have to go back and change all the visitors to accept a JapanPayroll type. In the first solution it was easy to add a new type, and in the second solution it's easy to add an operation. But you want a solution that lets you change in both dimensions. In the next section you'll learn how to solve this problem in Scala using abstract type members and trait mixins.

SOLVING THE EXPRESSION PROBLEM

You'll use Scala traits and abstract type members to solve the expression problem. Using the same payroll system, I'll show you how to easily add new operations to the payroll system without breaking type-safety and at the same time add a new type.

Start by defining the base payroll system as a trait with an abstract type member for payroll:

```
trait PayrollSystem {
  case class Employee(name: String, id: Long)
  type P <: Payroll
  trait Payroll {
    def processEmployees(
      employees: Vector[Employee]): Either[String, Throwable]
  }
  def processPayroll(p: P): Either[String, Throwable]
}
```
> Abstract type member for payroll

Again you'll nest everything inside a trait so that you can treat it as a module. The type P denotes some subtype of the Payroll trait, which declares an abstract method to process salaries for employees. The processPayroll method needs to be implemented to process payrolls for a given Payroll type. Here's how the trait could be extended for U.S. and Canada payrolls:

```
trait USPayrollSystem extends PayrollSystem {
  class USPayroll extends Payroll {
    def processEmployees(employees: Vector[Employee]) =
      Left("US payroll")
  }
}
```

```
trait CanadaPayrollSystem extends PayrollSystem {
  class CanadaPayroll extends Payroll {
    def processEmployees(employees: Vector[Employee]) =
      Left("Canada payroll")  }
}
```

I've omitted the details of processing a payroll because it's not important in this context. To process the payroll for U.S. employees, you can implement a USPayroll-System by providing an implementation of the processPayroll method:

```
object USPayrollInstance extends USPayrollSystem {
  type P = USPayroll
  def processPayroll(p: USPayroll) = {
    val employees: Vector[Employee] = ...
    val result = p.processEmployees(employees)
    ...
  }
}
```

In these settings it will be easy to add a new Payroll type for Japan. Create a trait that extends the PayrollSystem:

```
trait JapanPayrollSystem extends PayrollSystem {
  class JapanPayroll extends Payroll {
    def processEmployees(employees: Vector[Employee]) = ...
  }
}
```

Now add a new method to the Payroll trait without recompiling everything, using the shadowing feature of Scala:

```
trait ContractorPayrollSystem extends PayrollSystem {
  type P <: Payroll
  case class Contractor(name: String)

  trait Payroll extends super.Payroll {
    def processContractors(
      contractors: Vector[Contractor]): Either[String, Throwable]
  }
}
```

Shadowing the Payroll trait defined in PayrollSystem

The Payroll trait defined inside the ContractorPayrollSystem doesn't override but instead shadows the former definition of Payroll type from PayrollSystem. The former definition of Payroll is accessible in the context of ContractPayrollSystem using the super keyword. Shadowing can introduce unintended errors in your code, but in this context it lets you extend the old definition of Payroll without overriding it.

Another thing to notice is that you're redefining the abstract type member P. P needs to be any subtype of Payroll that understands both the processEmployees and processContractors methods. To process contractors for both the U.S. and Canada, extend the ContractPayrollSystem trait:

```
trait USContractorPayrollSystem extends USPayrollSystem with
  ContractorPayrollSystem {

  class USPayroll extends super.USPayroll with Payroll {
    def processContractors(contractors: Vector[Contractor]) =
      Left("US contract payroll")
  }
}

trait CanadaContractorPayrollSystem extends CanadaPayrollSystem with
  ContractorPayrollSystem {

  class CanadaPayroll extends super.CanadaPayroll with Payroll {
    def processContractors(contractors: Vector[Contractor]) =
      Left("Canada contract payroll")
  }
}
```

You're shadowing the former definition of USPayroll and CanadaPayroll. Also note that you're mixing in the new definition of the Payroll trait to implement the processContractors method. Keep type-safety requirements in mind: if you don't mix in the Payroll trait, you'll get an error when you try to create a concrete implementation of the USContractorPayrollSystem or CanadaContractorPayrollSystem. Similarly you can add the processContractors operation to JapanPayrollSystem:

```
trait JapanContractorPayrollSystem extends JapanPayrollSystem with
  ContractorPayrollSystem {

  class JapanPayroll extends super.JapanPayroll with Payroll {
    def processContractors(contractors: Vector[Contractor]) =
      Left("Japan contract payroll")
  }
}
```

At this point you've successfully solved the expression problem. The following listing shows the complete example.

Listing 8.4 Solution to the expression problem using `PayrollSystem`

```
package chap08.payroll

trait PayrollSystem {                              ◁┐ Initial interface of
  case class Employee(name: String, id: Long)        │ the PayrollSystem
  type P <: Payroll
  trait Payroll {
    def processEmployees(
        employees: Vector[Employee]): Either[String, Throwable]
  }
  def processPayroll(p: P): Either[String, Throwable]
}

trait USPayrollSystem extends PayrollSystem {
  class USPayroll extends Payroll {
    def processEmployees(employees: Vector[Employee]) = Left("US payroll")
  }
}
```

```
trait CanadaPayrollSystem extends PayrollSystem {
  class CanadaPayroll extends Payroll {
    def processEmployees(employees: Vector[Employee]) =
      Left("Canada payroll")
  }
}

trait JapanPayrollSystem extends PayrollSystem {
  class JapanPayroll extends Payroll {
    def processEmployees(employees: Vector[Employee]) =
      Left("Japan payroll")
  }
}

trait ContractorPayrollSystem extends PayrollSystem {
  type P <: Payroll
  case class Contractor(name: String)

  trait Payroll extends super.Payroll {
    def processContractors(
      contractors: Vector[Contractor]): Either[String, Throwable]
  }
}

trait USContractorPayrollSystem extends USPayrollSystem with
  ContractorPayrollSystem {

  class USPayroll extends super.USPayroll with Payroll {
    def processContractors(
      contractors: Vector[Contractor]) = Left("US contract payroll")
  }
}

trait CanadaContractorPayrollSystem extends CanadaPayrollSystem with
  ContractorPayrollSystem {

  class CanadaPayroll extends super.CanadaPayroll with Payroll {
    def processContractors(
      contractors: Vector[Contractor]) = Left("Canada contract payroll")
  }
}

trait JapanContractorPayrollSystem extends JapanPayrollSystem with
  ContractorPayrollSystem {

  class JapanPayroll extends super.JapanPayroll with Payroll {
    def processContractors(
      contractors: Vector[Contractor]) = Left("Japan contract payroll")
  }
}
```

**Interface of
PayrollSystem
after changes**

Using Scala first-class module support, you can wrap all the traits and classes inside an object and extend an existing software component without forcing everything to recompile and at the same time maintain type-safety. Note that both old and new interfaces of the Payroll are available, and the behavior is driven by what traits you compose. To use the new Payroll so you can process both employees and contractors, you have to mix in one of the ContractorPayrollSystem traits. The following

example demonstrates how you can create an instance of USContractorPayroll-
System and use it:

```
object RunNewPayroll {
  object USNewPayrollInstance extends USContractorPayrollSystem {      ◁┐ Create
    type P = USPayroll                                                   │  instance of
    def processPayroll(p: USPayroll) = {                                 │  new payroll
      p.processEmployees(Vector(Employee("a", 1)))                       │  system
      p.processContractors(Vector(Contractor("b")))
      Left("payroll processed successfully")
    }
  }
  def main(args: Array[String]): Unit = run
  def run = {                                                            │ Process payroll
    val usPayroll = new USPayroll                                        │ for employees
    USNewPayrollInstance.processPayroll(usPayroll)                     ◁┘ and contractors
  }
}
```

The processPayroll method invokes both the processEmployees and process-
Contractors methods of the Payroll trait, but you could instead have easily used an
existing payroll system that knows how to process salaries for U.S. employees, because
you're still confirming the USPayroll trait. All that remains is to implement the additional processContractors part.

   This is a good example that demonstrates the power of Scala's type system and the
abstractions available to build both scalable and extensible components. We solved
this problem using the object-oriented abstractions available in Scala. In section 8.3,
I'll show you how to solve this problem using the functional programming side of
things. But first I'll go over another powerful type of abstraction available in Scala.

8.2   *Types of types in Scala*

One of Scala's unique features is its rich type system. Like any good type system, it
doesn't work against you but rather provides the abstractions necessary to build reusable components. This section explores various types offered by the Scala type system.

8.2.1   *Structural types*

Structural typing in Scala is the way to describe types by their structure, not by their
names, as with other typing. If you've used dynamically typed languages, a structural
type may give you the feel of duck typing (a style of dynamic typing) in a type-safe
manner. Let's say you want to close any resource after use as long as it's closable. One
way to do that would be to define a trait that declares a close method and have all the
resources implement the trait. But using a structural type, you can easily define a new
type by specifying its structure, like the following:

```
def close(closable: { def close: Unit }) = {
   closable.close
}
```

The type of the parameter is defined by the { def close: Unit } structure. The flexibility of this approach is that now you can pass instances of any type to this function as long as it implements the def close: Unit method. Currently this new type doesn't have any name, but using the type keyword you can easily provide a name (type alias):

```
type Closable = { def close: Unit }
def close(closable: { def close: Unit }) = {
  closable.close
}
```

Structural types aren't limited to a single method, but when defining multiple methods make sure you use the type keyword to give it a name—otherwise, your function signatures will look confusing:

```
type Profile = {
  def name: String
  def address: String
}
```

You can also create new values of a structural type using the new keyword. For example:

```
val nilanjanProfile = new {
  def name = "Nilanjan"
  def address = "Boulder, CO"
}
```

You can use a structural type to reduce class hierarchies and simplify a code base. Let's say you have the following class hierarchies to represent various types of workers for a department store:

```
trait Worker {
  def salary: BigDecimal
    def bonusPercentage: Double
}

trait HourlyWorker {
  def hours: Int
  def salary: BigDecimal
}

case class FullTimeWorker(val salary: BigDecimal, ...)
    extends Worker
case class PartTimeWorker(val hours: Int, val salary: BigDecimal, ...)
    extends HourlyWorker
case class StudentWorker(val hours: Int, val salary: BigDecimal, ...)
    extends HourlyWorker
```

This is a small hierarchy, but you get the idea. Each type of worker is different; there are hourly and full-time workers. The only thing they have in common is they all get paid. If you have to calculate the money spent on paying salaries to workers in a given month, you have to define another common type that represents salaried workers:

```
trait SalariedWorker {
  def salary: BigDecimal
}
```

```
trait Worker extends SalariedWorker {
  def bonusPercentage: Double
}

trait HourlyWorker extends SalariedWorker {
  def hours: Int
}

def amountPaidAsSalary(workers: Vector[SalariedWorker]) = {
  ...
}
```

The benefit of duck typing is that it lets you abstract out commonalities without being part of the same type. Using a structural type you can easily rewrite a function like the following without defining new types:

```
def amountPaidAsSalary2(workers: Vector[{def salary: BigDecimal }]) = {
}
```

Now you can pass instances of any worker to the previous function without conforming to some common type. Structural type is a good technique to get rid of unnecessary class hierarchies, but the downside is that it's comparatively slow because it uses reflection under the hood.

8.2.2   *Higher-kinded types*

Higher-kinded types are types that know how to create a new type from the type argument. That's why higher-kinded types are also known as *type constructors*—they accept other types as a parameter and create a new type. The `scala.collections.immutable.List[+A]` is an example of a higher-kinded type. It takes a type parameter and creates a new concrete type. `List[String]` and `List[Int]` are examples of types you can create from the `List` kind. Kinds are to types as types are to values (see figure 8.2).

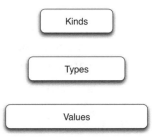

Figure 8.2   **Types classify values, and kinds classify types.**

> **MODULARIZING LANGUAGE FEATURES**
>
> Scala defines large sets of powerful features but not every programmer needs to use all of them.
>
> Starting with Scala 2.10 you must first enable the advanced features of the language. This is part of the effort to modularize Scala's language features.
>
> The `scala.language` object controls the language features available to the programmer. Take a look at the scaladoc of scala.language to find all the language features that you can control. For large projects, for example, you can disable some advanced Scala features so that they don't get abused. If a disabled feature is used, the compiler generates a warning (using a `-feature` compiler flag to display the warning

message). For example, a higher-kinded type is an advanced feature and you must explicitly import `scala.language.higherKinds` to enable it. You can also use the `-language:higherKinds` compiler flag to accomplish the same thing.

To enable all the advanced features pass `-language:_ parameter` to the Scala compiler.

Most of the collections classes are good examples of why kinds are such a powerful abstraction tool. You saw examples using higher-kinded types in chapter 5. Let's look at more examples to understand their usefulness. You'll try to build a function that takes another function as a parameter and applies that function to elements of a given type. For example, you have a vector of elements and want to apply a function to each element of the vector:

```
def fmap[A, B](xs: Vector[A], f: A => B): Vector[B] = xs map f
```

fmap applies the given f function to all the elements of vector. Similarly, if you want to apply the function to `Option`, you have to create another function:

```
def fmap[A, B](r: Option[A], f: A => B): Option[B] = r map f
```

Both functions look similar and only differ by the first parameter. The question is: how can you define a common fmap function signature for various types? Using a higher-kinded type, you can abstract out the type of the first parameter, as in the following:

```
trait Mapper[F[_]] {
    def fmap[A, B](xs: F[A], f: A => B): F[B]
}
```

The `Mapper` trait is parameterized by the `F[_]` type. F is a higher-kinded type because it takes another type parameter denoted by _. If you have to implement fmap for `Vector`, you'll do something like the following:

```
def VectorMapper = new Mapper[Vector] {
  def fmap[A, B](xs: Vector[A], f: A => B): Vector[B] = xs map f
}
```

Similarly, you can define one for `Option`:

```
def OptionMapper = new Mapper[Option] {
  def fmap[A, B](r: Option[A], f: A => B): Option[B] = r map f
}
```

Using higher-kinded types, you can raise the abstraction level higher and define interfaces that work across various types. For instance, you can use the `Mapper` trait to implement fmap for the `Function0` as follows:

```
def Function0Mapper = new Mapper[Function0] {
   def fmap[A, B](r: Function0[A], f: A => B) = new Function0[B] {
      def apply = f(r.apply)
   }
}
```

Function0 represents a function that doesn't take any parameters. For example, you can use the preceding Function0Mapper to compose two functions and create a new one:

```
Val newFunction = Function0Mapper.fmap(() => "one",
  (s: String) => s.toUpperCase)
```

The newFunction.apply will result in "ONE." The first parameter defines a function that takes zero parameters and returns "one." And the second parameter defines another function that takes a String parameter and makes it uppercase. Remember that calling apply on a Function type invokes the function.

Type projection

Before leaving this example, I want to explain one trick called *type projection* that comes in handy at times. Type projection T#x references the type member x of type T. The type projection allows for accessing members of the given type. You could do something like the following:

```
trait X {
  type E
}
type EE = X#E
```

That creates a new type alias of type member E defined inside the trait X. How could this be useful in the real world? Take the example of Either. Either is a type constructor (higher-kinded type) that takes two type parameters, one for Left and another for Right. You could create an instance of Left or Right like the following:

```
scala> Either.cond(true, "one", new RuntimeException)
res4: Either[java.lang.RuntimeException,java.lang.String] = Right(one)
```

Depending on whether the first parameter returns true or false, it creates either an instance of Right or Left. Can you use your fmap over Either type? Not easily because fmap only accepts types that take one type parameter, and Either takes two type parameters. But you can use type projection to hide one type parameter and make it constant.

First, you'll only apply the function if it's Right, because Right by convention implies success and Left implies failure. The fmap implementation would look something like the following:

```
def fmap[A, B](r: Either[X, A], f: A => B): Either[X, B] = r match {
    case Left(a) => Left(a)
    case Right(a) => Right(f(a))
  }
```

The interesting part of the implementation is type parameter X. Here X is specified by the function that creates Mapper, and using type projection you'll hide the X to the Mapper trait:

```
def EitherMapper[X] = new Mapper[({type E[A] = Either[X, A]})#E ] {
    def fmap[A, B](r: Either[X, A], f: A => B): Either[X, B] = r match
        {
```

```
        case Left(a)  => Left(a)
        case Right(a) => Right(f(a))
    }
  }
```

The (`{type E[A] = Either[X, A]}`)`#E` type projection references the type alias type `E[A] = Either[X, A]`. In the example, `X` denotes the type of `Left`, and you decided to not worry about `Left`—that's why you're hiding it and exposing the type of `Right` denoted by `A`. The type projection looks a little unusual, but it's helpful when you need one.

It's a little hard to come up with generic functions like `fmap` on your first try. I recommend always starting with specific implementations (even if you see duplications) to understand the pattern before creating abstractions. Once you understand the pattern, higher-kinded types help to create abstractions. I encourage you to look into Scala collections[2] to see various usages of higher-kinded types.

8.2.3 Phantom types

Phantom types are types that don't provide any constructors to create values. You only need these types during compile time to enforce constraints. It's hard to understand their application without an example. Again, let's consider an ordering system. An order is represented by an item and a shipping address:

```
case class Order(itemId: Option[Item], address: Option[String])
```

To place an order, you have to specify both item and shipping address. The client of the ordering system provides an item, specifies the shipping address, then places an order:

```
def addItem(item: String, o: Order) =
    Order (Some(item), o.shippingAddress)
def addShipping(address: String, o: Order) =
    Order (o.itemId, Some(address))
def placeOrder (o: Order) = { ... }
```

The problem with this approach is that the methods could get called out of order. For example, some clients could by mistake call `placeOrder` without specifying the shipping address. Well, you could implement necessary validations inside the `placeOrder` function, but using the type system to enforce an order would be even better. This is where you could use phantom types to enforce some constraints on the order object and the way it's used by various functions. First let's look into the following phantom types to represent states of order:

```
sealed trait OrderCompleted
sealed trait InCompleteOrder
```

---

[2] Martin Odersky and Lex Spoon, "The Architecture of Scala Collections," adapted from *Programming in Scala*, second edition, Odersky, Spoon and Venners, Artima Inc., 2011, http://mng.bz/Bso8.

```
sealed trait ItemProvided
sealed trait NoItem
sealed trait AddressProvided
sealed trait NoAddress
```

Each of these types represents a certain order state, and you'll use them as you progress through the ordering process. When the order is first initialized, it has no item and no address, and it's incomplete. You can easily represent that using the phantom types:

```
case class Order[A, B, C](itemId: Option[String],
  shippingAddress: Option[String])

def emptyOrder = Order[InCompleteOrder, NoItem, NoAddress](None, None)
```

The `Order` type now takes three type parameters, and an empty order is initialized with `InCompleteOrder`, `NoItem`, and `NoAddress` types. To enforce some constraints on each operation performed on the order, you'll use combinations of these types. For example, you can only add an item to an order when it doesn't have any items, and once an item is added its type parameter changes from `NoItem` to `ItemProvided`:

```
def addItem[A, B](item: String, o: Order[A, NoItem, B]) =
  o.copy[A, ItemProvided, B](itemId = Some(item))
```

`addItem` creates a new order by adding the item and changing the second type parameter from `NoItem` to `ItemProvided`. Similarly, `addShipping` creates a new order by updating the address:

```
def addShipping[A, B](address: String, o: Order[A, B, NoAddress]) =
  o.copy[A, B, AddressProvided](shippingAddress = Some(address))
```

To place an order, it needs to have both item and address, and you can easily verify that at compile time using types:

```
def placeOrder (o: Order[InCompleteOrder, ItemProvided, AddressProvided]) ={
  ...
  o.copy[OrderCompleted, ItemProvided, AddressProvided]()
}
```

`placeOrder` only accepts an order that's complete with item and address. If you try to invoke `placeOrder` without an item or address, you'll get a compile error. If I invoke `placeOrder` without specifying a shipping address, I get the following error:

```
[error]  found   :
    phantomtypes.Order[phantomtypes.InCompleteOrder,phantomtypes.ItemProvide
    d,phantomtypes.NoAddress]
[error]  required:
    phantomtypes.Order[phantomtypes.InCompleteOrder,phantomtypes.ItemProvide
    d,phantomtypes.AddressProvided]
```

The following listing shows the complete ordering system example with phantom types.

Listing 8.5 Ordering system with phantom types

```
package phantomtypes

sealed trait OrderCompleted              ◁——— Various order states
sealed trait InCompleteOrder
sealed trait ItemProvided
sealed trait NoItem
sealed trait AddressProvided
sealed trait NoAddress

case class Order[A, B, C](itemId: Option[String],
   shippingAddress: Option[String])

object Order {
  def emptyOrder = Order[InCompleteOrder, NoItem, NoAddress](None, None)
}

object OrderingSystem {
  def addItem[A, B](item: String, o: Order[A, NoItem, B]) =
     o.copy[A, ItemProvided, B](itemId = Some(item))
  def addShipping[A, B](address: String, o: Order[A, B, NoAddress]) =
     o.copy[A, B, AddressProvided](shippingAddress = Some(address))
  def placeOrder (o: Order[InCompleteOrder, ItemProvided, AddressProvided])=
  {
    o.copy[OrderCompleted, ItemProvided, AddressProvided]()
  }
}
```

To use this ordering system, you can create an empty order and then add the details as follows:

```
val o = Order.emptyOrder
val o1 = addItem("some book", o)
val o2 = addShipping("some address", o1)
placeOrder (o2)
```

This time you know that if the client of the ordering system doesn't properly populate the order, it will get a compilation error. You can also use this technique to implement the type-safe Builder pattern where, using phantom types, you can ensure all the required values are populated. In the next section, you'll use phantom types to implement type classes.

Scala isn't limited to only these types. It comes with many more varieties than I've covered here. There's a type called the *method dependent type*[3] that allows you to specify the return type based on the type of the parameter, path-dependent types that allow you to constrain types by objects, and many more. My advice is to keep playing with the language, and I am sure you'll become comfortable with Scala types.

---

[3] "What are some compelling use cases for dependent method types?" Answered by Miles Sabin on stackoverflow, Oct 22, 2011, http://mng.bz/uCj3.

8.3   Ad hoc polymorphism with type classes

A *type class* is a type system construct that supports ad hoc polymorphism. Ad hoc polymorphism is a kind of polymorphism in which polymorphic functions can be applied to arguments of different types. Ad hoc polymorphism lets you add features to a type any time you want. Don't think of type classes as classes in OOP; think of them as a category. Type classes are a way to define commonalities among sets of types. In this section you'll learn how type classes can help in building abstractions.

8.3.1   Modeling orthogonal concerns using type classes

A simple example can demonstrate how to implement type classes in Scala. The following example implements an adapter pattern using type classes. In an object adapter pattern, the adapter (the wrapper object) contains an instance of the class it wraps. The adapter pattern is a great way to add functionality to a type through composition. Here's the problem you're trying to solve: you have a `Movie` type represented by a case class and you want to convert it to XML:

```
case class Movie(name: String, year: Int, rating: Double)
```

One quick and dirty solution could be to add a `toXml` method inside the case class. But in most cases that would be inappropriate because converting to XML is a completely orthogonal responsibility for the `Movie` class and should not be part of the `Movie` type.

The second solution is to use the object adapter pattern. Define a generic interface for `XmlConverter` and parameterize it with a type so you can use it for multiple types:

```
trait XmlConverter [A] {
  def toXml(a: A): String
}
```

And provide an object adapter for the `Movie` instance like the following:

```
object MovieXmlConverter extends XmlConverter[Movie] {
  def toXml(a: Movie) =
    <movie>
      <name>{a.name}</name>
      <year>{a.year}</year>
      <rating>{a.rating}</rating>
    </movie>.toString
}
```

`MovieXmlConverter` implements the `toXml` method for the `Movie` type. To convert an instance of `Movie` to XML, all you have to do from client code is the following:

```
val p = Movie("Inception", 2010, 10)
MovieXmlConverter.toXml(p)
```

The problem with the following implementation is the incidental complexity introduced by the `MovieXmlConverter`. The converter is hiding the object you're dealing with, which is `movie`. Going to a `toXml` method inside the `Movie` class almost feels like an elegant solution. The second problem with that implementation is the rigidity of the design. It's going to be hard to provide a separate XML converter for the `Movie` type. Let's see how you can improve the solution with type classes.

The first role of a type class is to define a concept. The concept is XML conversion and could be easily represented by the `XmlConverter` trait:

```
trait XmlConverter [A] {
  def toXml(a: A): String
}
```

The trait is generalized for any type A. You don't have any constraints yet. The second role of a type class is to propagate constraints automatically to a generic algorithm. For example, you can create a new method called `toXml` that takes an instance of a type and a converter to convert it to XML:

```
def toXml[A](a: A)(converter: XmlConverter [A]) = converter.toXml(a)
```

But this isn't much of an improvement because you still have to create an instance of a converter and pass it to the method. What makes type classes practical in Scala is the `implicit` keyword. Making the converter parameter implicit allows the Scala compiler to jump in and provide the parameter when it's missing:

```
def toXml[A](a: A)(implicit converter: XmlConverter[A]) =
  converter.toXml(a)
```

Now you can invoke `toXml` by passing an instance of `Movie`, and the Scala compiler will automatically provide the converter for you. In fact, you can pass in an instance of any type as long as you have an implicit definition of an `XmlConverter` that knows how to convert that type. The following listing shows the complete example.

Listing 8.6 Type class to convert a type to XML

```
package chap08.typeclasses

trait XmlConverter[A] {                                    Type class for
  def toXml(a: A): String                                  XmlConverter
}

case class Movie(name: String, year: Int, rating: Double)
                                                           ❶ Implicit
object Converters {                                          converter
  implicit object MovieConverter extends XmlConverter[Movie] {  for Movie
    def toXml(a: Movie) = <movie>
                      <name>{a.name}</name>
                      <year>{a.year}</year>
                      <rating>{a.rating}</rating>
                   </movie>.toString
  }
}
object Main {                                              Import implicit
  import Converters._                                      converters
```

```
def toXml[A](a: A)(implicit converter: XmlConverter[A]) =
    converter.toXml(a)

def main(args: Array[String]) = {
  val p = Movie("Inception", 2010, 10)
  toXml(p)
  }
}
```

◁ **Method
that
converts
❷ to XML**

You created a type class called `XmlConverter` and then provided an implicit definition of it ❶. When using the `toXml` ❷ method, you have to make sure the implicit definition is available in the compiler scope, and the Scala compiler will do the rest. The flexibility of this implementation is that now if you want to provide a different XML conversion for `Movie`, you could do that and pass it to the `toXml` method as a parameter explicitly:

```
object MovieConverterWithoutRating extends XmlConverter [Movie] {
    def toXml(a: Movie) = <movie>
                            <name>{a.name}</name>
                            <year>{a.year}</year>
                          </movie>.toString
}
val p = Movie("Inception", 2010, 10)
toXml(p)(MovieConverterWithoutRating)
```

In fact, you can also make a `MovieConverterWithoutRating` implicit definition like the other converter. But make sure both definitions aren't in the compiler scope at the same time—otherwise, you'll get an "ambiguous implicit values" compile error. One way to use multiple implicit definitions for a given type is to import them in a much narrower scope, such as inside a method. The following two methods use a different XML converter for the `Movie` type:

```
def toXmlDefault(a: Movie) = {
  import Converters._
  toXml(a)
}

def toXmlSpecial[A](a: Movie) = {
  import SpecialConverters._
  toXml(a)
}
```

The `MovieConverterWithoutRating` is defined as an implicit object inside the `SpecialConverter` object.

Type classes are so useful that they're used in many places across the standard library. For example, look at the `sum` method available for `List`:

```
def sum [B >: A] (implicit num: Numeric[B]): B
```

The `Numeric[B]` trait is nothing but a type class. Let's see it in action:

```
scala> val l = List(1, 2, 3)
l: List[Int] = List(1, 2, 3)
```

```
scala> l.sum
res0: Int = 6

scala> val ll = List("a", "b", "c")
ll: List[java.lang.String] = List(a, b, c)

scala> ll.sum
<console>:9: error: could not find implicit value for parameter num:
    Numeric[java.lang.String]
            ll.sum
                ^
```

The Scala library provides implicit definitions for `Numeric[Int]` but not for
`Numeric[String]`, and that's why you get the implicit missing compilation error.
Similarly, the following `min` method defined in the Scala collection library also uses
`Ordering[B]` as a type class:

```
def min[B >: A](implicit cmp: Ordering[B]): A
```

> ### New syntax for declaring implicit parameters
> Beginning with Scala 2.8, there's a succinct way of declaring implicit parameters for
> methods and functions that makes the implicit parameter name anonymous:
>
> ```
> def toXml[A: XmlConverter](a: A) =
>         implicitly[XmlConverter[A]].toXml(a)
> ```
>
> Using `A: XmlConverter`, you're declaring that the `toXml` method takes an implicit
> parameter of type `XmlConverter[A]`. Because the implicit parameter name isn't
> available, you can use the `implicitly` method defined by `scala.Predef` to get ref-
> erence to the implicit parameter. Here's how that method is defined inside
> `scala.Predef`:
>
> ```
> def implicitly[T](implicit e: T) = e
> ```
>
> To describe code easily I still declare implicit parameters explicitly. But in cases
> where adding an additional implicit parameter doesn't help in readability, you can
> start using the new syntax.

The common confusion about type classes is that people tend to think of them as an
interface. But the key difference between an interface and a type class is that with
interface your focus is on subtype polymorphism, and with a type class your focus is on
parametric polymorphism. In the Java world you might know parametric polymorphism as *generics*, but a more appropriate name is *parametric polymorphism*. Another way
to understand the difference is that subtyping is common in the OOP world, and parametric polymorphism is common in the functional programming world. In fact, the
type-class concept is first found in the Haskell programming language, which is a
purely functional language.

Type classes are a flexible way to model orthogonal concerns of an abstraction
without hardwiring to the abstraction. Type classes are also useful in retroactive modeling because you can add a type class for a type anytime you want. The only limitation

of type-class implementation is that everything happens statically—there's no dynamic dispatch. The upside of this limitation is that all the implicit resolution happens during compile time, and there's no runtime cost associated with it. Type classes have everything you need to solve the expression problem, so let's see how.

8.3.2 Solving the expression problem using type classes

The payroll process is driven by two abstractions. One is the country for which you have to process the payroll, and the other is the payee. The USPayroll class will look something like this:

```
case class USPayroll[A](payees: Seq[A]) {
  def processPayroll = ...
}
```

The A type represents a type of payee; it could represent an employee or contractor. Similarly, the payroll class for Canada would look something like the following:

```
case class CanadaPayroll[A](payees: Seq[A]){
  def processPayroll = ...
}
```

To represent the type class for a family of payroll processors, you could define the following trait by parameterizing both country and the type of payee:

```
import scala.language.higherKinds
trait PayrollProcessor[C[_], A] {
  def processPayroll(payees: Seq[A]): Either[String, Throwable]
}
```

C is a higher-kinded type that represents a payroll type. The reason it's a higher-kinded type is because both USPayroll and CanadaPayroll take a type parameter. And A represents the type of payee. Note that you aren't using C anywhere except as a parameterized type, like a phantom type. It will make sense once I introduce the second building block of type class, the implicit definitions of the PayrollProcessor trait:

```
case class Employee(name: String, id: Long)
implicit object USPayrollProcessor
    extends PayrollProcessor[USPayroll, Employee] {

    def processPayroll(
        payees: Seq[Employee]) = Left("us employees are processed")
}

implicit object CanadaPayrollProcessor
    extends PayrollProcessor[CanadaPayroll, Employee] {

    def processPayroll(
        payees: Seq[Employee]) = Left("canada employees are processed")
}
```

Notice how you're using the first type parameter of PayrollProcessor to identify the appropriate definition of PayrollProcessor based on the country. To use these implicit definitions, you could use implicit class parameters for both USPayroll and CanadaPayroll types:

```
case class USPayroll[A](
  payees: Seq[A])(implicit processor: PayrollProcessor[USPayroll, A]) {

    def processPayroll = processor.processPayroll(payees)
}
case class CanadaPayroll[A](
  payees: Seq[A])(implicit processor: PayrollProcessor[CanadaPayroll, A]){

    def processPayroll = processor.processPayroll(payees)
}
```

The preceding code snippet also demonstrates another important point: you can use implicit parameters in class definitions as well. Now when you create an instance of USPayroll or CanadaPayroll, the Scala compiler will try to provide values for implicit parameters. Here's what you have so far.

Listing 8.7 Payroll system implemented with type class

```
package chap08.payroll.typeclass
import scala.langage.higherkinds

object PayrollSystemWithTypeclass {
  case class Employee(name: String, id: Long)          Type class for
                                                       payroll
  trait PayrollProcessor[C[_], A] {                    processor
    def processPayroll(payees: Seq[A]): Either[String, Throwable]
  }

  case class USPayroll[A](
    payees: Seq[A])(implicit processor: PayrollProcessor[USPayroll, A]) {

    def processPayroll = processor.processPayroll(payees)
  }
  case class CanadaPayroll[A](
    payees: Seq[A])(implicit processor: PayrollProcessor[CanadaPayroll, A])
  {
    def processPayroll = processor.processPayroll(payees)
  }
}                                                   ① Provide all
                                                       the implicit
object PayrollProcessors {                             definitions
  import PayrollSystemWithTypeclass._

  implicit object USPayrollProcessor                   U.S. payroll
    extends PayrollProcessor[USPayroll, Employee] {    processor

    def processPayroll(
      payees: Seq[Employee]) = Left("us employees are processed")
  }

  implicit object CanadaPayrollProcessor               Canada payroll
    extends PayrollProcessor[CanadaPayroll, Employee] {  processor
    def processPayroll(
      payees: Seq[Employee]) = Left("canada employees are processed")
```

```
    }
}

object RunPayroll {
  import PayrollSystemWithTypeclass._
  import PayrollProcessors._

  def main(args: Array[String]): Unit = run
  def run = {
    val r = USPayroll(Vector(Employee("a", 1))).processPayroll
    println(r)
  }
}
```

Create
instance of
USPayroll

Again, all the implicit definitions are grouped together ❶ to help you import them, as inside the RunPayroll object. Notice when you're instantiating USPayroll that you're providing a collection of employees, and the implicit processor will be provided by the Scala compiler. In this case, that's USPayrollProcessor. Now assert that you also have type-safety. Create a new type called Contractor:

```
case class Contractor(name: String)
```

Because there's no restriction on the type of payee (it's denoted by A without any bounds), you could easily create a collection of contractors and pass it to USPayroll:

```
USPayroll(Vector(Contractor("a"))).processPayroll
```

But the moment you try to compile the preceding line, you'll get a compilation error, because there's no implicit definition for USPayroll and Contractor type yet. You're still protected by the type system—it's all good.

> **NOTE** You can annotate your type classes with @implicitnotfound to get helpful error messages when the compiler can't find an implicit value of the annotated type.

Let's move on with the quest of solving the expression problem using type classes. Adding a new type in the current settings is trivial; add a new class and the implicit definition of the payroll processor:

```
object PayrollSystemWithTypeclassExtension {
  import PayrollSystemWithTypeclass._

  case class JapanPayroll[A](payees: Vector[A])(
    implicit processor: PayrollProcessor[JapanPayroll, A]) {

    def processPayroll = processor.processPayroll(payees)
  }
  case class Contractor(name: String)
}

object PayrollProcessorsExtension {
  import PayrollSystemWithTypeclassExtension._
  import PayrollSystemWithTypeclass._

  implicit object JapanPayrollProcessor
    extends PayrollProcessor[JapanPayroll, Employee] {
```

❶ Case class for
   Contractor type

```
    def processPayroll(payees: Seq[Employee]) =
      Left("japan employees are processed")
  }
}
```

Adding a new operation to process pay for contractors ❶ is also trivial because all you have to do is provide implicit definitions of payroll processors for contractors, as in the following:

```
implicit object USContractorPayrollProcessor
    extends PayrollProcessor[USPayroll, Contractor] {

    def processPayroll(payees: Seq[Contractor]) =
      Left("us contractors are processed")
}

implicit object CanadaContractorPayrollProcessor
    extends PayrollProcessor[CanadaPayroll, Contractor] {

    def processPayroll(payees: Seq[Contractor]) =
      Left("canada contractors are processed")
}

implicit object JapanContractorPayrollProcessor
    extends PayrollProcessor[JapanPayroll, Contractor] {

    def processPayroll(payees: Seq[Contractor]) =
      Left("japan contractors are processed")
  }
```

Add the preceding implicit definitions inside the `PayrollProcessorsExtension` object so that you can group them all together. The following code snippet shows how to use the preceding code to process the payroll of both employees and contractors:

```
object RunNewPayroll {
  import PayrollSystemWithTypeclass._
  import PayrollProcessors._
  import PayrollSystemWithTypeclassExtension._
  import PayrollProcessorsExtension._

  def main(args: Array[String]): Unit = run
  def run = {
    val r1 = JapanPayroll(Vector(Employee("a", 1))).processPayroll
    val r2 = JapanPayroll(Vector(Contractor("a"))).processPayroll
  }
}
```

You import all the necessary classes and implicit definition and process the payroll for Japan. You again successfully solved the expression problem, this time using a functional programming technique.

If you're a Java programmer, type classes might take a little while to get used to, but once you get comfortable with them they'll provide the power of retroactive modeling, which in turn will allow you to respond to change quickly.

8.4   *Summary*

This chapter is an important milestone in understanding the various applications of Scala's type system. Once understood and explored, Scala's type system helps in building reusable and scalable components. And a good type system not only provides type-safety, it also provides enough abstraction to build components or libraries much more quickly. You learned about abstract type members and self-type annotation and how to build components using them. You also explored various types of types provided by Scala and saw how they can be used to build applications and create abstractions.

One of the most common ways to identify the weakness and strengths of programming languages is the expression problem. You implemented the expression problem in two different ways, clearly demonstrating the power of Scala's type system. Scala being multiparadigm, you solved this problem using both object-oriented and functional paradigms. The object-oriented solution is implemented using abstract type members and traits. To solve this using functional programming, you learned about type classes. Type classes are a powerful way to provide polymorphic behavior at runtime, which is an important design technique for programmers. But I've only scratched the surface of Scala's type system. It has more things to offer than I could possibly cover in this chapter, but I'm certain that your curiosity will entice you to explore this subject further.

The next chapter covers one of the Scala's most popular features: actors. Scala actors make building concurrent applications easy and hassle-free.

Making concurrent
programming
easy with actors

This chapter covers

- Challenges with concurrent programming
- The actor programming model
- Handling faults in actors
- Composing concurrent programs with
  `Future` and `Promise`

In this chapter I introduce the most exciting feature of Scala: its actor library. Think of an actor as an object that processes a message (your request) and encapsulates state (state is not shared with other actors). The ability to perform an action in response to an incoming message is what makes an object an actor. At the high level, actors are the way you should do OOP. Remember that the actor model encourages no shared state architecture. In this chapter, I explain why that's an important property to have for any concurrent program.

Future and Promise provide abstractions to perform concurrent operations in a nonblocking fashion. They are a great way to create multiple concurrent and parallel computations and join them to complete your job. This is very similar to how you compose functions, but, in this case, functions are executed concurrently or in parallel. Think of Future as a proxy object that you can create for a result that will be available at some later time. You can use Promise to complete a Future by providing the result. We will explore Promise and Future as this chapter progresses. First let's understand what I mean by concurrent and parallel programming.

9.1   What is concurrent programming?

Concurrency is when more than one task can start and complete in overlapping time periods. It doesn't matter whether they're running at the same instant. You can write concurrent programs on a single CPU (single execution core) machine where only one task can execute at a given point of time. Typically multiple tasks are executed in a time-slice manner, where a scheduler (such as the JVM) will guarantee each process a regular "slice" of operating time. This gives the illusion of parallelism to the users. And the common de facto standard way to implement a multitasking application is to use threads. Figure 9.1 shows how a multitasking application shares a single CPU.

As you can see in figure 9.1, two threads are executing instructions generated by the application in a time-sliced manner. The group of instructions varies in size because you don't know how much code will be executed before the scheduler decides to take the running thread out and give another thread the opportunity to execute. Remember that other processes running at the same time might need some CPU time—you can see it's pretty unpredictable. Sometimes schedulers use a priority mechanism to schedule a thread to run when there's more than one thread in a ready-to-run state.[1] Things become more interesting when you have code that blocks for

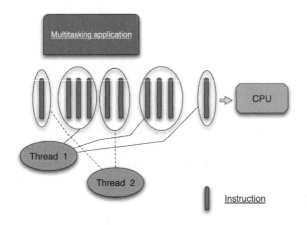

Figure 9.1   A concurrent application running in a single CPU core with two threads

---

[1] Java thread states (download), http://mng.bz/w1VH.

resources, such as reading data from a socket or reading from the filesystem. In this case, even though the thread has the opportunity to use the CPU, it can't because it's waiting for the data, and the CPU is sitting idle. I'll revisit this topic in section 9.4.

Most people use *concurrency* and *parallel programming* interchangeably, but there's a difference. In parallel programming (figure 9.2), you can literally run multiple tasks at the same time, and it's possible with multicore processors.

A concurrent program sometimes (in the next section I will explain why not always) becomes a parallel program when it's running in a multicore environment. This sounds great, because all the CPU vendors are moving toward manufacturing CPUs with multiple cores. But it poses a problem for software developers because writing concurrent, parallel applications is hard. Imagine that, while executing the multitasking application in parallel mode (figure 9.2), Thread 1 needs data from Thread 2 before proceeding further, but the data isn't available. In this case, Thread 1 will wait until it gets the data, and the application is no longer parallel. The more data and state sharing you have among threads, the more difficult it'll be for the scheduler to run threads in parallel. Throughout this chapter you'll try to make your concurrent program run in parallel mode as much as you can.

Another term that's used often with concurrency is *distributed computing*. The way I define distributed computing is multiple computing nodes (computers, virtual machines) spanned across the network, working together on a given problem. A parallel process could be a distributed process when it's running on multiple network nodes. You'll see an example of this in chapter 12 when we deploy actors in remote nodes so they can communicate across the network. But now let's look at the tools you can use to solve concurrency issues and the challenges associated with it.

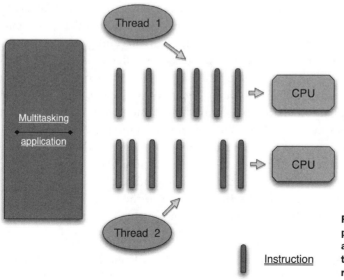

Figure 9.2 A concurrent and parallel application running in a two-CPU core with two threads. Both threads are running at the same time.

9.2   *Challenges with concurrent programming*

Chapter 1 discusses the current crisis[2] we're facing with the end of Moore's law. As a software engineer, I don't think we have a choice but to support multicore processors. The CPU manufacturers are already moving toward building multicore CPUs.[3] The future will see machines with 16, 32, and 64 cores. And the types of problems we're solving in enterprise software development are getting bigger and bigger. As the demand for processing power increases, we have to figure out a way to take advantage of these multicore processors—otherwise, our programs will become slower and slower.

But it's hard to write a correct and bug-free concurrent program. Here are some reasons why:

- Only a handful of programmers know how to write a correct, concurrent application or program. The *correctness* of the program is important.
- Debugging multithreaded programs is difficult. The same program that causes deadlock in production might not have any locking issues when debugging locally. Sometimes threading issues show up after years of running in production.
- Threading encourages shared state concurrency, and it's hard to make programs run in parallel because of locks, semaphores, and dependencies between threads.

Even though multithreading comes up as the main reason why writing concurrent programs is difficult, the main culprit is mutable state. Threading encourages shared-state concurrency. The next section explores the difficulties of shared-state concurrency.

9.2.1   *Difficulties of shared-state concurrency with threads*

The issue with using threads is it's a low level of abstraction for concurrency. Threads are too close to hardware and represent the way work is scheduled or executed by the CPU. You need something that can encapsulate threads and give you something that's easier to program with. Take the example of Scala collections: the `Traversable` trait defines an abstract method called `def foreach[U](f: Elem => U)`, which other collection library classes and traits implement. Imagine you have to use only `foreach` to do any sort of manipulation on the collection without using other useful methods like `map`, `fold`, `filters`, and so on. Well, in that case programming in Scala will become a little more difficult. This is exactly what I think about threads: they're too low-level for programmers. For example, in Java, before the introduction of the `java.util.concurrent` package, we had only `java.lang.Thread` and a handful of other classes to implement concurrent applications. After the introduction of the `java.util.concurrent` package, things improved. The new `java.util.concurrent` package provides a number of

---

[2]   Herb Sutter, "The Free Lunch Is Over: A Fundamental Turn Toward Concurrency in Software," December 2004, CPU trends graph updated August 2009, www.gotw.ca/publications/concurrency-ddj.htm.

[3]   Multicore CPU trend (graphic), www.gotw.ca/images/CPU.png.

nice utilities and implements popular concurrent design patterns, but it's still hard to avoid the fact that the main complexity behind using threads comes from using mutable shared data. It's a design issue that we programmers have to deal with when working with threads. To protect against data corruption and have consistency across many threads, we use locks. Using locks, we control the way the shared data is modified and accessed, but locks introduce problems to the program (see table 9.1).

Table 9.1 Challenges with shared state concurrency

Problem	Description
Locks don't compose	You can't implement a higher-level, thread-safe behavior by composing smaller thread-safe operations.
Using too many or too few locks	You don't know until you hit a problem. The problem might not show until in production (sometimes after years).[a] Acquiring and releasing locks are expensive operations.
Deadlocks and race conditions	This goes to the nondeterministic nature of the threads. It's almost impossible to make any deterministic reasoning of multithreaded code. You can use design patterns, such as always acquiring locks in a certain order, to avoid deadlocks, but this mechanism adds more responsibility to the developer.
Error recovery is hard	This is more of a threading issue than the shared-state issue, but it's a huge issue nonetheless. There's no clear mechanism to recover from errors in multithreaded programs. Usually a feedback loop is looking at the stack trace inside a log file.

a. Edward A. Lee, "The Problem with Threads," Jan. 10, 2006, http://mng.bz/Y4Co.

Last but not least, shared mutable data makes it hard to run programs in parallel, as discussed in section 9.1. The bigger question is: if threads are so hard to use, why are so many programs written using them? Almost all multithreaded programs have bugs, but this hasn't been a huge problem until recently. As multicore architectures become more popular, these bugs will be more apparent.

Threading should be left to only a few experts; the rest of us need to find a much higher level of abstraction that will hide the complexity of the multithreading and provide an easy-to-use API. Although there will be situations where threading may be your only option, for 99 percent of the cases you should be falling back to other alternatives. This change will come with a price, and the price is that we all have to start learning a new way to write and design concurrent applications. This chapter explores one of these new techniques.

9.2.2 *New trends in concurrency*

Enough talking about problems with threads and locks—let's turn our attention to the solutions. Table 9.2 lists the three most popular trends in implementing concurrent applications.

Table 9.2 Three most popular trends in concurrency

Name	Description
Software transactional memory (STM)	STM is a concurrency control mechanism similar to database transactions. Instead of working with tables and rows, STM controls the access to shared memory. An STM transaction executes a piece of code that reads and writes a shared memory. This is typically implemented in a lock-free way and is composable. I talk about STM in chapter 12 in more detail.
Dataflow concurrency	The principle behind the dataflow concurrency is to share variables across multiple tasks or threads. These variables can only be assigned a value once in its lifetime. But the values from these variables can be read multiple times, even when the value isn't assigned to the variable. This gives you programs that are more deterministic, with no race conditions and deterministic deadlocks. Chapter 12 covers dataflow concurrency constructs available in the Akka framework.
Message-passing concurrency	This is where you'll spend most of your time in this chapter. In this concurrency model, components communicate by sending messages. Messages can be sent both synchronously and asynchronously, but asynchronously sending messages to other components is more common. These messages are immutable and are separated from the state of individual components. You don't have to worry about shared state—in fact, message-passing concurrency encourages shared nothing (SN) architecture. The most successful implementation of message passing concurrency is the actor model, and it became popular after the Erlang programming language demonstrated the success of using the actor model as a concurrency model for building large-scale, distributed, parallel telecom applications. The Scala actor library is another implementation of the message passing concurrency model.

The remainder of this chapter focuses on message-passing concurrency using Scala actors. Let's jump right in.

9.3 *Implementing message-passing concurrency with actors*

In this concurrency model, actors communicate with each other through sending and receiving messages. An actor processes incoming messages and executes the actions associated with it. Typically, these messages are immutable because you shouldn't share state between them for reasons discussed previously.

There are two main communication abstractions in actor: send and receive. To send a message to an actor, you can use the following expression:

```
a ! msg
```

You're sending the `msg` message to actor `a` by invoking the `!` method. When you send a message to an actor, it's an asynchronous operation, and the call immediately returns. The messages are stored in a queue and are processed in first-in, first-out fashion. Think of this queue as a mailbox where messages get stored for an actor. Each actor gets its own mailbox. The `receive` operation is defined as a set of patterns matching messages to actions:

```
receive {
  case pattern1 =>
        ...
  case pattern =>
}
```

What differentiates an actor from any other object is the ability to perform actions in response to an incoming message.

The default actor library that ships with Scala, starting with Scala 2.10, is Akka (http://akka.io/) actors. There are many actor libraries but Akka is the most popular and powerful.

> **NOTE** Beginning with the Scala 2.10.1 release, the Scala actor library is deprecated and may be removed in a future release. To help with the migration Scala provides an Actor Migration Kit (AMK) and migration guide[4] so old Scala actor code can be easily migrated to the Akka actor library.

To create an actor, extend the `Actor` trait provided by the Akka library and implement the `receive` method. The following example creates a simple actor that prints a greeting message to the console when it receives a `Name` message:

```
import akka.actor.Actor

case class Name(name: String)

class GreetingsActor extends Actor {
  def receive = {
    case Name(n) => println("Hello " + n)
  }
}
```

The `GreetingsActor` can only process messages of type `Name`, and I will cover what will happen when you send messages that don't match any pattern in a moment. Please note that you don't necessarily have to create messages from `case` classes—you can send strings, lists, or whatever you can match using Scala's pattern matching. For example, to match string type messages, you could do something like the following:

```
case name: String => println("Hello " + name)
```

Before sending any messages to the `GreetingsActor` actor, the actor needs to be instantiated by creating an `ActorSystem`. Think of an `ActorSystem` as the manager of one or more actors. (`ActorSystem` is covered in the next section.) The actor system provides a method called `actorOf` that takes the configuration object (`akka.actor.Props`) and, optionally, the name of the actor:

```
import akka.actor.Props
import akka.actor.ActorSystem

val system = ActorSystem("greetings")
```

---

[4] See "The Scala Actors Migration Guide," http://docs.scala-lang.org/overviews/core/actors-migration-guide.html.

```
val a = system.actorOf(Props[GreetingsActor], name = "greetings-actor")

a ! Name("Nilanjan")                          Wait for message to be
                                              processed before shutdown
system.shutdown()
```

The actor system will create the infrastructure required for the actor to run. When you are done, `system.shutdown()` shuts down the infrastructure and all its actors. Messages are processed asynchronously so `system.shutdown()` might stop actors that still have unprocessed messages. Before running the previous snippet, make sure you add the following dependency in your build file:

```
libraryDependencies += "com.typesafe.akka" %% "akka-actor" % "2.1.0"
```

The following listing shows the complete code for `GreetingsActor`.

Listing 9.1   GreetingsActor

```
object GreetingsActor extends App {

  import akka.actor.Props
  import akka.actor.ActorSystem
  import akka.actor.Actor

  case class Name(name: String)

  class GreetingsActor extends Actor {
    def receive = {
      case Name(n) => println("Hello " + n)
    }
  }

  val system = ActorSystem("greetings")
  val a = system.actorOf(Props[GreetingsActor], name = "greetings-actor")

  a ! Name("Nilanjan")

  Thread.sleep(50)                     ←――――――┐  Wait to make sure
  system.shutdown()                            │  message is processed
}
```

If everything works as planned you should see the "Hello Nilanjan" message in the console. Congratulations! You have written your first Scala actors. Now let's step back to understand why we need an actor system.

9.3.1   What is ActorSystem?

An actor system is a hierarchical group of actors that share a common configuration. It's also the entry point for creating and looking up actors. Typically a design of an actor-based application resembles the way an organization works in the real world. In an organization the work is divided among departments. Each department may further divide the work until it becomes a size manageable by an employee. Similarly actors form a hierarchy where parent actors spawn child actors to delegate work until it is small enough to be handled by an individual actor.

NOTE An `ActorSystem` is a heavyweight structure that will allocate 1. . .*N* threads, so create one per logical subsystem of your application. For example, you can have one actor system to handle the backend database, another to handle all the web service calls, and so forth. Actors are very cheap. A given actor consumes only 300 bytes so you can easily create millions of them.

At the top of the hierarchy is the guardian actor, created automatically with each actor system. All other actors created by the given actor system become the child of the guardian actor. In the actor system, each actor has one supervisor (the parent actor) that automatically takes care of the fault handling. So if an actor crashes, its parent will automatically restart that actor (more about this later).

The simplest way to create an actor is to create an `ActorSystem` and use its `actorOf` method:

```
val system = ActorSystem(name = "word-count")
val m: ActorRef = system.actorOf(Props[SomeActor],
                                 name = "someActor")
```

The preceding snippet creates an `ActorSystem` named `"word-count"`, and the `actorOf` method is used to create an actor instance for the `SomeActor` class. `Props` is an `ActorRef` configuration object that's thread-safe and shareable. `Props` has a lot of utility methods to create actors.

Note here that when you create an actor in Akka, you never get the direct reference to the actor. Instead you get back a handle to the actor called `ActorRef` (actor reference). The foremost purpose of `ActorRef` is to send messages to the actor it represents. It also acts as a protection layer so you can't access the actor directly and mutate its state. `ActorRef` is also serializable, so if an actor crashes, as a fault-handling mechanism, you can possibly serialize the `ActorRef`, send it to another node, and start the actor there. Clients of the actor will not notice. There are different types of actor references. In this chapter we will look into local actor reference (meaning all the actors are running locally in a single JVM); chapter 12 will look into remote actor references (actors running on another remote JVM).

The second part of the actor system is actor path. An actor path uniquely identifies an actor in the actor system. Because actors are created in a hierarchical structure, they form a similar structure to a filesystem. As a path in a filesystem points to an individual resource, an actor path identifies an actor reference in an actor system. Note that these actors don't have to be in a

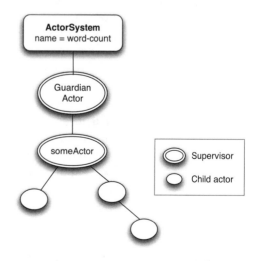

Figure 0.1 Actor system with hierarchy of actors

single machine—they can be distributed to multiple nodes. Using the methods
defined in ActorSystem, you can look up an actor reference of an existing actor in the
actor system. The following example uses the system / method to retrieve the actor
reference of the WordCountWorker actor:

```
class WordCountWorker extends Actor { ... }
...
val system = ActorSystem(name = "word-count")
system.actorOf(Props[WordCountWorker], name = "wordCountWorker")
...
val path: ActorPath = system / "WordCountWorker"
val actorRef: ActorRef = system.actorFor(path)
actorRef ! "some message"
```

The system / method returns the actor path, and the actorFor method returns the
actor reference mapped to the given path. If the actorFor fails to find an actor
pointed to by the path, it returns a reference to the dead-letter mailbox of the actor
system. It's a synthetic actor where all the undelivered messages are delivered.

   You can also create the actor path from scratch and look up actors. See the Akka
documentation for more details on the actor path.[5]

   To shut down all the actors in the actor system, invoke the shutdown method,
which gracefully stops all the actors in the system. The parent actor first stops all the
child actors and sends all unprocessed messages to the dead-letter mailbox before ter-
minating itself. The last important part of the actor system is message dispatcher. The
MessageDispatcher is the engine that makes all the actors work. The next section
explains how actors work.

9.3.2 How do Scala actors work?

Every actor system comes with a default MessageDispatcher component. Its responsibility is to send a message to the actor's mailbox and execute the actor by invoking the
receive block. Every MessageDispatcher is backed by a thread pool, which is easily
configured using the configuration file (more about this in chapter 12). You can also
configure various types of dispatchers for your actor system or specific actors. For this
chapter we are going to use the default dispatcher (a.k.a event-based dispatcher). Figure 9.4 shows how sending and receiving messages works inside actors.

   Sending a message to an actor is quite simple. To send a message to an actor mailbox the ActorRef first sends the message to the MessageDispatcher associated with
the actor (which in most cases is the MessageDispatcher configured for the actor system). The MessageDispatcher immediately queues the message in the mailbox of the
actor. The control is immediately returned to the sender of the message. This is
exactly how it worked when we sent a message to our greetings actor.

---

[5]   See "Actor References, Paths, and Addresses," version 2.1.0, http://doc.akka.io/docs/akka/2.1.0/general/
    addressing.html.

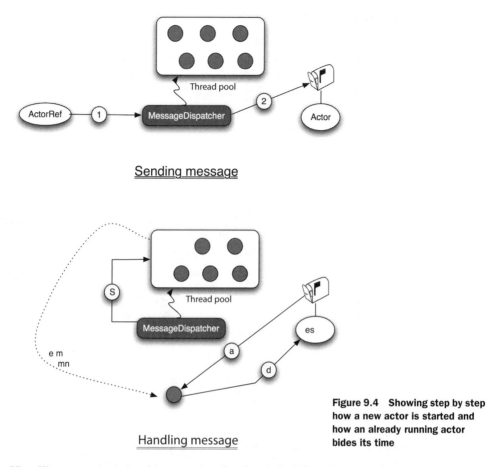

Sending message

Handling message

Figure 9.4   Showing step by step how a new actor is started and how an already running actor bides its time

Handling a message is a bit more involved so let's follow the steps in figure 9.4:

1 When an actor receives a message in its mailbox, MessageDispatcher schedules the actor for execution. Sending and handling messages happens in two different threads. If a free thread is available in the thread pool that thread is selected for execution of the actor. If all the threads are busy, the actor will be executed when threads becomes available.
2 The available thread reads the messages from the mailbox.
3 The receive method of the actor is invoked by passing one message at a time.

The message dispatcher always makes sure that a single thread always executes a given actor. It might not be the same thread all the time but it is always going to be one. This is a huge guarantee to have in the concurrent world because now you can safely use mutable state inside an actor as long as it's not shared. Now I think we are ready to build an application using actors.

9.3.3 *Divide and conquer using actors*

In the following example, the challenge is to count the number of words in each file in a given directory and sort them in ascending order. One way of doing it would be to loop through all the files in a given directory in a single thread, count the words in each file, and sort them all together. But that's sequential. To make it concurrent, we will implement the *divide-and-conquer*[6] (also called a *fork-join*) pattern with actors. We will have a set of worker actors handling individual files and a master actor sorting and accumulating the result.

> **Actor API**
>
> The `akka.actor.Actor` trait defines only one abstract method `receive` to implement the behavior of the actor. Additionally the `Actor` trait defines methods that are useful for lifecycle hooks and fault handling. Here is the list of some of the important methods. (Please check the scaladoc for a complete list of methods.)
>
> ```
> def unhandled(message: Any): Unit
> ```
>
> If a given message doesn't match any pattern inside the receive method then the unhandled method is called with the `akka.actor.UnhandledMessage` message. The default behavior of this method is to publish the message to an actor system's event stream. You can configure the event stream to log these unhandled messages in the log file.
>
> ```
> val self: ActorRef
> ```
>
> This field holds the actor reference of this actor. You can use `self` to send a message to itself.
>
> ```
> final def sender: ActorRef
> ```
>
> This is the `ActorRef` of the actor that sent the last received message. It is very useful when you want to reply to the sender of the message.
>
> ```
> val context: ActorContext
> ```
>
> This provides the contextual information for the actor, the current message, and the factory methods to create child actors. The context also provides access to the actor system and lifecycle hooks to monitor other actors.
>
> ```
> def supervisorStrategy: SupervisorStrategy
> ```
>
> This supervisor strategy defines what will happen when a failure is detected in an actor. You can override to define your own supervisor strategy. We will cover this topic later in this chapter.
>
> ```
> def preStart()
> ```
>
> This method is called when an actor is started for the first time. This method will be called before any message is handled. This method could be used to initialize any resources the actor needs to function properly.
>
> ```
> def preRestart()
> ```

6   Brian Goetz, "Java theory and practice: Stick a fork in it, Part 1," developerWorks, Nov. 13, 2007, http://mng.bz/aNZn.

Actors might be restarted in case of an exception thrown while handling a message. This method is called on the current instance of the actor. This is a great place to clean up. The default implementation is to stop all the child actors and then invoke the `postStop` method.

```
def postStop()
```
This method is called after the current actor instance is stopped.

```
def postRestart()
```
When an actor is restarted, the old instance of an actor is discarded and a fresh new instance of an actor is created using the `actorOf` method. Then the `postRestart` is invoked on the fresh instance. The default implementation is to invoke the `preStart` method.

To solve the word count problem with actors, you'll create two actor classes: one that will scan the directory for all the files and accumulate results, called `WordCount-Master`, and another one called `WordCountWorker` to count words in each file. It's always a good idea to start thinking about the messages that these actors will use to communicate with each other. First you need a message that will initiate the counting by passing in the directory location and the number of worker actors:

```
case class StartCounting(docRoot: String, numActors: Int)
```

The `docRoot` will specify the location of the files and `numActors` will create the number of worker actors. The main program will start the counting process by passing this message to the main actor. WordCountMaster and WordCountWorker will communicate with each other via messages. The `WordCountMaster` needs a message that will send the filename to the worker actor to count, and in return `WordCountWorker` needs a message that will send the word count information with the filename back to the master actor. Here are those messages:

```
case class FileToCount(fileName:String)
case class WordCount(fileName:String, count: Int)
```

To understand how these messages are consumed, look at figure 9.5. The figure shows only one worker actor, but the number of worker actors will depend upon the number you send through the `StartCounting` message.

Let's start with the `WordCountWorker` actor because it's the easiest one. This actor processes only `FileToCount` type messages, and the action associated with the message is to open the file and count all the words in it. Counting words in a file is exactly the same as the threading example you saw previously:

```
def countWords(fileName:String) = {
    val dataFile = new File(fileName)
    Source.fromFile(dataFile).getLines.foldRight(0)(_.split(" ").size + _)
  }
```

You're using `scala.io.Source` to open the file and count all the words in it—pretty straightforward. Now comes the most interesting part: the `receive` method. You

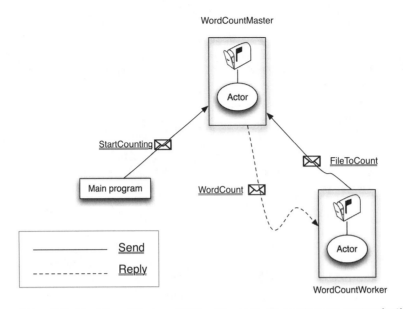

Figure 9.5 `WordCountMaster` and `WordCountWorker` actors are communicating by sending messages. The main program in the figure starts the word count process.

already know the message you need to handle, but one new thing you have to worry about is sending the reply to the `WordCountMaster` actor when you're done counting words for a given file.

The good news is, the Akka actor runtime sends the actor reference of `sender` implicitly with every message:

```
def receive {
    case FileToCount(fileName:String) =>
        val count = countWords(fileName)
        sender ! WordCount (fileName, count)
}
```

In reply you're sending the `WordCount` message back to the `WordCountMaster` actor.

What if an actor performs a blocking operation?

Usually it's recommended that you don't perform any blocking operation from actors. When you make a blocking call from an actor you are also blocking a thread. As mentioned earlier, a thread is a limited resource. So if you end up with many of these blocking actors you will soon run out of threads and halt the actor system.

At times you will not have any option other than blocking. In that case the recommended approach is to separate blocking actors from nonblocking actors by assigning different message dispatchers. This provides the flexibility to configure the blocking dispatcher with additional threads, throughput, and so on. An added benefit of this approach is if a part of the system is overloaded with messages (all the threads are busy in a message dispatcher) other parts can still function.

Here's the complete `WordCountWorker` class:

```
class WordCountWorker extends Actor {
  def countWords(fileName:String) = {
    val dataFile = new File(fileName)
    Source.fromFile(dataFile).getLines.foldRight(0)(_.split(" ").size + _)
  }
  def receive = {
    case FileToCount(fileName:String) =>
      val count = countWords(fileName)
      sender ! WordCount(fileName, count)
  }
  override def postStop(): Unit = {
    println(s"Worker actor is stopped: ${self}")
  }
}
```

In this case the `postStop` method is overridden to print a message in the console when the actor is stopped. This is not necessary. We will instead use this as a debug message to ensure that the actor is stopped correctly. Currently the `WordCountWorker` actor responds only to the `FileToCount` message. When it receives the message, it will count words inside the file and reply to the master actor to sort the response. Any other message will be discarded and handled by the `unhandled` method as described in the following side note.

What is ActorDSL?

If you are familiar with old Scala actors, `ActorDSL` will look quite similar to Scala actors. This is a new addition to the Akka actor library to help create one-off workers or even try in the REPL. To bring in all the DSL goodies into the scope import:

```
import akka.actor.ActorDSL._
```

To create a simple actor use the `actor` method defined in `ActorDSL` by passing an instance of the `Act` trait:

```
val testActor = actor(new Act {
  become {
    case "ping" => sender ! "pong"
  }
})
```

The `become` method adds the message patterns the actor needs to handle. Behind the scene `Act` extends the `Actor` trait and `become` adds the behavior of the receive block. Using this DSL syntax you no longer have to create a class. Here is an example of two actors communicating with each other by sending ping-pong messages:

```
object ActorDSLExample extends App {
  import akka.actor.ActorDSL._
  import akka.actor.ActorSystem
  implicit val system = ActorSystem("actor-dsl")
```

(continued)

```
val testActor = actor(new Act {
  become {
    case "ping" => sender ! "pong"
  }
})
actor(new Act {
  whenStarting { testActor ! "ping"}
  become {
    case x =>
      println(x)
      context.system.shutdown()
  }
})
}
```

The actor system is assigned to an implicit value so we don't have to pass it explicitly to the actor method. The whenStarting is the DSL for a lifecycle hook of the prestart method of the actor.

The WordCountMaster actor will start counting when it receives a StartCounting message. This message will contain the directory name that needs to be processed and the number of worker actors that could be used for the job. To scan the directory, use the list method defined in the java.io.File class that lists all the files in the directory:

```
private def scanFiles(docRoot: String) =
  new File(docRoot).list.map(docRoot + _)
```

The map method is used to create a list of all the filenames with a complete file path. At this point, don't worry about subdirectories. To create work actors, we use the numActors value passed to the StartCounting message and create that many actors:

```
private def createWorkers(numActors: Int) = {
for (i <- 0 until numActors) yield
  context.actorOf(Props[WordCountWorker], name = s"worker-${i}")
}
```

Since the worker actors will be the children of the WordCountMaster, the actor context.actorOf factory method is used.

To begin sorting, we need a method that will loop through all the filenames and send a FileToCount message to these worker actors. Because the number of files to process could be higher than the number of actors available, files are sent to each actor in a round-robin fashion:

```
private[this] def beginSorting(fileNames: Seq[String],
                               workers: Seq[ActorRef]) {
  fileNames.zipWithIndex.foreach( e => {
    workers(e._2 % workers.size) ! FileToCount(e._1)
  })
}
```

The `zipWithIndex` method pairs each element with its index. Here's one example:

```
scala> List("a", "b", "c").zipWithIndex
res2: List[(java.lang.String, Int)] = List((a,0), (b,1), (c,2))
```

When the `WordCountMaster` actor receives the `StartCounting` message it will create the worker actors and scan the files, then send these files to each worker. Here is how the `WordCountMaster` looks so far:

```
class WordCountMaster extends Actor {

  var fileNames: Seq[String] = Nil
  var sortedCount : Seq[(String, Int)] = Nil

  def receive = {
    case StartCounting(docRoot, numActors) =>
      val workers = createWorkers(numActors)
      fileNames = scanFiles(docRoot)
      beginSorting(fileNames, workers)
  }

  private def createWorkers(numActors: Int) = {
    for (i <- 0 until numActors) yield
      context.actorOf(Props[WordCountWorker], name = s"worker-${i}")
  }

  private def scanFiles(docRoot: String) =
    new File(docRoot).list.map(docRoot + _)

  private[this] def beginSorting(fileNames: Seq[String],
                                 workers: Seq[ActorRef]) {
    fileNames.zipWithIndex.foreach( e => {
      workers(e._2 % workers.size) ! FileToCount(e._1)
    })
  }
}
```

The `fileNames` field stores all the files we need to process. We will use this field later on to ensure we have received all the replies. The `sortedCount` field is used to store the result. An important point to note here is that it is safe to use mutable state inside an actor because the actor system will ensure that no two threads will execute an instance of an actor at the same time. You must make sure you don't leak the state outside the actor.

Next the `WordCountMaster` actor needs to handle the `WordCount` message sent from the `WordCountWorker` actor. This message will have the filename and the word count. This information is stored in `sortedCount` and sorted:

```
case WordCount(fileName, count) =>
    sortedCount ::= (fileName, count)
    sortedCount = sortedCount.sortWith(_._2 < _._2)
```

The last step is to determine when all the files are processed. One way to do that is to compare the size of `sortedCount` with the number of files to determine whether all the responses from the worker actors are received. When that happens we need to print the result in the console and terminate all the actors:

```
if(sortedCount.size == fileNames.size) {
  println("final result " + sortedCount)
  finishSorting()
}
```

We could use `context.children` to access all the worker actors and stop them like the following:

```
context.children.foreach(context.stop(_))
```

The simplest way to shut down an actor system is to use the `shutdown` method of the actor system. We can access the actor system from context using `context.system` like the following:

```
private[this] def finishSorting() {
  context.system.shutdown()
}
```

The following listing shows the complete implementation of `WordCountWorker` and `WordCountMaster` actors.

> **Listing 9.2 `WordCount` implementation using actors**

```
import akka.actor.Actor
import akka.actor.Props
import akka.actor.ActorRef
import java.io._
import scala.io._

case class FileToCount(fileName:String)
case class WordCount(fileName:String, count: Int)
case class StartCounting(docRoot: String, numActors: Int)

class WordCountWorker extends Actor {
  def countWords(fileName:String) = {
    val dataFile = new File(fileName)
    Source.fromFile(dataFile).getLines.foldRight(0)(_.split(" ").size + _)
  }

  def receive = {
    case FileToCount(fileName:String) =>
      val count = countWords(fileName)
      sender ! WordCount(fileName, count)
  }

  override def postStop(): Unit = {
    println(s"Worker actor is stopped: ${self}")
  }

}

class WordCountMaster extends Actor {

  var fileNames: Seq[String] = Nil
  var sortedCount : Seq[(String, Int)] = Nil

  def receive = {
```

```
    case StartCounting(docRoot, numActors) =>
      val workers = createWorkers(numActors)
      fileNames = scanFiles(docRoot)
      beginSorting(fileNames, workers)

    case WordCount(fileName, count) =>
      sortedCount = sortedCount :+ (fileName, count)
      sortedCount = sortedCount.sortWith(_._2 < _._2)
      if(sortedCount.size == fileNames.size) {
        println("final result " + sortedCount)
        finishSorting()
      }
  }

  override def postStop(): Unit = {
    println(s"Master actor is stopped: ${self}")
  }

  private def createWorkers(numActors: Int) = {
    for (i <- 0 until numActors) yield context.actorOf(Props[WordCount-
    Worker], name = s"worker-${i}")
  }

  private def scanFiles(docRoot: String) =
    new File(docRoot).list.map(docRoot + _)

  private[this] def beginSorting(fileNames: Seq[String], workers: Seq[Actor-
    Ref]) {
    fileNames.zipWithIndex.foreach( e => {
      workers(e._2 % workers.size) ! FileToCount(e._1)
    })
  }

  private[this] def finishSorting() {
    context.system.shutdown()
  }
}
```

`WordCountWorker` and `WordCountMaster` are both defined as actors. The communication between them is happening through immutable messages. When the `WordCount-Master` actor receives the `StartCounting` message, it creates worker actors based on the number passed in by the message. Once the actors are started, the `WordCount-Master` actor sends `FileToCount` messages to all the worker actors in round-robin fashion. When the worker actor is done counting the words inside the file, it sends the `WordCount` message back to the master actor. If the size of the `sortedCount` matches the number of files, it kills all the worker actors including the master actor.

The final piece missing from the preceding code is the main actor you saw in figure 9.4. For that, you're not going to create a new actor but instead create an object with the `Main` method.

Listing 9.3 Main program to start counting process

```
import akka.actor.ActorSystem
import akka.actor.Props
```

```
object Main {
  def main(args: Array[String]) {
    val system = ActorSystem("word-count-system")

    val m = system.actorOf(Props[WordCountMaster], name="master")
    m ! StartCounting("src/main/resources/", 2)
  }
}
```

You've learned lots of interesting things about actors in this section. And you learned how to design your applications using actors. Creating self-contained immutable messages and determining the communication between actors are important steps when working with actors. It's also important to understand that when working with actors, all the communication happens through messages, and *only* through messages. This brings up a similarity between actors and OOP. When Alan Kay[7] first thought about OOP, his big idea was "message passing."[8] In fact, working with actors is more object-oriented than you think.

What happens if something fails? So many things can go wrong in the concurrent/parallel programming world. What if we get an IOException while reading the file? Let's learn how to handle faults in an actor-based application.

9.3.4 *Fault tolerance made easy with a supervisor*

Akka encourages nondefensive programming in which failure is a valid state in the lifecycle of an application. As a programmer you know you can't prevent every error, so it's better to prepare your application for the errors. You can easily do this through fault-tolerance support provided by Akka through the supervisor hierarchy.

Think of this supervisor as an actor that links to supervised actors and restarts them when one dies. The responsibility of a supervisor is to start, stop, and monitor child actors. It's the same mechanism as linking, but Akka provides better abstractions, called *supervision strategies.*

Figure 9.6 shows an example of supervisor hierarchy.

You aren't limited to one supervisor. You can have one supervisor linked to another supervisor. That way you can supervise a supervisor in case of a crash. It's hard to build a fault-tolerant system with one box, so I

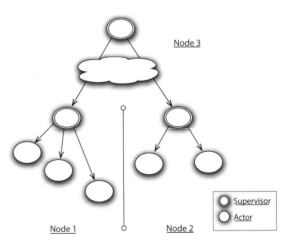

Figure 9.6 Supervisor hierarchy in Akka

---

[7] Alan Curtis Kay, http://en.wikipedia.org/wiki/Alan_Kay.

[8] Alan Kay, "Prototypes vs. classes was: Re: Sun's HotSpot," Oct 10, 1998, http://mng.bz/L12u.

recommend having your supervisor hierarchy spread across multiple machines. That way, if a node (machine) is down, you can restart an actor in a different box. Always remember to delegate the work so that if a crash occurs, another supervisor can recover. Now let's look into the fault-tolerant strategies available in Akka.

SUPERVISION STRATEGIES IN AKKA

Akka comes with two restarting strategies: One-for-One and All-for-One. In the One-for-One strategy (see figure 9.7), if one actor dies, it's recreated. This is a great strategy if actors are independent in the system. It doesn't require other actors to function properly.

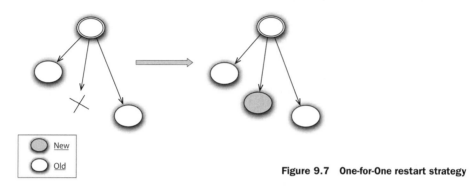

Figure 9.7   One-for-One restart strategy

If you have multiple actors that participate in one workflow, restarting a single actor might not work. In that case, use the All-for-One restart strategy (see figure 9.8), in which all actors supervised by a supervisor are restarted when one of the actors dies.

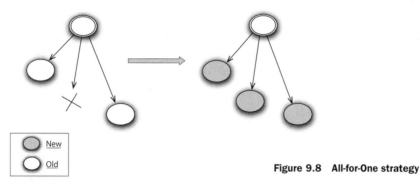

Figure 9.8   All-for-One strategy

So how do these look in code? In Akka, by default, each actor has one supervisor, and the parent actor becomes the supervisor for the child actors. When no supervisor strategy is defined, it uses the default strategy (OneForOne), which restarts the failing child actor in case of Exception. The following example configures the WordCount-Worker with OneForOneStrategy with retries:

```
import akka.actor.SupervisorStrategy._
class WordCountWorker extends Actor {
    . . .
```

```
    override val supervisorStrategy = OneForOneStrategy(maxNrOfRetries = 3,
withinTimeRange = 5 seconds) {
        case _: Exception => Restart
    }
. . .
}
```

You're overriding the supervisorStrategy property of the actor with your own fault handler. For example, in the case of java.lang.Exception your pattern will match and give a restart directive to the parent to discard the old instance of the actor and replace it with a new instance. If no pattern matches, the fault is escalated to the parent. Similarly, the following example configures the WordCountMaster actor with All-ForOneStrategy:

```
class WordCountMaster extends Actor {
. . .
  override val supervisorStrategy = AllForOneStrategy() {
      case _: Exception =>
        println("Restarting...")
              Restart
      }
. . .
}
```

A working example of a supervisor with the word-count example is in this chapter's code base. The next section talks about working with mutable data in a concurrent world.

9.4   Composing concurrent programs with Future and Promise

A Future is an object that can hold a value that may become available, as its name suggests, at a later time. It essentially acts as proxy to an actual value that does not yet exist. Usually this value is produced by some computation performed asynchronously. The simplest way to create a Future is to use the apply method:

```
def someFuture[T]: Future[T] = Future {
  someComputation()
}
```

In this case someFuture will hold the result of the computation and T represents the type of the result. Since the Future is executed asynchronously we need to specify the scala.concurrent.ExecutionContext. ExecutionContext is an abstraction over a thread pool that is responsible for executing all the tasks submitted to it. Here the task is the computation performed by the Future. There are many ways to configure and create ExecutionContext but in this chapter we will use the default global execution context available in the Scala library.

```
import ExecutionContext.Implicits.global
```

When the `Future` has the value it is considered completed. A `Future` could also be completed with an exception. To do an operation after the `Future` is completed we can use the `onComplete` callback method as in following:

```
someFuture.onComplete {
  case Success(result) => println(result)
  case Failure(t) => t.printStackTrace
}
```

Since a `Future` could be a success or failed state, the `onComplete` allows you to handle both conditions. (Check the scala.concurrent.Future scaladoc for more details.)

Futures can also be created using `Promise`. Consider `Promise` as a writable, single assignment container. You can use `Promise` to create a `Future`, which will be completed when `Promise` is fulfilled with a value:

```
val promise: Promise[String] = Promise[String]()
val future = promise.future
...
val anotherFuture = Future {
  ...
  promise.success("Done")
  doSomethingElse()
}
...
future.onSuccess { case msg => startTheNextStep() }
```

Here we have created two `Futures`, one using the `future` method and the other from `Promise`. `anotherFuture` completes the `promise` by invoking the `success` method (you can also complete `promise` with the `failure` method). Once the `promise` is completed you cannot invoke `success` again. If you do, it will throw an exception. And `promise` will automatically complete the `future` and the `onSuccess` callback will be invoked automatically. Please note that callbacks registered with `Future` will only be executed once the `future` is completed. The Scala Future and Promise APIs have many useful methods so please check the scaladoc for details.

By now you might be wondering when to use `Future` and when to use actors. A common use case of `Future` is to perform some computation concurrently without needing the extra utility of an actor. The most compelling feature of the Scala Future library is it allows us to compose concurrent operations, which is hard to achieve with actors. To see them in action let's implement the word count problem using `Future` and `Promise`.

9.4.1 Divide and conquer with Future

You are going to reimplement the word count problem using `Future`. First let's break down the word count problem into small steps so that we can solve them individually. Since `Future` allows functional composition we should be able to combine small steps to solve our problem. We can find a solution in four steps:

- Scan for all the files in a given directory
- Count words in a given file
- Accumulate and sort the result
- Produce the result

We already know how to scan the files in a given directory but this time we will perform it asynchronously:

```
private def scanFiles(docRoot: String): Future[Seq[String]] = Future {
    new File(docRoot).list.map(docRoot + _)
}
```

Similarly we can count words for a given file inside a Future. If something goes wrong we can use the recover method to register a fallback:

```
private def processFile(fileName: String): Future[(String, Int)] =
  Future {
    val dataFile = new File(fileName)
    val wordCount =
      Source
        .fromFile(dataFile).getLines.foldRight(0)(_.split(" ").size + _)
    (fileName, wordCount)
  } recover {
    case e: java.io.IOException =>
      println("Something went wrong " + e)
      (fileName, 0)
  }
```

The recover callback will be invoked if IOException is thrown inside the Future. Since each file is processed inside a Future we will end up with a collection of futures like the following:

```
val futures: Seq[Future[(String, Int)]] =
  fileNames.map(name => processFile(name))
```

Now this is a problem. How will we know when all the futures will complete? We cannot possibly register callbacks with each future since each one is independent and can complete at a different time. Rather than Seq[Future[(String, Int)]], we need Future[Seq[(String, Int)]] so we can accumulate the results and sort them. This is exactly what Future.sequence is designed for. It takes collections of futures and reduces them to one Future:

```
val singleFuture: Future[Seq[(String, Int)]] = Future.sequence(futures)
```

You can invoke the map method on future to sort the result:

```
private def processFiles(
    fileNames: Seq[String]): Future[Seq[(String, Int)]] = {
  val futures: Seq[Future[(String, Int)]] =
      fileNames.map(name => processFile(name))
  val singleFuture: Future[Seq[(String, Int)]] = Future.sequence(futures)
  singleFuture.map(r => r.sortWith(_._2 < _._2))
}
```

If you haven't guessed, `Future` is an example of a monad. It implements `map`, `flatMap`, and `filter` operations, necessary ingredients of functional composition. Now you can compose `scanFiles` and `processFiles` to produce the sorted result:

```
val path = "src/main/resources/"

  val futureWithResult: Future[Seq[(String, Int)]] = for {
    files <- scanFiles(path)
    result <- processFiles(files)
  } yield {
    result
  }
```

The for-comprehensions here are composing `scanFiles` and `processFiles` operations together to produce another `future`. Note here that each operation is performed asynchronously and we are composing `futures` in a nonblocking fashion. The for-comprehensions are creating another `future` that only completes when both the `scanFiles` and `processFiles` future complete. It is also acting as the pipe between two operations where the output of the `scanFiles` is sent to `processFiles`.

For the last step we can use a `Promise` that will be fulfilled when futureWith-Result completes. Here is the complete implementation of the word count example using `Future`:

Listing 9.4 Word count example using `Future`

```
import scala.concurrent._
import ExecutionContext.Implicits.global
import scala.util.{Success, Failure}
import java.io.File
import scala.io.Source

object Main {
  def main(args: Array[String]) {
    val promiseOfFinalResult = Promise[Seq[(String, Int)]]()          ◁── Promise that
    val path = "src/main/resources/"                                       holds the
                                                                           final result
    val futureWithResult: Future[Seq[(String, Int)]] = for {
      files <- scanFiles(path)
      result <- processFiles(files)
    } yield {
      result
    }

    futureWithResult.onSuccess {
      case r => promiseOfFinalResult.success(r)                        ◁── Promise is
    }     promiseOfFinalResult.future.onComplete {                         fulfilled with
                                                                           the result
      case Success(result) => println(result)
      case Failure(t) => t.printStackTrace
    }
  }

  private def processFiles(fileNames: Seq[String]): Future[Seq[(String,
    Int)]] = {
```

```
    val futures: Seq[Future[(String, Int)]] = fileNames.map(name =>
      processFile(name))
    val singleFuture: Future[Seq[(String, Int)]] =          Converting sequence of
        Future.sequence(futures)                            future to single future
    singleFuture.map(r => r.sortWith(_._2 < _._2))
  }

  private def processFile(fileName: String): Future[(String, Int)] =
  Future {
    val dataFile = new File(fileName)
    val wordCount = Source.fromFile(dataFile).getLines.foldRight(0)(_.split("
      ").size + _)
    (fileName, wordCount)
  } recover {
    case e: java.io.IOException =>
      println("Something went wrong " + e)
      (fileName, 0)
  }

  private def scanFiles(docRoot: String):Future[Seq[String]] = Future { new
      File(docRoot).list.map(docRoot + _) }

}
```

As you can see it's very easy to get started with Future and it is very powerful because it allows you to do functional composition. On the other hand, actors allow you to structure your application and provide fault-handling strategies. You don't have to choose between them. You can have your application broken down into actors and then have actors use futures as building blocks to perform asynchronous operations. In the next section we will see how we can use futures inside actors.

9.4.2 *Mixing Future with actors*

As you work your way through Akka actors two common patterns will evolve:

- Send a message to an actor and receive a response from it. So far we have only used fire-and-forget using the ! method. But getting a response is also a very common use case (a.k.a ask pattern).
- Reply to sender when some concurrent task (Future) completes (a.k.a pipe pattern).

Let's take an example to demonstrate these two patterns in action. In the following code snippet we have two actors, parent and the child:

```
import akka.pattern.{ask, pipe}
implicit val timeout = Timeout(5 seconds)

class GreetingsActor extends Actor {
  val messageActor = context.actorOf(Props[GreetingsChildActor])
  def receive = {
    case name =>
      val f: Future[String] = (messageActor ask name).mapTo[String]
      f pipeTo sender
  }
}
```

```
class GreetingsChildActor extends Actor {
  def receive = { ...
    }
  }
```

GreetingsActor accepts name and sends the message to a child actor to generate a greeting message. In this case we are using the ask method (you can use ? as well) of the ActorRef to send and receive a response. Since messages are processed asynchronously the ask method returns a Future. The mapTo message allows us to transform the message from Future[Any] to Future[String]. The challenge is we don't know when the message will be ready so that we can send the reply to the sender. The pipeTo pattern solves that problem by hooking up with the Future so that when the future completes it can take the response inside the future and send it to the sender. To see the complete working example please look at the chapter codebase.

9.5   *When should you not use actors?*

This chapter has highlighted the benefits of actors in building message-oriented concurrent applications. It's also discussed why shared mutable data is the root cause of most of the concurrency problems, and how actors eliminate that using shared nothing architecture. But what if you have to have a shared state across multiple components?

- *Shared state*—A classic example is where you want to transfer money from one account to another, and you want to have a consistent view across the application. You need more than actors. You need transaction support. Alternatives like STM would be a great fit for this kind of problem, or you have to build transactions over message passing. (You'll see an example of this in chapter 12.)
- *Cost of asynchronous programming*—For many programmers, it's a paradigm shift to get used to asynchronous programming. It takes time and effort to get comfortable if you are not used to it. Debugging and testing large message-oriented applications is hard. At times, asynchronous message passing makes it difficult to track and isolate a problem (knowing the starting point of the message helps). This has nothing to do with the actor model specifically, but more to do with the inherited complexity of messaging-based applications. Lately Akka TestKit[9] and Typesafe console[10] are helping to mitigate the testing and debugging issues.
- *Performance*—If your application has to have the highest performance, then because actors may add an overhead, you may be better off using a much lower level of abstraction, like threads. But again, for 99.9 percent of applications, I think the performance of actors is good enough.

9.6   *Summary*

In this chapter you learned about new concurrency trends and the problems with shared-state concurrency. It became clear that if you raise the level of abstraction

---

[9] "Testing Actor Systems (Scala), TestKit Example," http://doc.akka.io/docs/akka/2.1.0/scala/testing.html.
[10] "Typesafe Console," http://typesafe.com/products/console.

higher, you can easily build concurrent applications. This chapter focused on message-passing concurrency and how to use actors to implement it.

We also learned about the Future and Promise APIs and how we can use functional composition to construct larger programs by combining small concurrent operations. One of the big challenges with building fault-tolerant applications is handling errors effectively and recovering from them. You learned how the supervisor strategy works to handle errors in actor-based applications. This makes it easy to build long-running applications that can automatically recover from errors and exceptions.

The next chapter focuses on writing automated tests for Scala applications and explores how Scala helps with writing tests and the various tools available to you for testing. It's not as hard as you may think. It also shows you how to write tests around actors.

Building confidence
with testing

10

This chapter covers
- Automated testing using ScalaCheck
- Using JUnit to test Scala code
- Writing better tests with dependency injection
- Behavior-driven development using Specs
- Testing actor-based systems

So far, I've been showing you code without writing tests—so why worry about that right now? The answer is, I wrote tests around the code but didn't mention doing so because I wanted you to focus more on the Scala language. Now that's going to change. My goal for this chapter is to make you comfortable writing automated tests in Scala so that you can build production-quality software.

The path to writing well-crafted code[1] is the path where you write tests for your code. The common perception about writing tests is that it's hard, but this chapter will change that mindset. I'm going to show you how you can get started

---

[1] "Manifesto for Software Craftsmanship," http://manifesto.softwarecraftsmanship.org.

with practices like test-driven development and continuous integration for your Scala project. The idea of test-driven development (TDD) is to write the test before you write code. I know this seems backward, but I promise you that by the end of this chapter it will make sense. You'll learn that writing tests is more like doing a design exercise than testing, and it makes sense to design your software. Your design tool will be code—more specifically, test code.

I'll start by introducing automated testing and how developers use it in real-world projects. There are two kinds of automated tests: ones you write (the most common) and ones you generate for your code. First I discuss how you can generate tests for your code using the ScalaCheck tool, because it's easy. Scala, being a statically typed language, enjoys a unique position where tools like ScalaCheck can generate tests for your functions or classes based on types. ScalaCheck is a great way to get started with automated tests. But to truly get the benefit of automated tests, you also have to write them manually.

The majority of this chapter focuses on writing automated tests. Many testing tools are available for writing tests for your Scala code but this chapter walks you through using two tools: JUnit (www.junit.org) and Specs (http://etorreborre.github.com/specs2/).

If you're a Java developer and have used JUnit before, using it to test your Scala code is easy. Specs is a testing tool written in Scala for Scala and provides more expressiveness in your tests. I'll take you through the process of writing tests, the tools available to you, and design techniques you can use to make your design testable. The testability property of your design determines how easy it is to write tests. I'll show you how to implement dependency injection in Scala.

Dependency injection is a design pattern used by developers to make their code more testable (read more about this in section 10.5). As a hybrid language, Scala provides a number of abstraction techniques you can use to implement dependency injection. This chapter explores all of them. I'll also show you how to use a framework like Spring (www.springsource.org), a popular dependency injection framework in Java, in your Scala project.

Writing automated tests is commonly said to be hard, but the reality is if you use the right tools and techniques it's easy. Without any further delay, let's get started by asking: what are automated tests? And how do they fit into the software development process?

10.1 *Importance of automated testing*

> I don't care how good you think your design is, if I can't walk in and write a test for an arbitrary method of yours in five minutes it's not as good as you think it is, and whether you know it or not, you're paying a price for it.
> —Michael Feathers

Automated tests are tests that are recorded or prewritten and can be run by a machine without any manual intervention. The tool that allows you to run these tests is called an *automated testing tool.* As mentioned earlier, there are two kinds of automated tests: ones you write and ones generated by a tool. Regardless of how the automated tests are created, it's important to understand the value of having them around and running them as often as you can. To grasp their benefits, let's explore how automated tests fit into the agile software development process. Chances are you're already doing agile software development,[2] but if you aren't, having these tests available is still valuable.

In the agile software development process, teams don't analyze and design the application up front; they build it using an evolutionary design.[3] In this process developers only design for today, not tomorrow. They design an application based on what they know today, understanding that some of the design decisions made today might be wrong tomorrow. They also implement functionality of the application incrementally. In this model, application design evolves and goes through lots of changes. Two important questions need to be answered:

- What does evolving design have to do with automated testing?
- Why is evolving the design better than designing the application up front?

The first question is more important in the context of this chapter. Automated tests are important because your application goes through lots of changes and you might break existing functionality. In this ever-changing environment, you won't be able to keep up using manual testing. You need automated tests that can run repeatedly to ensure that your application is behaving as expected and that nothing unexpected has changed.

The next question asks why evolutionary design is better. Why not design the application up front so you don't have to change so frequently? In some cases you have to do an upfront design, like integrating with an external commercial product, and you don't have control over its source code.

But most of the time you have to cope with requirements that change over time. Agile software development tries to reduce the cost of change, and getting a correct upfront design is hard in the face of changing requirements. It becomes costly to maintain and change a big upfront design.[4]

You can't think of all the features your application will implement or how the various components of your application will work with each other. The larger the application becomes, the harder it becomes to design up front. Agile processes embrace more of an incremental approach to software development, where you build a little, test a little, and review the application features with users to get their feedback. In this process it's vital to have automated tests that give you feedback to assure you that your application is working.

Automated tests not only help you find problems, they also work as documentation for the application. If you want to understand the behavior of a class or component,

---

[2] "Agile software development," http://en.wikipedia.org/wiki/Agile_software_development.

[3] Martin Fowler, "Is Design Dead?," May 2004, http://martinfowler.com/articles/designDead.html.

[4] "Waterfall model," http://en.wikipedia.org/wiki/Waterfall_model.

you can look at the associated tests. Section 10.6 shows you how to develop executable documentation in Scala using Specs. The problem with the traditional way of documenting code is that the documentation goes stale quickly because most of us forget to keep it up-to-date with code changes. But if you have tests that act as documentation, you'll keep them up to date with code changes because every code change is preceded by or is the result of a test change.

There are varied types of automated tests: specification-based, unit, integration, functional, and regression, to name a few. This chapter focuses on specification-based tests and test-driving software using unit tests. Other types of tests also play an important role in software development but are beyond the scope of this chapter. In specification-based testing you express the behavior of your application in an executable description, and the tool generates tests to break it. On the other hand, unit tests are something you write to design and verify your application.

If you haven't done any sort of automated testing, it might take a while to get used to it. Don't worry too much at the beginning, and don't give up, because the benefits mentioned earlier will pay you back. You'll be able to respond to change quickly because now you have tests to provide feedback.

I begin by discussing how to generate automated tests using ScalaCheck so that you can start getting the benefits of automated tests while you learn how to write them for your Scala project.

10.2 *Automated test generation using ScalaCheck*

ScalaCheck is a tool for testing Scala and Java programs by generating test data based on property specifications. The basic idea is that you define a property that specifies the behavior of a piece of code, and ScalaCheck automatically generates random test data to check whether the property holds true. Don't confuse the ScalaCheck property with a JavaBean property. In ScalaCheck, a property is a testable unit. To create a new property in ScalaCheck, you have to make a statement that describes the behavior you want to test. For example, I'm making the following claim about the reverse method defined in the String class:

```
val anyString = "some string value"
anyString.reverse.reverse == anyString
```

My claim is that if the reverse method is invoked twice on an instance of a String, I get the same value back. The job of ScalaCheck would be to falsify this statement by generating random test data. Without going any further, let's try a little example with ScalaCheck. Create a new directory called scalacheck and add the following build.sbt file to the root of the directory:

```
name := "ScalaCheckExample"

version := "1.0"

organization := "Scala in Action"

scalaVersion := "2.10.0"
```

```
resolvers ++= Seq(
  "Sonatype Snapshots" at "http://oss.sonatype.org/content/repositories/
    snapshots",
  "Sonatype Releases" at "http://oss.sonatype.org/content/repositories/
    releases"
)

libraryDependencies ++= Seq (
  "org.scalacheck" %% "scalacheck" % "1.10.0" % "test"
)

// append options passed to the Scala compiler
scalacOptions ++= Seq("-deprecation", "-unchecked", "-feature")
```

This project file will download and add the ScalaCheck dependency to your project
(don't forget to do a reload and an update). You can also download the latest
ScalaCheck (http://code.google.com/p/scalacheck/downloads/list) and play with it
using Scala REPL. In this chapter I show all the examples using the SBT project
because it's more convenient to build and compile. In the next section, you'll create
your first ScalaCheck test to verify the claim about the reverse method.

10.2.1 *Testing the behavior of a string with ScalaCheck*

To create a new property in ScalaCheck, you have to use the org.scalacheck.Prop
trait. The property in ScalaCheck is represented by instances of the Prop trait. There
are several ways to create an instance of a property in ScalaCheck but the one you're
going to use here is org.scalacheck.Prop.forAll.

    forAll is a factory method that creates a property that can be tested by
ScalaCheck. This method takes a function as an argument that should return a Boolean and can take any type of parameter as long as there's a generator. *Generators* are
components used by ScalaCheck to generate test data. (You'll read more about generators later in this section.) Here's how the property would look for the statement I
made about reverse in the previous section:

```
Prop.forAll((a: String) => a.reverse.reverse == a)
```

The way to read the preceding property is this: for all strings, the expression (a:
String) => a.reverse.reverse == a should hold true (this matches with the claim in
the previous section). ScalaCheck will use the generator for String type to generate
random string data to validate the statement. To run this property with SBT, you need
to wrap it inside the Properties class (later I show you how to use ScalaCheck with
your tests). The org.scalacheck.Properties represents a collection of ScalaCheck
properties, and SBT has built-in support for running Properties:

```
package checks
import org.scalacheck._

object StringSpecification extends Properties("String") {
  property("reverse of reverse gives you same string back") =
    Prop.forAll((a: String) => a.reverse.reverse == a)
}
```

```
> test
[info] Updating {file:/Users/n/mybook/code/chap10/scalacheck/}default-490062...
[info] Resolving org.scala-lang#scala-library;2.9.2 ...
[info] Resolving org.scalacheck#scalacheck_2.9.2;1.9 ...
[info] Resolving org.scala-tools.testing#test-interface;0.5 ...
[info] Done updating.
[info] Compiling 1 Scala source to /Users/n/mybook/code/chap10/scalacheck/target/scala-2.9.2/c
lasses...
[info] Compiling 1 Scala source to /Users/n/mybook/code/chap10/scalacheck/target/scala-2.9.2/t
est-classes...
[info] + String.reverse of reverse gives you same string back: OK, passed 100 tests.
[info] Passed: : Total 1, Failed 0, Errors 0, Passed 1, Skipped 0
[success] Total time: 8 s, completed Jun 18, 2012 3:26:03 PM
```

Figure 10.1 **The output from running ScalaCheck from the SBT prompt**

Save the preceding code in a StringSpecification.scala file under the src/test/scala folder of your project, and run the test action from the SBT prompt. If the setup is correct so far, you'll notice that ScalaCheck has tried 100 times to falsify your property but failed (see figure 10.1).

After 100 tests it should be safe to say that the property does hold true. Let's add another property that will check for any two strings x and y, where the expression x.startsWith(y) should be equivalent to x.reverse.endsWith(y.reverse). The ScalaCheck property should look like the following:

```
property("startsWith") = Prop.forAll {(x: String, y: String) =>
    x.startsWith(y) == x.reverse.endsWith(y.reverse)
}
```

Does this hold true? Go ahead and try this and see whether ScalaCheck can prove the property to be wrong. Again this property holds true after 100 tests. Let's try to create a property that's *not* always true and see whether ScalaCheck is able to catch it. The statement is this: for any two strings x and y, the expression x > y is equivalent to x.reverse > y.reverse. The ScalaCheck property looks like the following:

```
property("string comparison") = Prop.forAll {(x: String, y: String) =>
    x > y == x.reverse > y.reverse
}
```

In this case ScalaCheck will fail and show the arguments for which the expression doesn't hold true. The output may not always be visible to you because ScalaCheck uses character values from Char.MIN_VALUE to Char.MAX_VALUE. The following listing shows the complete String specification class.

Listing 10.1 String specification for ScalaCheck

```
package checks

import org.scalacheck._

object StringSpecification extends Properties("String") {
  property("reverse of reverse gives you same string back") =
      Prop.forAll((a: String) => a.reverse.reverse == a)
```

Property for reverse method

Define new specification

```
property("startsWith") = Prop.forAll {(x: String, y: String) =>
    x.startsWith(y) == x.reverse.endsWith(y.reverse)
}

property("string comparison - WILL FAIL") =
    Prop.forAll {(x: String, y: String) =>
      x > y == x.reverse > y.reverse
    }
}
```

Property for startsWith method

Property for string comparison

In listing 10.1 you create a specification for the `String` class. Granted, you haven't specified the complete behavior of the class, but you can see how ScalaCheck specifications work. You extend the `Properties` trait to make your specification runnable by SBT. Each statement that you want to verify is wrapped around a ScalaCheck property. You're using the `Prop.forAll` factory method to create a new property by passing a function that captures the statement that needs to be verified by ScalaCheck. ScalaCheck executes this function by passing random test data generated by built-in generators.

I hope by now you get the idea of how ScalaCheck properties are created and can be used to test the behavior of Scala code.

> **NOTE** The idea of automated testing didn't originate with ScalaCheck, but from a tool called QuickCheck,[5] a testing tool for the Haskell language. Sometime these tools are also called *specification-based unit testing tools*. You provide a specification of a class or method in terms of properties. This kind of specification-based testing tool relies heavily on the correctness of the type system. Because Scala and Java are both statically typed languages, ScalaCheck would be a great way to create specifications and add them to your project.

The next section discusses ScalaCheck generators so that when the time comes, you can create your own custom generator for a new type you create.

10.2.2 ScalaCheck generators

In the previous section you wrote your first ScalaCheck specification without worrying about generators, so why bother now? The reason you didn't worry about generators was that ScalaCheck knows how to generate test data for the `String` type (it knows about other types too[6])—but how about a new type that you created? In this case you're on your own. The good news is ScalaCheck provides all the building blocks you need to roll your own generator.

The ScalaCheck generators are responsible for generating test data, and the `org.scalacheck.Gen` class represents them. Think of generators as functions that take some generation parameters and return a generated value sometimes. For some combinations of parameters, the generator may not generate any value. A generator for

---

[5] "Introduction to QuickCheck," modified Oct 25, 2012, www.haskell.org/haskellwiki/Introduction_to _QuickCheck.

[6] "ScalaCheck user guide," updated April 12, 2012, http://code.google.com/p/scalacheck/wiki/UserGuide.

type T could be represented by a function of type `Gen.Params => T`. The ScalaCheck library already ships with various kinds of generators, but one in particular is quite important: the `arbitrary` generator. This is a special generator that generates arbitrary values for any supported type. It's the generator ScalaCheck used when testing the `String` specification you created in the previous section. To run any specification, ScalaCheck needs a generator to generate test data, so generators play an important role in ScalaCheck. The next section shows you how to create a custom generator in ScalaCheck.

10.2.3 *Working with ScalaCheck*

In this section I show you how to use ScalaCheck with a simple real-world use case. In the real world, you don't write specifications for the `String` class but rather for types (classes and traits) that you'll create. Instead of creating a new type on your own, let's take a look at the `scala.Either` class. This will be close, in terms of complexity, to the types you create or deal with in your project. In Scala, the `Either` type allows you to represent a value for one of two possible types: `Left` and `Right`. Usually, by convention, `Left` represents failure and `Right` represents success.

> **NOTE** Take a look at the scaladoc[7] of the `Either` type to get a feel for what you can do with this type.

In this section you'll add specification tests for some of its API methods. First I list the specifications you want to test. This is clearly not an exhaustive list, but it's a good starting point:

1 `Either` will have value on either `Left` or `Right`, but not both at any point in time.
2 `fold` on the `Left` should produce the value contained by `Left`.
3 `fold` on the `Right` should produce the value contained by `Right`.
4 `swap` returns the `Left` value to the `Right` and vice versa.
5 `getOrElse` on `Left` returns the value from `Left` or the given argument if this is `Right`.
6 `forAll` on `Right` returns true if `Left` or returns the result of the application of the given function to the `Right` value.

The complexity of the specifications grows as you go down the list, but you'll see how easy it is to implement them.

First, create a custom ScalaCheck generator for the `Either` type, because there's no built-in generator for this type. Creating new generators in ScalaCheck is as easy as combining the existing generators. To keep things simple, only create generators that can generate `Int` values for `Left` and `Right` (later I show you how to parameterize the generator). To create a new generator for `Left`, use the existing generator for the `Int` value to create instances for `Left`:

---

7 Scala Either, http://mng.bz/106L.

```
import Gen._
import Arbitrary.arbitrary

val leftValueGenerator = arbitrary[Int].map(Left(_))
```

The preceding code snippet creates a new instance of the `Int` type generator and maps it to create values for `Left`. Similarly, for creating instances of `Right`, use the following code:

```
val rightValueGenerator = arbitrary[Int].map(Right(_))
```

To successfully generate instances of the `Either` type, you have to randomly generate instances of `Left` or `Right`. To solve these kinds of problems, the ScalaCheck `Gen` object ships with helper methods like `oneOf` or `frequency`, called combinators. They allow you to combine multiple generators. For example, you could use `Gen.oneOf` to combine `leftValueGenerator` and `rightValueGenerator` to create a generator for the `Either` type. And `oneOf` ensures that `Left` and `Right` values are generated randomly:

```
implicit val eitherGenerator =
    oneOf(leftValueGenerator, rightValueGenerator)
```

By defining the generator as an `implicit val`, you don't have to pass it to ScalaCheck properties—ScalaCheck will pick it up. The generator you've defined here only generates `Int` values, but if you wanted to play with different types of values, you'd also define the generator like this:

```
implicit def arbitraryEither[X, Y](implicit xa: Arbitrary[X],
        ya: Arbitrary[Y]): Arbitrary[Either[X, Y]] =
    Arbitrary[Either[X, Y]](
        oneOf(arbitrary[X].map(Left(_)), arbitrary[Y].map(Right(_)))
    )
```

The generators for both `Left` and `Right` are type-parameterized so they'll take any type of parameter for which the `arbitrary` generator is defined in ScalaCheck.

You can also use `Gen.frequency` to get more control over each individual generator and its uses. If you wanted to use `leftValueGenerator` 75% of the time compared to the `rightValueGenerator`, you could use `Gen.frequency` like this:

```
implicit val eitherGenerator =
    frequency((3, leftValueGenerator), (1, rightValueGenerator))
```

The generator is created. Let's move on with your first specification. This specification is easy to implement—all you have to do is check that both `Left` and `Right` aren't present at the same time. In this case you'll use the `isLeft` and the `isRight` methods available in the `Either` type that return true or false based on whether it contains a value:

```
property("isLeft or isRight not both") = Prop.forAll((e: Either[Int, Int])
    => e.isLeft != e.isRight)
```

If `isLeft` and `isRight` are equal, your specification fails because it clearly states that both `Left` and `Right` can't have values at the same time.

For the second specification ("fold on the Left should produce the value contained by Left") and the third ("fold on the Right should produce the value contained by Right"), use the fold method defined in the Either type:

```
property("left value") = Prop.forAll{(n: Int) =>
        Left(n).fold(x => x, b => error("fail")) == n }

property("Right value") = Prop.forAll{(n: Int) =>
        Right(n).fold(b => error("fail"), x => x) == n }
```

Both cases will error out if they try to access the wrong value. The contract of the fold is like the following, where it only applies the appropriate function parameter:

```
def fold[X](fa: A => X, fb: B => X) = this match {
    case Left(a) => fa(a)
    case Right(b) => fb(b)
}
```

Go ahead and add these properties to a specification class and run them (see listing 10.2 for the complete specification).

Customizing the number of tests generated by ScalaCheck

ScalaCheck provides configurable options which allow you to control how ScalaCheck verifies your property. If you want to generate more than 100 successful tests before a property is declared successful, you can pass ScalaCheck arguments to your test through SBT. The trick is to use the SBT test-only action. This action allows you to provide test names as arguments and pass additional test arguments. If you don't specify any test names, it will run all the tests like the SBT test action. You can change the default setting for the minimum successful (-s) tests from 100 to 500 by passing test arguments to SBT like the following:

```
>test-only -- -s 500
```

By passing -s (ScalaCheck-specific configuration), you've configured the minimum successful tests that will be generated by ScalaCheck before a property is pronounced successful. Check the ScalaCheck documentation to learn about all the configuration options.

The fourth specification ("swap returns the Left value to Right and vice versa") is a little harder but nothing that can't be fixed. According to this specification, the swap method of the Either type could swap the value from Left to Right and vice versa. Here you can use pattern matching to check whether the value corresponds to Left or Right. For example, if it's Left, then after swap the value should be available on the Right side and vice versa for the Right value:

```
property("swap values") = Prop.forAll{(e: Either[Int, Int]) => e match {
        case Left(a) => e.swap.right.get == a
        case Right(b) => e.swap.left.get == b
    }
}
```

The following listing shows the complete specification for the Either type, including
specification numbers 5 and 6.

Listing 10.2   Complete EitherSpecification

```
object EitherSpecification extends Properties("Either") {
  import Gen._
  import Arbitrary.arbitrary
  val leftValueGenerator = arbitrary[Int].map(Left(_))
  val rightValueGenerator = arbitrary[Int].map(Right(_))
  implicit val eitherGenerator = oneOf(leftValueGenerator,
    rightValueGenerator)

  property("isLeft or isRight not both") =
    Prop.forAll((e: Either[Int, Int]) => e.isLeft != e.isRight)

  property("left value") =
    Prop.forAll{(n: Int) => Left(n).fold(x => x, b => error("fail")) == n }

  property("Right value") =
    Prop.forAll{(n: Int) =>
      Right(n).fold(b => error("fail"), x => x) == n }

  property("swap values") = Prop.forAll{(e: Either[Int, Int]) => e match {
    case Left(a) => e.swap.right.get == a
    case Right(b) => e.swap.left.get == b
  }
  }

  property("getOrElse") =
    Prop.forAll{(e: Either[Int, Int], or: Int) =>
        e.left.getOrElse(or) == (e match {
            case Left(a) => a
      case Right(_) => or
        })
  }

  property("forall") = Prop.forAll {(e: Either[Int, Int]) =>
    e.right.forall(_ % 2 == 0) == (e.isLeft || e.right.get % 2 == 0)
  }
}
```

Annotations:
- Generator for Either.Left → `val leftValueGenerator = arbitrary[Int].map(Left(_))`
- Generator for Either.Right → `val rightValueGenerator = arbitrary[Int].map(Right(_))`
- Define specification by extending Properties
- Generator for Either by using oneOf combinator

The previous listing creates a generator for the Either type by using the building
blocks provided by ScalaCheck. Arbitrary.arbitrary is one of those building blocks
that lets you create new custom generators. Using it, you create generators for both
Left and Right values of the Either type. Then, using the combinators available in
the Gen object, you create a generator for the Either type. The rest of the code is
defining ScalaCheck properties for all the specifications declared at the beginning of
the section.

There are plenty of Scala open source libraries, like Scalaz (https://github.com/
scalaz/scalaz) and Lift (https://github.com/lift/framework), that use ScalaCheck for
testing their classes. You can always download them and go through their ScalaCheck
tests to see various ways you can use them.

It's also easy to use ScalaCheck to test Java codebases. Because Scala and Java inter-operate, you don't have to do anything special to test java codebases. ScalaCheck also supports the generation of Java collection classes.

As you've already figured out, ScalaCheck is a powerful framework. For example, with 20–25 lines of code, you managed to generate 600 tests. With the ability to create custom generators, I'm sure you can think of places in your project where ScalaCheck will be valuable.

What about the new functionality you've yet to implement? You aren't sure how it should look yet—the classes, traits, and functions you'd need to implement the functionality. The next section introduces you to a design technique called test-driven development, which might solve your problem.

10.3 *Test-driven development cycle*

Test-driven development[8] (TDD) is a technique of using tests to drive the design of software (see figure 10.2). At first it sounds misleading because you usually associate tests with a verification of the software. You test your software to make sure it's working as expected. It's more like the last thing you do before releasing your software. TDD completely reverses that and makes testing a central part of the software development life-cycle. In agile software development, TDD is one of the most, if not the most, important practice. But you don't have to buy in to agile to reap the benefits of TDD—you can use it with any process. Remember: TDD is a design tool. In the end you get a test suite, but that's more of a secondary effect. Let's go through and understand how TDD works, and then I'll explain why it works.

The figure outlines how TDD works as a development practice. You always start with a failing end-to-end test. An end-to-end test (sometimes called an *integration* test) exercises your application from top to bottom. This could mean the test is making an HTTP request through a browser and checking the response back. Then you write a bunch of unit tests to break the problem into smaller pieces and make them pass. You only write production code when you have a failing test, and you only refactor when your tests are passing. One way to think about it is to take one of the acceptance criteria of the feature you're supposed to implement and write it as an executable test.

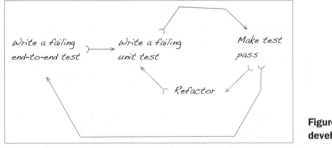

Figure 10.2   Test-driven development cycle

---

[8] "Test-driven Development," http://en.wikipedia.org/wiki/Test-driven_development.

Let's consider the following feature request. As a pricing analyst, you want to calculate a price for products so you can bill customers correctly:

Acceptance criteria:
  A 100 product code should use cost plus the percent amount.
  Example: 150 (cost) + 20% = $180
  All products whose ID starts with B should use an external price source to get the price.

In this case, if you pick the first acceptance criterion, your job would be to implement that criterion as a test. When you start to implement the acceptance criterion as a test, the following are the some of the questions that might pop into your head:

- Where should you implement the pricing logic?
- Should you create a trait or start with a simple function?
- What parameters will the function take?
- How should you test the output?
- Should it hit the database or filesystem to pull up the cost?

If this is the case, you have already started to think about the design. But at this point your focus should be only on the unit of work at hand. That means the acceptance criterion you're working on. The most common theme of TDD is to pick the simplest solution that could possibly work. In this case the simplest solution would be to create a function that takes a product code, looks it up in a `Map`, and returns the price using the formula specified in the acceptance criterion. Probably, using `Map` to look up the cost design decision you made might not hold true on the next test. When that happens, you'll make the necessary code changes and look up the cost from some persistence store—you get the idea. Do the simplest thing that could possibly work, and then incrementally design and build your application.

Once your test is running, you have the opportunity to refactor or clean up. *Refactoring* (www.refactoring.com) is a technique you can use to improve the design of existing code without changing the behavior. This test-code-refactor cycle repeats for each feature or step that you implement. Sometimes this cycle is called the *red-green-refactor* cycle. When a test is failing, you're in the red state; then you make the test pass and move to the green state. TDD is a development practice, and it takes some time to get used to it. As you go through some examples, it will become clearer.

The good news is that the Scala community is blessed with lots of testing tools to use. I'm going to focus on two of the most popular: JUnit and Specs. JUnit is more popular among Java developers and can be easily used to test Scala code. But most Scala programmers use Specs to test their Scala code.

As you start writing tests, you're also building a test suite. If you don't run them often, then you're not extracting the benefits from them. The next section discusses setting up a continuous integration[9] environment to get continuous benefits from them.

---

[9] Martin Fowler, "Continuous Integration," May 1, 2006, http://martinfowler.com/articles/continuous Integration.html.

10.3.1 *Setting up your environment for TDD*

Once you and your team get comfortable with TDD, you need a tool that checks out the latest code from your source code repository and runs all the tests after every check-in of the source control system. This ensures that you always have a working software application. A continuous integration (CI) tool does that automatically for you. Almost all the existing CI tools will work for Scala projects. Table 10.1 shows some Scala tools that you could use in your Scala project.

Table 10.1 Tools to set up your TDD environment

Name	Description
Jenkins CI[a]	Open source continuous integration tool that could build and test your project continuously. You can configure it to point to your source control and run builds every time the repository is updated. In essence, almost all the CI tools have these features. You could also use any other popular CI tool for your Scala project.
Jenkins SBT plugin[b]	Allows you to run SBT build actions from Jenkins and lets you configure SBT using Jenkins. For CI tools that don't have native support for SBT but support Maven, you can easily generate a POM file for your SBT project using the `make-pom` SBT command.
Code coverage[c]	Code coverage is a measurement of source code that's under automated tests. Code coverage tools help you to identify the area of the code that's not tested. Almost all Java code coverage tools will work for Scala projects, but using tools that work with your build tool, like SBT, is always better.

a. Jenkins home page, http://jenkins-ci.org.
b. sbt plug-in, edited on Aug. 27, 2011, http://wiki.jenkins-ci.org/display/JENKINS/sbt+plugin.
c. jacoco4sbt, https://bitbucket.org/jmhofer/jacoco4sbt/wiki/Home.

> **TIP** SBT is still fairly new compared to other build tools available in the market. If you have a testing tool or CI environment that doesn't work well with SBT, you can use Maven (http://maven.apache.org) as your build tool. There's a Maven Scala plug-in[10] that makes your Maven project Scala-aware and allows you to compile and run your Scala tests. You can also generate a .POM file (Maven build file) from your SBT project using the `make-pom` action.

I've mentioned only a handful of tools you can include in your project to have a continuous feedback cycle. The toolset around Scala is always evolving, so try out a few tools and pick the one that best fits your project. The next section explains how you can use JUnit to test your Scala code.

10.3.2 *Using JUnit to test Scala code*

JUnit (www.junit.org) is a simple testing framework written in Java that allows you to write automated tests. This is a popular framework used in many Java projects. If you've used the JUnit testing tool previously to write tests for Java code, I'm happy to

---

[10] maven-scala-plugin, version 2.14.2, Aug. 4, 2010, http://scala-tools.org/mvnsites/maven-scala-plugin/.

inform you that you can use it to test Scala code too. To use JUnit inside your SBT project, add the following dependency to your project file:

```
libraryDependencies += "junit" % "junit" % "4.10" % "test"
```

By default, SBT doesn't recognize JUnit-style test cases, so you have to add another dependency to your project to make SBT aware of JUnit test cases:

```
libraryDependencies += "com.novocode" % "junit-interface" % "0.8" % "test"
```

The `junit-interface`[11] tool implemented the test interface of SBT so that SBT can run JUnit test cases. After you reload and update your SBT project, you're ready to add JUnit test cases and run them using the test action from SBT console. This works out great if you have legacy JUnit tests that you want to retain while porting your application from Java to Scala, or you have both Java and Scala projects[12] that you're building with SBT.

JUnit is a good way to get started writing automated tests, but it's not an appropriate testing tool for Scala projects because it still doesn't understand Scala natively. There are multiple open source Scala testing tools you can use to write more expressive tests. Section 10.6 looks into a Scala testing tool called Specs that most Scala developers use, but for now let's try to understand an important concept called dependency injection, which helps in designing more testable applications.

10.4 Better tests with dependency injection

Dependency injection (DI) is a design pattern that separates behavior from dependency resolution (the way your components find other dependent components). This pattern also helps to design programs that are highly decoupled in nature. Let's look at a naïve example to understand how DI works (see figure 10.3).

This example is about calculating the price of a product based on various pricing rules. Typically any pricing system will have hundreds of rules, but to keep things simple I will only talk about two:

- The cost-plus rule determines the price by adding a percentage of the cost.
- Getting the price from an external pricing source.

With these rules in place, the calculate price service would look something like the next listing.

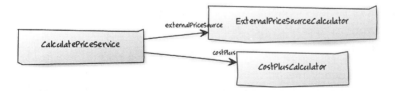

Figure 10.3 `CalculatePriceService` and its calculators

---

[11] Stefan Zeiger, szeiger/junit-interface, https://github.com/szeiger/junit-interface.
[12] SBT, https://github.com/harrah/xsbt.

Listing 10.3   Basic `CalculatePriceService`

Create price calculator for external source ❷

① Create cost-plus calculator

Map of all calculators as partial function

Calculates the price based on price type

Base trait for all calculators

```scala
sealed class CalculatePriceService {
  val costPlusCalculator = new CostPlusCalculator()
  val externalPriceSourceCalculator = new ExternalPriceSourceCalculator()

  val calculators = Map(
    "costPlus" -> calculate(costPlusCalculator) _ ,
    "externalPriceSource" -> calculate(externalPriceSourceCalculator) _)


  def calculate(priceType: String, productId: String): Double = {
    calculators(priceType)(productId)
  }
  private[this] def calculate(c: Calculator)(productId: String):Double =
    c.calculate(productId)
}
trait Calculator {
  def calculate(productId: String): Double
}

class CostPlusCalculator extends Calculator {
  def calculate(productId: String) = {
    ...
  }
}

class ExternalPriceSourceCalculator extends Calculator {
  def calculate(productId: String) = {
    ...
  }
}
```

The cost-plus rule is implemented by the costPlusCalculator ❶, and the external price source is handled by the externalPriceSourceCalculator ❷. Both calculators extend the Calculator trait. The CalculatePriceService class uses these calculators based on the parameter priceType. Right now the two possible values for priceType are "costPlus" and "externalPriceSource". Let's relate this example to the definition of DI. The behavior of the CalculatePriceService is to use the appropriate price calculator to determine the price for a given product. At the same time this class is also resolving its dependencies. Is there anything wrong with managing your own dependencies?

NOTE   Dependency injection is a specific form of inversion of control where the concern being inverted is the process of obtaining the needed dependencies.

Yes, there are some potential problems with this, in particular when your software is evolving. What if your client decides to use a different external pricing source to calculate the price or redefines the cost-plus calculation logic for some customers? In these cases you have to come up with different implementations of calculators and change the `CalculatePriceService` accordingly. This might be okay in some situations, but if you're planning to build this as a component that will be shared by projects, you have a problem.

Using DI, you can easily solve this problem. If the dependent calculators could be passed in (injected) to the `CalculatePriceService`, then the service could be easily configured with various implementations of calculators. In its simplest form, you could pass these calculators through the constructor:

```
sealed class CalculatePriceService(
    val costPlusCalculator: Calculator,            Calculators passed in as
    val externalPriceSourceCalculator: Calculator) {  ◁─ constructor arguments

    val calculators = Map(
      "costPlus" -> calculate(costPlusCalculator) _ ,
      "externalPriceSource" -> calculate(externalPriceSourceCalculator) _)

    def calculate(priceType: String, productId: String): Double = {
      calculators(priceType)(productId)
    }
    private[this] def calculate(c: Calculator)(productId: String):Double =
      c.calculate(productId)
  }
```

The only thing that's changed compared to the previous code listing is that now the instances of two calculators are passed in as constructor arguments. In this case, the caller of the service takes the responsibility to determine the dependent price calculators and inject them into the service. This makes the service highly decoupled because it doesn't care how the `costPlusCalculator` or `externalPriceSourceCalculator` is created or implemented. This also gives you flexibility in terms of design because now you can easily incorporate the changes your customer is talking about and come up with different implementations of pricing rules.

10.4.1 Techniques to implement DI

What does DI have to do with testing? In unit testing it's important to understand the unit you're testing. When you're testing the `calculate` method of `CalculatePrice-Service`, your system under test is the `CalculatePriceService`, not the `costPlusCalculator` or the `externalPriceSourceCalculator`. But if you don't isolate the calculators, your test will end up testing them as well. This is okay when you're testing your system end to end using an integration test, but not when you want to test only the behavior of the `CalculatePriceService`. In this small example, it might be hard to see the difference, but in a large application without isolation of dependencies, you'll end up initializing the system over and over again for each component you test. Isolation is important if you want to write simple and manageable unit tests.

The second problem with a closely coupled system is the speed of testing. It's important to have your tests run faster. Remember that your tests are your feedback mechanism, so if they run slowly you won't get faster feedback. In this example, each of your calculators might access the database or an external web service, and these will slow down your tests.

> **DEFINITION** *Test double* is a common umbrella term for a test-specific equivalent of a component that your system under test depends on.

Ideally you'll create a test version for each calculator so that you can focus your testing to verify only the system under test, which in this case is `CalculatePriceService`. In the test version of the calculator, you can return a hardcoded price or use an in-memory database to speed things up. This will also give you more control over the test data. One key aspect of TDD is rerunnable tests. If your tests are heavily dependent on the external data, they will become brittle because the external data could change and break your tests.

> **NOTE** A measure of a good unit test is that it should be free of side effects, the same as writing a pure function in functional programming.

If you follow TDD as a driver for your design, you don't have to worry too much about the coupling problem—your tests will force you to come up with a decoupled design. You'll notice that your functions, classes, and methods follow a DI pattern.

The following sections discuss ways you can implement dependency injection in Scala. Table 10.2 shows the list.

Table 10.2 Techniques to implement dependency injection

Technique	Description
Cake pattern	Handles dependency using trait mixins and abstract members.
Structural typing	Uses structural typing to manage dependencies. The Scala structural typing feature provides duck typing[a] in a type-safe manner. *Duck typing* is a style of dynamic typing in which the object's current behavior is determined by the methods and properties currently associated with the object.
Implicit parameters	Manages dependencies using implicit parameters so that as a caller you don't have to pass them. In this case, dependencies could be easily controlled using scope.
Functional programming style	Uses function currying to control dependencies. *Function currying* is a technique by which you can transform a function with multiple arguments into multiple functions that take a single argument and chain them together.
Using a DI framework	Most of the techniques mentioned here will be home-grown. I show you how to use a DI framework in your Scala project.

a. Duck typing, http://en.wikipedia.org/wiki/Duck_typing.

These techniques can help to write more testable code and provide a scalable solution in Scala. Let's take our favorite `CalculatePriceService` and apply each of the techniques mentioned in the table.

10.4.2 Cake pattern

A *cake pattern*[13] is a technique to build multiple layers of indirection in your application to help with managing dependencies. The cake pattern is built on the three abstraction techniques described in Table 10.3.

Table 10.3   Abstractions used in the cake pattern

Name	Description
Abstract members	Provides a way to abstract the concrete types of components. Using abstract types you can create components that don't depend on concrete types, and the type information could be provided by other components that use them. (See this chapter's codebase for an example.)
Self type annotation	Allows you to redefine `this` and is a way to declare the dependencies required by a component. Using a trait mixin, you can inject various implementations of dependencies. (See this chapter's codebase for an example.)
Mixin composition	You've already seen this in chapter 4. A mixin allows you to use Scala traits to override and add new functionality.

These concepts were covered in detail in chapter 7, so let's see how the cake pattern can help you decouple the `CalculatePriceService` from its calculators and make it more testable. The first thing you can do is extract the calculator instances from the service to its own namespace called `Calculators`:

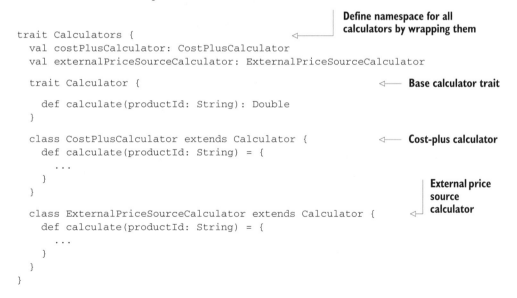

```
trait Calculators {                                 ┌─ Define namespace for all
  val costPlusCalculator: CostPlusCalculator        └─ calculators by wrapping them
  val externalPriceSourceCalculator: ExternalPriceSourceCalculator

  trait Calculator {                                ◁── Base calculator trait

    def calculate(productId: String): Double
  }

  class CostPlusCalculator extends Calculator {     ◁── Cost-plus calculator
    def calculate(productId: String) = {
      ...
    }
  }
                                                       External price
                                                       source
  class ExternalPriceSourceCalculator extends Calculator {  ◁─┘ calculator
    def calculate(productId: String) = {
      ...
    }
  }
}
```

---

[13] Martin Odersky and Matthias Zenger, "Scalable Component Abstractions," presented at OOPSLA'05, Oct. 16-20, 2005, http://lamp.epfl.ch/~odersky/papers/ScalableComponent.pdf

The idea behind this `Calculator` trait is to have a component namespace that has all the calculators in your application. Similarly, let's create a component namespace for the `CalculatePriceService` and declare its dependency to `Calculators` by self type:

```
trait CalculatePriceServiceComponent {this: Calculators =>
  class CalculatePriceService {
    val calculators = Map(
      "costPlus" -> calculate(costPlusCalculator) _
      "externalPriceSource" -> calculate(externalPriceSourceCalculator) _)

    def calculate(priceType: String, productId: String): Double = {
      calculators(priceType)(productId)
    }
    private[this] def calculate(c: Calculator)(productId: String):Double =
      c.calculate(productId)
  }
}
```

Create new namespace for CalculatePriceService

Map all the calculators with unique name

You're using the self type `this: Calculators` to redefine `this`. That will also allow you to statically ensure that no one can create `CalculatePriceService` without mixing in the `Calculators` trait. The benefit is that now you can reference both `costPlusCalculator` and `externalPriceSourceCalculator` freely. The self type will ensure that they're available during runtime.

You must be wondering why both calculators are declared as abstract inside the `Calculators` trait. It's because you want to control how these calculators are created. Remember from the tests, you don't want to use the calculators; instead you want to use a fake or `TestDouble` version of the calculators. At the same time, you want to use the real version of the calculators in production mode. This is where the trait mixin comes in handy. For production mode you could create a pricing system by composing all the real versions of these components, as in the following:

```
object PricingSystem extends CalculatePriceServiceComponent
            with Calculators {
  val costPlusCalculator = new CostPlusCalculator
  val externalPriceSourceCalculator = new ExternalPriceSourceCalculator
}
```

The pricing system is initialized with the real implementation of `costPlusCalculator` and `externalPriceSourceCalculator`, and for testing the pricing could be created using the fake implementation:

```
trait TestPricingSystem extends CalculatePriceServiceComponent
        with Calculators {
  class StubCostPlusCalculator extends CostPlusCalculator {
    override def calculate(productId: String) = 0.0
  }
  class StubExternalPriceSourceCalculator extends
      ExternalPriceSourceCalculator {
    override def calculate(productId: String) = 0.0
  }
  val costPlusCalculator = new StubCostPlusCalculator
  val externalPriceSourceCalculator = new StubExternalPriceSourceCalculator
}
```

Fake implementation for cost-plus calculator

Fake implementation of external price source calculator

In the case of the `TestPricingSystem`, the calculators are implemented using `TestDouble` so that it helps to write tests around the calculate price service. In your tests you'll use the `TestPricingSystem` shown in the following listing.

Listing 10.4 JUnit test case for calculating price service (cake pattern)

```
package scala.book.cakepatterntest {
  import junit.framework.Assert._
  import org.junit.Test
  import cakepattern._

  class CalculatePriceServiceTest extends TestPricingSystem {

    @Test
    def shouldUseCostPlusCalculatorWhenPriceTypeIsCostPlus() {
      val calculatePriceService = new CalculatePriceService
      val price = calculatePriceService.calculate("costPlus",
                              "some product")
      assertEquals(5.0D, price)
    }

    @Test
    def shouldUseExternalPriceSourceCalculator () {
      val calculatePriceService = new CalculatePriceService
      val price = calculatePriceService.calculate("externalPriceSource",
                         "dummy")
      assertEquals(10.0D, price)
    }
  }
}
```

Test case mixed in with test version of pricing

Test to assert cost-plus calculator used

Test to assert external price source calculator used

You mix the test version of the pricing system into your test class. This will automatically make the fake implementation of the calculators available inside the test. That simplifies your test and lets you focus testing on the `CalculatePriceService`. The two tests are testing whether the `CalculatePriceService` is using the right type of calculator when invoked with the name of the calculator.

This is a common technique used by Scala developers to manage dependencies. In smaller projects, it's reasonable to have the wiring of dependencies implemented like the `PricingSystem` and the `TestPricingSystem`, but for large projects it may become difficult to manage them. For large projects it makes more sense to use a DI framework (section 10.5.2 shows how to use off-the-shelf DI) that allows you to completely separate object creation and injection from business logic.

10.4.3 *Structural typing*

Structural typing in Scala is the way to describe types by their structure. The previous section created the `Calculators` trait as a namespace for all the calculators, and `CalculatePriceService` used it to get to individual calculators. The contract between these two traits is the two abstract vals: `costPlusCalculator` and `externalPrice-SourceCalculator`, because `CalculatePriceService` doesn't care about anything else. To create a structure that captures this information, make Scala treat that as a new type:

```
type Calculators = {
    val costPlusCalculator: Calculator
    val externalPriceSourceCalculator: Calculator
}
```

The code creates a new type called `Calculators` by specifying the structure. `type` is a keyword in Scala used to create new types or a type alias. Now you can use this type to inject various implementations of calculators into the `CalculatePriceService`:

```
class CalculatePriceService(c: Calculators) {
  val calculators = Map(
   "costPlus" -> calculate(c.costPlusCalculator) _ ,
   "externalPriceSource" -> calculate(c.externalPriceSourceCalculator) _)

  def calculate(priceType: String, productId: String): Double = {
    calculators(priceType)(productId)
  }

  private[this] def calculate(c: Calculator)(productId: String):Double =
     c.calculate(productId)
}
```

When using a structural type, you don't necessarily have to name your type—you can use it inline, as in the following:

```
import scala.language.reflectiveCalls
class CalculatePriceService(c: {
    val costPlusCalculator: Calculator
    val externalPriceSourceCalculator: Calculator
}) {
    val calculators = Map(
      "costPlus" -> calculate(c.costPlusCalculator) _ ,
      "externalPriceSource" -> calculate(c.externalPriceSourceCalculator)_)

    def calculate(priceType: String, productId: String): Double = {
      calculators(priceType)(productId)
    }
    private[this] def calculate(c: Calculator)(productId: String):Double =
     c.calculate(productId)
}
```

Enabling reflective access of structural type member (annotation pointing to `import scala.language.reflectiveCalls`)

Inline structural type passed as argument to ❶ constructor

In this case, the type of the constructor parameter is defined as inlined ❶. The advantage of structural typing in Scala is that it's immutable and type-safe. The Scala compiler will ensure that the constructor parameter of `CalculatePriceService` implements both the abstract vals `costPlusCalculator` and `externalPriceSource-Calculator`. Again, you could create two types of configuration—one for testing and another for production:

```
object ProductionConfig {
    val costPlusCalculator = new CostPlusCalculator
    val externalPriceSourceCalculator = new ExternalPriceSourceCalculator
    val priceService = new CalculatePriceService(this)
}
object TestConfig {
    val costPlusCalculator = new CostPlusCalculator {
```

Define test configuration with fake implementations

Define production configuration with real implementation

```
      override def calculate(productId: String) = 0.0
    }

    val externalPriceSourceCalculator = new ExternalPriceSourceCalculator {
      override def calculate(productId: String) = 0.0
    }
    val priceService = new CalculatePriceService(this)
  }
```

Based on what you're doing, you have the flexibility to pick the appropriate configuration. This is one of my favorite ways to handle dependencies because it's easy and simple. Yet it does come with a price. Internally, structural typing is implemented using reflection, so it's slower compared to other approaches. Sometimes that's acceptable, but be aware of it when using structural typing.

10.4.4 Implicit parameters

Implicit parameters provide a way to allow parameters to be found. Using this technique you can have the Scala compiler inject appropriate dependencies into your code. (You've already seen implicit parameters in action [section 10.2.2].) ScalaCheck uses implicit parameters to decide an appropriate generator to use for a given property. To declare a parameter implicit, you have to mark the parameter with the `implicit` keyword.

The following example injects the calculators as a parameter to `CalculatePrice-Service` and marks them as implicit:

```
class CalculatePriceService(
    implicit val costPlusCalculator: CostPlusCalculator,
    implicit val externalPriceSourceCalculator:
    ExternalPriceSourceCalculator
)
```

The beauty of implicit parameters is that if you don't supply them when creating the instance of `CalculatePriceService`, the Scala compiler will search for "implicit" values that match your parameter in the compilation scope. If the compiler fails to find an appropriate implicit value, it fails the compilation.

Create an object called `ProductionServices` that defines these implicit values for production code:

```
object ProductionServices {
    implicit val costPlusCalculator = new CostPlusCalculator
    implicit val externalPriceSourceCalculator =
    new ExternalPriceSourceCalculator
}
```

To provide values for implicit parameters, you also have to mark each value with `implicit`—otherwise the compiler won't recognize it. You have to import this object when running in production mode, and the easiest way to do that is use a configuration object like the following:

```
object ProductionConfig {
  import ProductionServices._
  val priceService = new CalculatePriceService
}
```

Similarly, for testing, create a separate configuration object and provide a test implementation of the services:

```
object TestServices {
    implicit val costPlusCalculator = new CostPlusCalculator {
      override def calculate(productId: String) = 0.0
    }

    implicit val externalPriceSourceCalculator =
      new ExternalPriceSourceCalculator {
      override def calculate(productId: String) = 0.0
    }
}

object TestConfig {
  import TestServices._
  val priceService = new CalculatePriceService
}
```

You don't necessarily have to always use implicit values for implicit parameters because you can always explicitly pass parameters the old-fashioned way. Using `implicit` to handle dependencies can easily get out of hand as your application grows in size, unless they're grouped together like the preceding configuration objects. Otherwise, your implicit declaration and imports will be scattered around the code and will make it hard to debug compilation issues. Note that implicit parameter resolution depends on types. Instead of defining both `costPlusCalculator` and `externalPriceSourceCalculator` as a type of `Calculator`, you had to provide more specific types. Sometimes this constraint can be too restrictive to build a scalable design.

10.4.5 *Dependency injection in functional style*

The general idea behind DI is inversion of control.[14] Instead of a component controlling its dependencies, it's passed from outside (usually by some container or framework). When you work with functions, then, DI is already happening automatically. If you consider a function as a component, then its dependencies are its parameters. This makes functions inherently testable. If you create function currying, you can also hide the dependencies as you did with other patterns. *Function currying* is a technique of transforming functions that takes multiple arguments into a chain of functions each with a single argument. The following is the new interface of `Calculators` that only uses functions:

```
trait Calculators {
    type Calculator = String => Double
    protected val findCalculator: String => Calculator
```

[14] Martin Fowler, "Inversion of Control Containers and the Dependency Injection Pattern," Jan. 23, 2004, http://martinfowler.com/articles/injection.html.

```
protected val calculate: (Calculator, String) => Double =
  (calculator, productId) => calculator(productId)
}
```

The type `Calculator` is an alias of function that takes product ID and returns the price. The `findCalculator` function determines the calculator for a given price type. And finally `calculate` is a function that takes an instance of `Calculator` and `productId` to calculate the price of the product. This is quite similar to the interfaces you designed earlier, but this time with only functions.

You can turn the `calculate` function into a `curried` function by invoking the `curried` method defined for all function types in Scala:

```
val f: Calculator => String => Double = calculate.curried
```

The `curried` method takes a function of *n* parameters and transforms it to *n* functions with one parameter. In this case it created a function that takes `Calculator` and returns a function that calculates the price for a `productid`. The benefit of doing this now is you have a function that knows how to calculate price but hides the `Calculator` from the users. The following is the example test implementation of the `Calculators`:

```
object TestCalculators extends Calculators {
  val costPlusCalculator: String => Double = productId => 0.0
  val externalPriceSource: String => Double = productId => 0.0

  override protected val findCalculator = Map(           ◁─┐ Map already
    "costPlus" -> costPlusCalculator,                        extends
    "externalPriceSource" -> externalPriceSource            Function1
  )

    def priceCalculator(priceType: String): String => Double = {
        val f: Calculator => String => Double = calculate.curried
        f(findCalculator(priceType))
      }
  }
}
```

The `priceCalculator` method returns a function that takes the `productId` and returns the price of the product that encapsulates the dependencies used to compute the price. This is an example of how you can do dependency injection using functional programming.

10.4.6　*Using a dependency injection framework: Spring*

Scala's abstract members, self type and mixin provide more abstraction techniques than are available in Java, but DI frameworks provide the following additional services that aren't available in these abstraction techniques:

- They create a clean separation between object initialization and creation from the business logic. These frameworks provide a separate lifecycle to create dependencies as part of the application initialization. This way, your wiring between components becomes transparent from the code.

- These frameworks help you to work with various other frameworks. For example, if you're planning to use existing Java web frameworks, then a DI framework will help to inject your Scala objects as dependencies.
- Most of the DI frameworks, like Spring (www.springsource.org) and Guice (http://code.google.com/p/google-guice/), provide aspect-oriented programming (AOP)[15] support to handle cross-cutting behaviors like transaction and logging out of the box.

The good news is you can use any Java DI framework with your Scala project. This section shows you how to use the Spring framework as a DI framework in your Scala project. (I won't explain how the Spring dependency injection framework works, but if you're new to it read the tutorials[16] available on the Spring framework website.)

The Spring framework allows you to configure dependencies in multiple ways. I'll show you how to configure it using the external XML configuration file. In the Spring world, all the dependencies are called beans, because all the objects follow the Java-Bean[17] convention. According to this convention a class should provide a default constructor, and class properties should be accessible using get, set, and is methods.

To make a property a bean property, Scala provides a handy annotation called @BeanProperty. This annotation tells the Scala compiler to generate getter and setter methods automatically so you don't have to worry about it. The following listing shows the beanified version of the CalculatePriceService.

Listing 10.5   Bean version of `CalculatePriceService`

```
package scala.book
import scala.reflect._
sealed class CalculatePriceService {
  @BeanProperty var costPlusCalculator: Calculator = _      ❶
  @BeanProperty var externalPriceSourceCalculator: Calculator = _   ❷

  def calculators = Map(
    "costPlus" -> calculate(costPlusCalculator) _ ,
    "externalPriceSource" -> calculate(externalPriceSourceCalculator) _)

  def calculate(priceType: String, productId: String): Double = {
    calculators(priceType)(productId)
  }
  private[this] def calculate(c: Calculator)(productId: String):Double =
    c.calculate(productId)
}
```

❷ Annotate **externalPriceSourceCalculator** as bean property

❶ Annotate **costPlusCalculator** as bean property

This version of CalculatePriceService looks almost identical to the version from section 10.3, except here both the costPlusCalculator ❶ and externalPriceSourceCalculator ❷ are declared as bean properties using @BeanProperty annota-

---

[15] "Aspect-oriented programming," http://en.wikipedia.org/wiki/Aspect-oriented_programming.
[16] "The IoC container," Spring Framework, http://static.springsource.org/spring/docs/2.5.x/reference/beans.html.
[17] "JavaBeans," http://en.wikipedia.org/wiki/JavaBean.

tions. The @BeanProperty annotations will generate the following getters and setters for costPlusCalculator and externalPriceSourceCalculator properties:

```
def getCostPlusCalculator: Calculator = this.costPlusCalculator
def setCostPlusCalculator(c: Calculator) { this.costPlusCalculator = c }

def getExternalPriceSourceCalculator: Calculator =
    this.externalPriceSourceCalculator
def setExternalPriceSourceCalculator (c: Calculator) {
    this. externalPriceSourceCalculator = c
}
```

Both price calculators are already beans because they provide a default constructor. The only missing piece is to wire up dependencies to the service, and in Spring you can do this by specifying a configuration file, as shown in the next listing.

Listing 10.6 Spring application context file

```
 <?xml version="1.0" encoding="UTF-8"?>
<beans xmlns="http://www.springframework.org/schema/beans"
    xmlns:xsi="http://www.w3.org/2001/XMLSchema-instance"
    xsi:schemaLocation=
      "http://www.springframework.org/schema/beans
      http://www.springframework.org/schema/beans/spring-beans-2.0.xsd">
    <bean id="costPlusCalculator" class="scala.book.CostPlusCalculator"/>
    <bean id="externalPriceSourceCalculator"
          class="scala.book.ExternalPriceSourceCalculator"/>

    <bean id="calculatePriceService"
          class="scala.book.CalculatePriceService">
      <property name="costPlusCalculator" ref="costPlusCalculator" />
    <property name="externalPriceSourceCalculator"
                            ref="externalPriceSourceCalculator" />
    </bean>
</beans>
```

Define bean for cost-plus calculator

Define bean for external price source calculator

❶ Define bean for service by setting dependencies

This is a standard version of a Spring configuration file, where the calculators and the CalculatePriceService are defined by setting up the dependencies ❶. Save this Spring application-context.xml file in your src/main/resources folder in your SBT project. This is the main configuration file for the pricing application. This file will be used to initialize the application beans. Similarly, you also have a test version of the configuration file under src/test/resources that refers to the fake implementation of calculators. You could also create fake instances inside the test and inject them. You'll use the latter one to see how you could inject fake versions of the calculators. But first add the following dependencies to your SBT project file:

```
val spring = "org.springframework" % "spring" % "2.5.6"
val springTest = "org.springframework" % "spring-test" % "2.5.6"
val junit = "junit" % "junit" % "4.4" % "test"

val junitInterface = "com.novocode" % "junit-interface" % "0.5" % "test"
```

Both the Spring framework and the Spring test framework are added as dependencies. Because you haven't learned about Specs yet, let's use JUnit as the testing tool. Again, junitInterface is the testing interface for SBT so that it can run the JUnit tests.

To test CalculatePriceService, you can use Spring to configure the beans and override the appropriate calculator inside the test. To use Spring with the JUnit test, add the following annotations along with the test class declaration:

```
@RunWith(classOf[SpringJUnit4ClassRunner])
@ContextConfiguration(
    locations = Array("classpath:/application-context.xml"))
```

The RunWith annotation allows JUnit tests to get access to instantiated beans as defined in the application context file. The ContextConfiguration lets you specify which configuration file to use to initialize beans. If you have a test version of the configuration file, specify that. Inside the test, if you declare a variable of CalculatePriceService with the @Resource annotation, Spring will create and inject an instance of it into the test. Here's the skeleton JUnit test with Spring configuration:

```
@RunWith(classOf[SpringJUnit4ClassRunner])
@ContextConfiguration(locations =
    Array("classpath:/application-context.xml"))
class CalculatePriceServiceTest {

  @Resource
  var calculatePriceService: CalculatePriceService = _
}
```

The instance of CalculatePriceService will be created by the Spring framework and injected inside the test for you. At this point, this test class is set up for testing the calculate price service. The following is the JUnit test to check that the calculate price service uses the cost-plus calculator to calculate price:

```
@Test
def shouldUseCostPlusCalculatorWhenPriceTypeIsCostPlus() {
  val fakeCostPlusCalculator = new Calculator {
    def calculate(productId: String) = 2.0D
  }
  calculatePriceService.setCostPlusCalculator(fakeCostPlusCalculator)
  val price = calculatePriceService.calculate("costPlus", "some product")
  assertEquals(2.0D, price)
}
```

The real implementation of the costPlusCalculator is replaced by a fake implementation. The test is passing "costPlus" as a price type, and according to the logic (see listing 10.5) it will use the cost-plus calculator. Similarly, the following is the test for an external price source calculator:

```
@Test
def testShouldReturnExternalPrice() {
  val fakeExternalPriceSourceCalculator = new Calculator {
      def calculate(productId: String) = 5.0D
  }
```

```
      calculatePriceService.setExternalPriceSourceCalculator(
        fakeExternalPriceSourceCalculator)
      val price = calculatePriceService.calculate("externalPriceSource",
        "dummy")
      assertEquals(5.0D, price)
    }
```

In a similar fashion, the real implementation is swapped with a fake version before invoking the service. The following listing shows the complete JUnit test.

Listing 10.7 Complete unit testing using Spring dependency injection

```
import javax.annotation.Resource
  import junit.framework.Assert._
  import org.junit.Test
  import org.junit.runner.RunWith
  import org.springframework.test.context.ContextConfiguration
  import org.springframework.test.context.junit4.SpringJUnit4ClassRunner

  @RunWith(classOf[SpringJUnit4ClassRunner])
  @ContextConfiguration(locations = Array("classpath:/application-
      context.xml"))
  class CalculatePriceServiceTest {

      @Resource
      var calculatePriceService: CalculatePriceService = _

      @Test
      def shouldUseCostPlusCalculatorWhenPriceTypeIsCostPlus() {
        val fakeCostPlusCalculator = new Calculator {
          def calculate(productId: String) = 2.0D
        }
        calculatePriceService.setCostPlusCalculator(fakeCostPlusCalculator)
        val price = calculatePriceService.calculate("costPlus",
            "some product")
        assertEquals(2.0D, price)
      }

      @Test
      def testShouldReturnExternalPrice() {
        val fakeExternalPriceSourceCalculator = new Calculator {
          def calculate(productId: String) = 5.0D
        }
        calculatePriceService.setExternalPriceSourceCalculator(
            fakeExternalPriceSourceCalculator)
        val price = calculatePriceService.calculate("externalPriceSource",
            "dummy")
        assertEquals(5.0D, price)
      }
  }
```

Allow JUnit test to access Spring beans ⊳ (points to `@RunWith(classOf[SpringJUnit4ClassRunner])`)

Configuration file used to initialize beans ◁ (points to `class CalculatePriceServiceTest {`)

Resource annotation lets Spring set bean value ◁ (points to `var calculatePriceService: CalculatePriceService = _`)

You annotate your JUnit test to allow it to see all the Spring beans using `RunWith` and specify the configuration file used to create the beans. Note that if you have a test version of the configuration, you should specify it here—that way you don't have to create a fake implementation per test. In large projects it's recommended to have a test version of a configuration file where you can configure all your beans with fake implementations of their dependencies. As you can see, there's nothing much to change to use Scala classes and traits with the Spring framework. And this is true for all other dependency injection frameworks available in Java. There's some up-front work to use a DI framework, but for large projects it's worth it—unless you're using some Scala framework that provides native support for managing dependencies.

I covered a lot of ground in this section, and I'm sure the techniques you've learned here will help you to write more decoupled and testable systems in Scala.

The next section covers another testing tool, called Specs. JUnit was great to get quickly up and running with testing Scala code, but now it's time to get used to the Scala-based testing framework, which is more expressive and easier to use.

10.5 *Behavior-driven development using Specs2*

Behavior-driven development (BDD) is about implementing an application by describing the behavior from the point of view of stakeholders. So far I've been talking about test-driven development in this chapter, so why bother discussing BBD? How is it different from TDD?

The answer is that it isn't different. BDD[18] is doing TDD the right way. The first thing to notice is that the definition of BDD doesn't talk about testing at all. This is on purpose, because one pitfall of doing TDD is that some people put more emphasis on testing than solving the business problem. And BDD puts more emphasis on solving business problems. In fact, it recommends looking at the application from the stakeholder's perspective. The end result of doing BDD in a project has the following two important outcomes:

- *Delivering value quickly*—Because you're focused on viewing the application from the stakeholder's point of view, you understand and deliver value quickly. It helps you to understand the problem and recommend appropriate solutions.
- *Focus on behavior*—This is the most important improvement because at the end of the day, behaviors that you implement are the ones your stakeholders want. Having a focus on behavior also reduces the effort spent on up-front design, analysis, and documentation, which rarely adds value to the project.

To get developers and stakeholders on the same page, you need the Ubiquitous[19] language, a common language everybody speaks when describing the behavior of an application. And you also need a tool so you can express these behaviors and write automated specifications that assert the behavior.

> **NOTE** I've been using *test* and *specification* synonymously, but *specification* is a better way to talk about behavior with stakeholders. Think of a specification as a list of examples.

[18] David Chelimsky, et al., *The RSpec Book: Behaviour-Driven Development with RSpec, Cucumber, and Friends,* Pragmatic Bookshelf, 2010, www.pragprog.com/book/achbd/the-rspec-book.
[19] "UbiquitousLanguage," http://martinfowler.com/bliki/UbiquitousLanguage.html.

In BDD, you still follow the red-green-refactor cycle during your development. The only thing that changes is the way you look at these tests or specifications. It's time to see some BDD in action, and the next section introduces you to the BDD tool that most Scala developers use: Specs2.

10.5.1 *Getting started with Specs2*

Specs2[20] is the BDD library for Scala, and it's written in Scala. At the time of this writing it's the de facto BDD library used by Scala developers. The easiest way to get started with Specs is to add it as a dependency to your SBT project. Add the following to your SBT build.sbt file:

```
scalaVersion := "2.10.0"
libraryDependencies += "org.specs2" %% "specs2" % "1.13" % "test"
```

If you're planning to use some other version of Specs, make sure it's compatible with the Scala version set in your SBT project. Once you reload and update your project, you're ready to use Specs. The best part is that SBT knows how to run the Specs specification natively. Write the first Specs specification using the same calculate price service you saw in the previous section. Create the empty specification for CalculatePriceService:

```
package scala.book
import org.specs._
class CalculatePriceServiceSpecification extends Specification
```

To declare a Specs specification, you always have to import org.specs2.mutable._ and extend the Specification trait. Next, specify the behaviors of the calculate price service:

```
package scala.book
import org.specs2.mutable._
class CalculatePriceServiceSpecification extends Specification {
  "Calculate price service" should {
    "calculate price for cost plus price type" in {}
    "calculate price for external price source type" in {}
  }
}
```

You've added a structure to the specification. First you use the should method to define the system, followed by the description of two behaviors of the service. The Specs framework adds methods like should and in to the String class using implicit conversion so that your specification can become more expressive and readable. When you run this specification using the SBT test action, you'll see the output shown in figure 10.4.

If you have a color-enabled terminal window, Specs will show the test output in different colors. Because I haven't implemented the specification, in figure 10.4, it's yellow. (If I had implemented the specification, green would indicate a passed test, red a failure.)

---

[20] Specs 2, http://etorreborre.github.com/specs2/.

```
[info] == scala.book.CalculatePriceServiceSpecification ==
[info] + Calculate price service should
[info]   o calculate price for cost plus price type
[info]   o calculate price for external price source type
[info] == scala.book.CalculatePriceServiceSpecification ==
[info]
[info] == test-complete ==
[info] == test-complete ==
[info]
[info] == test-finish ==
```

Figure 10.4 Specs output of running a specification

Implement these pending specifications using the cake pattern implementation of the service. In section 10.5.1, you created two versions of CalculatePriceService—one that uses the real calculators and another using the fake implementation of the calculators for testing. Here's the test version of CalculatePriceService:

```
trait TestPricingSystem
    extends CalculatePriceServiceComponent with Calculators {
  class StubCostPlusCalculator extends CostPlusCalculator {
    override def calculate(productId: String) = 5.0D
  }
  class StubExternalPriceSourceCalculator
      extends ExternalPriceSourceCalculator {
    override def calculate(productId: String) = 10.0D
  }
  val costPlusCalculator = new StubCostPlusCalculator
  val externalPriceSourceCalculator = new StubExternalPriceSourceCalculator
}
```

Both calculators return a hardcoded price. This is perfectly fine because the focus right now is on CalculatePriceService, and the assumption is that both calculators work correctly. To use this version of the pricing system, you need to mix this in with the specification, as shown in the following listing.

Listing 10.8 Specification for CalculatePriceService

```
import org.specs2.mutable._
import cakepattern._
class CalculatePriceServiceSpecification
    extends Specification with TestPricingSystem {

  "Calculate price service" should {
    "calculate price for cost plus price type" in {
      val service = new CalculatePriceService
      val price: Double = service.calculate("costPlus", "some product")
      price must
      beEqualTo(5.0D)                                    ⊲┐ Using specs2
    }                                                     ❶ beEqualTo matcher

    "calculate price for external price source type" in {
      val service = new CalculatePriceService
      val price: Double = service.calculate("externalPriceSource",
                          "some product")
```

```
      price must be_==(10.0D)
    }
  }
}
```

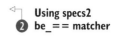

Using specs2
② be_ == matcher

The `TestPricingSystem` is mixed in with the `CalculatePriceService` using the fake implementation of calculators. **①** uses the Specs' built-in matcher called `beEqualTo`, and **②** uses an overloaded version of it. The `must` method is again added by Specs using implicit conversions to almost all the types to make the specification more readable. This example demonstrates how easy it is to write a good expressive specification with Specs. The next section explores Specs features available to you for writing expressive specifications.

10.5.2 *Working with specifications*

To effectively work with Specs, you need to get comfortable with specifications and the available matchers. The matchers are the way you add expectations in your specification. `beEqualTo` and `must be_==` are examples of matchers. Specs ships with many built-in matchers, and you can find the complete list in the Specs documentation.[21]

You saw a sample specification in the previous section. Now I'll show you a variation of that. Depending on the kind of behavior you're describing, pick the appropriate one.

The basic format of the Specs specification is that you extend the `Specification` trait and then provide examples:

```
package variousspecs
import org.specs2.mutable._
object MySpec extends Specification {
  "example1" in {}
  "example2" in {}
}
```

One way to look at a specification is as a group of examples that describe the behavior of your application. But typically, when writing specifications you'll have a component for which you're describing the behavior; this is your system under specification. You can organize the examples as a group for a system under specification:

```
object SUSSpec extends Specification {
  "my system" should {
    "do this" in {}
    "do that" in {}
  }
}
```

You can also nest examples if you want to refine your examples. You may want to add an example to describe the behavior of a cost-plus calculator when the product ID is

---

[21] Specs, MatchersGuide, "How to add expectations to your examples," http://code.google.com/p/specs/wiki/MatchersGuide.

empty. According to the stakeholder, the price in this case should be 0.0. Here's how the example looks:

```
"calculate price for cost plus price type" in {
    val service = new CalculatePriceService
    val price: Double = service.calculate("costPlus", "some product")
    price must beEqualTo(5.0D)

    "for empty product id return 0.0" in {
        val service = new CalculatePriceService
        service.calculate("costPlus", "") must beEqualTo(0.0D)
    }
}
```

You're nesting the example for the special case when the product is empty. By default, examples are run in isolation, and they don't share any state. What that means is that you have to take extra measures to share the variables and state. Because having shared state between examples is a bad idea, I'm not going to cover that here.

Another interesting way to declare specifications in Specs is to use data tables.[22] Data tables allow you to execute your example with a set of test data. For example, if you have to describe an example of how the cost-plus rule calculates price, having one example with one sample data isn't enough. To describe its behavior properly, you need a set of data that evaluates the rule. Specs data tables come in handy in these cases. They let you specify your sample data in a table format like the following:

```
"cost plus price is calculated using 'cost + 20% of cost + given service
  charge' rule" in {

    "cost" | "service charge" | "price" |>
    100.0  !    4              ! 124     |
    200.0  !    4              ! 244     |
    0.0    !    2              ! 2       | {
      (cost, serviceCharge, expected) =>
        applyCostPlusBusinessRule(cost, serviceCharge) must be_==(expected)
    }
}
```

The example describes the rule, and the data table helps capture the data you need to verify the applyCostPlusBusinessRule method. The first row of the table is the header and is used for readability purposes. The second and following rows have sample data followed by a closure that's invoked for each row of data. Inside the closure you're evaluating the applyCostPlusBusinessRule method and checking the expected result. To use data tables in your specification, you have to mix in the Data-Tables trait. And the > at the beginning of the table is also required—think of it as a play command. The > makes the table executable as part of the example.

Specs data tables are a great way to create examples with sets of example data. You can also use ScalaCheck with Specs and have it generate sample data for your example.

---

[22] Specs, "How to use Data Tables," updated March 30, 2010, http://code.google.com/p/specs/wiki/AdvancedSpecifications.

The next section explores how automated testing fits into the asynchronous messaging world. In chapter 9 you learned about actors as a specific example of messaging systems. Now let's see how to write tests around them.

10.6 *Testing asynchronous messaging systems*

So far this chapter has talked about testing or created examples for systems that are synchronous, where the test invokes the system and control comes back to the test when the system is done performing an action. But in asynchronous fire-and-forget systems, the control will come back to the test while the system is executing. From the test, you don't get the feedback you're looking for. To overcome this challenge, developers sometimes extract the business logic outside of the messaging layer (always a good idea) and test it separately. One drawback with this kind of approach is that you're no longer testing your system end to end. For example, to verify that one actor is sending a message to another actor after some action, you need to write an integration test that sends a message to one actor and waits for the reply. The general rule for writing integration tests around asynchronous systems is to detect invalid system state or wait for some expected notification with a timeout.

Writing automated tests around asynchronous systems is quite new, and the tools for it are still maturing. One tool worth mentioning here is Awaitility,[23] which provides a nice testing DSL for testing asynchronous systems. Let's see Awaitility work in a simple example. Imagine that you have an order-placing service that saves orders to the database asynchronously, and you place an order by sending a `PlaceOrder` message. Here's the dummy ordering service implemented as an actor:

```
package example.actors
case class PlaceOrder(productId: String, quantity: Int, customerId: String)

class OrderingService extends Actor {
    def act = {
      react {
        case PlaceOrder(productId, quantity, customer) =>
      }
    }
  }
```

Inside the specification you'll use Awaitility's await method to wait until the order is saved into the database. If the order isn't saved in the database, then you know that something went wrong while processing the message. Here's the specification for the ordering service:

```
import org.specs2.mutable._
import example.actors._
import com.jayway.awaitility.scala._
import com.jayway.awaitility.Awaitility._
class OrderServiceSpecification extends Specification
      with AwaitilitySupport {
```

---

[23] Awaitility, http://code.google.com/p/awaitility/.

```
"Ordering system" should {
  "place order asynchronously" in {                    ❶ Send
    val s = new OrderingService().start                  message
    s ! PlaceOrder("product id", 1, "some customer id")  to actor
    await until {orderSavedInDatabase("some customer id") }  ◁── Wait until
    1 must_== 1                                                    data is saved
  }                                                              in database
  def orderSavedInDatabase(customerId: String) = ...
}
}
```

The preceding example sends an asynchronous message to the ordering service ❶ and waits until the order is saved into the database. The default timeout for Awaitility is 10 seconds, and you can easily set your timeout by invoking the overloaded version of `await`. Inside the `orderSavedInDatabase`, you could go to the data source and check whether the order is saved for a given customer ID.

Awaitility doesn't provide any infrastructure to help you test asynchronous systems, but it does make your examples readable.

10.7 Summary

This chapter covered an important topic that is critical to developing high-quality software. Picking up a new programming language and trying to use it to build a large application is difficult. And one of the common hurdles is to find a way to write automated tests in the new language or programming environment. This chapter gave you that introduction and introduced tools you can use in Scala projects.

First I introduced you to automated testing and how you can generate automated tests using ScalaCheck. You learned how to define specifications in ScalaCheck and create custom test data generators. ScalaCheck is a great way to get test protection for your Scala project.

You learned about agile software development and the role test-driven development plays inside it. You also explored how TDD is beneficial to building reliable software and how it helps in evolving design. To use TDD as a practice in a Scala project, you need tool support. I explained how to set up a continuous environment and use SBT as a build tool. I listed some of the common tools used by Scala developers.

Building applications using automated tests requires that your design be testable. One of the critical properties for a testable design is inversion of control, used in Java, Ruby, and other languages. Scala, being both object-oriented and functional, has more options to create abstractions. Section 10.5 showed you ways of doing dependency injection in Scala. Concepts like self type and abstract members aren't only restricted to dependency injection—in fact, you can take these abstract ideas and build reusable components in Scala.

The most common mistake made by developers when doing TDD is putting focus on testing, whereas the most important thing is the behavior of the application. BDD fixes that confusion by putting the focus back on behavior and customer collaboration. I introduced you to a tool called Specs that allows you to write expressive specifications. I mentioned that you can use JUnit to test your Scala code, but noted that it isn't recommended. Using Scala specification/testing tools will improve the readability of your tests and will provide better integration with other Scala tools.

On the surface, writing automated tests looks difficult, but I'm confident you don't feel that way anymore. With Scala's rich ecosystem of tools, it's easy to get started with automated tests or specifications, and you don't have any excuse not to use them.

The next chapter discusses functional programming. You've seen some functional programming features of Scala in previous chapters and examples, but chapter 11 ties them together with functional programming concepts so you can write more reliable and correct Scala programs.

Part 3

Advanced steps

These last 2 chapters lead you through advanced steps in Scala.

One of the most exciting features of Scala is that it runs on the JVM. The benefit of running on a JVM, as you know by this point, is that you can integrate with other languages on it and take advantage of all the frameworks and tools built into other JVM languages. Chapter 11, while it encourages you to think Scala first, covers the interoperability between Scala and Java.

Chapter 12 introduces Akka, a Scala toolkit that allows you to build next-generation, event-based, fault-tolerant, scalable, and distributed applications for the JVM.

To understand how the individual pieces of Akka fit together, you're going to build a large real-time product search application using Akka called Akkaoogle. This application is similar to what used to be called Froogle.

Interoperability between Scala and Java

This chapter covers

- Using Java classes in Scala
- Working with Java generics and collections
- Solving integration challenges
- Building web applications using Java frameworks

One of the most exciting features of Scala is that it runs on the JVM. The benefit of running on a JVM is that you can take advantage of all the frameworks and tools built into other JVM languages. More companies are moving to the JVM even if they don't use Java as their primary programming language. I strongly believe that any language that doesn't have support for the JVM is almost a nonstarter, for most of the software projects in the enterprise.

One of the main design goals of Scala is to run on a JVM and provide interoperability with Java. Scala is compiled to Java bytecodes, and you can use tools like `javap` (Java class file disassembler) to disassemble bytecodes generated by the Scala compiler. In most cases, Scala features are translated to Java features so that Scala can easily integrate with Java. For example, Scala uses type erasure[1] to be compatible with Java. Type erasure also allows Scala to be easily integrated with dynamically typed languages for the JVM. Some Scala features (such as traits) don't directly map to Java, and in those cases you have to use workarounds (more about this in section 11.3).

Even though integration with Java is easy for the most part, I encourage you to use pure Scala as much as possible. When I'm working with the Java library or framework, I try to find something equivalent in Scala first, and use Java if there's no equivalent Scala library available. The downside of using the Java library is that you have to deal with mutability, exceptions, and nulls that are absolutely discouraged in the Scala world. Be extra careful when choosing a Java library or framework before using it in Scala. A good example of a well-written Java library is Joda-Time (http://joda-time.sourceforge.net).

The most common integration of Scala and Java has part of the project written in Scala. Section 11.4 shows how to use Scala with existing Java frameworks such as Hibernate and Spring to build a web application.

In most cases, the integration between Scala and Java is seamless, but be aware of some corner cases because they will occur when you're integrating Java code with Scala and vice versa. The goal of this chapter is to show you how easily you can integrate Scala with Java and which practices to follow to avoid integration problems. You've been integrating with Java classes and frameworks throughout the book without my pointing them out, but here you'll focus on integration so you can take advantage of both worlds.

The easiest way to introduce Scala in an existing Java project is to write some part of it in Scala and demonstrate the benefits the language has to offer over Java—and then gradually rewrite the Java parts to Scala. I've seen this transition path work successfully many times.

Let's kick off the chapter with some integration examples between Java and Scala. You'll learn how to handle features that are available in Java but not in Scala, such as static members and checked exceptions, and how to use Scala features like traits in Java code. You'll also learn how Scala annotations help in integration—for example, generating JavaBean-style get and set. At the end of the chapter you'll build a web application using Java frameworks.

11.1   Using Java classes in Scala

It's easy to integrate Java classes with Scala. Because working with dates in Java is always a painful process, the following Java code snippet uses the Joda-Time library to calculate the number of days between two dates:

```
package chap11.java;

import org.joda.time.DateTime;
import org.joda.time.Days;
import java.util.Date;
```

[1] Java Tutorials: Type erasure, http://download.oracle.com/javase/tutorial/java/generics/erasure.html.

```
public class DateCalculator {
  public int daysBetween(Date start, Date end) {
    Days d = Days.daysBetween(new DateTime(start.getTime()),
    new DateTime(end.getTime())));
    return d.getDays();
     }
   }
```

In a new SBT project, save the preceding code snippet to DateCalculator.java in the src/main/java/chap11/java folder. SBT knows how to cross-compile Java and Scala code. To use this class in Scala, extend the Java class as follows:

```
package chap11.scala

import chap11.java._
import java.util.Date

class PaymentCalculator(val payPerDay: Int = 100) extends DateCalculator {
  def calculatePayment(start: Date, end: Date) = {
    daysBetween(start, end) * payPerDay
  }
}
```

The Scala class is calculating the payment using the daysBetween method defined in the Date-Calculator Java class. The integration is so seamless, you won't even notice the difference.

In the next section you'll learn how to use Java static members in Scala.

11.1.1 *Working with Java static members*

When working with Java classes that declare static members, you need to understand how they're interpreted in Scala.

Scala doesn't have any static keywords, and Scala interprets Java static methods by thinking of them as methods of a companion object. Take a look at the following example to see how it works. This code adds a static method that returns the chronology (chronological calendar system) used by Joda-Time to represent time:

> ## Compiling Java and Scala together
>
> SBT knows how to build mixed Scala and Java projects out of the box. The Scala compiler allows you to build against both Java classes and Java source code. That way, if you have bidirectional dependency between Java and Scala, you can build them together without worrying about order.
>
> You can also use the Maven build tool to build mixed Java and Scala projects. To do so, you have to add an additional Maven plug-in. In this chapter's final example you'll use Maven to build an example project.

```
package chap11.java;

import org.joda.time.DateTime;
import org.joda.time.Days;
import org.joda.time.Chronology;
import java.util.Date;

public class DateCalculator {
  public int daysBetween(Date start, Date end) {
```

```
    Days d = Days.daysBetween(new DateTime(start.getTime()), new
      DateTime(end.getTime()));
    return d.getDays();
  }

  public static Chronology getChronologyUsed() {
    return DateTime.now().getChronology();
  }
}
```

Public static method to return chronology

To access the static member, you have to refer it as if it's defined in a companion object, like the following:

```
class PaymentCalculator(val payPerDay: Int = 100) extends DateCalculator {
  ...
  def chronologyUsed = DateCalculator.getChronologyUsed
}
```

You're accessing the static method defined in `DateCalculator` by using the class name like you access a companion object.

Visibility issues between Scala and Java

Scala and Java implement visibility differently.

Scala enforces visibility at compile time but makes everything public at runtime. There's a reason for that: in Scala, companion objects are allowed to access protected members of companion classes, and that can't be encoded at the bytecode level without making everything public.

Java enforces visibility rules both at compile time and runtime. This brings up some interesting corner cases. For example, if you have a protected static member defined in a Java class, there's no way to access that member in Scala. The only workaround is to wrap it in a public member so that can be accessed.

Up next, you'll see how to work with Java checked exceptions, because Scala doesn't have them.

11.1.2   *Working with Java checked exceptions*

Scala's lack of checked exceptions at times creates confusion when working with Java codebases where the compiler enforces checked exceptions. If you invoke the following Java method in Scala, you don't have to wrap the call in a `try/catch` block:

```
package chap11.java;
import java.io.*;

public class Writer {
  public void writeToFile(String content) throws IOException {
    File f = File.createTempFile("tmpFile", ".tmp");
    new FileWriter(f).write(content);
  }
}
```

In Scala, you can invoke the method without a `try/catch` block:

```
scala> def write(content: String) = {
     |   val w = new Writer
     |   w.writeToFile(content)
     | }
write: (content: String)Unit

scala> write("This is a test")
```

As a programmer, it's your responsibility to determine whether you need to catch the exception. The Scala compiler won't force you. In cases where you think you should catch the exception, don't rethrow the exception from Scala. It's a bad practice. A better way is to create an instance of the `Either` or `Option` type. The following code snippet invokes the `writeToFile` method and returns an instance of `Either[Exception, Boolean]`:

```
def write(content: String): Either[Exception, Boolean] = {
  val w = new Writer
  try {
    w.writeToFile(content)
    Right(true)
  }catch {
    case e: java.io.IOException => Left(e)
  }
}
```

The benefit is now you can compose with the result. Always remember that exceptions don't compose. But there may be cases where you have to throw an exception because some framework or client code expects it, and in these cases you can use Scala annotations to generate bytecodes that throw an exception (section 11.2.1 has more on this). For now, let's move on to Java generics. Understanding how Java generics work is important because they're used in Java collections.

11.1.3 *Working with Java generics using existential types*

Java generics translate straightforwardly to Scala type parameters. For example, `Comparator<T>` translates to `Comparator[T]`, and `ArrayList<T>` to `ArrayList[T]`. But things become interesting when you have classes defined in Java with wildcard types. Here are two examples of Java collections with wildcard types:

```
Vector<?> names = new Vector<?>()
List numbers = new ArrayList()
```

In both cases, the type parameter is unknown. These are called *raw types* in Scala, and existential types let you handle these raw types in Scala. `Vector<?>` could be represented as `Vector[T] forSome { type T }` in Scala. Reading from left to right, this type expression represents a vector of `T` for some type of `T`. This type `T` is unknown and could be anything. But `T` is fixed to some type for this vector.

Let's look at an example to see how to use Java raw types in Scala. The following creates a Java vector with a wildcard type:

```
import java.util.*;

class JavaRawType {
  public static Vector<?> languages() {
    Vector languages = new Vector();
    languages.add("Scala");
    languages.add("Java");
    languages.add("Haskell");
    return languages;
  }
}
```

`JavaRawType.languages` returns a vector of three languages, but with wildcard type `?`. To use the `languages` method in Scala, you have to use the existential type. The type signature will be `Vector[T] forSome { type T}`, as in the following:

```
import java.util.{Vector => JVector }

def printLanguages[C <: JVector[T] forSome { type T}](langs: C):Unit = {
  for(i <- 0 until langs.size) println(langs.get(i))
}
```

Working with Java collections

Working with Java collection classes in Scala is painful once you get used to the power of the Scala collections library. Ideally, you should work with Scala collections in Scala code and transform them into the Java collection equivalent when crossing into Java code, and vice versa. That way, you can use the power of the Scala collections library when needed and easily integrate with Java codebases that only understand Java collection classes. The Scala library ships with two utility classes that do exactly that for you:

```
scala.collection.JavaConversions
scala.collection.JavaConverters
```

Both of these classes provide the same set of features, but they're implemented differently. `JavaConversions` provides a series of implicit conversions that convert between a Java collection and the closest corresponding Scala collection, and vice versa. `JavaConverters` uses a "Pimp my Library" pattern to add the `asScala` method to Java collection and `asJava` method to Scala collection types. My recommendation would be to use `JavaConverters` because it makes the conversion explicit. The following example uses `JavaConverters` to convert `java.util.List` to Scala and back:

```
scala> import java.util.{ArrayList => JList }
import java.util.{ArrayList => JList}
scala> val jList = new JList[Int]()
jList: java.util.ArrayList[Int] = []
scala> jList.add(1)
res1: Boolean = true
scala> jList.add(2)
res2: Boolean = true
scala> import scala.collection.JavaConverters._
import scala.collection.JavaConverters._

scala> jList.asScala foreach println
```

The asScala on jList transforms the java.util.ArrayList to scala.collection.mutable.Buffer so that you can invoke foreach on it. The following transforms scala List to java.util.List:

```
scala> List(1, 2).asJava
res4: java.util.List[Int] = [1, 2]
```

The existential type sets the upper bound of the type C and prints all the elements of the Java vector.

There's placeholder syntax for existential type JVector[_]. It means the same thing as JVector[T] forSome { type T }. The preceding printLanguages method could also be written as follows:

```
def printLanguages[C <: JVector[_]](langs: C):Unit = {
    for(i <- 0 until langs.size) println(langs.get(i))
  }
```

11.2 *Using Scala classes in Java*

One of the most interesting language features of Scala is traits, which are used a lot in Scala codebases. If you define a trait with only abstract methods, it gets compiled in the Java interface, and you can use it in Java without any issues. But if you have a trait with concrete methods, things become interesting. Let's take an example where you'll have a trait with concrete methods and see how that's compiled into Java bytecode.

The following example has a Scala trait that makes objects persistable to a database when mixed in:

```
package chap11.scala

trait Persistable[T]{
  def getEntity: T

  def save(): T = {
    persistToDb(getEntity)
    getEntity
  }
  private def persistToDb(t: T) = {...}
}
```

You have an abstract method called getEntity and two concrete methods, save and persistToDb. When this code is compiled, the Scala compiler generates two class files, Persistable.class and Persistable$class. To verify the content of each class file, you can use the :javap option in the SBT console:

```
scala> :javap chap11.scala.Persistable
Compiled from "ScalaJavaMash.scala"
public interface chap11.scala.Persistable extends scala.ScalaObject{
    public abstract java.lang.Object getEntity();
    public abstract java.lang.Object save();
}
```

```
scala> :javap chap11.scala.Persistable$class
Compiled from "ScalaJavaMash.scala"
public abstract class chap11.scala.Persistable$class extends
  java.lang.Object{
    public static java.lang.Object save(chap11.scala.Persistable);
    public static void $init$(chap11.scala.Persistable);
}
```

The `Persistable.class` file represents the Java interface, with all the public methods declared in the `Persistable` trait, and extends `scala.ScalaObject`. Every user-defined class in Scala extends `scala.ScalaObject`. On the other hand, the `Persistable $class` file defines an abstract class that defines all the concrete methods of the trait. Think of this abstract class as a façade to all the concrete methods defined in the trait.

On the Java side, take the help of both classes. You'll extend the interface and use the abstract class as a façade to access the concrete methods of the trait. The following example has an `Account` type that implements the `Persistable` interface and uses the static methods in `Persistable$class` to access concrete methods of the `Persistable` trait:

```
package chap11.java;

import chap11.scala.*;

public class Account implements Persistable<Account> {
  public Account getEntity() { return this; }
  public Account save() {                              ◁── Access save
    return (Account)Persistable$class.save(this);          method
  }                                                        from trait
}
```

The implementation of the `Persistable` interface is straightforward. `getEntity` returns an instance of the `Account` object, and the save method delegates to the static save method of the `Persistable$class` class to access the implementation-defined trait. Note that when working with stackable traits, it's much better to create a concrete class in Scala and then directly use it or extend it in Java. (This chapter's accompanying codebase has an example of that.)

One of the first hurdles people face when integrating Scala with Java frameworks is that Scala classes don't have JavaBean-style `get` and `set` methods. Scala annotations provide the flexibility to specify how you want the Scala compiler to generate bytecodes and are helpful in cases like these.

11.2.1 *Using Scala annotations*

Scala doesn't follow the standard Java getter and setter pattern. In Scala, getters and setters look different. For example, to create a Scala class with a Scala-style getter and setter, all you have to do is declare members as `var`, as in the following:

```
class ScalaBean(var name: String)
```

When compiled, this class generates the following bytecode:

```
scala> :javap chap11.scala.ScalaBean
Compiled from "ScalaJavaMash.scala"
public class chap11.scala.ScalaBean extends java.lang.Object
  implements scala.ScalaObject{
    public java.lang.String name();                    ◁──── get method
    public void name_$eq(java.lang.String);            ◁──── set method
    public chap11.scala.ScalaBean(java.lang.String);
}
```

If you compare the following code with the code generated in the preceding snippet, it will make sense:

```
scala> val s = new chap11.scala.ScalaBean("Nima")
s: chap11.scala.ScalaBean = chap11.scala.ScalaBean@6cd4be25

scala> s.name
res0: String = Nima

scala> s.name = "Paul"
s.name: String = Paul
```

If you add the `scala.reflect.BeanProperty` annotation to a property, the Scala compiler will generate corresponding `get` and `set` methods. In the case of `name`, it will generate `getName` and `setName` methods:

```
class ScalaBean(@scala.reflect.BeanProperty var name: String)
```

Here's how it looks when inspected using `javap`:

```
scala> :javap chap11.scala.ScalaBean
Compiled from "ScalaJavaMash.scala"
public class chap11.scala.ScalaBean extends java.lang.Object implements
     scala.ScalaObject{
    public java.lang.String name();
    public void name_$eq(java.lang.String);
    public void setName(java.lang.String);              ◁──── JavaBean-style set method
    public java.lang.String getName();                  ◁──── JavaBean-style get method
    public chap11.scala.ScalaBean(java.lang.String);
}
```

Note here that when using the `BeanProperty` annotation, the Scala compiler will generate both Scala and Java-style `get` and `set` methods. Using `BeanProperty` does increase the size of the class file generated, but that's a small price to pay for the interoperability with Java. Now if you want to generate JavaBean-compliant `BeanInfo`, you can use `scala.reflect.BeanInfo`.

Section 11.1 showed that Scala doesn't have checked exceptions, and Scala doesn't have a `throws` keywords to declare methods that throw exceptions. This at times causes problems. For example, if you want to use Scala to declare a `java.rmi.Remote` interface, you'll have trouble because each method declared in the `Remote` interface needs to throw `RemoteException`. Again, using annotations you could instruct the

Scala compiler to generate methods with a `throws` clause. The following code defines an RMI interface in Scala:

```
trait RemoteLogger extends java.rmi.Remote {
  @throws(classOf[java.rmi.RemoteException])
  def log(m: String)
}
```

The `RemoteLogger` trait extends the standard `java.rmi.Remote` to mark the interface as an RMI remote interface; to generate the `throws` clause it's using the `scala.throws` annotation defined in the Scala standard library. Look into the generated bytecode, and you'll see the `throws` clause:

```
scala> :javap chap11.scala.RemoteLogger
Compiled from "ScalaJavaMash.scala"
public interface chap11.scala.RemoteLogger extends java.rmi.Remote{
  public abstract void log(java.lang.String) throws
    java.rmi.RemoteException;
}
```

You can also use Scala's target meta annotation to control where annotations on fields and class parameters are copied. In the following code the `Id` annotation will only be added to the Bean getter `getX`:

```
import javax.persistence.Id
class A {   @(Id @beanGetter) @BeanProperty val x = 0 }
```

Otherwise, by default, annotations on fields end up on the fields. This becomes important when you're dealing with Java frameworks that are particular about where the annotation is defined. In the next section you'll see some usage of the target annotation and how to use popular frameworks like Spring and Hibernate in the Scala codebase.

11.3 *Building web applications in Scala using Java frameworks*

In this section you'll build a web application using Scala classes with Java frameworks. This example will show how you can use Scala in a Java-heavy environment, so when adopting or migrating to Scala you don't have to throw away all your investment in Java frameworks and infrastructure. Obviously, some of the boilerplate code goes away when you use frameworks built for Scala. Nonetheless, learning to work with Java frameworks is important for cases where you don't have the option to select Scala-based frameworks. In this section you're going to build a web application using the Spring framework (www.springsource.org) and Hibernate (www.hibernate.org). You'll also let go of your favorite build tool, SBT, and use Maven to build your Java because it's the most common build tool used in Java projects.

> **NOTE** This section assumes that you've previously used Spring, Hibernate, and Maven to build Java web applications. If you haven't, it may become hard to follow. It's also safe to skip this section if you aren't interested in working with Java frameworks.

Before going any further, let's identify the type of application you're going to build. You'll build a small web application called topArtists that displays top artists from Last.fm (www.last.fm). Last.fm is a popular music website that lets visitors access internet radio stations. Last.fm also provides an API you can use to retrieve various charts about songs and artists. You'll be using its `chart.getTopArtists` REST API to retrieve all the current top artists and save them in your local database. You'll also display all the artists stored in your local database to the user. Let's move on and set up the Maven build.

> **NOTE** You first need to get an API key from Last.fm. Make sure you have it before you run this example. You can acquire an API key at the Last.fm website (www.last.fm/api/authentication).

If you've done Java development, then most likely you've already used Maven. But if Maven isn't set up, download the latest version of the Maven build tool (http://maven.apache.org/download.html). Maven knows how to compile Java source files, but to make it compile Scala source files you need to add the Maven Scala plug-in.[2] To create an empty web application using Maven, execute the following command:

```
mvn archetype:generate -DgroupId=scala.in.action -DartifactId=top.artists
  -DarchetypeArtifactId=maven-archetype-webapp
```

That command will create an empty web project for you. The structure of the project should be familiar because it's exactly the same as an SBT project (SBT follows Maven conventions). Once you have the pom.xml file (the Maven build file generated by the preceding command), you can configure all the dependencies. As mentioned, you'll use the Hibernate and Spring frameworks to build the application. To save time, you can copy the pom.xml file from the codebase associated with the project.

There's no need to explain how Maven works because once you configure all the dependencies, it gets out of your way. But if you've never used Maven, remember that pom.xml is the build file you use to configure Maven and specify all the dependencies.

For the topArtists application you'll use Spring to build the web layer and also use it as a dependency injection framework. Hibernate will be your ORM layer and will save all the artists retrieved from Last.fm to the database. For your toy application, you'll be using the database HSQLDB (http://hsqldb.org). But to make a REST request to Last.fm, you'll use a pure Scala library called dispatch.[3] Dispatch is a Scala library, built on top of the Async Http Client library, that makes it easy to work with web services.[4]

> **NOTE** The complete version of the topArtists web application is available in the code that accompanies this chapter.

Let's move on and write the code necessary to build the application.

---

[2] Maven Scala plug-in download, http://scala-tools.org/mvnsites/maven-scala-plugin/.
[3] Dispatch Scala library: http://dispatch.databinder.net/Dispatch.html.
[4] See "AsyncHttpClient/async-http-client," https:/github.com/AsyncHttpClient/async-http-client.

Compiling Scala code with Maven

By default, Maven knows how to compile Java code. If you take a look at the pom.xml file associated with the codebase of this chapter, you'll notice the following snippet:

```
...
<groupId>org.scala-tools</groupId>
<artifactId>maven-scala-plugin</artifactId>
<version>2.15.2</version>
...
```

This adds the Maven Scala plug-in. As you can see, this code calls for the 2.15.2 version of the plug-in, but make sure you always use the latest version. Once you add the plug-in, it will create goals (tasks) to compile and run Scala classes. For example, you can use Maven's `scala:compile` to compile Scala code and `scala:cc` to have a continuous compilation (similar to `~compile` in SBT). You can find more options at the Maven Scala plug-in documentation page.

11.3.1 *Building the model, view, and controller*

The topArtists application displays artists retrieved from the REST API call from Last.fm. To see what information you can retrieve from Last.fm, invoke the following URL from any web browser window:

```
http://ws.audioscrobbler.com/2.0/?method=chart.gettopartists&api_key=
<your api key>
```

Make sure you use your Last.fm API key before invoking the URL. If the request is successful, you'll see information about artists, including name, number of times the songs have been played, listeners, URL, and other attributes. To keep things simple, use only the result from the first page and store the name of the artist, play count, and listeners. Your simple domain object will look like the following:

```
package chap11.top.artists.model

class Artist {
  var name: String = ""
  var playCount: Long = 0
  var listeners: Long = 0
}
```

This model class represents an artist by name, number of times songs by the artist have been played, and number of listeners. You'll retrieve all this data from the Last.fm feed.

Because you're using Hibernate as your ORM tool, you need to make your domain object compatible with Hibernate. First use `@BeanProperty` to generate JavaBean-style `get`/`set` methods. Then use necessary `javax.persistence` annotations so that Hibernate knows how to retrieve and save `Artist` domain objects into the database. The following listing shows the complete `Artist` domain object.

Listing 11.1 `Artist` Hibernate domain object

```
package chap11.top.artists.model

import reflect.BeanProperty
import javax.persistence._
import scala.annotation.target.field

@Entity
class Artist {
  @(Id @field) @(GeneratedValue @field) @BeanProperty
  var id: Long = 0
  @BeanProperty
  var name: String = ""
  @BeanProperty
  var playCount: Long = 0
  @BeanProperty
  var listeners: Long = 0
}
object Artist {
  def apply(name: String, playCount: Long, listeners: Long) = {
    val a = new Artist
    a.name = name
    a.playCount = playCount
    a.listeners = listeners
    a
  }
}
```

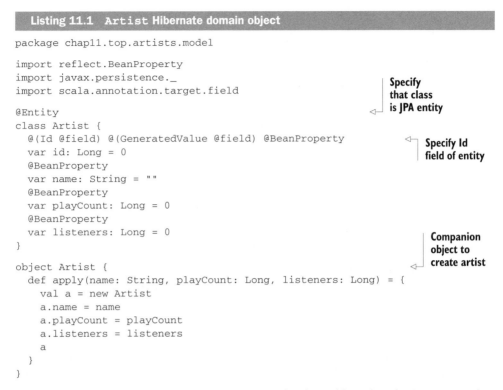

Specify
that class
is JPA entity

Specify Id
field of entity

Companion
object to
create artist

Hibernate implements the Java Persistence API (JPA), and by using the JPA annotation `Entity` you're specifying Hibernate to persist the object to the database. You're using the `Id` annotation to specify the ID field of the class and `scala.annotation.target` to generate the `Id` and `GeneratedValue` annotation at the field level.

Now, to save and retrieve the artist from the database, you have to work with the Hibernate session factory. Create a new class to encapsulate that and call it `ArtistDb`. This class will help you hide Hibernate-specific details from the rest of the code. Think of this class as a data access object. Because you're using Spring, you can easily inject the necessary Hibernate dependencies into this new class. The following listing shows the complete implementation of the `ArtistDb` class.

Listing 11.2 `ArtistDb.scala` database access with Hibernate

```
package chap11.top.artists.db

import org.springframework.stereotype.Repository
import org.springframework.transaction.annotation.Transactional
import org.springframework.beans.factory.annotation.Autowired
import org.hibernate.{Session, SessionFactory}
import java.util.{List => JList }
import chap11.top.artists.model.Artist

trait ArtistDb {
  def findAll: JList[Artist]
```

Interface
of data access
layer

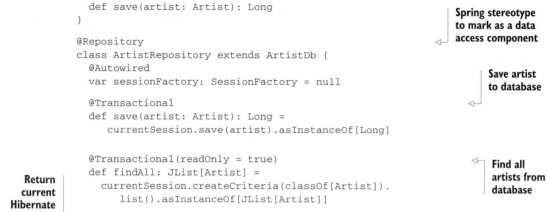

```
    def save(artist: Artist): Long                          Spring stereotype
}                                                            to mark as a data
                                                          ⟵┘ access component
@Repository
class ArtistRepository extends ArtistDb {
  @Autowired
  var sessionFactory: SessionFactory = null                 Save artist
                                                            to database
  @Transactional
  def save(artist: Artist): Long =                        ⟵┘
    currentSession.save(artist).asInstanceOf[Long]

  @Transactional(readOnly = true)                        ⟵┐ Find all
  def findAll: JList[Artist] =                              artists from
    currentSession.createCriteria(classOf[Artist]).         database
        list().asInstanceOf[JList[Artist]]

  private def currentSession = sessionFactory.getCurrentSession

}
```

Return current Hibernate session ⟶ (annotation pointing to `private def currentSession`)

The `ArtistRepository` class is marked with the Spring stereotype annotation `Repository` so that the Spring framework can automatically scan and load the component from the classpath. When Spring loads the class, it also sets the `sessionFactory` dependency. In the next section, you'll see how all these components are configured. For now, assume that the `sessionFactory` will be available in the `ArtistRepository` class to make database calls using Hibernate. The `save` method is straightforward: using the current Hibernate session, it saves an instance of `Artist` to the database. `asInstanceOf[Long]` typecasts the return value of the save to `Long`. In this case, you know that the save operation will return the `Id` value of the object saved. `findAll` queries the database and returns all the artists stored in the database. You typecast using `asInstanceOf` because by default the Hibernate `list` method returns a `List` of objects. At this point, you have enough code to save and retrieve domain objects from the database. Let's move on to build the controller.

As discussed earlier, you're going to use Spring to build your web tier. Again, you'll use Spring's stereotype annotation `@Controller` to mark a class as a controller. The job of the controller you'll build will be to get the top artists from Last.fm and display artists stored in the local database. Start off with the action that retrieves the list from the local database and sends it to the view to render. You already have an `ArtistDb` that knows how to retrieve artists from the database, and you'll use Spring to inject an instance of `ArtistDb` to the controller:

```
@Controller
class ArtistsController {
  @Autowired
  val db: ArtistDb = null
}
```

Add a method in the controller that maps to a URL and returns a list of artists to the view:

```
@RequestMapping(value = Array("/artists"), method = Array(GET))
def loadArtists() =
   new ModelAndView("artists", "topArtists", db.findAll)
```

The @RequestMapping annotation maps the "/artists" URI to the method load-
Artists. And in the method it uses db.findAll to find all the artists from the database. The first parameter to ModelAndView is the name of the view that will be
rendered as a result of the method. The topArtists parameter is a handy way to
name the response of db.findAll. Using the topArtists name inside the view, you
can access all artists returned from the findAll call. But before you can return a list of
artists successfully, you have to first get the list from Last.fm. Allow the user to refresh
the artists saved in the local database. To implement refresh, invoke the REST API
specified by Last.fm. Use the Dispatch library to make a REST call to Last.fm. Dispatch
provides a nice DSL or wrapper over the Apache HttpClient library. The following
code snippet creates an Http request object from the URL:

```
val rootUrl = "http://ws.audioscrobbler.com/2.0/"
val apiMethod = "chart.gettopartists"
val apiKey = sys.props("api.key")
val req = url(rootUrl + "?method=" + apiMethod + "&api_key=" + apiKey)
```

The API key is retrieved from the system property. When running the application, you
have to specify the API as a system property. The url method takes a string URL as an
input and returns an instance of Http request. But creating an Http request won't do
much unless you tell Dispatch how to process the response received from the request.
You can easily do that by specifying a handler. In this case we will use the built-in
handler as.xml.Elem to handle the XHTML response:

```
Http(req OK as.xml.Elem).map {resp => ...}
```

Http returns the Promise of scala.xml.Elem (since every HTTP request is handled
asynchronously) and we are using map to access the contents of the Promise object.
Since we are not using Spring's asynchronous support, we will wait for the Promise (by
invoking the apply method) to finish before rendering the result. The response from
Last.fm consists of an XML with a list of artists and looks something like the following:

```
<lfm status="ok">
  <artists page="1" perPage="50" totalPages="20"
    total="1000">
    <artist>
      ...
    </artist>
    <artist>
      ...
    </artist>
    ...
  </artists>
</lfm>
```

You'll use Scala's awesome native XML support to parse the result. Dispatch already
converted the response to an instance of NodeSeq, and now you have to extract all the

artists from the response, create a Hibernate `Artist` object, and save it to the database. Here's the method that does exactly that:

```scala
private def retrieveAndLoadArtists() {
  val rootUrl = "http://ws.audioscrobbler.com/2.0/"
  val apiMethod = "chart.gettopartists"
  val apiKey = sys.props("api.key")
  val req = url(rootUrl +
    "?method=" + apiMethod + "&api_key=" + apiKey)
  Http(req OK as.xml.Elem).map {resp =>
    val artists = resp \\ "artist"
    artists.foreach {node =>
      val artist = makeArtist(node)
      println(artist.name)
      db.save(artist)
    }
  }()
}
private def makeArtist(n: Node) = {
  val name = (n \ "name").text
  val playCount = (n \ "playcount").text.toLong
  val listeners = (n \ "listeners").text.toLong
  Artist(name = name, playCount = playCount, listeners = listeners)
}
```

Request to get top artists

Make HTTP request and receive response

Applying the Promise to get the result

Parse XML response

The refresh action of the controller needs to use the `retrieveAndLoad` method to load and save the artists to the database and display the artists view. The following listing shows the complete controller implementation.

Listing 11.3 Completed `ArtistsController.scala`

```scala
package chap11.top.artists.controller

import org.springframework.stereotype.Controller
import org.springframework.beans.factory.annotation.Autowired
import org.springframework.web.bind.annotation.RequestMapping
import org.springframework.web.bind.annotation.RequestMethod._
import chap11.top.artists.db.ArtistDb
import chap11.top.artists.model.Artist
import org.springframework.web.servlet.ModelAndView
import dispatch._
import scala.xml.Node

@Controller
class ArtistsController {
  @Autowired
  val db: ArtistDb = null

  @RequestMapping(value = Array("/artists"), method = Array(GET))
  def loadArtists() =
    new ModelAndView("artists", "topArtists", db.findAll)

  @RequestMapping(value = Array("/refresh"), method = Array(GET))
  def refresh() = {
    retrieveAndLoadArtists()
```

Find all artists and render artists view

Refresh artists from Last.fm

```scala
    new ModelAndView("artists", "topArtists", db.findAll)
  }

  private def retrieveAndLoadArtists() {
    val rootUrl = "http://ws.audioscrobbler.com/2.0/"
    val apiMethod = "chart.gettopartists"
    val apiKey = sys.props("api.key")
    val req = url(rootUrl + "?method=" + apiMethod + "&api_key=" + apiKey)
    Http(req </> { resp =>
      val artists = resp \\ "artist"
      artists.foreach {node =>
        val artist = makeArtist(node)
        println(artist.name)
        db.save(artist)
      }
    }()                     //applying the Promise
  }

  private def makeArtist(n: Node) = {
    val name = (n \ "name").text
    val playCount = (n \ "playcount").text.toLong
    val listeners = (n \ "listeners").text.toLong
    Artist(name = name, playCount = playCount, listeners = listeners)
  }
}
```

Now that you have the code for the model and controller, it's time to turn to the view. This simple view will take the response from the controller and render that using Java-Server Pages (JSP). The example uses a pure Java solution for the view, but you can experiment with template libraries written in Java, like Scalate (http://scalate .fusesource.org). Your JSP view will take the topArtists parameter returned from the controller and iterate through it to render the response. The following listing shows what the view looks like.

Listing 11.4   artists.jsp to render all the artists

```
<%@page contentType="text/html;charset=utf-8"%>
<%@taglib prefix="c" uri="http://java.sun.com/jsp/jstl/core"%>
<%@ taglib uri="http://java.sun.com/jsp/jstl/functions" prefix="fn" %>
<!DOCTYPE HTML PUBLIC "-//W3C//DTD HTML 4.01 Transitional//EN" "http://
    www.w3.org/TR/html4/loose.dtd">
<html>
<head>
  <title>Top Artists from Last.fm</title>
</head>
<body>
 <p>
   <a href="<c:url value="/refresh.html"/>">Refresh from Last.fm</a>
 </p>
<h2>Top artists</h2>
<p>
  <c:if test="${fn:length(topArtists) == 0}">
    <h3>No artists found in database. Refresh from Last.fm</h3>
  </c:if>
```

```
<table>
  <tr>
    <th>Name</th>
    <th>Play count</th>
    <th>Listeners</th>
  </tr>
  <c:forEach items="${topArtists}" var="artist">
    <tr>
      <td>${artist.name}</td>
      <td>${artist.playCount}</td>
      <td>${artist.listeners}</td>
    </tr>
  </c:forEach>
</table>
</p>
</body>
</html>
```

Iterate through topArtists list

You use the `topArtists` to access the list of artists returned from the controller and display them. In the next section you'll integrate all the pieces using Spring configuration files.

11.3.2 *Configuring and running the application*

You'll use the Spring configuration to configure both Spring MVC and Hibernate. This way Spring will ensure that all the necessary dependencies you need for your model and controller objects are properly initialized and injected. Because you followed all the conventions using Scala and Java annotations at the Spring configuration level, you won't have any problem configuring Scala classes. This is a great benefit of smooth interoperability between Scala and Java. In the following listing's spring-context-data.xml file, you're configuring the model and controller objects.

Listing 11.5   Configuring the model and Hibernate using Spring

```
<?xml version="1.0" encoding="UTF-8"?>
<beans xmlns="http://www.springframework.org/schema/beans"
       xmlns:xsi="http://www.w3.org/2001/XMLSchema-instance"
       xmlns:context="http://www.springframework.org/schema/context"
       xmlns:tx="http://www.springframework.org/schema/tx"
       xsi:schemaLocation="
         http://www.springframework.org/schema/beans
   http://www.springframework.org/schema/beans/spring-beans-3.0.xsd
         http://www.springframework.org/schema/context
   http://www.springframework.org/schema/context/spring-context-3.0.xsd
         http://www.springframework.org/schema/tx
   http://www.springframework.org/schema/tx/spring-tx-3.0.xsd">

    <tx:annotation-driven/>

    <context:component-scan base-package="chap11.top.artists.db"/>

    <bean id="transactionManager" class=
   "org.springframework.jdbc.datasource.DataSourceTransactionManager">
        <property name="dataSource" ref="dataSource"/>
```

Look for data access objects

```
        </bean>

        <bean id="dataSource" class="org.apache.commons.dbcp.BasicDataSource"
➥destroy-method="close">
            <property name="driverClassName" value="org.hsqldb.jdbcDriver"/>
            <property name="url" value="jdbc:hsqldb:mem:scala-spring-
➥hibernate"/>
            <property name="username" value="sa"/>
            <property name="password" value=""/>
        </bean>

        <bean id="sessionFactory" class=                                       ⎫ Configure
➥"org.springframework.orm.hibernate3.annotation.                              ⎬ Hibernate
➥AnnotationSessionFactoryBean">                                                ⎭
            <property name="dataSource" ref="dataSource"/>
            <property name="annotatedClasses">
                <list>
                    <value>chap11.top.artists.model.Artist</value>     ◁── Specify
                </list>                                                     domain
            </property>                                                      object for
            <property name="hibernateProperties">                           Hibernate
                <props>
                    <prop key=
➥"hibernate.dialect">org.hibernate.dialect.HSQLDialect</prop>
                    <prop key="hibernate.show_sql">true</prop>
                    <prop key="hibernate.hbm2ddl.auto">create</prop>
                </props>
            </property>
        </bean>
</beans>
```

Using this file, you're configuring Hibernate with HSQLDB and the domain objects
that are used with Hibernate. You're also using Spring's component scan to look for
`ArtistDb` so that it gets initialized with the necessary Hibernate dependencies. Check
Spring's documentation for more about the tags used in the configuration file. In the
following listing's spring-context-web.xml file, you're configuring the controller and
the Spring servlets you're going to use to intercept HTTP requests.

Listing 11.6 Configuring the controller and web using Spring

```
<?xml version="1.0" encoding="UTF-8"?>
<beans xmlns="http://www.springframework.org/schema/beans"
       xmlns:xsi="http://www.w3.org/2001/XMLSchema-instance"
       xmlns:context="http://www.springframework.org/schema/context"
       xsi:schemaLocation="
         http://www.springframework.org/schema/beans
➥http://www.springframework.org/schema/beans/spring-beans-3.0.xsd
         http://www.springframework.org/schema/context
➥http://www.springframework.org/schema/context/spring-context-3.0.xsd">

Configure
controller ▷  <context:component-scan base-package="chap11.top.artists.controller"/>

Main
HTTP   ▷      <bean id="viewResolver"
request
handler ❶      class="org.springframework.web.servlet.view.UrlBasedViewResolver">
                <property name="viewClass" value=
```

```
"org.springframework.web.servlet.view.JstlView"/>
      <property name="prefix" value="/WEB-INF/jsp/"/>
      <property name="suffix" value=".jsp"/>
   </bean>

   <bean id="openSessionInViewInterceptor"
        class=
"org.springframework.orm.hibernate3.support.
OpenSessionInViewInterceptor">
      <property name="sessionFactory" ref="sessionFactory"/>
   </bean>

   <bean class=
"org.springframework.web.servlet.mvc.annotation.
DefaultAnnotationHandlerMapping">
      <property name="interceptors">
         <list><ref bean="openSessionInViewInterceptor"/></list>
      </property>
   </bean>

</beans>
```

❶ Suffix for all
❷ the pages

The `UrlBasedViewResolver` class from Spring is used to intercept the HTTP
request ❶ and forward the request to the appropriate controller. In this case, it's Art-
istsController. You also configure suffix with .jsp ❷ so that when you return
`ModelAndView` with "artists" from the controller, it can look for the artists.jsp file in
the WEB-INF/jsp folder. To load these configuration files when the application starts,
add them to the web.xml file. The following listing shows the complete web.xml.

Listing 11.7   web.xml of the topArtists web application

```
<?xml version="1.0" encoding="UTF-8"?>
<web-app xmlns="http://java.sun.com/xml/ns/javaee"
         xmlns:xsi="http://www.w3.org/2001/XMLSchema-instance"
         xsi:schemaLocation="http://java.sun.com/xml/ns/javaee
http://java.sun.com/xml/ns/javaee/web-app_2_5.xsd"
         id="scala-spring-hibernate"
         version="2.5">

   <context-param>
      <param-name>contextConfigLocation</param-name>
      <param-value>/WEB-INF/spring-context-data.xml</param-value>
   </context-param>

   <listener>
      <listener-class>
org.springframework.web.context.ContextLoaderListener
</listener-class>
   </listener>
   <servlet>
      <servlet-name>dispatcher</servlet-name>
      <servlet-class>
org.springframework.web.servlet.DispatcherServlet</servlet-class>
      <init-param>
         <param-name>contextConfigLocation</param-name>
         <param-value>/WEB-INF/spring-context-web.xml</param-value>
      </init-param>
```

❶ Spring configuration file

❷ Listener that configures Spring

Handle all HTTP requests

```
            <load-on-startup>1</load-on-startup>
        </servlet>
        <servlet-mapping>
            <servlet-name>dispatcher</servlet-name>
            <url-pattern>*.html</url-pattern>
        </servlet-mapping>
        <welcome-file-list>
            <welcome-file>index.jsp</welcome-file>
        </welcome-file-list>
    </web-app>
```

Most of the content of this file should be familiar to you if you've built a web application for the JVM. All the Java web containers read the web.xml to initialize Java-based web applications. The listener attribute ❷ allows applications to listen to events generated by containers, such as when an application is loaded or unloaded. In this case, the listener configured is `ContextLoaderListener`, and this class knows how to configure Spring by reading `context-param` ❶. To run the application, you can use the already configured Jetty web server using the following command:

```
mvn -Dapi.key=<your-last.fm-pai-key> jetty:run
```

As you can see, setting up and creating web applications using Scala and Java frameworks is easy. Some of the boilerplate configuration is unavoidable when working with Java frameworks, but you can still have fun writing Scala code.

11.4 Summary

One thing that should be clear from this chapter is that Scala's interoperability with Java is pain-free. There are a few places where you have to take extra precautions, but for the most part you can integrate with existing Java codebases without thinking too much. The extra carefulness comes when you have to integrate some features of Scala that aren't supported in Java and vice versa. You learned how to deal with situations like that throughout this chapter. Because Scala is designed from the ground up to interoperate with Java, most of the workarounds are also simple to implement and learn.

The benefit of simple integration with Java means you can easily get started with Scala in existing codebases. As the final example demonstrates, you can use Scala with existing popular Java frameworks without rewriting entire applications.

The next chapter looks into one of the most exciting Scala frameworks: Akka. This framework lets you build large, scalable, and distributed applications using various concurrency models. I know you've been waiting for this for a long time—so without further delay, let's jump into the exciting world of Akka.

12

Scalable and distributed applications using Akka

This chapter covers

- The philosophy behind Akka
- Simpler concurrency with actors, STM, agents, and dataflow
- Building a large scalable application with Akka called Akkaoogle

This chapter introduces an exciting Scala toolkit called Akka, which allows you to build next-generation, event-based, fault-tolerant, scalable, and distributed applications for the JVM. Akka provides multiple concurrency abstractions (mentioned in section 9.2.3), and this chapter explores each one of them. So far, you've only seen how actors can be used to build message-oriented concurrency. Here we'll go beyond actors and look into concurrency abstractions like STM, Agent, and Dataflow.

To understand how the pieces of Akka fit together, you're going to build a real-time product search application using Akka called Akkaoogle. This application is similar to Froogle (www.google.com/products), Google's service that finds the lowest price on products you search for. You'll build this product incrementally so you can see which Akka features you can use in which situations.

> **NOTE** All of the Akka features covered in this chapter are also available as a Java API. I can't cover the Java side of things in this chapter, but you can check out the latest documentation at http://akka.io/docs/ for details.

Akka is written in Scala but exposes all its features through both the Java and Scala APIs. Because this is a Scala book, in this chapter I mainly discuss the Scala API, but I include Java examples as well. You can build the Akkaoogle application in Java by following the Scala examples because both APIs look almost the same. First I'll talk about the philosophy behind Akka so you understand the goal behind the Akka project and the problems it tries to solve.

12.1 *The philosophy behind Akka*

The philosophy behind Akka is simple: make it easier for developers to build correct, concurrent, scalable, and fault-tolerant applications. To that end, Akka provides a higher level of abstractions to deal with concurrency, scalability, and faults. Figure 12.1 shows the three core modules provided by Akka for concurrency, scalability, and fault tolerance.

The concurrency module provides options to solve concurrency-related problems. By now I'm sure you're comfortable with actors (message-oriented concurrency). But actors aren't a be-all-end-all solution for concurrency. You need to understand alternative concurrency models available in Akka, and in the next section you'll explore all of

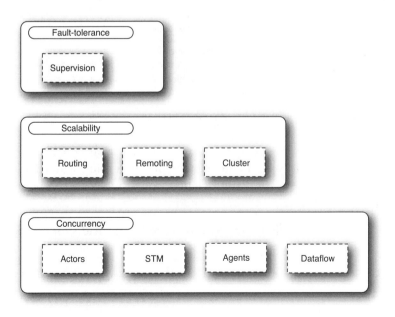

Figure 12.1   Akka core modules

them. At the core, Akka is an event-based platform and relies on actors for message passing and scalability. Akka puts both local and remote actors at your disposal. Using local actors with routing (the ability to send work with multiple instances of an actor) you can scale up and you can use remote actors to help you scale out. We'll look into this in more detail when you build a sample application at the end of the chapter.

12.2 *Simple concurrency with Akka*

To scale up your applications, use concurrency. In chapter 9 you learned that threads are a difficult and error-prone way to implement concurrency and should be the tool you choose last. The question then becomes what are your first, second, or third options? This section introduces you to those options and helps you decide which are appropriate. Table 12.1 describes all the concurrency techniques available in Akka. The good news is you can combine all these concurrency techniques, which is what most Akka developers end up doing.

Table 12.1 Concurrency alternatives available in Akka

Name	Description
Actors	An actor is an object that processes messages asynchronously and encapsulates state. Actors implement message-passing concurrency. We explored actors in chapter 9.
Software transactional memory (STM)	Software transactional memory is a concurrency model analogous to database transactions for controlling access to a shared state. It's a better alternative to locks and provides composability.
Agents	Agents provide abstraction over mutable data. They only allow you to mutate the data through an asynchronous write action.
Dataflow	Dataflow concurrency is deterministic. This means that it behaves the same every time you execute it. So if your problem deadlocks the first time, it will always dead-lock, helping you to debug the problem. Akka implements Oz-style[a] dataflow concurrency using `Future`.

a. "Concurrency," Oz documentation, www.mozart-oz.org/documentation/tutorial/node8.html.

These options provide the flexibility you need to design your concurrency applications correctly. For example, you can model an application using actors, handle mutable state with STM or agents, and use dataflow concurrency to compose multiple concurrent processes. The possibilities are endless.

NOTE   Akka no longer includes the STM module but instead supports Scala STM.[1]

Let's begin the journey into the world of Akka concurrency—it will be a fun ride.

---

[1] Information on Scala STM, http://nbronson.github.com/scala-stm/.

12.2.1 *Remote actors*

In chapter 9 we explored actors in detail. Actor programming is not restricted to only a single JVM, so actors can communicate with each other across multiple JVMs (figure 12.2). Akka remote actors allow you to deploy actors in remote machines and send messages back and forth transparently. Remote actors are a great way to make your application scalable and distributed. The messages are automatically serialized using the Google protocol buffer (http://code.google.com/p/protobuf/), and communication between the two nodes is handled using JBoss Netty (www.jboss.org/netty). Think of the Google protocol buffer as XML but smaller and faster, and Netty as a non-blocking I/O (NIO) implementation, which allows Akka to efficiently use threads for I/O operations.

Akka implements transparent remoting, where the remoteness of the actor is completely configured at deployment time. You can work with local actors while building the solution and configure remote details of each individual actor during deployment.

> **NOTE** In a future version of Akka, Netty will be replaced with an actor-based I/O library called Actor I/O.

Before we proceed further let's add dependencies for remote actors. Akka is modular, so instead of pulling in the entire Akka library, you're only depending on the Akka actors. You can find the complete build.sbt file in the accompanying codebase for this chapter.

```
resolvers ++= Seq(
  "Akka Repo" at "http://akka.io/repository",
  "Typesafe Repo" at "http://repo.typesafe.com/typesafe/repo"
)

libraryDependencies ++= Seq(
  "com.typesafe.akka" %% "akka-actor" % "2.1.0",
  "com.typesafe.akka" %% "akka-remote % "2.1.0"
)
```

The `resolvers` define the location of the dependencies, and the `library-Dependencies` add remote actors.

We will take the same word count example we built in chapter 9 and change the worker actor to implement it in Java and, instead of files, we will work with a list of

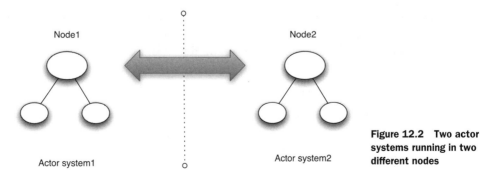

Figure 12.2 Two actor systems running in two different nodes

URLs. The goal is to connect to the URL and count all the words on the page. To create an Akka actor in Java you have to extend the `akka.actor.UntypedActor` class and override the `onReceive` method:

```
import akka.actor.UntypedActor;
public class WordCountWorker extends UntypedActor {
    @Override
    public void onReceive(Object message) {
    }
}
```

The class is called `UntypedActor` because Akka includes the concept of a `TypedActor`. The typed actors implement the active object[2] pattern, which turns any POJO interface into an asynchronous API using actors.

> **NOTE**   Akka typed actors are an implementation of the active object pattern. It turns synchronous method invocations into asynchronous dispatches. The one advantage using typed actors has over untyped actors is that you can have a static compile-type contract and you don't have to define messages. Read more about Akka typed actors in the Akka documentation.

Because your `WordCountWorker` needs to handle the `FileToCount` message, you need to typecast the message received as a parameter to `FileToCount`:

```
if (message instanceof FileToCount) {
  FileToCount c = (FileToCount)message;
} else {
  throw new IllegalArgumentException("Unknown message: " + message);
}
```

The code is checking the type of message received using the `instanceof` operator, and if the message isn't of type `FileToCount`, an exception is thrown. Because you want to write most, if not all, of your code in Scala, add the `countWords` method to the `FileToCount` case class that counts all the words in a resource, to which the URL points:

```
case class FileToCount(url:String) {
  def countWords = {
    Source.fromURL(new URL(url))
          .getLines.foldRight(0)(_.split(" ").size + _)
  }
}
```

The `countWords` method counts the number of words in a resource using the `scala.io.Source` class provided in the Scala library. From the `WordCountWorker` actor, you can invoke the `countWords` method to count words:

```
FileToCount c = (FileToCount)message;
Integer count = c.countWords();
```

---

[2] "Active object," http://en.wikipedia.org/wiki/Active_object.

To reply with a response to the sender, use the getSender().tell(...) method. The tell method allows actors to reply to the sender. To reply to the master, the worker actor needs to construct the WordCount message by passing the filename and the word count:

```
FileToCount c = (FileToCount)message;
Integer count = c.countWords();
getSender().tell(new WordCount(c.url(), count));
```

The getSelf method returns the actor reference to the current actor. The following listing shows the complete WordCountWorker actor in Java. Save this in the src/main/java folder of your SBT project.

Listing 12.1   WordCountWorker Akka actor in Java

```
package countwords;

import akka.actor.UntypedActor;

public class WordCountWorker extends UntypedActor {
    @Override
    public void onReceive(Object message) {
        if (message instanceof FileToCount) {
            FileToCount c = (FileToCount)message;
            Integer count = c.countWords();
            getSender().tell(new WordCount (c.url(), count),
                getSelf());
        }
        else {
            throw new IllegalArgumentException(
                "Unknown message: " + message);
        }
    }
}
```

Send reply to sender

To take advantage of the remote actors, we run all the worker actors in a JVM separate from the master actor. To achieve that, let's create two actor systems with different properties. The easiest way to configure Akka actors is by providing a configuration file in the classpath. You can find the details of all the configuration properties in the Akka documentation.[3] The following example defines two actor systems: the main actor system and the worker actor system:

```
workersystem {
  akka {
    actor.provider = "akka.remote.RemoteActorRefProvider"
    remote.netty.hostname = "127.0.0.1"
    remote.netty.port = 2560
  }
}
mainsystem {
akka {
```

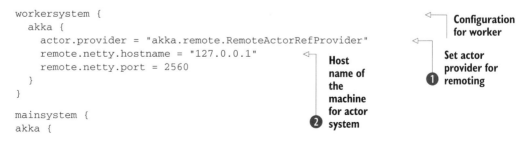

Configuration for worker

Set actor provider for remoting ❶

Host name of the machine for actor system ❷

---

[3]   Configuration version 2.0.3, http://mng.bz/vmsQ.

```
actor.provider = "akka.remote.RemoteActorRefProvider"
remote.netty.hostname = "127.0.0.1"
actor {
deployment {
  /wordCountMaster {
    remote = "akka://workersystem@127.0.0.1:2560"
  }
 }
 }
}
}
```

◄─────── **Deployment location for the accumulatorActor ❸ actor**

Separating the configuration by actor systems provides the flexibility to define settings for each actor system. The following elements add remoteness to your actor system:

- Change the actor provider to `akka.remote.RemoteActorRefProvider` ❶.
- Add the host name of the machine in which the actor system will be running ❷. Make sure this IP address is reachable.
- The port number which the remote actor system should listen on.
- Map the actor name to the actor system in which it will be deployed ❸.

Now save the preceding configuration into the `application.conf` file under the src/ main/resources folder of the project. This will make the application.conf file available in the classpath. To make the `workersystem` run on a different JVM, run the following code in a different terminal:

```
package countwords

import akka.actor._
import com.typesafe.config.ConfigFactory

object WorkerSystem extends App {
    val workerSystem = ActorSystem("workersystem",
        ConfigFactory.load.getConfig("workersystem"))
}
```

◄─ **Start "workersystem" actor system**

This will start the `"workersystem"` running and listening for messages on port number 2560. Now let's create a new actor that will tie all the pieces together. It will run on the main actor system:

Listing 12.2 `MainActor` running on a main actor system

```
package countwords

import akka.actor._
import com.typesafe.config.ConfigFactory
import scala.io.Source
import java.net.URL

case class FileToCount(url:String) {
  def countWords = {
    Source.fromURL(
      new URL(url)).getLines.foldRight(0)(_.split(" ").size + _)
  }
```

```
}
case class WordCount(url:String, count: Int)
case class StartCounting(urls: Seq[String], numActors: Int)

object MainSystem {
  class MainActor(accumulator: ActorRef) extends Actor {
    def receive = {
      case "start" =>
        val urls = List("http://www.infoq.com/",
          "http://www.dzone.com/links/index.html",
          "http://www.manning.com/",
          "http://www.reddit.com/")
        accumulator ! StartCounting(urls, 2)

    }
  }

  def main(args: Array[String]) = run

  private def run = {                                        Loading the
    val mainSystem = ActorSystem("main",                     mainsystem
      ConfigFactory.load.getConfig("mainsystem"))         ⊲─ configuration
    val accumulator = mainSystem.actorOf(Props[WordCountMaster],
      name ="wordCountMaster")
    val m = mainSystem.actorOf(Props(new MainActor(accumulator)))
    m ! "start"
  }
}
```

Now if you start the WorkerSystem and the MainSystem in two different JVM instances you will have the workers running on one JVM and the main actor running on another. This opens up myriad possibilities to scale, because now you can distribute work to multiple machines.

12.2.2 *Making mutable data safe with STM*

Software transactional memory (STM) turns a Java heap into a transactional dataset. STM is similar to database transactions, but is used for memory instead. Because memory isn't durable with STM, you only get the first three properties of ACID (atomicity, consistency, isolation, durability):

- *Atomicity*—This property states that all modifications should follow the "all or nothing" rule. In STM, all the modification is done through an atomic transaction, and if one change fails all the other changes are rolled back.
- *Consistency*—This property ensures that an STM transaction takes the system from one consistent state to another. If you want to delete one element from a Map and insert into another Map, then at the end of the STM transaction both Maps will be modified appropriately.
- *Isolation*—This property requires that no other STM transaction sees partial changes from other transactions.

The best part of STM is freedom from locks. It rolls back from exceptions and is composable. You can also take two smaller STM operations and combine them to create bigger STM operations. Before I show you STM examples, let's step back in order to understand what state is and how it's represented in STM.

HOW STATE IS DEFINED IN STM

Let's look at how state is handled in imperative programming. Figure 12.3 shows how state is handled in an imperative world. You directly access the data in memory and mutate it. In the figure, an object, A, is directly accessing the data represented by B and C. The problem with this approach is that it doesn't work in the concurrent world. What will happen when some other thread or process tries to access the data residing in B or C when A is trying to mutate that data? The result is unexpected behavior.

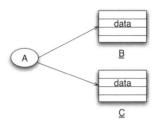

Figure 12.3   State represented in imperative programming

To solve the problem with this approach, STM defines mutable state differently. In STM, *state* is defined as the value that an entity with a specific identity has at a particular point. A *value* is something that doesn't change (it's immutable). And *identity* is a stable reference to a value at a given point in time. Figure 12.4 shows how the previous structure would be represented in STM. The mutable part here is the identity, which gets associated with a series of values. And STM makes the mutation of reference from one value to another atomic. What will happen in this case when some other thread or process tries to access the data residing in B or C when A is trying to mutate it? You'll see the value associated with B or C, because STM transactions are isolated and no partial change is visible outside the transaction.

This idea of defining state in terms of identities and values is derived from the programming language Clojure (http://clojure.org). Now let's see how STM works in Akka through examples.

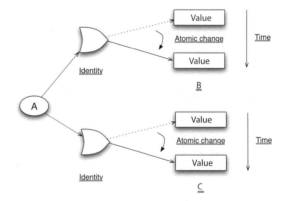

Figure 12.4   State represented in STM

HANDLING MUTABLE DATA IN AKKA USING STM

Akka uses the Scala STM library for its STM. To add the library to your SBT project use the following snippet:

```
resolvers += ("Typesafe Repository" at "http://repo.typesafe.com/typesafe/
    releases/")

libraryDependencies ++= Seq(
  "org.scala-stm" %% "scala-stm" % "0.7",
  "org.specs2" %% "specs2" % "1.13" % "test"
)
```

To demonstrate how STM works let's take a simple example in which you create atomic operations for deleting and inserting elements into an immutable Map. To manage this mutability, wrap the value (in this case, the immutable HashMap) in the scala.concurrent.stm.Ref object as follows:

```
val ref1 = Ref(HashMap[String, Any](
    "service1" -> "10",
    "service2" -> "20",
    "service3" -> null))
val ref2 = Ref(HashMap[String, Int]())
```

Refs are nothing but mutable references to values that you can share safely with multiple concurrent participants. The preceding snippet creates two refs pointing to the immutable HashMap. To perform any operation on Ref you have to use the atomic method defined in the STM package by passing an in-transaction parameter. The Scala STM library creates the transaction object and grants the caller permission to perform transactional reads and writes. Any refs you change in the closure will be done in an STM transaction. For example, in the following code you're trying to add a new element to the Map managed by ref2:

```
def atomicInsert(key: String, value: Int) = atomic { implicit txn =>
    val oldMap = ref2.get
    val newMap = oldMap + ( key -> value)
    ref2.swap(newMap)
}
```

By invoking ref2.get you're getting the value currently associated with the Ref and using swap to replace the old value with the new value. If the operation fails, the changes will be rolled back. The transaction parameter is marked as implicit so you don't have to pass it around.

To implement atomic deletion of key from ref1, you can use the transform method defined in Ref. The transform method allows you to transform the value referenced by Ref by applying the given function:

```
def atomicDelete(key: String): Option[Any] = atomic {
    val oldMap = ref1.get
    val value = oldMap.get(key)
    ref1.transform(_ - key)
    value
}
```

The atomicDelete function returns the value that's deleted. Why return the old value from the function? I have a plan to use it later, so hang in there.

I keep talking about the composability of STM, but haven't yet shown you an example. Your wait is over. Imagine you have to build an atomic swap function that moves one item from one Map to another. With STM, it's easy: all you have to do is wrap both the atomicDelete and atomicInsert functions in an atomic function, as in the following:

```
def atomicSwap(key: String) = atomic { implicit txn =>
    val value: Option[Any] = atomicDelete(key)
```

```
        atomicInsert(key, Integer.parseInt(value.get.toString))
}
```

Because `ref2` only holds an `Int` type value, you have to parse it to `Int` before insertion. To fully understand the beauty of the `swap` function, look at the following specification:

```
"Atomic operations in composition" should {
    "rollback on exception" in {
        swap("service3")
        ref1.single().contains("service3") must beEqualTo(true)
        ref2.single().contains("service3") must beEqualTo(false)
    }
}
```

The `single` method of STM lets you access the contents of `Ref` without requiring a transaction. When you try to swap `"service3"` (which maps to a null value), the `Integer`
`.parseInt` will throw an exception. At that point the delete is already successful, but thanks to STM it will roll back the entire transaction. Can your locks do that? No.

STM is a great way to build smaller atomic operations and large ones by composition, similar to how functions are composed in functional programming. To learn more about STM, consult the Scala STM documentation.[4] Let's move our attention to another concurrency abstraction called `Agent`.

12.2.3   *Agents*

`Agents` provide asynchronous changes to any individual storage location bound to it. An agent only lets you mutate the location by applying an action. Actions in this case are functions that asynchronously are applied to the state of `Agent` and in which the return value of the function becomes the new value of `Agent`. However, reading a value from `Agent` is synchronous and instantaneous. The difference between `Ref` and `Agent` is that `Ref` is a synchronous read and write; `Agent` is reactive. To apply any action asynchronously, Akka provides two methods: `send` and `sendOff`. The `send` method uses the reactive thread pool allocated for agents, and `sendOff` uses a dedicated thread, ideal for a long-running processes. Here's an example of `Agent` associated with a file writer that logs messages to the log file through `send` actions:

```
import akka.agent.Agent
implicit val system = ActorSystem("agentExample")
val writer = new FileWriter("src/test/resources/log.txt")
val a = Agent(writer)
a.send { w => w.write("This is a log message"); w}
a.close                                                     ◁————————❶ Shut Agent down
writer.close
```

`Agent` will be running until you invoke the `close` method ❶. An actor system is created for the agent because, behind the scenes, agents are implemented using actors. If you have to do more than logging to a file, something that will take time, use the `sendOff` method:

```
a.sendOff { someLongRunningProcess }
```

---

4   Scala STM Expert Group, http://nbronson.github.com/scala-stm/index.html.

Note that at any time, only one `send` action is invoked. Even if actions are sent from multiple concurrent processes, the actions will be executed in sequential order. Note that actions might get interleaved between multiple threads.

To use `Agents` in your project you must add the following to your SBT `library-Dependencies`:

```
libraryDependencies ++= Seq(
  "com.typesafe.akka" %% "akka-actor" % "2.1.0",
  "com.typesafe.akka" %% "akka-agent" % "2.1.0",
  "org.specs2" %% "specs2" % "1.13" % "test"
)
```

Agents also participant in STM transactions when used in the `atomic` block and messages are held until the transaction is completed. This is important because if you have a side-effect action, like logging to a file, you don't want to do that with STM. Why? Because if STM transactions fail, they retry automatically, meaning your side-effecting operation is executed multiple times. This might not be what you want, so combining agents with STM is a great pattern to execute side-effecting actions along with STM transactions. Sometimes the asynchronous nature of `Agent` confuses people into thinking that agents are similar to actors, but they're completely different in the way you design them. `Agent` is associated with data, and you send behavior to `Agent` from outside, in the form of a function. In the case of actors, the behavior is defined inside the actor, and you send data in the form of a message.

You'll revisit agents when using Akkaoogle to log transactions, but now let's continue with our next concurrency model: dataflow. Dataflow is a great way to encapsulate concurrency from a program. It can be read sequentially.

12.2.4 Dataflow

Dataflow concurrency is a deterministic concurrency model. If you run it and it works, it will always work without deadlock. Alternatively, if it deadlocks the first time, it will always deadlock. This is a powerful guarantee to have in a concurrent application because you can easily understand the code. The dataflow concurrency allows you to write sequential code that performs parallel operations. The limitation is that your code should be completely side-effect free. You can't have deterministic behavior if your code is performing side-effecting operations.

Dataflow is implemented in Akka using Scala's delimited continuations compiler plug-in. To enable the plug-in within your SBT project, add the following lines to the build.sbt file:

```
autoCompilerPlugins := true

libraryDependencies <+= scalaVersion { v => compilerPlugin(
    "org.scala-lang.plugins" % "continuations" % v) }

scalacOptions += "-P:continuations:enable"

libraryDependencies += "com.typesafe.akka." %% " akka-dataflow" % "2.1.0"
```

To work with dataflow concurrency, you have to work with dataflow variables. A dataflow variable is like a single-assignment variable. Once the value is bound, it won't change, and any subsequent attempt to bind a new value will be ignored. The following example defines a dataflow variable:

```
val messageFromFuture = Promise[String]()
```

Here Akka `Promise` is used to create a dataflow variable. A `Promise` is a read handle to a value that will be available at some point in the future. Any dataflow operation is performed in the `Future.flow` block:

```
Future.flow {
    messageFromFuture()
}
```

The preceding call will wait in a thread unless a value is bound to `messageFromFuture`. `Future.flow` returns a `Future` so you can perform other operations without blocking the main thread of execution. Think of a `Future` as a data structure to retrieve the result of some concurrent operation. To assign a value to a dataflow variable, use the `<<` method as in the following:

```
Future.flow {
    messsageFromFuture << "Future looks very cool"
}
```

Once a value is bound to a dataflow variable, all the `Futures` that are waiting on the value will be unblocked and able to continue with execution. The following listing shows a complete example of using the dataflow variable.

Listing 12.3   Complete dataflow concurrency example

```
import akka.actor._
import akka.dispatch._
import Future.flow

object Main extends App {
    implicit val system = ActorSystem("dataflow")
    val messageFromFuture, rawMessage, parsedMessage = Promise[String]()
    flow {
        messageFromFuture << parsedMessage()
        println("z = " + messageFromFuture())
    }
    flow { rawMessage << "olleh" }
    flow { parsedMessage << toPresentFormat(rawMessage()) }

    def toPresentFormat (s: String) = s.reverse
}
```

The next section dives into building an application using some of the Akka concepts you have learned so that you can see practical use cases of Akka concurrency.

12.3   *Building a real-time pricing system: Akkaoogle*

You've covered a lot of ground so far in this chapter, you've learned new concepts, and you've seen several examples. But now it's time to see how these concepts are applied

Figure 12.4   Homepage of the Akkaoogle application

in a large application. In this section you'll build a large web-based product search site called Akkaoogle (see figure 12.4). It will be similar to Google's product search application (www.google.com/products) except that, instead of returning all products matching your criteria, your application will only return the cheapest deal found on the web.

So how does this application work? It gets the product price from two types of vendors that are offering the product. You can pay money to Akkaoogle and become an internal vendor. In this case, the product information is stored in Akkaoogle, and you pay a small service charge. You can also sign up as external vendor, in which case Akkaoogle makes a RESTful web service call to fetch the price—but the downside is you pay a bigger service charge. When the user is looking for the cheapest deal, Akkaoogle checks with all the vendors (internal and external) and finds the lowest price for the user. Because this all has to be done in real time and you want your Akkaoogle users to have a good experience, you have to find the cheapest deal in no more than 200 to 300 milliseconds. That's a challenge if you have to implement it using primitive concurrency constructs. But with Akka? Let's see how you could implement this.

12.3.1   The high-level architecture of Akkaoogle

Figure 12.5 shows you the high-level view of how Akkaoogle will be implemented. At first glance it may look complicated, but don't worry—you're going to build it in small pieces. Keep this figure in mind when building the application so you know where you're heading.

Here are the descriptions for each important component in figure 12.5 that you'll now start building:

- *Request handler*—This is an actor that handles HTTP requests from the user. You'll use an asynchronous HTTP library called Mist, provided by Akka, to implement this actor.
- *Search cheapest product*—This is the main entry point to execute a search to find the cheapest deal. This actor will search both internal and external vendors.

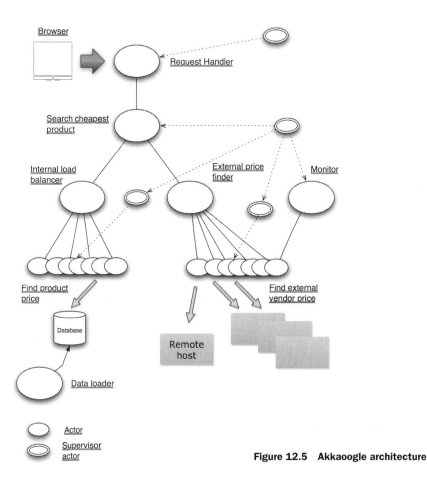

Figure 12.5   Akkaoogle architecture

- *Internal load balancer*—This is a load-balancing actor that sends messages to worker actors to find the cheapest product available in the internal database.
- *External load balancer*—This actor invokes all the external vendor services and finds the cheapest price among them.
- *Find product price and find vendor price*—The worker actors do the work of finding the price.
- *Monitor*—A simple monitor actor logs the failures that happen in external vendor services.
- *Data loader*—An actor that loads data to the database. This could be used to load product data for internal vendors.

You're also going to build a supervisor hierarchy to handle failures. You don't want Akkaoogle going down because you'll lose new business and money. Let's begin the fun by setting up the product with all the dependencies you need.

12.3.2 *Setting up the project for Akkaoogle*

Create an SBT project as shown in figure 12.6. Use the Build.scala file as your definition file and build.properties to configure the version of SBT. This project uses SBT 0.11.2, but you can easily upgrade to a newer version by modifying the build.properties file.

The first thing to configure is the database, and for that you'll use our old friends Squeryl (http://squeryl.org) and H2 (www.h2database.com). You used them extensively in chapter 7. To make your life easier, use the custom tasks in the following listing to start and stop the H2 database.

Figure 12.6 Akkaoogle project structure

Listing 12.4   H2 start and stop actions

```scala
object H2TaskManager {
  var process: Option[Process] = None
  lazy val H2 = config("h2") extend(Compile)

  val startH2 = TaskKey[Unit]("start", "Starts H2 database")
  val startH2Task =
    startH2 in H2 <<= (fullClasspath in Compile) map { cp =>
    startDatabase(cp.map(_.data).map(_.getAbsolutePath()).filter(_.contains(
    "h2database"))))}

    def startDatabase(paths: Seq[String]) = {
      process match {
        case None =>
          val cp = paths.mkString(System.getProperty("path.seperator"))
          val command = "java -cp " + cp + " org.h2.tools.Server"
          println("Starting Database with command: " + command)
          process = Some(Process(command).run())
          println("Database started ! ")
        case Some(_) =>
          println("H2 Database already started")
      }
    }
  val stopH2 = TaskKey[Unit]("stop", "Stops H2 database")
  val stopH2Task = stopH2 in H2 :={
    process match {
      case None => println("Database already stopped")
      case Some(_) =>
        println("Stopping database...")
        process.foreach{_.destroy()}
        process = None
        println("Database stopped...")
    }
  }
}
```

The detailed explanation of how these tasks are implemented is in chapter 7, but in a nutshell, the h2-start and h2-stop tasks allow you to start and stop the H2 in-memory database from the SBT command prompt. The following listing shows the complete project definition file with all the dependencies you need for the Akkaoogle project.

Listing 12.5   Akkaoogle build.scala file

```scala
object AkkaoogleBuild extends Build with ConfigureScalaBuild {

  import H2TaskManager._
  lazy val root = project(id = "akkaoogle", base = file("."))
   .settings(startH2Task, stopH2Task)
   .settings(
      organization := "scalainaction",
      scalaVersion := "2.10.0",
      scalacOptions ++= Seq("-unchecked", "-deprecation"),
      resolvers +=
        "Typesafe Repo" at "http://repo.typesafe.com/typesafe/repo",
        parallelExecution in Test := false
    )
   .settings(
        libraryDependencies ++= Seq(
        "com.typesafe.akka" % "akka-actor" % "2.1.0",
        "com.typesafe.akka" % "akka-remote" % "2.1.0",
        "com.typesafe.akka" % "akka-agent" % "2.1.0",
        "org.specs2" %% "specs2" % "1.13" % "test",
        "com.h2database" % "h2" % "1.2.127",
        "org.squeryl" % "squeryl_2.10.0-RC5" % "0.9.5-5",
        "org.eclipse.jetty" % "jetty-distribution" % "8.0.0.M2"
      ))
}
```

Add H2-related tasks to project ⟵

Add library dependencies ⟵

The build.scala file declares all the dependences and settings you need to start working on the Akkaoogle project. Once all the dependencies are downloaded you're ready to implement the Akkaoogle application. The next section builds the domain models you need to implement the internal vendor service. I test drove most of the application, but I won't show you test cases here. I encourage you to go through the test cases in this chapter's accompanying codebase. Even better, write tests for the code used throughout the rest of the chapter.

12.3.3   *Implementing the domain models*

You need a way to implement the products provided by internal vendors and also a model that represents external vendors. To reduce duplication between domain models, create a common trait called Model that extends the KeyedEntity trait provided by Squeryl. This trait provides an id field that acts as a primary key in the database for all the domain models:

```scala
trait Model[A] extends KeyedEntity[Long] { this: A =>
   val id: Long = 0
}
```

Here the `Model` also declares that it will get mixed in with a type represented by A. You're declaring a self type here because later on it will let you add generic methods that work on all the model objects (more about this later). Now you can create model classes that represent products and external vendors by extending the `Model` trait:

```
class Product(val description: String,
              val vendorName: String,
              val basePrice: Double,
              val plusPercent: Double)
    extends Model[Product]

class ExternalVendor(val name: String, val url: String)
    extends Model[ExternalVendor]
```

You're keeping these models simple so you can focus more on the Akka-related features you'll implement. The `url` property of the external vendor specifies the `url` you'll use to invoke the remote RESTful service. Add a method to the `Product` class to calculate the price using the `basePrice` and the `plusPercentage` fields:

```
def calculatePrice = basePrice + (basePrice * plusPercent / 100)
```

You'll need this method to determine the price of products offered by internal vendors. Because Akkaoogle cares about quality, you need to track the service availability of all the external vendors so you can rate them quarterly. You'll log (to the database) every time a call to an external vendor service fails and you'll need a domain model to represent it:

```
class TransactionFailure(val vendorId: String,
                         val message: String,
                         val timestamp: Date)
    extends Model[TransactionFailure]
```

The following listing creates an Akkaoogle `schema` object that will create the necessary tables in the database and provide helper methods to work with domain models.

Listing 12.6   Akkaoogle schema

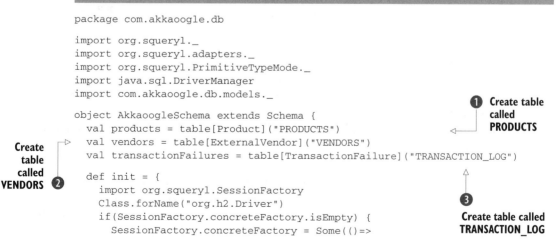

```
package com.akkaoogle.db

import org.squeryl._
import org.squeryl.adapters._
import org.squeryl.PrimitiveTypeMode._
import java.sql.DriverManager
import com.akkaoogle.db.models._
                                                              ❶ Create table
                                                                 called
object AkkaoogleSchema extends Schema {                          PRODUCTS
  val products = table[Product]("PRODUCTS")      ◁─────────┘
  val vendors = table[ExternalVendor]("VENDORS")
  val transactionFailures = table[TransactionFailure]("TRANSACTION_LOG")

  def init = {                                                  ▲
    import org.squeryl.SessionFactory                           │
    Class.forName("org.h2.Driver")                            ❸
    if(SessionFactory.concreteFactory.isEmpty) {          Create table called
      SessionFactory.concreteFactory = Some(()=>          TRANSACTION_LOG
```

Create table called VENDORS ❷

```
        Session.create(
          DriverManager.getConnection(
            "jdbc:h2:tcp://localhost/~/test", "sa", ""),
          new H2Adapter))
    }
  }

  def tx[A](a: =>A): A = {                    ④ Execute function
    init                                         within transaction
    inTransaction(a)
  }

  def createSchema() {                        ◁─── Create new schema
    tx { drop ; create }
  }
}
```

The listing defines the schema you'll use for Akkaoogle. The schema defines three tables of products ❶, vendors ❷, and transactionFailures ❸. The init method makes the database connection (in this case to the H2 database) and is used by the tx method ❹ to make sure the application is connected before initiating the transaction.

To fetch values back from the database, you can define finder methods in the companion objects of the domain models:

```
object TransactionFailure {
    def findAll = tx {
        from(transactionFailures)(s => select(s)) map(s => s)    ◁─┐ Find all
    }                                                              │ transaction
}                                                              ❶ failures

object Product {
    def findByDescription(description: String): Option[Product] =
        tx {
        products.where(p => p.description like description).headOption
    }
}

object ExternalVendor {
    def findAll = tx {                                      ❸ Find all
        from(vendors)(s => select(s)) map(s => s)              external vendors
    }                                                      ◁─┘
}
```

Find first product matched with description ❷

The TransactionFailure, Product, and ExternalVendor companion objects define finder methods to help fetch the values from the database. TransactionFailure .findAll ❶ returns all the transaction failures stored in the database (for large database tables, you should define finders that take some criteria to filter data). The findByDescription ❷ returns the first matching product from the database, and the ExternalVendor.findAll ❸ returns all the vendors that are registered with Akkaoogle.

Using the same technique you used in chapter 7, you'll add a save method to each domain model. The save method for all the domain objects is almost identical, except for the Squeryl table object. Create a generalized version of the save method that works with all the domain models that extend the Model trait:

```scala
trait Model[A] extends KeyedEntity[Long] { this: A =>
  val id: Long = 0
  def save(implicit table: Table[A]): Either[Throwable, String] = {
    tx {
      try {
        table.insert(this)
        Right("Domain object is saved successfully")
      } catch {
        case exception => Left(exception)
      }
    }
  }
}
```

The `save` method takes an implicit parameter that's of type `org.squeryl.Table`, which can handle type `A`. For example, when the `Model` is an instance of `Product`, then `A` is going to be of type `Product`, and `Table[A]` is going to be a table that knows how to save `Product`, which is the `products` property defined in the `AkkaoogleSchema` object. Because the parameter is defined as an implicit parameter, the compiler will now look for a value that matches the parameter type within the scope. This way, the caller won't have to specify the parameter when saving an instance of a domain model. The following listing shows the complete `models` package.

Listing 12.7 Complete `models` package of Akkaoogle

```scala
package com.akkaoogle.db

import AkkaoogleSchema._
import org.squeryl._
import org.squeryl.PrimitiveTypeMode._
import java.util.Date

package models {

  implicit val transactionFailures: Table[TransactionFailure] =
    AkkaoogleSchema.transactionFailures
  implicit val vendors: Table[ExternalVendor] = AkkaoogleSchema.vendors
  implicit val products: Table[Product] = AkkaoogleSchema.products

  trait Model[A] extends KeyedEntity[Long] { this: A =>
    val id: Long = 0
    def save[T[A] <: Table[A]](
        implicit table: T[A]): Either[Throwable, String] = {
      tx {
        try {
          table.insert(this)
          Right("Domain object is saved successfully")
        } catch {
          case exception => Left(exception)
        }
      }
    }
  }
}
```

1 Implicit TransactionFailure table for save

2 Implicit ExternalVendor table for save

3 Implicit Products table for save

4 Insert row into database

```
class TransactionFailure(val vendorId: String,
                         val message: String,
                         val timestamp: Date) extends
                         Model[TransactionFailure]

  object TransactionFailure {
  def findAll = tx {
    from(transactionFailures)(s => select(s)) map(s => s) }
}

class ExternalVendor(
  val name: String, val url: String) extends Model[ExternalVendor]

object ExternalVendor {
  def findAll = tx { from(vendors)(s => select(s)) map(s => s) }
}

class Product(val description: String,
              val vendorName: String,
              val basePrice: Double,
              val plusPercent: Double)
  extends Model[Product] {
  def calculatePrice = basePrice + (basePrice * plusPercent / 100)
}

object Product {
  def findByDescription(description: String): Option[Product] =
    tx {
      products.where(p => p.description like description).headOption
    }
  }
}
```

The `models` package defines all the classes you need to make Akkaoogle work with the database. It defines a parameterized version of save ❹ that works with all the `table` objects created inside the package. To make `save` work for all these `table` types, you have defined implicit values (❶ ❷ ❸) for each `table` so that the Scala compiler picks the appropriate one when saving your domain objects.

It's time to move to the core of the application: implementing the price lookup actors for both the internal and external vendors.

12.3.4 *Implementing the core with actors*

The core of Akkaoogle is to find the cheapest deal on the web and track the availability of the external services for quality purposes. To support these functionalities, the Akkaoogle application needs to handle the message types shown in the following listing.

Listing 12.8   List of message types supported by Akkaoogle (messages.scala)

```
package com.akkaoogle.calculators

object messages {
  case class FindPrice(productDescription: String, quantity: Int)
  case class LowestPrice(vendorName: String,
```

```
                        productDescription: String,
                        price: Double)
    case class LogTimeout(actorId: String, msg: String)

    case class FindStats(actorId: String)
    case class Stats(actorId: String, timeouts: Int)
}
```

The `FindPrice` message type represents a request triggered by a user looking for the cheapest deal. Needless to say, it's the most important message type in the application. The response of the `FindPrice` message is represented by the `LowestPrice` message, and it contains all the information the user needs about the cheapest deal. Akkaoogle internally uses the rest of the message types to track the availability of external services. Every time an external service times out, the `LogTimeout` message is sent to an actor to log the details. The `FindStats` and `Stats` messages are used for administration purposes.

First, implement a way to find the cheapest price for the products offered by the internal providers. Remember: products offered by internal providers are stored in a database. The `InternalPriceCalculator` actor calculates the lowest price by looking up the product by description, shown in the following listing.

Listing 12.9 Actor that calculates lowest price for internal products

```
package com.akkaoogle.calculators

import messages._
import com.akkaoogle.db.models._
import akka.actor._

class InternalPriceCalculator extends Actor {
  def receive = {
    case FindPrice(productDescription, quantity) =>
      val price = calculatePrice(productDescription, quantity)
      sender ! price
  }

  def calculatePrice( productDescription: String, qty: Int):
    Option[LowestPrice] = {
    Product.findByDescription(productDescription) map { product =>
      Some(LowestPrice(product.vendorName,
        product.description,
        product.calculatePrice * qty))
    } getOrElse Option.empty[LowestPrice]
  }
}
```

This actor is simple. When it receives the `FindPrice` message, it uses the product description provided to find the product in the database and calculate the price using the `calculatePrice` method, as defined in the `Product` domain class. At the end it returns the `LowestPrice` response. The current implementation only considers the first matching product, which in some cases isn't the right behavior. It should match all the products with a description (even a partial description) and derive the lowest price. I leave it to you to make the necessary changes to the calculation. For now, let's move on to the external providers.

Because you can have many external vendors for your application, you can't make the remote service calls sequentially because it would increase the response time and affect your users. You have to invoke the service calls in parallel and find a way to set a timeout for each service so you can respond to the user within a reasonable time. Actors are a nice and easy way to achieve parallelism. You'll next create an actor for each external vendor and broadcast the FindPrice message to these actors. These actors will act as a proxy client to the remote service. The following listing shows how the proxy actor for each external vendor is implemented.

Listing 12.10 The external vendor proxy actor

```
class ExternalVendorProxyActor(val v: ExternalVendor) extends Actor {
    def receive = {
      case fp: FindPrice =>
        var result: Option[LowestPrice] = Option.empty[LowestPrice]
        val f = Future({
          val params = "?pd=" + fp.productDescription + "&q=" + fp.quantity
          val price = Source.fromURL(v.url + params).mkString.toDouble
          Some(LowestPrice(v.name,
            fp.productDescription, price * fp.quantity))
        }) recover { case t => Option.empty[LowestPrice] }
        f pipeTo sender
    }
}
```

Make web service call ❶

Reply to sender when future completes ❸

Send message to sender on Future complete ❷

Source.fromURL makes the REST call to the vendor web service ❶. Because the web service might take some time to respond, it's wrapped in a Future. A Future is a data structure to retrieve the result of some concurrent operation without blocking. Typically, some other actor does the work and completes the Future so you aren't blocked. Future is a great and easy way to execute code asynchronously. Akka Future can also monadically (using map and flatMap) compose with other Futures.

The reference of the Future is then piped to a sender ❸. This is a common pattern in Akka, called the pipeTo pattern. Instead of waiting for the Future to complete and send the result to the sender, you're piping Future to the sender. pipeTo adds an onComplete callback to the Future so that when it completes, its output can be sent to the sender. If the Future fails with an exception, the recover ❷ method returns the empty option. The Future construct in Akka is powerful. Make sure you explore it in the Akka documentation(http://mng.bz/wc7D).

You need the actor in the following listing to broadcast the FindPrice message to each proxy actor and, at the end, find the lowest price out of all the responses.

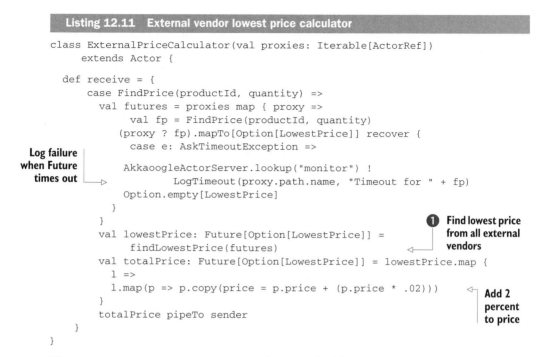

Listing 12.11 External vendor lowest price calculator

```
class ExternalPriceCalculator(val proxies: Iterable[ActorRef])
    extends Actor {

  def receive = {
    case FindPrice(productId, quantity) =>
      val futures = proxies map { proxy =>
        val fp = FindPrice(productId, quantity)
        (proxy ? fp).mapTo[Option[LowestPrice]] recover {
          case e: AskTimeoutException =>

            AkkaoogleActorServer.lookup("monitor") !
                LogTimeout(proxy.path.name, "Timeout for " + fp)
            Option.empty[LowestPrice]
        }
      }
      val lowestPrice: Future[Option[LowestPrice]] =
        findLowestPrice(futures)
      val totalPrice: Future[Option[LowestPrice]] = lowestPrice.map {
        l =>
        l.map(p => p.copy(price = p.price + (p.price * .02)))
      }
      totalPrice pipeTo sender
  }
}
```

Log failure when Future times out ⤷

1 Find lowest price from all external vendors ◁

Add 2 percent to price ◁

The `ExternalPriceCalculator` actor is created with references to `ExternalVendor-ProxyActor`. The `FindPrice` message is broadcast to all the proxy actors using the `?` method (ask pattern). The `ask` method implements the Request Reply pattern. But instead of waiting for the reply, it returns a `Future`. This way you're even-handed in terms of dispatching messages to each proxy so that all the external vendors get their fair share of time to respond with prices. The `findLowestPrice` method at line **1** determines the lowest price out of all the responses, and here's how it's implemented:

```
def findLowestPrice(
    futures: Iterable[Future[Option[LowestPrice]]]):
    Future[Option[LowestPrice]] = {
  val f: Future[Option[LowestPrice]] =
    Future.fold(futures)(Option.empty[LowestPrice]) {
      (lowestPrice: Option[LowestPrice], currentPrice: Option[LowestPrice])
      => {
        currentPrice match {
          case Some(first) if (lowestPrice.isEmpty) => Some(first)
          case Some(c) if (c.price < lowestPrice.get.price) => Some(c)
          case _ => lowestPrice
        }
      }
    }
  f
}
```

Match first price ⤷

Compare and set lowest price ⤷

No current price, return previous price ◁

The findLowestPrice method uses the fold operation over all the Futures to find the lowest price. The beauty of this fold is it's performed in a nonblocking fashion. This is an important criterion—otherwise, the entire operation would take more time. The fold method creates a new Future that wraps the entire operation and is performed on the thread of the Future that completes last. If any of the Futures throws an exception, the result of the fold becomes that exception.

So far, you've implemented actors to get both the internal and external lowest price. The following listing shows one more actor you need; it can find the lowest price from both internal and external vendors and return the result.

Listing 12.12 Cheapest deal finder actor

```
class CheapestDealFinder extends Actor {
  def receive = {
    case req: FindPrice =>
      val internalPrice =
        (AkkaoogleActorServer.lookup("internal-load-balancer") ?        Send
          req).mapTo[Option[LowestPrice]]                               message to
                                                                        internal load
      val externalPrice =                                               balancer
        (AkkaoogleActorServer.lookup("external-load-balancer") ?
          req).mapTo[Option[LowestPrice]] recover {                     Send message
            case e: AskTimeoutException =>                              to external
              Option.empty[LowestPrice]                                 load balancer
      }
      val lowestPrice: Future[Option[LowestPrice]] =
        findLowestPrice(internalPrice :: externalPrice :: Nil)
      lowestPrice pipeTo sender
  }
}
```

The actor uses AkkaoogleActorServer (you'll implement this in section 12.3.6) to look up the "internal-load-balancer" actor in order to calculate the internal price. This actor acts as a router for InternalPriceCalculator (you'll learn about Akka routers in the next section). Similarly, "external-load-balancer" finds the router actor for the ExternalPriceCalculator actor. The CheapestDealFinder actor finds the lowest price from both internal and external vendors and then finds the cheapest price among them.

You use the router actors to increase the scalability of the application because they help in routing messages to multiple instances of actors, based on an algorithm. The next section discusses routers and dispatchers, two of the neat features of Akka.

12.3.5 *Increase scalability with remote actors, dispatchers, and routers*

I haven't discussed Akka dispatchers and message routing on purpose, because to truly understand them you need a context where they're valuable—like our current example. What will happen if you deploy the current application in production?

SETTING UP MESSAGE ROUTING

For one user at a time, the current setup would work fine, but with multiple concurrent users it won't scale. When the `CheapestDealFinder` actor is processing a message, other messages are waiting in the mailbox for processing. In some cases you may want that behavior, but in this case you can't do that. If you could create multiple instances of the `CheapestDealFinder` actor, you could process messages in parallel. Then you'd have to route messages to these actors effectively so you don't overload some actors. But how will the caller know which actor instance has the fewest messages to process? The good news is Akka comes with special kinds of actors called routers, which can effectively route messages between multiple instances of actors. The router actor acts as a gateway to a collection of actors. You send a message to the router actor, and the router actor forwards the message to one of the actors, based on some routing policy. For example, the `SmallestMailboxRouter` router routes messages based on the mailbox. The actor with the least number of messages in the mailbox wins. The following code snippet creates 10 instances of `CheapestDealFinder` actors and creates a `SmallestMailboxRouter` to route messages to them:

```
val cheapestDealFinderLoadBalancer = system.actorOf(
  Props[CheapestDealFinder]
     .withRouter(SmallestMailboxRouter(nrOfInstances = 10)),
       name = "cheapest-deal-finder-balancer")
```

Here the `CheapestDealFinder` actor is created with `SmallestMailboxRouter` by passing the number of instances that this router will manage. Note that the router will automatically create `CheapestDealFinder` actors. To create your own routing logic, you need to extend `RouterConfig`.

Similarly, the following code example creates routers for both `InternalPriceCalculator` and `ExternalPriceCalculator` using `RoundRobinRouter`:

```
val internalPriceCalculators: List[ActorRef] =
    createInternalPriceCalculators(10)

val internalLoadBalancer = system.actorOf(
        Props[InternalPriceCalculator]
      .withRouter(RoundRobinRouter (routees = internalPriceCalculators)),
       name = "internal-load-balancer")

val proxies = createExternalProxyActors(ExternalVendor.findAll)

val externalPriceCalculators: List[ActorRef] =
    createExternalPriceCalculators(10, proxies)

val externalLoadBalancer = system.actorOf(
        Props [ExternalPriceCalculator]
      .withRouter(RoundRobinRouter(routees = externalPriceCalculators)),
       name="external-load-balancer")
```

`RoundRobinRouter` routes messages to actors in round-robin fashion. Instead of allowing the router to create the actor instances, the instances are passed as a parameter (they are called *routees*). The reason is that you want to specify additional parameters to customize them further (discussed in the next section).

These routers let you scale and handle multiple users at a time. But what about performance? You still need the underlying threads to run all the event-based actors you've created. The next section explores how to customize Akka to allocate dedicated threads for each actor type.

IMPROVE PERFORMANCE WITH DISPATCHERS

Every actor system has a default dispatcher that's used if nothing is configured. In Akka, message dispatchers are the engine behind the actors that makes `Actor` run. Think of a dispatcher as a service with a thread pool that knows how to execute actors when a message is received. In most scenarios, the default settings work best. In fact, when you're building an Akka application, I recommend starting with that—don't create a special configuration.

But if you notice some contention on a single dispatcher, you can start creating dedicated dispatchers for a group of actors. Assume you're in that situation. You notice that your `InternalPriceCalculatorActor` and `ExternalVendorProxyActor` actors aren't getting executed as quickly as you want, and it's because of the contention in the default dispatcher. Remember, all the actors are created from the same actor system. You can easily configure the default dispatcher by adding more threads to it, but for learning purposes you're going to use different dispatchers. Akka comes with four types of message dispatchers:

- *Dispatcher*—The default dispatcher used by the actor system. It's an event-based dispatcher that binds actors to a thread pool. It creates one mailbox per actor.
- *PinnedDispatcher*—Dedicates one thread per actor. It's like creating thread-based actors.
- *BalancingDispatcher*—This event-driven dispatcher redistributes work from busy actors to idle actors. All the actors of the same type share one mailbox.
- *CallingThreadDispatcher*—It runs the actor on the calling thread. It doesn't create any new thread. Great for unit testing purposes.

Using dispatchers in Akka is a simple two-step process: first, specify them in the configuration file, then set up the actor with the dispatcher. The following configuration snippet declares the dispatcher you'll use for the `ExternalPriceCalculator` actor:

```
akkaoogle {
  dispatchers {
    external-price-calculator-actor-dispatcher {
      # Dispatcher is the name of the event-based dispatcher
      type = Dispatcher
      # What kind of ExecutionService to use
      executor = "fork-join-executor"
      # Configuration for the fork-join pool
      fork-join-executor {
        # Min number of threads to cap factor-based parallelism number to
        parallelism-min = 2
        # Parallelism (threads) ... ceil(available processors * factor)
        parallelism-factor = 2.0
        # Max number of threads to cap factor-based parallelism number to
```

```
         parallelism-max = 100
      }
      # Throughput defines the maximum number of messages to be
      # processed per actor before the thread jumps to the next actor.
      # Set to 1 for as fair as possible.
      throughput = 100
    }
  }
}
```

The external-price-calculator-actor-dispatcher uses a Dispatcher (the default event-based dispatcher) with a fork-join thread pool. The fork-join thread pool is configured with additional properties. Akka dispatchers are configurable (read the Akka documentation for details). Similarly, the following dispatcher could be used for the InternalPriceCalculator actor:

```
akkaoogle {
  dispatchers {
    ...
    ...
    internal-price-calculator-actor-dispatcher {
        # Dispatcher is the name of the event-based dispatcher
        type = BalancingDispatcher
        # What kind of ExecutionService to use
        executor = "thread-pool-executor"
        thread-pool-executor {
          # Min number of threads to cap factor-based core number to
          core-pool-size-min = 5
        }
      }
      ...
  }
}
```

This time the internal-price-calculator-actor-dispatcher uses Balancing-Dispatcher with the thread pool executor, with the minimum number of threads set to 5. In the real world, you should do performance testing before choosing a configuration that works for everybody.

To use these dispatchers you will use the withDispatcher method of Props, as in the following:

```
private def createInternalPriceCalculators(initialLoad: Int)(
  implicit system: ActorSystem) = {
  (for (i <- 0 until initialLoad) yield
     system.actorOf(Props[InternalPriceCalculator]
       .withDispatcher
       ("dispatchers.internal-price-calculator-actor-dispatcher"),
     name=("internal-price-calculator" + i))).toList
}

 private def createExternalPriceCalculators(initialLoad: Int,
   proxies: List[ActorRef])(implicit system: ActorSystem) = {
   (for (i <- 0 until initialLoad) yield system.actorOf(
     Props(new ExternalPriceCalculator(proxies))
```

```
    .withDispatcher(
        "dispatchers.external-price-calculator-actor-dispatcher"),
    name = ("external-price-calculator" + i))).toList
}
```

The `createInternalPriceCalculators` method creates all the `InternalPrice-`
`Calculator` actors and configures the `dispatchers.internal-price-calculator-`
`actor-dispatcher`. Now these actors will no longer use the default dispatcher that
comes with `ActorSystem` but rather the one that's configured. Similarly, `create-`
`ExternalPriceCalculators` configures the `ExternalPriceCalculator` actors. The
following listing shows the completed `AkkaoogleActorServer` which creates and configures all the actors used in the Akkaoogle application.

Listing 12.13   Akkaoogle actor server

```
package com.akkaoogle.infrastructure

import com.akkaoogle.calculators._
import akka.actor._
import com.akkaoogle.db.models._
import akka.actor.{ActorRef, Actor}
import akka.routing._
import com.typesafe.config.ConfigFactory

object AkkaoogleActorServer {

  var system: Option[ActorSystem] = None                        | Initialize
                                                                 ⊲┘ all actors
  def run(): Unit = {
    println("starting the remote server...")
    system = Some(ActorSystem("akkaoogle",
          ConfigFactory.load.getConfig("akkaoogle")))
    system.foreach(s => register(s))
  }

  private def register(implicit system: ActorSystem) {
    val monitor = system.actorOf(Props[MonitorActor], name = "monitor")

    val cheapestDealFinderLoadBalancer = system.actorOf(
      Props[CheapestDealFinder]
        .withRouter(SmallestMailboxRouter(nrOfInstances = 10)),
              name = "cheapest-deal-finder-balancer")

    val internalPriceCalculators: List[ActorRef] =
        createInternalPriceCalculators(10)

    val internalLoadBalancer = system.actorOf(
    Props[InternalPriceCalculator]
      .withRouter(RoundRobinRouter(routees = internalPriceCalculators)),
      name = "internal-load-balancer")

    val proxies = createExternalProxyActors(ExternalVendor.findAll)
    val externalPriceCalculators: List[ActorRef] =
        createExternalPriceCalculators(10, proxies)

    val externalLoadBalancer = system.actorOf(
        Props [ExternalPriceCalculator]
```

```
            .withRouter(RoundRobinRouter(routees = externalPriceCalculators)),
              name="external-load-balancer")
    }

    def lookup(name: String): ActorRef = {                           ⊲  Look up
        system map { s =>                                               ActorRef
            val path = s / name                                         by name
            s.actorFor(path)
        } getOrElse(throw new RuntimeException("No actor found"))
    }

    def stop(){                                                      ⊲  Stop actor system
      system.foreach(_.shutdown())                                      and actors
    }

    private def createExternalProxyActors(vendors:
      Iterable[ExternalVendor])(implicit system: ActorSystem) = {
      val proxies = for(v <- vendors) yield  {
            println("Creating vendor proxies for " + v.name)
            val ref = system.actorOf(Props(new ExternalVendorProxyActor(v))

        .withDispatcher("dispatchers.proxy-actor-dispatcher"), name=v.name)
          ref
      }
      proxies.toList
    }

    private def createInternalPriceCalculators(
      initialLoad: Int)(implicit system: ActorSystem) = {
      (for (i <- 0 until initialLoad) yield
        system.actorOf(Props [InternalPriceCalculator]
          .withDispatcher("dispatchers.internal-price-calculator-actor-
          dispatcher"),
          name=("internal-price-calculator" + i))).toList
    }

    private def createExternalPriceCalculators(
      initialLoad: Int, proxies: List[ActorRef])(
      implicit system: ActorSystem) = {
      (for (i <- 0 until initialLoad) yield system.actorOf(
          Props(new ExternalPriceCalculator(proxies))
            .withDispatcher(
              "dispatchers.external-price-calculator-actor-dispatcher"),
          name = ("external-price-calculator" + i))).toList
    }
}
```

Where do the remote actors fit in? Making an actor remote is a matter of changing the configuration at deployment time. There's no special API for remote actors. This lets you scale further by deploying them into multiple remote machines, if required. Refer to the codebase for this chapter for an example. So far, you've implemented the Find-Price message. The next section implements the LogTimeout message using Agents.

12.3.6 *Handling shared resources with Agent*

To build the monitoring piece for the Akkaoogle application, you have to rely on a shared mutable state, and this section shows you how to put Agent to use.

The monitor actor needs to log any transaction failure with external vendors. You can always extend its functionality for internal use, but for now it needs to handle the following two message types:

```
case class LogTimeout(actorId: String, msg: String)
case class FindStats(actorId: String)
```

On receiving a LogTimeout message, it needs to save the transaction failure information to the database and also keep track of the number of times a particular service failed. Agent fits the requirement well. It can store shared data and, if required, participate in the STM transaction.

To keep things simple you'll use the Map provided by Akka. The side effect that's saving information to the database can't be done safely within an STM transaction, because an STM transaction could retry the operations in a transaction multiple times if there's any read/write inconsistency. If you try to save information to the database within the transaction, it may get saved more than once. If you use Agent, it can participate in the STM transaction and get executed only when the STM transaction completes successfully. Here's how to increment the failure counter and save the information in the database in an atomic operation:

```
val errorLogger = Agent(Map.empty[String, Int])

...
...
private def logTimeout(actorId: String, msg: String): Unit = {
  errorLogger send { errorLog =>
    val current = errorLog.getOrElse(actorId, 0)
    val newErrorLog =  errorLog + (actorId -> (current + 1))
    val l = new TransactionFailure(actorId, msg,
      new Date(System.currentTimeMillis))
    l.save
    newErrorLog
  }
}
```

The logTimeout method first gets the actorId and the message that needs to be logged in the database. The send method of Agent takes a function that increments the failure counts and saves the message into the database. With this setup, implementing the FindStats message is easy:

```
case FindStats(actorId) =>
  val timeouts = errorLogger().getOrElse(actorId, 0)
  sender ! Stats(actorId, timeouts = timeouts)
```

Get the latest count from the map and return it. In the real world, you'll monitor other information, but as of now you're done with the monitor actor. The following is the complete code.

Listing 12.14   Complete `monitor` actor

```
package com.akkaoogle.infrastructure
import akka.agent.Agent
import akka.actor.Actor
import com.akkaoogle.calculators.messages.{Stats, FindStats, LogTimeout}
import java.util.Date
import com.akkaoogle.db.models._

class MonitorActor extends Actor {
  import context._
  val errorLogger = Agent(Map.empty[String, Int])

  def preRestart = errorLogger send { old => Map.empty[String, Int] }

  def receive = {                                          ⟵─── Message handler
    case LogTimeout(actorId, msg) =>
      logTimeout(actorId, msg)
    case FindStats(actorId) =>
      val timeouts = errorLogger().getOrElse(actorId, 0)
      sender ! Stats(actorId, timeouts = timeouts)
  }

  private def logTimeout(actorId: String, msg: String): Unit = {
    errorLogger send { errorLog =>
        val current = errorLog.getOrElse(actorId, 0)
      val newErrorLog =  errorLog + (actorId -> (current + 1))
      val l = new TransactionFailure(actorId, msg,
        new Date(System.currentTimeMillis))
      l.save
      newErrorLog
    }
  }
}
```

Clear out logs before restart ❶ (annotation pointing to `preRestart` line)

`MonitorActor` checks the health of external vendor services and provides stats. The `preRestart` ❶ is a callback method defined by the Akka `actor` trait, which is invoked when the actor is about to be restarted. In the `preRestart` you're clearing up the log count but ideally you may want to save the existing error count in some persistence storage so you can fetch the errors for later use. Now let's hook all these actors with a simple UI.

12.4   Adding asynchronous HTTP support with Play2-mini

Play2-mini is a lightweight REST framework on top of the Play2 framework. It maps an HTTP request to a function that takes an HTTP request and returns a response. Behind the scenes, all the requests are handled using actors. It also provides support for nonblocking, asynchronous HTTP support of the Play2 framework. Behind the scenes, the Play2 framework uses the Netty server that implements the Java NIO API. The next section sets up the Akkaoogle project to use the Play2-mini framework.

12.4.1 *Setting up Play2-mini*

To make your Akkaoogle project aware of the Play2-mini project, you need to add the necessary `libraryDependencies` to the SBT build definition. Because you're also going to use the Netty server built into Play2-mini as your web server, you'll configure `play.core.server.NettyServer` as the main entry point. To run the Akkaoogle application, all you have to do is enter `"sbt run"`. The following trait captures the necessary settings to convert the Akkaoogle project to Play2-mini:

```
trait ConfigureScalaBuild {
  lazy val typesafe = "Typesafe Repository" at "http://repo.typesafe.com/
    typesafe/releases/"

  lazy val typesafeSnapshot = "Typesafe Snapshots Repository" at "http://
    repo.typesafe.com/typesafe/snapshots/"

  val netty = Some("play.core.server.NettyServer")

  def scalaMiniProject(org: String, name: String, buildVersion: String,
    baseFile: java.io.File = file(".")) = Project(id = name, base =
    baseFile, settings = Project.defaultSettings).settings(
    version := buildVersion,
    organization := org,
    resolvers += typesafe,
    resolvers += typesafeSnapshot,
    libraryDependencies += "com.typesafe" %% "play-mini" % "2.1=RC2",
    mainClass in (Compile, run) := netty,
    ivyXML := <dependencies> <exclude org="org.springframework"/>
</dependencies>
  )
}
```

The `scalaMiniProject` method creates an SBT project with all the Play2-mini dependencies. For Akkaoogle, you'll mix in this trait and use the `scalaMiniProject` method to create the project, as in the following listing.

Listing 12.15 Akkaoogle SBT project with Play2-mini

```
import sbt._
import Keys._

object AkkaoogleBuild extends Build with ConfigureScalaBuild {

  import H2TaskManager._
  lazy val root = scalaMiniProject("com.akkaoogle","akkaoogle","1.0")
   .settings(startH2Task, stopH2Task)
   .settings(
      organization := "scalainaction",
      scalaVersion := "2.10.0",
      scalacOptions ++= Seq("-unchecked", "-deprecation"),
      resolvers += "Typesafe Repo" at "http://repo.typesafe.com/typesafe/
     repo",
      parallelExecution in Test := false
    )
   .settings(
      libraryDependencies ++= Seq(
```

```
            "com.typesafe.akka" %% "akka-actor" % "2.1.0",
            "com.typesafe.akka" %% "akka-remote" % "2.1.0",
            "com.typesafe.akka" %% "akka-agent" % "2.1.0",
            "com.h2database" % "h2" % "1.2.127",
            "org.squeryl" % "squeryl_2.10-RC5" % "0.9.5-5",
            "org.specs2" %% "specs2" % "1.13" % "test",
        "org.eclipse.jetty" % "jetty-distribution" % "8.0.0.M2" % "test"
        ))
}
```

After you save and reload the build definition, you should have everything you need to give a UI look to your application. In the next section, you'll build your first Play2-mini action, which can take the HTTP request and send messages to the actors.

12.4.2 *Running with Play2-mini*

When you start a Play2-mini–based application, the first thing it does is look for an implementation of `com.typesafe.play.mini.Setup`. Every Play2-mini–based application needs to implement this class:

```
package com.typesafe.play.mini
 class Setup(a: Application) extends GlobalSettings {
 ...
 }
```

This class takes an instance of `Application` as a parameter. Think of `Application` as a controller of the MVC model that handles all the requests. In the case of Play2-mini, the only abstract method you have to implement is the `routes` method:

```
package com.typesafe.play.mini
trait Application {
  def route: PartialFunction[RequestHeader, Handler]
}
```

For your application to work with Play2-mini, you need to implement the `Setup` by passing a concrete implementation of the `Application` trait. Here's the implementation of the `Setup`:

```
import com.akkaoogle.infrastructure._
import org.h2.tools.Server
import com.akkaoogle.db.AkkaoogleSchema._

object Global extends com.typesafe.play.mini.Setup(com.akkaoogle.http.App)
{
  println("initializing the Akkaoogle schema")
  createSchema()
  AkkaoogleActorServer.run()
}
```

The `Global` object extends the `Setup` class by passing `com.akkaoogle.http.App` as an implementation of the `Application` trait. `com.akkaoogle.http.App` will handle all the HTTP requests for the Akkaoogle application. `Global` is also a great place to initialize the various parts of the system. In this case, you're creating the schema, and `AkkaoogleActorServer` starts all the actors. Here's the complete implementation of the `com.akkaoogle.http.App` Play2-mini `Application`:

Listing 12.16   Akkaoogle Play2-mini Application

```
package com.akkaoogle.http

import com.typesafe.play.mini._
import play.api.mvc._
import play.api.mvc.Results._
import com.akkaoogle.infrastructure._
import akka.pattern.{ ask, pipe, AskTimeoutException }
import com.akkaoogle.calculators.messages._
import play.api.libs.concurrent._
import scala.collection.JavaConverters._

/**
 * this application is registered via Global
 */
object App extends Application {
  def route = {
      case GET(Path("/")) => Action { request =>        Get homepage
        Ok(views.index()).as("text/html")               of Akkaoogle
      }
      case GET(Path("/akkaoogle/search")) & QueryString(qs) =>
       Action { request =>
         val desc = QueryString(qs, "productDescription").get.asScala
         val f =
        (AkkaoogleActorServer
          .lookup("cheapest-deal-finder-balancer") ? FindPrice(
              desc.head, 1)).mapTo[Option[LowestPrice]]
         val result = f.map({
         case Some(lowestPrice)=>
           Ok(lowestPrice.toString).as("text/html")
         case _ =>
           Ok("No price found").as("text/html")         Return
        })                                               asynchronous
        AsyncResult(result.asPromise)                    result
        }
    }
  }
}
```

(margin note, left) Get cheapest price for given description

The `routes` method is a partial function that matches the HTTP URL to an action.
`Action` is nothing but a function object that takes an HTTP request and returns a
`Result`. For example, case `GET(Path("/"))` matches the HTTP `GET` to `"/"` URL. The
Play2-mini framework provides a nice DSL to parse the HTTP URL and verb. The following action returns `Ok`(HTTP 200 response code) with the output of the
`views.index()` method:

```
Action { request =>
  Ok(views.index()).as("text/html")
}
```

`views.index` returns the HTML code to render the Akkaoogle homepage shown in
figure 12.4. The following `GET` pattern match for product search is more interesting:

```
GET(Path("/akkaoogle/search"))  & QueryString(qs)
```

In this case, you're using the `QueryString` helper of Play2-mini to parse the query parameters and give you a value mapped to a parameter. In the action, you extract the description given by the user to create the `FindPrice` message, which in turn is sent to `cheapest-deal-finder-balancer` to find the cheapest price available for the product. You can find the complete working version of the Akkaoogle project in the chapter's codebase. The Akkaoogle application isn't completed yet, so you can take over and add more features to make it better. That's the best way to learn and explore Akka.

12.5 Summary

Akka is a powerful toolkit that you can use to build frameworks or applications. Akka makes concurrency easy for programmers by raising the abstraction level. Akka is a concurrency framework built on actors, but it provides all the popular concurrency abstractions available on the market. It provides the flexibility you need to build your next enterprise application. Akka's STM support lets you safely operate on mutable data structures without leaving the comfort of actor-based concurrency. Most importantly, you learned that STM composes, so you can build smaller atomic operations and compose them to solve problems. You also explored agents as another concurrency model that lets you send behavior from outside to manipulate data in a safe manner. Exploring dataflow concurrency was also interesting because it lets you write sequential programs without worrying about concurrency. And dataflow concurrency code is very easy to understand and follow.

By building Akkaoogle, you explored various considerations, constraints, and design decisions that typically arise when building large concurrent applications. I'm sure that the insights you gained will enable you to build your next Akka application. Always remember that Akka provides lots of options and configuration flexibility, and you should pick the features and options that work best for your application requirements. Akka is already used in various real-world applications,[5] and now you can use it too. From here on, let's keep all our CPU cores busy.

---

[5] Akka use cases, http://akka.io/docs/akka/1.1.2/intro/use-cases.html.

index

RELATED MANNING TITLES

Scala in Depth
by Joshua D. Suereth

ISBN: 978-1-935182-70-2
304 pages, $49.99
May 2012

Akka in Action
by Raymond Roestenburg and Rob Bakker

ISBN: 978-1-617291-01-2
475 pages, $49.99
October 2013

Play for Scala
by Peter Hilton, Erik Bakker,
   and Francisco Canedo

ISBN: 978-1-617290-79-4
300 pages, $49.99
June 2013

Functional Programming in Scala
by Paul Chiusano and Rúnar Bjarnason

ISBN: 978-1-617290-65-7
325 pages, $44.99
August 2013

For ordering information go to www.manning.com